25 YEARS • BUILT to LAST

THE LISTENER'S GUIDE TO AUDIO BOOKS

REVIEWS, RECOMMENDATIONS, AND LISTINGS FOR MORE THAN 2,000 TITLES

John Wynne

A FIRESIDE BOOK
PUBLISHED BY SIMON & SCHUSTER
NEW YORK LONDON TORONTO SYDNEY TOKYO SINGAPORE

FIRESIDE
Rockefeller Center
1230 Avenue of the Americas
New York, NY 10020

Designed by Chris Welch

Manufactured in the United States of America

10 9 8 7 6 5 4 3 2 1

Library of Congress Cataloging-in-Publication Data

Wynne, John.
The listener's guide to audio books : reviews, recommendations, and listings for more than 2,000 titles / John Wynne.
p. cm.
"A Fireside book."
Includes index.
1. Audiobooks—Reviews. I. Title.
ML156.9.W96 1995
028.1'37—dc20 95-18782
CIP
MN

ISBN-0-684-80239-2

Dedicated to my Dad, Tom Wynne, for all his appreciated support over the years.

I would like to thank my editor, Becky Cabaza, for her faith in this project and her editorial expertise;
my agent, Harold Schmidt, for his diligence and skill in helping to assemble this book;
John Cassaras for his unflagging assistance in the trenches and his valuable insights;
Lisa Dolin for her professionalism and for giving me a start and a hand in this industry.

CONTENTS

CONTRIBUTORS

Gregory and Patricia Kishel ("Business and Motivation") are business consultants and the authors of numerous books and articles on entrepreneurship, including the best-selling *How to Start, Run, and Stay in Business* (John Wiley & Sons) and *Growing Your Own Business* (Perigee Books). The Kishels also conduct business seminars and frequently speak to groups and the media. Gregory is currently the director of the Orange County Small Business Development Center in southern California, and Patricia is an assistant professor of management and marketing at Cypress College.

Anthony Martone ("Plays and Poetry") is a professor of English at Suffolk County Community College on Long Island. He has specialized in dramatic literature at the college for the past fifteen years and is presently teaching theater history at The American Academy of Dramatic Arts. Besides his work in drama, he has devoted much study to film and the lyrics of classical popular American music.

Although **Chris Pfouts** ("Humor" and "Nonfiction") has made much of his literary reputation writing about violence, his sense of humor runs deep and he has contributed a number of comedy items to American periodicals and newspapers. His books *Lead Poisoning, True Tales of American Violence,* and *Safe in the City* (all from Paladin Press) broke new ground in the study of modern violence and its prevention. Pfouts is currently editor of *International Tattoo Art* magazine, a job that allows more room for humor than one might expect.

A graduate of the North Carolina School of the Arts, **Kevin Thomsen** ("Action and Adventure") has performed extensively in television, theater, and film. As a writer, he has developed numerous screenplays (almost all in the action/adventure genre). Together with Garet Scott, he directs and produces for their Off-Off-Broadway theater company Punch. He also produces, directs, and writes in the audio book field.

Ron Wolfe ("Horror" and "Science Fiction and Fantasy") is a feature writer and cartoonist for the *Arkansas Democrat-Gazette* in Little Rock, Arkansas. He is the coauthor (with John Wooley) of three horror novels, *Death's Door* the most recent. His short stories have appeared in *Twilight Zone* magazine, *Asimov's* magazine, *The Year's Best Horror,* and Epic Comics' *Clive Barker's Hellraiser.* After years as a movie critic, he would just as soon sit back and listen. As for the best of all audio tapes, he likes the ones that don't get snarled in the machine.

Journalist, novelist, and pop-culture aficionado **John Wooley** ("Nonfiction," "Radio Drama and Documentaries," and "Religion") is an entertainment writer for the *Tulsa World,* a columnist for *Baby Boomer Collectibles,* and a regular contributor to *Discoveries* and *Fangoria.* His recent work includes the drive-in movie book *Hot Schlock Horror* (Dreamtrip Press), the horror novel *Death's Door* (Dell/Abyss, written with Ron Wolfe), the *Mamie Van Doren* and *Confidential* trading card sets (Kitchen Sink Press), and the feature-length video documentary *Still Swingin'* (VCI), which he wrote and associate-produced. His qualifications as a contributor to *The Listener's Guide to Audio Books* include a longtime love for old-time radio, which he began collecting on tape in the sixties.

INTRODUCTION

The audio book industry is one of the fastest-growing areas in publishing today. In fact, it's a billion dollar industry. Yet I realized there was no guide available for the rapidly growing number of listeners. No way for audio book fans to know what tapes were available, whether they were good, bad, or mediocre, or how to order them. I decided the time had come to create a comprehensive, user-friendly compilation that gave listeners the information they needed to make informed choices about what to buy. Having been in the industry over ten years and having produced over a hundred audio books (several of them award winners), I felt qualified to undertake the task.

The audio books reviewed here are commercial releases by well-known authors. These are the tapes usually obtainable at the retail level—at your bookstore or record store or by mail order. They are often abridged (or edited) to a three-hour format and use celebrity readers or are read by the authors themselves. (There are many full-length, unabridged recordings, usually available for rental by mail order, but due to considerations of the length of this book, are not included here.)

This guide was assembled by my contacting major audio book publishers and asking them to send me those releases they wanted reviewed or listed. I have tried to review all the materials submitted to me. If I have been unable to include every entry or audio book publisher, bear with me. Hopefully, we will include you in upcoming editions.

History

Sometimes I hear people complain that audio books are a "replacement" for reading. In my mind, nothing replaces reading. Audio books take something that exists in one medium and put it in another—much as when a film, TV show, or stage play uses a book as its source material. The title is now in a new medium—and with an actor involved, it could be argued, a dramatic medium.

And let's not put the cart before the horse. The oral tradition of storytelling is the oldest form of artful communication—older than books. Look at Homer. His great art of storytelling did not appear in book form until hundreds of years after the blind poet created *The Iliad* and *The Odyssey.* Audio books are not a replacement for reading but a distillation of ideas or dramatic events that can be conveyed to the listener by the most personal and intimate of instruments—the human voice.

Discovering an author on audio can spur the listener to pursue that author's other works (in book or tape format) or, after an audio program has whetted the appetite, to read the unabridged version of a book that would otherwise have been left on the shelf.

Time considerations do intrude into our busy lives as we approach the twenty-first century. We simply don't have time to read everything. We have to pick and choose. And, obviously, when we're commuting behind the wheel, we are unable to read. Why stare vacantly at the bumper in front of us? Or listen to constant radio commercials and the same old songs over and over? Isn't it better to challenge ourselves by listening to information and entertainment available on audio books?

The audio book, as we know it today, could be said to have had its start in 1952, when the spoken-word record company Caedmon (named after the Greek poet) was inaugurated by two literature majors at Columbia University. They put a microphone in front of Dylan Thomas, who read *A Child's Christmas in Wales.* Not only was a company launched—but an industry!

For thirty years, Caedmon was the main game in town, with the emphasis on authors reading their own work. But by the early eighties, mainstream publishing houses began to see the commercial possibilities in simultaneous book and tape releases of current best-sellers. In the next decade, it's fair to say there was a virtual explosion of books being read on tape. Today it is unusual for a best-seller—or even a book bubbling under best-seller status—not to be recorded.

While most audio books have a one book–one reader ratio, there has been a trend in the past two years to broaden the spectrum. Heavily dramatized multiple-cast recordings seem to be proliferating, often with pointed musical underscoring and elaborate sound effects. Serials from the golden age of radio are recalled and yet today's technology (including binaural 3-D sound and Dolby Surround) add vital new dimensions that speak solely to the nineties. Where does the future of audio books lie? We can only guess in this rapidly changing, fluid medium.

How to Use This Guide

The Listener's Guide to Audio Books is divided into categories defined by subject, such as "Action and Adventure," "Business and Motivation," and "Nonfiction."

Each category begins with a "Highly Recommended" list of titles I've selected as the very best. The reviews are next and are broken down into the following:

Title
Author
Reader (Performer)
Rating
Review
Number of Cassettes **Length of Program** **Publisher**

The rating system is as follows:

★★★★ Highly Recommended
★★★ **Very Good**
★★ **Good**
★ **Below Par**
Bomb

In a very few instances, length of program is not provided because the publisher has not provided that information. But by the number of cassettes listed, the timing can be estimated (for example, two cassettes will run from two to three hours, or from one to one and a half hours per cassette).

The publisher has been listed according to the information on the box itself. For example, Bantam Audio and BDD Audio (Bantam Doubleday Dell) are one and the same publisher. In the ordering information section of this book, all the names of the same publisher are listed so that there will be no confusion.

After the reviews in each category are *listings* of recommended audio books that are currently in print. These provide the following information:

Title
Author
Reader (Performer)
Publisher

Occasionally a reader's name will not appear in the lists as the project was not yet cast as this book went to print, or the reader has not been identified by the publisher.

As the Spanish language market is growing, some Spanish language titles are included in the listings.

Following the review and listing chapters is a section of Grammy Award–

winning and –nominated recordings from the inception of the spoken-word category of the awards in 1958 to the present.

"Ordering Information" follows, giving you the information necessary to place an order for any audio book reviewed or listed in this guide. Just note the publisher indicated in the review or listing, then locate it in the ordering information section, and a phone number and address are provided for easy ordering.

An index with titles and author names appears at the back of the book for easy reference.

I hope you will use and enjoy this guide to audio books.

ACTION AND ADVENTURE

Thousands of years ago, before the invention of the written word, there was the spoken word. Our early ancestors would huddle around blazing fires and tell one another action-packed stories of brutal hunts, savage crusades, glorious conquests, and epic battles. When you consider this rich and exciting storytelling tradition, it's no wonder that there are so many excellent choices in "Action and Adventure."

As you flip through the following selections, you're bound to notice that I've given almost all of John Le Carré's recordings four stars. That's not a fluke. Simply put, Mr. Le Carré himself reads all of his books, and Mr. Le Carré is an extraordinary narrator. With Mr. Le Carré's recordings, the listener is given the unique opportunity of hearing every word, every character, every nuance, jump right off the page. Even if you've never thought of yourself as a Le Carré fan, I can strongly recommend you try one of his books-on-tape. And if you are a fan, and have already read all of his books, I can also recommend you listen to his tapes. (His readings are so inspired that he'll make you think you read a *different* book!)

Although many of the books in this category have been successfully adapted to either film or television, you shouldn't let this put you off. The experience of hearing a single reader interpret a book dramatically holds many of its own rewards. Whether you enjoy the high-tech high jinks of Tom Clancy, the international spy tinglers of Robert Ludlum, the war-torn heroics of Ken Follett, or the courtroom wrangling of John Grisham, there's an audio tape in this section that will raise your blood pressure.

HIGHLY RECOMMENDED (★★★★)

The Bourne Identity
The Bourne Supremacy
The Bourne Ultimatum
Congo
A Dangerous Fortune
The Deceiver
Eye of the Needle
Honor among Thieves
Jurassic Park
The Looking Glass War
A Murder of Quality
The Night Manager
The Pelican Brief
A Perfect Spy
The Russia House
A Small Town in Germany
"The Spy in His Prime" (from The Secret Pilgrim)
The Spy Who Came in from the Cold

The Andromeda Strain
Author: Michael Crichton
Reader: Chris Noth
★★★

When an unmanned research satellite returns to earth mysteriously and lethally contaminated, four American scientists are summoned to a secret laboratory. They work against the threat of a worldwide epidemic until, terrifyingly, their microbacterial "adversary" ruptures the sterile seal of the lab and their already desperate search for an answer becomes a split-second race against time. A good, clear reading by Mr. Noth helps the listener to follow all of the details and reasoning behind Mr. Crichton's microbiological, apocalyptic nightmare. Let the nail biting begin. . . .

2 css 3 hr Random House AudioBooks

Battleground
Author: W.E.B. Griffin
Reader: Gerald McRaney
★★★

It was a battle whose name would reverberate through a generation of Americans and go down in history as the bloodiest of World War II—Guadalcanal. W.E.B. Griffin presents this heralded saga of the Marine Corps. As a reader, Mr. McRaney brings a strong sense of conviction to the book, although he does miss some of the subtler points of the story. But don't worry. When the first shots are fired, you'll find yourself scrambling for a foxhole.

2 css 3 hr Simon & Schuster Audio

Beast
Author: Peter Benchley
Reader: David Rasche
★★★

A couple disappears while sailing off the coast of Bermuda, leaving evidence of a devastating accident. As investigators piece together the clues, they begin to wonder: Have the oceans been so destroyed by man—and the balance of nature so completely upset—that a legendary beast has been forced up from the deep, and has begun to kill . . . and kill again? A beautiful presentation by Mr. Rasche makes for a level of tension Benchley fans haven't enjoyed since *Jaws.* I *would not* recommend listening to this on the beach.

2 css 3 hr Random House AudioBooks

The Bourne Identity
Author: Robert Ludlum
Performer: Darren McGavin
★★★★

Dragged from the sea and riddled with bullets, his face altered by plastic surgery, Jason Bourne is a man with an unknown past and an uncertain future. Now he's running for his life, the target of professional assassins, at the center of a maddening, deadly puzzle. *Who is Jason Bourne?* To answer that question, he must find the secret buried deep in his own past. The answer for espionage fans is that the *Bourne* trilogy is the best Ludlum you'll find on audio. Darren McGavin, with his gravelly, rumbling voice, gives a sensitive and haunting performance that makes for a smart, sexy, sizzling adventure.

2 css 2 hr Bantam Audio

The Bourne Supremacy
Author: Robert Ludlum
Performer: Darren McGavin
★★★★

Who is the "new" Jason Bourne and why has he suddenly appeared? Who is paying him? Who is the next target on his list? The vice premier of the People's Republic of China is brutally slain, and all the clues point to the legendary assassin, Jason Bourne. But Bourne never existed! Now someone else has resurrected the Bourne identity, and our hero is forced to use his murderous skills to stop him. If he does not succeed, the Far East and the world will pay a devastating price. Bourne and McGavin are together again for more of the best Ludlum on tape.

2 css 3 hr Bantam Audio

The Bourne Ultimatum
Author: Robert Ludlum
Performer: Darren McGavin
★★★★

Thirteen years have passed since our hero was last forced to assume the alias of the assassin Jason Bourne. Now, with one phone call, he is thrust back into the madness. His greatest enemy, Carlos the Jackal, is hunting again. Bourne must penetrate Carlos's private army as well as a clandestine paramilitary group that has infiltrated the U.S. military, every level of industry, and even the highest corridors of the government. . . . Thankfully, good things come in threes, and Darren McGavin completed the *Bourne* trilogy. Hurrah!

3 css 3½ hr Bantam Audio

Call for the Dead
Author/Reader: John Le Carré
★★★

Call for the Dead is the book that introduces us to John Le Carré's lugubrious hero George Smiley. Why did a high-ranking official at the foreign office commit suicide? And why did he book an alarm call the next morning? Smiley investigates. This is one of Le Carré's "early" recordings, and is not as smooth or as bold as his later readings. Still, it's a great two hours.

2 css 2 hrs Listen for Pleasure

The Cardinal of the Kremlin
Author: Tom Clancy
Reader: David Ogden Stiers
★★★

Mikhail Filitov is a war hero and a Red Army colonel, but to the CIA he is known as the Cardinal. A chance encounter in a Moscow subway leads the KGB to begin a hunt for the spy. What the Cardinal knows could change the course of history. What the maverick CIA man named Ryan must do is outduel the KGB and bring the Cardinal out alive. Mr. Stiers gives a solid performance, effortlessly handling all of Mr. Clancy's technobabble while deftly spinning out the plot. Some effective music and sound effects are dotted throughout.

2 css 3 hr Simon & Schuster Audio

The Careful Man
Author: Frederick Forsyth
Reader: Robert Powell
★★

Timothy Hanson is a careful man who has six months to live. How should he plan his life and the disposal of his wealth? There are surprises in store for his greedy relatives. Mr. Powell finds some humor in this clever little tale but, unfortunately, none of the tension or suspense. I'd advise bringing a seat cushion for this bumbling and bumpy ride.

1 css 1½ hr Durkin Hayes Audio

The Chamber
Author: John Grisham
Reader: Michael Beck
★★

In 1967, in Mississippi, Klan member Sam Cayhall is accused of bombing the law offices of Jewish civil rights activist Marvin Kramer, killing Kramer's two sons. Now, decades later, Cayhall is still on death row for the crime, with time running out. A young lawyer asks to work on the case, which his firm has handled on a pro bono basis for years. Why in the world would he want to get involved? And considering Michael Beck's ho-hum narration of this book, why should the listener? He gives a warm, clear reading that clarifies all of Mr. Grisham's complex legalese but completely misses all of the emotional punch.

4 css 6 hr Bantam Audio

Clear and Present Danger
Author: Tom Clancy
Reader: David Ogden Stiers
★★★

The U.S. ambassador to Colombia has been murdered by drug lords. Covert enemy agents filter into the jungles of South America, and Central America is ready to explode. Jack Ryan is in the eye of the storm—and for the United States the stakes have never been greater. A clean, tight abridgment of the novel and an intelligent performance by Mr. Stiers make for a flashy, rollicking adventure.

2 css 3 hr Simon & Schuster Audio

The Client
Author: John Grisham
Reader: Blair Brown
★★★

Just before a New Orleans attorney committed suicide, he told eleven-year-old Mark Sway a deadly secret about the murder of a senator and the mafia thug accused of killing him. Everyone's pressuring Mark to share the secret, but he knows the mob is watching his every move. So Mark, streetwise and old beyond his years, hires a lawyer: a fifty-two-year-old divorcée who's been through more than anyone could imagine and survived. Some nice, haunting music underscores the tender, powerful narration of Ms. Brown. Especially wonderful is her ability to climb inside the thoughts of young Mr. Sway.

4 css 6 hr Bantam Audio

Congo
Author: Michael Crichton
Reader: Judith Ivey
★★★★

Deep in the heart of the Congo, the eight members of a field expedition die in a matter of minutes. In Houston, a supervisor watches a gruesome video transmission of that ill-fated team . . . and the grainy, moving image of a dark, blurred shape. A new expedition is sent into the Congo, only to descend into a secret world where the only way out may be through the grisliest of deaths. For the audiophile, this tape is a real hidden treasure—Judith Ivey is *spectacular.* She successfully combines *Congo*'s gritty, detail-laden tension with a sensitive interpretation of the characters involved.

2 css 3 hr Random House AudioBooks

A Dangerous Fortune
Author: Ken Follett
Reader: Tim Curry
★★★★

In 1866, tragedy strikes at the exclusive Winfield School when a young student drowns in a mysterious accident involving an elite group of boys. The drowning and its aftermath initiate a spiraling circle of treachery that spans three decades and entwines many lives. Mr. Curry's expressive voice spins this epic yarn stunningly. He paints every scene vividly, carefully etching every detail and line of dialogue. The beautiful music that underscores some of the action ensures that this is a real audio treat.

4 css 6 hr Bantam Audio

Day of the Cheetah
Author: Dale Brown
Reader: Joseph Campanella
★★

DreamStar—a new fighter developed by the U.S. Air Force—possesses what might be the ultimate edge: a piloting system that not only responds directly to its pilot's thought commands but also issues commands of its own. Captain Kenneth Francis James is the only man trained to control this flying bomb and to manage its traumatic effects on the nervous system . . . but he is also Andrei Maraklov, a KGB mole ordered to steal DreamStar. A surprisingly light touch by Mr. Campanella helps a lot of this heavy techno-thriller fly by, but, alas for the listener, most of it is earthbound.

2 css 3 hr Dove Audio

The Deceiver
Author: Frederick Forsyth
Reader: Charles Keating
★★★★

Sam McCready has served with distinction as chief of the covert operations desk of Britain's Secret Intelligence Service. But times have changed. A high-level policy decision demands that SIS strip away its old-style operatives, and the first to be targeted for retirement is the freewheeling McCready. Presented to a panel of his peers, McCready's cxploits may be dazzling evidence of his value—or damning proof that he must be put aside. Working with a crisp abridgment, Mr. Keating gives a bright and aggressive reading that manages to make the action both clear and exciting.

4 css 4 hr Bantam Audio

The Devil's Alternative
Author: Frederick Forsyth
Reader: Peter Egan
★★

The Soviet wheat crop is disastrous; the Russian people face starvation unless they can persuade the U.S. government to sell their grain surplus. The United States is willing, but for a price: arms concessions. A deal could be struck; the unthinkable alternative is war. . . . A particularly weak reading by Mr. Egan turns this gung ho thriller into a screeching, ho-hum yawn. For the audiophile, I suggest the *alternative* of "off."

2 css 2½ hr Listen for Pleasure

Disclosure
Author: Michael Crichton
Reader: John Lithgow
★★

Tom Sanders is an up-and-coming executive, a man whose corporate future is certain. After a closed-door meeting with his new boss—a woman who was his lover ten years before—he is accused of sexually harassing her. Now, as he scrambles to defend himself, he finds himself trapped between what he knows to be true and what he knows others will assume to be the truth. At first, I quite enjoyed Mr. Lithgow's laid-back reading, but after a few minutes I found my attention wandering. The story is clearly there, it just takes some concentration on the listener's part to keep it clear.

4 css 4 hr Random House AudioBooks

Dragon
Author: Clive Cussler
Reader: John Rubinstein
★★★

Deep beneath the Pacific lies the greatest secret of World War II—a crashed B-29 bomber and the nuclear payload it carried toward Japan in 1945. Now, a group of Japanese extremists are placing nuclear devices in compact cars shipped to strategic U.S. cities. While America is held hostage, Dirk Pitt is called on to spearhead a desperate counterattack. Mr. Rubinstein has such a good time reading this story, you'll easily find yourself swept up into the action.

2 css 3 hr Simon & Schuster Audio

"The Emperor"
Author: Frederick Forsyth
Reader: Edward de Souza
★★★

A short story from Forsyth's *No Comebacks* collection. An exotic tropical island is the setting for some fishy business. A droll reading by Mr. de Souza makes Frederick Forsyth much funnier than I'd ever thought him.

1 css 1½ hr Durkin Hayes Audio

Eye of the Needle
Author: Ken Follet
Reader: Edward Woodward
★★★★

His code name is the Needle. He is a tall, handsome German aristocrat of extraordinary intelligence—England's most dangerous enemy. He knows the secret that could win the war for Hitler. She is Lucy Rose, a beautiful young Englishwoman torn between her burning desire and her binding duty. She is the only one who can stop him. A powerful reading by the old action/adventure hand Edward Woodward drives this thrilling tale home.

2 css 2½ hr Durkin Hayes Audio

Firebreak
Author: Richard Herman, Jr.
Reader: Joseph Campanella
Bomb

After the smoke has cleared in Kuwait, preparations for a new war have already begun. The Iraqis have perfected a new nerve gas that can overwhelm the most advanced gas masks and a missile that can deliver the gas straight into the heart of Israel. Israel's embattled prime minister sees only one path to his country's survival—nuclear retaliation. A desperate gamble by the U.S. president could postpone the outbreak of the final world war . . . or hasten its arrival. Despite Mr.

Campanella's valiant effort, he was simply the wrong choice for this thrilling page-turner. It pains me to say this, but . . . *read the book.*

2 css 3 hr Dove Audio

The Firm
Author: John Grisham
Performer: D. W. Moffett
★★

A bright young lawyer, fresh out of law school, is aggressively courted by a small, but mysteriously wealthy, legal practice in Memphis. He and his wife barely arrive in Memphis when he starts to figure out that there's more to the firm than meets the eye. It's a shame, however, that there's not more to meet the ear from Mr. Moffett. His reading has a charming, youthful quality, but he doesn't find the power in any of the older characters—which there are plenty of.

2 css 3 hr Bantam Audio

The Fist of God
Author: Frederick Forsyth
Reader: Simon Jones
★★★

Unless the Allies can penetrate the Iraqi regime during the Persian Gulf War, they realize they may be sending their vast coalition of air and land forces into a bloody desert Armageddon. Then word leaks out to British intelligence that Israel's Mossad once had a mole in Iraq. Major Mike Martin heads into Baghdad, and under the very eyes of Iraq's fearsome secret police, seeks to reestablish a connection with "Jericho." Thanks to Mr. Jones's sparkling performance, this six-hour journey doesn't seem like sixteen. There's some lovely music included, although its placement sounds arbitrary and confusing.

4 css 6 hr BDD Audio

Flight into Danger
Authors: Arthur Hailey and John Castle
Reader: Edward Albert
Bomb

The story of a major airline disaster. When the entire crew and half the passengers collapse from food poisoning during a routine flight, it is left to one passenger with wartime flying experience to take over the controls and try to maneuver the plane to safety. As a listener, you'd better bring a life jacket. A tentative, halting reading by Mr. Albert, coupled with poor production values, makes this tape enjoyable only for those Arthur Hailey and John Castle fans out there.

2 css 2 hr Listen for Pleasure

The Gemini Contenders
Author: Robert Ludlum
Performer: Anthony Heald
★★★

Dead of night. Salonika, Greece, December 1939. A clandestine order of monks embarks on a desperate mission: to transport a mysterious vault to a hiding place high in the Italian Alps. Its sinister contents, concealed for centuries, could rip apart the Christian world. Now, as the Nazi threat marches inexorably closer, men of good and evil are drawn into a violent and deadly hunt, sparking a relentless struggle that could forever change the world. With Mr. Heald's remarkable ear for dialects and characters, a rogues' gallery of heroes and villains spring to life. A thrilling, edge-of-your-seat journey.

4 css 4 hr Bantam Audio

Honor among Thieves
Author: Jeffrey Archer
Reader: Martin Jarvis
★★★★

In the impoverished streets of Baghdad, there is a growing disillusionment with Saddam Hussein. Sensing this, he moves boldly to settle scores with the United States. Saddam gathers into his web three key players: a powerful American Mafia boss; the world's greatest forger; and a special assistant to the president of the United States. In Mr. Jarvis's capable hands, I found myself catapulted immediately into Jeffrey Archer's deft plot, twisted and turned for a solid six hours, then released breathless at the end.

4 css 6 hr Harper Audio

The Hunt for Red October
Author: Tom Clancy
Reader: Richard Crenna
★★★

The *Red October,* the most valuable submarine in the Russian fleet, is a new ballistic-missile vessel with a virtually undetectable silent propulsion system. Marko Ramius, the highly skilled commander of *Red October,* is confident of his ship's ability to avoid detection and determined to settle a bitter score with the Russian state. A taut, suspenseful tale filled with authentic details of the most sophisticated technology, and also the introduction of Jack Ryan. Richard Crenna's gripping, solid performance is just the thing for this underwater thriller. Even though this is Mr. Clancy's first novel, it's one of his best on tape.

2 css 2 hr 40 min Audio Editions

Inca Gold
Author: Clive Cussler
Reader: Howard McGillin
★★★

When a group of archaeologists are nearly drowned in a Peruvian sacrificial pool, only Dirk Pitt can save them. But soon Pitt and his friends are plunged into a vicious, no-holds-barred struggle to survive involving art thieves, a tribe of local Indians, U.S. FBI and Customs agents . . . and the priceless treasure of the last Inca ruler that sets off a race against danger and time, rushing toward a wild climax in a subterranean world of darkness and death. A crisp, tight story matched with Howard McGillin's delicate touch makes for a terrific time.

4 css 4½ hr Simon & Schuster Audio

Jurassic Park
Author: Michael Crichton
Reader: John Heard
★★★★

A shroud of secrecy covers a privately owned island where an American bioengineering firm is building a theme park. Local doctors are mystified when a park worker arrives at the hospital, apparently mauled by an animal of monstrous proportions. A year later, when the first invited guests preview "Jurassic Park," the amazement, the shock, and, finally, the terror they experience offer a horrifying solution to this puzzle. Even if you've read the best-selling book, or have seen the blockbuster movie, I can recommend, without hesitation, that you listen to the tape. In the best storytelling tradition, Mr. Heard delivers the story, just the story, and nothing more. Wonderful.

2 css 3 hr Random House AudioBooks

The Kaisho
Author: Eric Lustbader
Performer: B. D. Wong
★★

Bound to honor a promise to his father, Nicholas Linnear arrives in Venice to aid the Kaisho, boss of the bosses of the *Yakuza,* the Japanese underworld. Mikio Okami has been marked for death by an assassin whose motives are shrouded in mysticism and madness. At the same time, in America, a Mafia godfather is slain in a brutal ritual . . . his exotic sister is about to embrace a forbidden power . . . and ex-detective Lew Croaker uncovers evidence of a vast conspiracy linking the Mafia and the *Yakuza.* B. D. Wong graces Mr. Lustbader's book with a gentle, sensitive touch, but, alas, not with one ounce of excitement.

2 css 3 hr Dove Audio

The Key to Rebecca
Author: Ken Follett
Reader: Anthony Quayle
★★★

In all of Cairo there are only two people who can stop a brilliant Nazi agent from passing crucial secrets to Rommel's advancing army. One is a down-on-his-luck English officer; the other, a beautiful young Jewish girl whom he has to persuade to become sexual bait in a trap. Mr. Quayle, with his many years of experience in the theater and in films, graces this story with just the right dramatic touch, finding plenty of charm and interest in all the characters. He isn't Le Carré, but awfully close.

2 css 2½ hr Listen for Pleasure

Lie Down with Lions
Author: Ken Follett
Reader: Peter Marinker
★★

A thriller about idealism and betrayal, terrorism and loyalty, and passions so fierce that they nearly destroy everything. This tale of deadly intrigue and even deadlier love is played out by Ellis, the secretive and daring American agent; Jean-Pierre, the charming doctor and Soviet sympathizer; Jane, the gutsy woman who finds herself a pawn; and the guerrillas, ruthless, resilient, and almost as mysterious to their allies as they are to their enemies. A valiant effort by Mr. Marinker to keep this story taut on audio fails utterly.

2 css 3 hr Simon & Schuster Audio

The Looking Glass War
Author/Reader: John Le Carré
★★★★

It's been twenty years since the end of World War II and things just haven't been the same in British intelligence. But now comes word that Russian missiles have been sighted in East Germany. Suddenly, the department's old juices begin to flow as the Cold War rapidly heats up. And three British subjects find themselves undertaking the most perilous mission of their careers. Surprisingly fresh and alive, with a cast of well-portrayed characters. All the depth and nuance you'd expect from Le Carré.

2 css 3 hr Random House AudioBooks

The Manchurian Candidate
Author: Richard Condon
Reader: Robert Vaughn
Bomb

Raymond Shaw is plucked off a battlefield in Korea by the Chinese and brainwashed. He is then restored to his own side without any recollection of what occurred. After the war, Raymond takes his place in the American political scene.

He is rich, socially accepted, and a "Medal of Honor" man. He is also the perfect assassin—ready and able to kill without question whenever his "controller" decides that the time is right to activate him. Unfortunately, somebody "*activated*" Robert Vaughn, and he assassinates Mr. Condon's *Candidate* with rhythmic monotony. If you've been searching for something to help you sleep at night, try this. If you're looking for a cracking post–Korean War thriller, try Mr. Condon's book or the film of the same.

2 css 3 hr Listen for Pleasure

"Money with Menaces"
Author: Frederick Forsyth
Reader: Edward de Souza
★★★

A short story from Forsyth's *No Comebacks* collection, about a man leaving his glasses case on a commuter train, followed by all sorts of dirty doings, including blackmail. A tidy little romp with Mr. de Souza if you have an hour to kill. And I do mean kill. . . .

1 css 1 hr Durkin Hayes Audio

A Murder of Quality
Author/Reader: John Le Carré
★★★★

There is a murder in one of England's leading private schools: One of the schoolmasters finds that his wife has been killed in their home. But before she died, the victim wrote a letter in which she forecast her own murder—at the hands of her husband. George Smiley, Le Carré's mild-mannered and unlikely hero, investigates. A real treat for murder mystery fans who also dabble in action/adventure, or vice versa.

2 css 2 hr Listen for Pleasure

The Night Manager
Author/Reader: John Le Carré
★★★★

In *The Night Manager,* Le Carré presents a new arena where the old rivalries of great nations have been supplanted by the ravages of individual greed. Where the rules of espionage forged by past generations are put to more shocking use. Where arms dealers and drug smugglers rise to unheard-of power. It is this world, in all its brilliant corruption, that Mr. Le Carré opens up for us. One of his newest recordings, showing that Le Carré, like fine English sherry, ages extremely well.

4 css 4 hr Random House AudioBooks

Night Shadows
Author/Reader: Ron Ely
★★

Jake Sands, now retired, once worked for a special government unit and then as a "recoverer" of stolen or missing objects . . . and people. Jogging one night, he literally stumbles upon a body. As the fates would have it, Jake is back in business. And so is the actor Ron Ely, of television Tarzan fame. While Mr. Ely's writing is clearly exciting, his reading is clearly not. This tape is more proof that most authors should not read their own words.

2 css 3 hr Dove Audio

No Comebacks
Author: Frederick Forsyth
Reader: Edward de Souza
★★★

Three selected short stories ("No Comebacks," "Money with Menaces," and "Privilege") from Forsyth. Within these stories lives a wealth of characters irrevocably trapped in a world of no comebacks, beyond the point of no return—from the manipulators and the manipulated, to the ultrarich capable of buying and selling human lives, to the everyday man maneuvered by circumstances into performing deadly acts of violence. A solid professional reading by Mr. de Souza keeps the suspense on track. When short stories are done as well as these, it's a wonder there aren't more on audio.

2 css 3 hr Listen for Pleasure

The Osterman Weekend
Author: Robert Ludlum
Reader: Robert Loggia
★★★

A group of radical Soviets are trained to infiltrate the social and professional ranks of the U.S. financial community. If they succeed, the future of global peace will be placed in jeopardy. The CIA has identified three American couples as possible suspects. And the agency has found one man uniquely qualified to uncover who among them are actually foreign agents. John Tanner, a friend to all three couples, has agreed to entertain them for a weekend. . . . Mr. Loggia and his gruff reading wrings every bit of action out of this book, even though he's out of breath at the end. (Perhaps it's from fighting the dated seventies music that's included?)

2 css 3 hr Random House AudioBooks

Patriot Games
Author: Tom Clancy
Reader: Martin Sheen
★★★

Years before his appearance in *The Hunt for Red October*, Jack Ryan, historian, ex-marine, and CIA analyst, is vacationing in London, when the Ulster Liberation Army makes a terrorist attack on the Prince and Princess of Wales. By instinctively diving forward to break up the attack, he gains both the gratitude of a nation and the hatred of its most dangerous men. Jack Ryan must summon all of the skills and knowledge at his command to battle his nemesis. The distinctive voice of Martin Sheen is a great match for this thriller. He handles the many dialects of the British Isles remarkably, as well as the action sequences (appropriately fast-paced without ever being rushed). Overall, a good production with some effective music.

2 css 3 hr Random House AudioBooks

The Pelican Brief
Author: John Grisham
Performer: Anthony Heald
★★★★

Late one October night, Justice Abe Rosenberg, at ninety-one the Supreme Court's liberal legend, is shot to death in his Georgetown home. Two hours later, Glenn Jensen, the court's youngest and most conservative justice, is strangled. The country is stunned; the FBI has no clues. But Darby Shaw, a brilliant law student at Tulane, thinks she has the answer. Days of digging through the law library's computers have led her to draft a brief speculating on an obscure connection between the two justices—and a most likely suspect. Mr. Heald brings lots of heart, plenty of fun, and forceful intelligence to Mr. Grisham's best-selling page-turner.

4 css 5 hr 40 min Bantam Audio

A Perfect Spy
Author/Reader: John Le Carré
★★★★

Magnus Pym, lifetime secret agent and presently counselor for certain unmentionable matters at the British embassy in Vienna, is missing, believed defected. The chase is on: for a missing person, for the truth about a charming man. It is conducted by Pym himself as well as by his pursuers. While Pym with desperate affection recounts his quest for love and faith, and his first steps in deception, his pursuers unearth such a trail of duplicity as would make Kim Philby look like a patriotic Boy Scout. Yet the man they all loved remains mysteriously, maddeningly intact. Mr. Le Carré himself narrates his complex novel simply, yet with utter clarity. A virtual seminar on dialects and characterizations.

4 css 5½ hr Listen for Pleasure

Red Storm Rising
Author: Tom Clancy
Reader: F. Murray Abraham
★★★

"Allah!" With that shrill cry, three Muslim terrorists blow up a key Soviet oil complex, creating a critical oil shortage that threatens the stability of the USSR. To offset the effects of this disaster, members of the politburo and KBG devise a brilliant plan of diplomatic trickery. But as the story nears its climax, the Soviets are faced with another prospect, one they hadn't planned on: a full-scale conflict in which nobody can win. F. Murray Abraham is able to create so many wonderful, individual voices that you'll think you're listening to a full-cast radio play. The effect is supported by some complex sound effects.

2 css 2 hr Sound Editions

Rising Sun
Author: Michael Crichton
Reader: Keith Szarabajka
★★

Two cops are plunged into the Los Angeles Japanese community as they investigate the death of a beautiful young woman at the U.S. headquarters of a powerful Japanese electronics corporation. Their search for the killer uncovers an insidious, widespread pattern of bribery, corruption, and extortion that reaches from Tokyo to Capitol Hill. While Mr. Szarabajka is a gifted actor with a pleasant voice, his handling of this material is uninspired and his interpretation weak.

2 css 3 hr Random House AudioBooks

The Road to Omaha
Author: Robert Ludlum
Reader: Joseph Campanella
★★★

A lovable romp that reunites General MacKenzie Hawkins, the loose cannon, and Sam Devereaux, the legal wizard, last seen in *The Road to Gandolfo*. Together, Hawkins and Devereaux plan to take possession of a prime piece of real estate—the state of Nebraska! Secret treaties with Indian tribes, the Air Force's SAC headquarters in Omaha, and a mysterious Supreme Court opinion. . . . Joseph Campanella gives a bright and brassy performance, full of vim and vigor, whipping off the snappy dialogue at brisk clip.

4 css 4 hr Random House AudioBooks

The Russia House
Author/Reader: John Le Carré
★★★★

We are in the third year of perestroika and glasnost. The place is Moscow. The man is Barley: a derelict English publisher with a passion for jazz and a penchant for booze, who visits the Moscow book fair. The woman is Katya: a beautiful Russian with a mission to mankind and access to some of the hottest defense intelligence to come out of the Soviet Union in years. The action moves from Moscow to a safe house in London to a CIA-owned island off the coast of Maine and back again to the Soviet Union. Another lucid reading by Mr. Le Carré that finds every nuance in each syllable. Mr. Le Carré's rendering of Barley is especially humorous and a real treat for Le Carré fans.

2 css 3 hr Random House AudioBooks

Sahara
Author: Clive Cussler
Reader: Tom Wopat
Bomb

A deadly toxic compound in the middle of the African desert is killing thousands of people and threatening marine life in the world's seas. As Dirk Pitt crosses the Sahara to uncover an unholy conspiracy, he discovers the truth about Kitty Mannock, an Australian pilot missing since 1931, and an incredible secret held in a Confederate ironclad. . . . Dirk Pitt might strike again in *Sahara,* but he strikes out with Mr. Wopat. To put it in one word—boring.

2 css 3 hr Simon & Schuster Audio

The Sands of Time
Author/Reader: Sidney Sheldon
Bomb

The tale of four nuns who are forced to flee their Spanish convent and face a hostile world they long ago abandoned. Suddenly these four women find themselves pawns in a violent struggle between the outlawed Basque underground movement, led by the charismatic Jaime Miro, and the Spanish army, under the command of the vengeful Colonel Ramón Acoca, who is bent on destroying them all. To put it delicately, Mr. Sheldon lacks the reading skills of Mr. Le Carré. With Mr. Le Carré you get a strong sense of the author's lack of ego, while with Mr. Sheldon . . .

2 css 3 hr Dove Audio

The Scarlatti Inheritance
Author: Robert Ludlum
Reader: David Dukes
★★★

Elizabeth Wyndham Scarlatti is the powerful matriarch of an influential and wealthy family. But just how powerful is she? And is she influential enough to stop her own son, who, going under the name of Heinrich Kroeger, is about to give Hitler's Third Reich control of the most powerful instrument on earth? She summons the key figures of the Western world to Switzerland to propose a plan to stop Kroeger. But can she? After all, a mother has just so much power over her son. . . . Mr. Dukes succeeds in getting both hands around this epic story and then doling it out intrigue by intrigue. I found his German dialects beautifully convincing.

2 css 3 hr Random House AudioBooks

The Scorpio Illusion
Author: Robert Ludlum
Performer: Robert Lansing
★★★

Amaya Bajaratt is beautiful, elusive—and deadly. Born in a remote Basque village, she was forced to look on as soldiers brutally killed her parents, and at that moment she vowed death to all authority. Now an accomplished assassin, when the man she loves is killed in a terrorist raid she strikes out in a bold act of vengeance that involves the heads of Israel, England, France, and the United States in one violent act. Desperate to find her, the intelligence community turns to former naval officer Tye Hawthorne. A breathtaking performance by Robert Lansing delivers all of the moody atmospheres required by Robert Ludlum over the course of this epic saga.

4 css 6 hr Bantam Audio

"Sharp Practice"
Author: Frederick Forsyth
Reader: Edward de Souza
★★★

A story from Forsyth's *No Comebacks.* On a train bound for Tralee, a priest, a judge, and a horse buyer find themselves involved in a game of poker. None expected to see the others again . . . especially in a court of law. A deceptively smooth reading by Mr. de Souza makes this the perfect tape to plug into your Walkman [for a short trip.]

1 css 1 hr Durkin Hayes Audio

The Shepherd
Author: Frederick Forsyth
Reader: Robert Powell
★★★

It is Christmas Eve, 1957, and a man is flying home alone, on leave from Germany. His plane cuts through the clear, frosty night, destination England. Then, out over the North Sea, the fog begins to close in. Radio contact ceases, the compass fails, and the vertical speed indicator no longer functions. All he knows is how fast he is flying. Suddenly, out of the mist comes another plane, an old World War II bomber, flying below him—as if trying to make contact. Robert Powell tells the story in a steady, fully realized manner, making for a short but exciting trip.

1 css 1 hr Durkin Hayes Audio

Shuttle
Author: David C. Onley
Reader: Robert Lansing
★★

The giant hyperspace jet *Yorktown* climbs into the sky above Edwards Air Force Base with the space shuttle *Columbia* clasped to her back. Her mission is to launch the shuttle into space from the edge of the earth's atmosphere. But disaster looms and one craft will never return. With the shattered craft locked in a fatal orbit, Mission Control races against time to mount a final rescue attempt. A pedestrian reading by Robert Lansing doesn't help to give this tale much excitement.

2 css 3 hr Durkin Hayes Audio

Sky Masters
Author: Dale Brown
Reader: Joseph Campanella
★★

In the near future, U.S. forces are completing their final withdrawal from bases in the Philippines. The Chinese navy lays claim to the Spratly Islands, decimating a Philippine drilling platform when its occupants refuse to knuckle under. The confrontation quickly escalates when the Chinese use a tactical nuke to wipe out the Filipino flotilla. The United States counterattacks, with Colonel Patrick "Mac" MacLanahan of the original "Old Dog" flight playing a key role. Joseph Campanella, normally an enchanting reader, is miscast with this blood-and-guts saga. His usual warmth and humor are here, but none of the gritty machismo Mr. Brown's book needs to succeed on audio.

2 css 3 hr Dove Audio

A Small Town in Germany
Author/Reader: John Le Carré
★★★★

There are political demonstrations and riots in Bonn. Federal authorities confess themselves "deeply concerned." The British ambassador reluctantly agrees to impose a voluntary curfew on his staff. Then Leo Harting goes missing, taking with him a batch of sensitive files. "What's all this about Leo being ill? He hasn't had a day's illness in his life. What's Leo been up to?" Alan Turner, a cynical and weary service professional, is sent from London to find out. Mr. Le Carré uses a particularly light touch in narrating the witty dialogue, while at the same time untangling the complex plot.

2 css 2 hr Listen for Pleasure

Solo
Author: Jack Higgins
Reader: Tim Pigott-Smith
★★★

John Mikali is a brilliant but psychotic pianist who lives a double life as a contract hit man. But he slips up on a job in London and accidentally kills the teenage daughter of a tough SAS soldier, a trained and brutal killer himself. As Colonel Asa Morgan hunts the man who murdered his daughter, the story builds to a satisfying climax. Tim Pigott-Smith's rendering of Mr. Higgins's tragic tale is solid throughout, hitting all the right buttons.

2 css 3 hr Listen for Pleasure

Sphere
Author: Michael Crichton
Reader: Edward Asner
Bomb

A spaceship has been found resting on the ocean floor—a spaceship at least 300 years old. Has it come from an alien culture? From a different universe? Four scientists rush to the scene and descend together into the depths of the sea to search for answers. What they find there only raises more—and increasingly ominous—questions. Yet the biggest question of all is why Mr. Asner couldn't come up with any sense of excitement for this book. Unclear and boring.

2 css 3 hr Random House AudioBooks

"The Spy in His Prime" (from The Secret Pilgrim)
Author/Reader: John Le Carré
★★★★

The Berlin Wall has toppled, the Iron Curtain has been swept aside, the Cold War has ended. . . . Le Carré himself narrates the inner turmoils of Ned, a shrewd, loyal, decent soldier in British intelligence, revisiting his life as a spy and as a middle-aged man. Unfortunately, this in not Le Carré at his very best. Fortunately, Le Carré not at his very best is only slightly less than perfect.

2 css 3 hr Random House AudioBooks

The Spy Who Came in from the Cold
Author/Reader: John Le Carré
★★★★

No one at headquarters is very surprised when Alec Leamas is withdrawn from operational work and put "on the shelf." The Berlin network has been a failure for years, they say, and someone has to take the rap for it. Besides, Leamas is part of the old school. What no one knows is that Leamas's apparent degradation is part of the intricate deception devised by Control to lead Leamas to the top man behind the Berlin Wall: Mundt. "This is your last job," Control assures him. "Then you can come in from the cold." This was Le Carré's third novel and the one that brought him worldwide acclaim. For the audiophile, here is the master himself, performing a virtual Cold War aria.

2 css 2½ hr Durkin Hayes Audio

Stealth
Author: Guy Durham
Reader: Ken Howard
Bomb

Despite Mr. Durham's being a weapons expert and a navy veteran, his story of clandestine intrigue at an intelligence training facility and at the air force's supersecret Nellis testing range is muddled beyond recognition in the hands of Ken Howard. Perhaps one day they'll invent subtitles for audio.

2 css 3 hr Durkin Hayes Audio

Stolen Thunder
Author: David Axton
Reader: James Naughton
★★★

Rows of B-52 bombers—the gargantuan aircraft that once decimated North Vietnam—now stand obsolete on the dry desert floor of Arizona. A group of six ex-military personnel, including a woman pilot, hijack one of the planes as the instrument of their revenge. Twelve thousand miles away awaits a Libyan terrorist training camp whose annihilation is their mission. The reason: to avenge the murder of a young pilot whose father and widow are in the B-52 crew. With James Naughton's relaxed and comfortable hand at the wheel, *Stolen Thunder* is a clean, smooth ride.

2 css 3 hr Durkin Hayes Audio

Stony Man Doctrine
Author: Don Pendleton
Reader: George Maharis
★★★

Colonel John Phoenix, better known as Mack Bolan, the Executioner, blasts into action with his paramilitary strike squads, Phoenix Force and Able Team. Their mission is to wage a dirty war for the president of the United States: a war that is merciless, outside the Geneva Convention, and mindless of national borders. It is a desperate war to stop the carnage being unleashed throughout the United States by an international troika of terror. An aggressive reading by Mr. Maharis brings a healthy dose of machismo to this action-packed tale of derring-do.

2 css 3 hr Durkin Hayes Audio

The Sum of All Fears
Author: Tom Clancy
Reader: David Ogden Stiers
★★

Peace may finally be at hand in the Middle East—as Jack Ryan lays the groundwork for a plan that could end centuries of conflict. But ruthless terrorists have a final, desperate card to play; with one terrible act, distrust mounts, forces collide, and the floundering U.S. president seems unable to cope with the crisis. With the world on the verge of nuclear disaster, Ryan must frantically seek a solution—before the chiefs of state lose control of themselves and the world. Mr. Stiers somehow misses with this Tom Clancy title. His usual intelligent reading, so useful for untying Mr. Clancy's technical knots, comes off here as pedantic and plodding.

4 css 6 hr Simon & Schuster Audio

The Swiss Account
Author: Paul Erdman
Reader: Edward Woodward
★★★

Switzerland, World War II: Spymaster Allen Dulles discovers that Germany is close to developing a nuclear bomb. But the Nazis are not his only enemy. He must also battle the immensely powerful, ruthless Swiss banking and industrial interests who are profiting enormously by financing Hitler's war machine and selling high-tech military hardware to the Third Reich. In 1945, Dulles dispatches a team of operatives on a mission with three objectives: to stop the shipment of Swiss arms to Germany, to sabotage the German atomic bomb project, and, against all odds, to stay alive. A terrific job by Edward Woodward—an old hand at espionage characters—lends this period nail-biter all the immediacy of today's headlines.

2 css 3 hr Audio Renaissance Tapes

Tarzan
Author: Edgar Rice Burroughs
Readers: Multiple Cast
★★★

Authorized versions of four classics: *Tarzan of the Apes, The Return of Tarzan, Tarzan and the Jewels of Opar,* and *Tarzan and the City of Gold.* Directed by Johnny Weissmuller, Jr. A refreshingly faithful rendition of the classic stories.

4 css 6 hr The Mind's Eye

A Time to Kill
Author: John Grisham
Performer: Michael Beck
★★

Clanton, Mississippi. The life of a ten-year-old girl is shattered by two drunken and remorseless young men. The mostly white town reacts with shock and horror at the inhuman crime, until her black father acquires an assault rifle and takes justice into his own outraged hands. For ten days, as burning crosses and the crack of sniper fire spread through the streets of Clanton, the nation sits spellbound while young defense attorney Jack Brigance struggles to save his client's life . . . and then his own. Yet as exciting as the story is, it suffers dramatically from Mr. Beck's strained, workmanlike effort at narration. This book deserves much better.

2 css 3 hrs Bantam Audio

Touch the Devil
Author: Jack Higgins
Reader: Ian Holm
★★★

Hitler's war, Vietnam, and Belfast were the training grounds for three of the most professional and deadly international terrorists. First there is Frank Barry, seasoned killer, whose sole motivation is money and who will work for anyone. The only man capable of stopping him is Martin Brosnam, a killer schooled in Vietnam, graduate of the IRA, and now rotting away in the French prison fortress of Belle Isle. And there is Liam Devlin, weary after a lifetime supporting the IRA cause but wily enough to spring Brosnam and help him track down Barry. Ian Holm throws himself into this book with wild abandon. He grabs each life-and-death situation and shakes it for all it's worth. Very stirring.

2 css 2½ hr Listen for Pleasure

Trevayne
Author: Robert Ludlum
Performer: Philip Bosco
★★★

A self-made millionaire at thirty-five, Andrew Trevayne has lived his life with honesty and integrity to become one of the most admired men in the nation. Now, at the express wish of the president, Trevayne has undertaken a special assignment: an investigation into "the secret government within the government." It's a job that will sweep him into a nightmare maze of intrigue and peril far beyond the corridors of official power, where Mafia and big business mingle, money is all, and anything can be bought—including the government itself. Mr. Bosco, while maybe sounding a touch elderly for the material, manages to pull off a cunning bedtime story for adults.

3 css 3½ hr Bantam Audio

Tripwire
Author: Jay Brandon
Reader: Gregory Harrison
★★

Elizabeth Truett's quiet life is ripped apart when she is the only witness to a brutal murder. Suddenly she must accept protective custody from the police, and Captain Bill Jerek is the only person who knows where she is hiding. But two other people are desperately looking for her: One is the killer, and the other is a war-ravaged POW named Tripwire, returned from Vietnam to reclaim his life. Mr. Harrison lacks the technical ability to bring this story all of the color it demands.

2 css 3 hr The Publishing Mills

Weapon
Author: Robert Mason
Reader: Tim Matheson
★★

The U.S. military has constructed Solo—the ultimate war machine. Solo walks, talks, reasons, kills, and looks like a man—and is unstoppable. Solo is so human that when the military sends him to Nicaragua for a "test kill," he decides to find things out for himself. And what he discovers is that he has been lied to by his creators. Now this six-foot-two, 300-pound war machine is determined to teach his own government what honor means. Even though Mr. Matheson has the means to make the story clear, he doesn't have the guts-and-glory sensibility this book desperately needs.

2 css 3 hr Dove Audio

The White Ninja
Author: Eric Lustbader
Reader: Tim Matheson
★★

Nicholas Linnear, the "White Ninja," has returned to Japan, home of his spiritual heart. Here, where he usually finds serenity and beauty, he must watch, helpless, as his life unravels. He can no longer summon the discipline most vital to a ninja. An enemy has invaded his spirit, robbing him of the ninja balance that is the source of his power. A weak and rushed performance by Tim Matheson makes this story incomprehensible. True, there's some nice atmospheric music included, but this isn't supposed to be just a sound track . . . is it?

2 css 3 hr Dove Audio

White Shark
Author: Peter Benchley
Reader: Stephen Collins
★★★

At a small marine institute, a young marine biologist, Simon Chase, begins to notice strange behavior among the creatures of the sea—something in the ocean is throwing off the balance of nature. Then the body of a diver washes ashore. When more victims are discovered, Chase realizes that while the killer resembles a white shark, it is far more dangerous and malevolent than any shark he has ever encountered. A professional job by Stephen Collins keeps Mr. Benchley's terrifying tale on an even keel. Not quite *Jaws*, but plenty of bite.

2 css 3 hr Random House AudioBooks

The Wind Chill Factor
Author: Thomas Gifford
Reader: Ron Vawter
★★★

Some of the Nazis who survive view Hitler's defeat as a mere temporary setback. Their plans are in motion. Their key personnel are in place inside the corporations and capitals of every major nation. By the end of the century, it will all be theirs. John Cooper is an heir to this evil—an evil he'd turned his back on. Until now. For the dark legacy has finally caught up with him, thrusting into his hands a secret too explosive to be kept. Mr. Vawter brings just the right amount of creepy intimacy to Mr. Gifford's words. I listened to this one with all the lights on.

2 css 3 hr Bantam Audio

Without Remorse
Author: Tom Clancy
Reader: David Dukes
★★

John Kelly, former navy SEAL and Vietnam veteran, is still getting over the accidental death of his wife six months before, when he befriends a young woman with a checkered past. When the past reaches out for her in a particularly horrifying fashion, he vows revenge and sets out to track down the men responsible. At the same time, the Pentagon is readying an operation to rescue a key group of prisoners in a North Vietnamese prisoner-of-war camp. John Kelly has his own mission. The Pentagon wants him for theirs. Once again, one of Mr. Clancy's thrillers is torn to little, boring pieces by an inferior audio performance.

4 css 6 hr Random House AudioBooks

Angel Eyes
A: Eric Lustbader
R: Adrienne Barbeau
DOVE

The Apocalypse Watch
A: Robert Ludlum
R: Edward Hermann
BDD

As the Crow Flies
A: Jeffrey Archer
R: Alec McCowen
HARP

Assumed Identity
A: David Morrell
R: Ed Asner
DOVE

Black Blade
A: Eric Lustbader
R: Michael Nouri
DOVE

Bolt
A: Dick Francis
R: Nigel Havers
DURK

Break In
A: Dick Francis
R: Nigel Havers
DURK

Bright Orange for the Shroud
A: John D. MacDonald
R: Darren McGavin
RH

Bright Star
A: Harold Coyle
R: Jerry Orbach
S&S

The Burning
A: Graham Masterton
R: David Dukes
DOVE

Chains of Command
A: Dale Brown
R: Robert Culp
DOVE

The Chamber
A: John Grisham
R: Michael Beck
BDD

The Chancellor Manuscript
A: Robert Ludlum
R: Michael Moriarty
BDD

Clancy and Coonts: Two Techno-Thrillers (The Hunt for Red October and Flight of the Intruder)
A: Tom Clancy and Stephen Coonts
R: Richard Crenna and Frank Converse
PART

Close Combat
A: W.E.B. Griffin
R: Edward Herrmann
HARP

Cold Harbour
A: Jack Higgins
R: David McCallum
S&S

Counterattack
A: W.E.B. Griffin
R: Gerald McRaney
S&S

CW2
A: Layne Heath
R: Michael O'Keefe
S&S

Cyclops
A: Clive Cussler
R: John Rubinstein
S&S

Dark Side of the Street
A: Jack Higgins
R: Edward Woodward
DOVE

The Day after Tomorrow
A: Allan Folsom
R: Edward Herrmann
BDD

Day of Judgment
A: Jack Higgins
R: Edward Woodward
DOVE

Debt of Honor
A: Tom Clancy
R: John Rubinstein
RH

Declarations of War
A: Len Deighton
DURK

Desert Fire
A: David Hagberg
R: David McCallum
DURK

The Doomsday Conspiracy
A/R: Sidney Sheldon
DOVE

The Eagle Has Flown
A: Jack Higgins
R: David McCallum
S&S

Eagles at War
A: Walter J. Boyne
R: Paul Hecht
RH

Edge of Honor
A: P. T. Deutermann
BRILL

Embrace the Serpent
A/R: Marilyn Quayle and Nancy Northcott
DOVE

Eye of the Storm
A: Jack Higgins
R: Patrick MacNee
DOVE

The Fifth Profession
A: David Morrell
R: David McCallum
DOVE

A Fine Night for Dying
A: Jack Higgins
R: Nicholas Ball
DOVE

First among Equals
A: Jeffrey Archer
R: Michael York
HARP

The First Sacrifice
A: Thomas Gifford
R: Ron Rifkin
BDD

"The Fledgling Spy" (from The Secret Pilgrim)
A/R: John Le Carré
DURK

"The Fledgling Spy" (from The Secret Pilgrim)
A/R: John Le Carré
RH

Flight of the Intruder
A: Stephen Coonts
R: Frank Converse
PART

Floating City
A: Eric Lustbader
DOVE

The Fourth K
A: Mario Puzo
R: David Dukes
RH

A Game for Heroes
A: Jack Higgins
R: Christopher Lee
DOVE

The General's Daughter
A: Nelson DeMille
R: Ken Howard
RH

The Gold Coast
A: Nelson DeMille
R: David Dukes
RH

The Guest of Honor
A: Irving Wallace
R: Roddy McDowall
DOVE

Hammerheads
A: Dale Brown
R: Joseph Campanella
DOVE

Heat
A: Stuart Woods
R: Tony Roberts
HARP

Hell Is Always Tonight
A: Jack Higgins
R: Patrick MacNee
DOVE

Honor Bound
A: W.E.B. Griffin
BRILL

Honorable Enemies
A: Joe Weber
BRILL

The Hunt for Red October
A: Tom Clancy
R: Frank Muller
PART

If Tomorrow Comes
A: Sidney Sheldon
R: Roger Moore
DOVE

Imperfect Strangers
A: Stuart Woods
R: Anthony Heald
HARP

Inca Gold
A: Clive Cussler
R: Howard McGillin
S&S

Indiana Jones and the Last Crusade
A: Novelization by Rob MacGregor; story by George Lucas and Menno Meyjes; screenplay by Jeffrey Boam
R: William Conrad
DOVE

Killshot
A: Elmore Leonard
R: Bruce Boxleitner
DOVE

Kolymsky Heights
A: Lionel Davidson
R: Theodore Bikel
ART

A Lesson before Dying
A: Ernest J. Gaines
TW

Line of Fire: Continuing the Saga of the Corps
A: W.E.B. Griffin
R: Joel Higgins
S&S

The Living Daylights and A Quantum of Solace
A: Ian Fleming
R: Anthony Valentine
DURK

Luciano's Luck
A: Jack Higgins
R: Patrick MacNee
DOVE

Master of the Game
A: Sidney Sheldon
R: Roddy McDowall
DOVE

The Matarese Circle
A: Robert Ludlum
R: Martin Balsam
BDD

McNally's Trial
A: Lawrence Sanders
R: Boyd Gaines
S&S

Memoirs of a Dance-Hall Romeo
A: Jack Higgins
R: Christopher Cazenove
DOVE

Memorias de Media Noche (Memories of Midnight)
(Spanish)
A: Sidney Sheldon
R: Elizabeth Pena
DOVE

Memories of Midnight
A: Sidney Sheldon
R: Jenny Agutter
DOVE

The Memories of Midnight Collection
A: Sidney Sheldon
R: Jenny Agutter
DOVE

The Modigliani Scandal
A: Ken Follett
R: Michael York
DOVE

The Murders
A: W.E.B. Griffin
R: Dick Hill
BRILL

The Naked Face
A: Sidney Sheldon
R: Roger Moore
DOVE

The Negotiator
A: Frederick Forsyth
R: Anthony Zerbe
BDD

The New Breed
A: W.E.B. Griffin
R: Kevin McCarthy
S&S

Night of the Fox
A: Jack Higgins
R: David Birney
DOVE

Night of the Fox
A: Jack Higgins
R: Paul Sorvino
S&S

Night of the Hawk
A: Dale Brown
R: Joseph Campanella
DOVE

Night over Water
A: Ken Follett
R: Tim Curry
S&S

On Dangerous Ground
A: Jack Higgins
R: Patrick MacNee
DOVE

On Wings of Eagles
A: Ken Follett
R: Ron Rifkin
DURK

The Other Side of Midnight
A: Sidney Sheldon
R: Jenny Agutter
DOVE

Our Game
A/R: John Le Carré
RH

Paper Money
A: Ken Follett
R: John Standing
DOVE

Paradise Junction
A: Phillip Finch
DURK

Prodigal Daughter
A: Jeffrey Archer
R: Paula Prentiss
HARP

Rage of Angels
A: Sidney Sheldon
R: Susannah York
DOVE

Red Square
A: Martin Cruz Smith
R: Robert O'Keefe
RH

Red Storm Rising and Patriot Games
A: Tom Clancy
R: F. Murray Abraham and Martin Sheen
RH

The Rhinemann Exchange
A: Robert Ludlum
R: Bob Gunton
BDD

Riding the Rap
A: Elmore Leonard
R: Joe Mantegna
BDD

River God
A: Wilbur Smith
BRILL

The River Sorrow
A: Craig Holden
BDD

Rogue Warrior III: Green Team
A: Richard Marcinko and John Weisman
R: Richard Marcinko
S&S

A Season in Hell
A: Jack Higgins
R: David McCallum
S&S

The Seventh Secret
A: Irving Wallace
R: Paul Scofield
DOVE

Sheba
A: Jack Higgins
R: Patrick MacNee
DOVE

Siro
A: David Ignatius
R: Joseph Campanella
DOVE

Storm Warning
A: Jack Higgins
R: Nicholas Ball
DOVE

Storming Heaven
A: Dale Brown
R: Robert Foxworth
DOVE

A Stranger in the Mirror
A: Sidney Sheldon
R: Alan King
DOVE

Sword Point
A: Harold Coyle
R: Richard Masur
S&S

The Ten Thousand
A: Harold Coyle
R: Robert Foxworth
S&S

Thunder Point
A: Jack Higgins
R: Roger Moore
DOVE

To Catch a King
A: Jack Higgins
R: Christopher Lee
DOVE

To Catch a King, Day of Judgment and Toll for the Brave
A: Jack Higgins
R: Christopher Lee, Edward Woodward, and Nicol Williamson
DOVE

Toll for the Brave
A: Jack Higgins
R: Nicol Williamson
DOVE

The Tom Clancy Gift Set
A: Tom Clancy
R: David Ogden Stiers
S&S

Tom Clancy's Op Center
A: Created by Tom Clancy with Steve Pieczenik
R: Edward Herrmann
RH

Treasure
A: Clive Cussler
R: James Keach
S&S

Trial by Fire
A: Harold Coyle
R: John Schneider
S&S

Trinities
A: Nick Tosches
R: Jerry Orbach
BDD

Triple
A: Ken Follett
R: Edward Woodward
S&S

A Trophy for Eagles
A: Walter J. Boyne
R: Peter MacNicol
RH

Twelve Red Herrings
A: Jeffrey Archer
R: Alec McCowen
HARP

Windmills of the Gods
A: Sidney Sheldon
R: Lee Remick
DOVE

Word of Honor
A: Nelson DeMille
R: Brian Murray
RH

The Wrath of God
A: Jack Higgins
R: Christopher Cazenove
DOVE

Wrath of the Lion
A: Jack Higgins
R: Nicol Williamson
DOVE

BUSINESS AND MOTIVATION

The audiotapes included here represent the best of the best on the subject of business, covering a broad array of topics from management and marketing to sales and service; from building self-esteem to building teams. Bringing the authors' books to life, these tapes provide a wealth of information on business concepts, strategies, and techniques that can help make you more successful. Though differing in style, approach, and purpose, each taped program shares a common bond—the refusal to accept the status quo and a desire to effect meaningful change in our lives.

Countless years of business experience and academic research have gone into creating the audio selections that follow. Containing wit and wisdom, insight and inspiration, the programs should have the answers to many of your business questions.

We hope that our reviews make it easier for you to pick and choose the tapes that will be of the greatest use to you. Access to information is critical if one is to accomplish one's personal and professional goals. One key bit of data or new idea can make all the difference.

Some of the authors' names are sure to be familiar to you. Sam Walton. Lee Iacocca. Tom Peters. John Naisbitt and Patricia Aburdene. Og Mandino. Peter Lynch. Zig Ziglar. Harvey Mackay. Kenneth Blanchard. Best-selling authors all, each one is an acknowledged business expert. Other authors, whom you may not have heard of yet, are waiting to be discovered. They, too, have much to share with you.

Whether your immediate goal is to start a business, or to get a job, a promotion, or a raise, help is at hand to assist you in achieving your objective. You'll get tips and strategies on managing your money, motivating others, maximizing your potential, from the likes of Napoleon Hill, Stephen Covey, and Brian Tracy. For a look at the future listen to what trend-spotter Faith Popcorn has to say, or pull up a chair and get the inside scoop on business from ice-cream moguls Ben and Jerry.

The business information you need to help you thrive on chaos, build customers for life, get what you want, and find the winner within is just a cassette away.

HIGHLY RECOMMENDED (★★★★)

Ben and Jerry's: The Inside Scoop
Dr. Robert Anthony's "The Ultimate Secrets of Total Self-confidence"
How to Sell Anything to Anybody
Iacocca
The One Minute Manager
The One Minute Manager Meets the Monkey
One Up on Wall Street
The Power of Positive Thinking
The Science of Personal Achievement
Think and Grow Rich
The Tom Peters Seminar
Zig Ziglar's Secrets of Closing the Sale

Anthony Robbins' Powertalk
Author/Reader: Anthony Robbins
★★

The first part of the program, which was recorded at Robbins's resort in Fiji, is as much promo for the resort as motivational program. Drawing on various laboratory experiments in human and animal behavior, Robbins outlines his strategies for changing negative beliefs and taking control of one's life. The second part consists of an interview Robbins conducted with economist Paul Zane Pitzer, who discusses the economic decisions people make and their lifestyle expectations. Robbins's fast-paced delivery is his strong suit here, but the disjointedness of the programs works against them.

2 css 2 hr 20 min Audio Renaissance Tapes

The Art of Negotiation
Author/Reader: Gerard I. Nierenberg
★★★

Nierenberg shares his negotiating techniques for winning people over to your point of view whether it's at home or at work, in your personal or professional dealings. Practical and down-to-earth, Nierenberg gives specifics on how to get a raise, buy a car, plan a vacation, resolve conflicts, and more. Emphasizing the need to keep an open mind and recognize negotiating as an ongoing part of life, the author is ably assisted by performers "Frank" and "Edna," who act out his examples and bring the mock negotiations to life.

1 css 45 min Random House AudioBooks

Beating the Street
Author/Reader: Peter Lynch
★★★

Lynch, the best-selling author of *One Up on Wall Street* (see page 57), offers advice ("Peter's Prescription") for making the right investment choices. Expressing his egalitarian view that anyone who keeps an eye on the products in demand at the local shopping mall can be a successful investor, Lynch does a good job of demystifying the market.

2 css 3 hr Simon & Schuster Audio

Ben and Jerry's: The Inside Scoop
Author: Fred "Chico" Lager
Reader: Joseph Campanella
★★★★

This tape is excellent, delivering much more than a single scoop of information on what it took to create Ben and Jerry's Ice Cream and what it takes to succeed in business. Told from the perspective of "Chico" Lager, the company's former CEO, the program omits nothing, starting at the beginning as Ben Cohen and Jerry Greenfield search for a business to start, teach themselves to make ice cream, and overcome every financial, marketing, and management obstacle that gets in their path. This is a classic lesson on entrepreneurship. Campanella's reading—even-paced and compelling—adds just the right dollop of whipped cream.

2 css 3 hr Dove Audio

Beware the Naked Man Who Offers You His Shirt
Author/Reader: Harvey Mackay
★★★

Mackay, the man who told people who to "swim with the sharks and not be eaten alive," provides strategies for getting to the top and staying there. Structuring the tape in the form of "short courses," he delves into business topics ranging from getting a job, a raise, or a promotion, to starting a business. Organized and methodical, he covers a lot of ground and offers many valuable suggestions.

1 css 1½ hr Simon & Schuster Audio

Beyond a Passion for Excellence
Author/Reader: Tom Peters
★★★

An original program based on Peters's management concepts and findings, this focuses on what it takes to achieve business excellence in a highly competitive and rapidly changing environment. Noting that foreign competitors keep getting better and standards of performance keep getting raised, Peters says it isn't enough just to make incremental improvements in service. Nothing short of exponential gains will do. Citing successful companies in industries ranging from shoe manufacturing to steel, cars to computers, Peters makes his case with force and verve.

1 css 1 hr Random House AudioBooks

Blow Your Own Horn
Author/Reader: Jeffrey P. Davidson
★★★

Davidson outlines a step-by-step program for successful self-promotion covering five critical areas of career marketing. Showing how to become your own career coach and gain additional exposure on the job, he provides strategies for getting noticed and getting ahead. The tape is clear and concise, with information on developing communications skills, networking, assessing personal strengths and weaknesses, and preparing a plan of action.

1 css 50 min Simon & Schuster Audio

Control Your Destiny or Someone Else Will
Authors: Noel M. Tichy and Stratford Sherman
Reader: Stratford Sherman
★★★

In an excellent reading of his book, Sherman discusses the revolutionary changes that CEO Jack Welch implemented at General Electric in the 1980s. In addition to sharing Welch's basic philosophy (i.e., either you're number one or two in your industry or you're not in it), the authors show the strategies and techniques Welch employed at G.E. This includes an inside look at the company's mergers, acquisitions, and downsizing activities (buying RCA, selling its appliance division to Black & Decker, and cutting some 170,000 positions).

2 css 2 hr Harper Audio

Coping with Difficult People
Author/Reader: Robert M. Bramson, Ph.D.
★★★

Bramson identifies seven difficult-to-deal-with personality types, ranging from "snipers" to "clams," "bulldozers" to "balloons," and shows effective ways of coping with them. Whether it's standing up for yourself or stepping aside, hearing them out or cutting them off, Bramson shows which strategies work best with which people. The tape uses dramatizations to illustrate the various situations, and Bramson's voice of reason ties everything together.

1 css 1 hr Simon & Schuster Audio

The Corporate Coach
Authors: James B. Miller with Paul B. Brown
Reader: James B. Miller
★★★

Miller, who turned a failing office supplies business with $50,000 in annual sales into a $150 million company in twenty-five years, shares his philosophy on teamwork. Packing his story with numerous anecdotes, do's and don'ts, and an abundance of common sense, Miller does an outstanding job of telling what goes into making a successful team and developing a customer-driven company. It's clear that he enjoys his work and wants his employees and customers to derive satisfaction from his business.

1 cc 1½ hr Harper Audio

Creating Character Voices for Fun and Profit
Author/Reader: Patrick Fraley
★★

While the obvious audience for this program is actors and comedians, it can be of use to businesspeople and others, as well. Fraley, a successful voice-over actor, shows how you can turn your voice into a powerful tool, enlivening your conversations and presentations and enhancing communication. Outlining the steps involved in creating characters and developing the right voices for them, he's backed up by an able cast of his own vocal creations.

2 css 2 hr Audio Editions

Customers for Life
Authors: Carl Sewell and Paul Brown
Reader: Charles Dean
★★★

Drawing on his experience running the number-one Cadillac dealership in Dallas, Sewell tells how his business achieved that position and what it does to stay there. Crediting satisfied, repeat customers for the dealership's success, Sewell provides helpful, real-world advice on using focus groups, market research, and other techniques to find out what customers really want. Along with this, he shows how to set up a system that inspires and empowers employees to deliver superior service on a continual basis.

2 css 2 hr Bantam Audio

Doing It Now
Author/Reader: Edwin Bliss
★★★

The program focuses on the reasons people procrastinate and provides a twelve-step plan for overcoming them. Presented in a question-and-answer format that brushes aside each excuse for not taking action, the tape includes exercises for building self-mastery and the confidence to tackle the tasks at hand.

1 css 50 min Simon & Schuster Audio

Don't Fire Them, Fire Them Up
Authors: Frank Pacetta with Roger Gittines
Reader: Frank Pacetta
★★★

Pacetta, a district manager in Xerox's Cleveland sales office, shows how to turn underperforming workers into winners. Practicing what he preaches, he turned one of Xerox's worst districts into one of its best by getting his team members to believe in their product and to believe in themselves. Pacetta offers basic advice on the nuts and bolts of being a sales professional.

1 css 1½ hr Simon & Schuster Audio

Dr. Robert Anthony's "The Ultimate Secrets of Total Self-confidence"
Author/Reader: Robert Anthony
★★★★

Dr. Anthony offers clear-cut strategies for developing self-awareness and self-confidence and for managing feelings of guilt. Emphasizing the need to take control over one's actions and to look within for guidance, Dr. Anthony says that each person possesses self-healing powers and the ability to find health, happiness, and peace of mind. To achieve these states, though, one must first break the bonds of negative thinking. Proceeding in a step-by-step manner, Dr. Anthony explains why self-imposed barriers to personal fulfillment exist and what you must do to remove them.

2 css 3 hr Dove Audio

Effective Listening
Author/Reader: Kevin J. Murphy
★★

Stating that listening is the most important skill a manager can have, Murphy warns that what you don't hear *can* hurt you. People are often so preoccupied with the past or the future (what they have done or are about to do) that they have difficulty tuning into the present and listening to what's being said. Interrupting others, finishing people's sentences, and monopolizing conversations are all signs of listening problems that need to be corrected. The tape includes self-assessments and techniques you can use to monitor your listening ability and build your skills.

1 css 50 min Simon & Schuster Audio

Everyone's Money Book
Authors/Readers: Jordan E. Goodman and Sonny Bloch
★★★

The tape is divided into seven parts covering the various kinds of investments one can make from cash to stocks and bonds to commodities. It also provides strategies on which investments to make based on your age, detailing how your portfolio should look at different times in your life from youth to retirement. Novice investors will find this tape excellent, and experienced investors should pick up valuable tips as well. As an added benefit, purchasers of the tape can receive a free investment newsletter.

1 css 1½ hr Random House AudioBooks

The Executive Memory Guide
Author/Reader: Hermine Hilton
★★★

This tape offers specific memory techniques for overcoming the "seven-second syndrome"—having information go in one ear and out the other. Saying there's no such thing as a bad memory, only an untrained memory, Hilton shows how to lock in information and file it away for future use. "Mnemonics are the key," she points out, explaining how to use word association, visualization, and mental memos to expand your memory power. Hilton's presentation is good and the dramatizations of typical memory loss situations (giving a presentation, meeting a new client, etc.) enliven the program.

1 css 50 min Simon & Schuster Audio

First Things First
Author/Reader: Stephen R. Covey
★★

Covey, the author of *The 7 Habits of Highly Effective People,* outlines a "principle-centered" approach to organizing your life and finding time for the things that are really important to you. As he points out, it's not just a matter of doing more, but of doing what matters. Emphasizing the importance of making moral choices and the spiritual side of life, Covey delivers his message in a deliberate fashion.

1 css 1½ hr Simon & Schuster Audio

Get to the Point
Authors: Karen Berg and Andrew Gilman with Edward P. Stevenson
Readers: Karen Berg and Andrew Gilman
★★

Communications experts Berg and Gilman share their methods for improving presentation skills and overcoming speaking anxiety. Although packed with information—how to use body language and visual props; strategies; and analogies—the tape is uneven in sections due to the readers' different styles. More choreography is needed to blend their parts into a cohesive whole.

1 css 1 hr Bantam Audio

Getting Past No
Author/Reader: William Ury
★★★

Ury details his five-part system for overcoming resistance and convincing others to see your point of view. Numerous examples are provided throughout the tape, with tips on how to deal with anyone from an angry boss to an unruly teenager. Rather than going head-to-head with an opponent, Ury stresses noncombative alternatives (silence, stepping back for a moment, etc.) that shift the situation from face-to-face confrontation to side-by-side cooperation. The reading is well paced and utilizes the additional voices in the anecdotes well.

2 css 2 hr Bantam Audio

Getting to Yes
Authors: Roger Fisher and William Ury
Reader: Roger Fisher
★★★

Using examples and sample dialogues from real-life situations, the program outlines ways to strengthen your negotiating ability without weakening your relationships. Fisher, the director of the Harvard Negotiation Project, describes a number of techniques you can use to avoid confrontation ("negotiation jujitsu," third-party mediators, etc.) and achieve positive results. Observing that often what's needed is a *third* position that addresses *both* parties' needs, Fisher makes his points well.

1 css 50 min Simon & Schuster Audio

The Greatest Salesman in the World
Author/Reader: Og Mandino
★★★

Mandino uses a story format to share his techniques on becoming a successful salesperson. Recounting the tale of Hafid, a camel boy during the time of Christ who resolves to become the greatest salesman the world has ever known, Mandino reveals that the secrets to success are contained in a set of scrolls. These scrolls—each one outlining a valuable principle to live by—set forth the steps one must take to achieve greatness. Mandino's reading works well as he pens this story of faith and fortitude.

1 css 1½ hr Bantam Audio

Part II The Greatest Salesman in the World
Author/Reader: Og Mandino
★★★

This continues the story of Hafid (above), the camel boy who rises to become one of the wealthiest men of his time by following the principles in a set of ancient scrolls. Now old and uncomfortable in his retirement, Hafid is looking for new challenges. The task he ultimately pursues is to write his own "Ten Vows of

Success," emphasizing the importance of personal responsibility, positive action, and faith.

1 css 1½ hr Bantam Audio

How to Get What You Want
Author/Reader: Zig Ziglar
★★★

Recorded live in front of an audience, this tape features motivation expert Zig Ziglar's formula for setting goals and achieving them. Asking the question "Are you a wandering generality or a meaningful specific?" Ziglar says that most people's problem isn't a lack of time, but a lack of direction. Ziglar's spirit and enthusiasm never flag as he moves from one anecdote to the next, motivating, prodding, and inspiring.

1 css 1 hr 10 min Simon & Schuster Audio

How to Sell Anything to Anybody
Author/Reader: Joe Girard
★★★★

Joe Girard, the man picked by *The Guinness Book of Records* as "the world's greatest salesman" for twelve consecutive years, provides street-smart tips on selling. Girard delivers the goods in a straightforward, no-nonsense style that covers everything from getting leads and making the sale to building lasting customer relationships. Emphasizing the need to behave in a professional manner, Girard offers advice on virtually every aspect of what it takes to be a top salesperson.

1 css 1½ hr Harper Audio

Iacocca
Authors: Lee Iacocca with William Novak
Reader: Lee Iacocca
★★★★

Iacocca tells about his childhood, career, and management philosophy and the role he played in developing the Ford Mustang and turning around Chrysler. A fearless risk taker who bounced back to even greater heights after being fired by Henry Ford II, Iacocca comes across as surprisingly low-key and unassuming about his accomplishments.

1 css 1 hr Bantam Audio

If You Haven't Got the Time to Do It Right, When Will You Find the Time to Do It Over?
Author/Reader: Jeffrey J. Mayer
★★

Office organization expert Mayer explains how to organize your desk, your office, and your day. Step by step, he demonstrates how to cut through clutter, streamline routines, and save up to an hour a day. Nicknamed Mr. Neat, Mayer covers everything from how to label and store files to ways to use an agenda and prioritize activities.

1 css 1 hr Simon & Schuster Audio

Imagineering
Author/Reader: Michael LeBoeuf
★★★

LeBoeuf, the author of *Working Smart,* offers suggestions and techniques for unlocking your creativity. Telling how such inventors and innovators as Edison, Einstein, and Bell developed systematic methods for harnessing their imagination, he says that each of us is capable of "imagineering"—giving form to creative new ideas. Supportive and specific, LeBoeuf shows that creativity is much more widely spread than you might think and that the only barriers to it are the ones we impose on ourselves.

1 css 50 min Simon & Schuster Audio

The Leader in You
Authors: Dale Carnegie and Associates, Inc./Stuart R. Levine and Michael A. Crom
★★★

Carrying on the teachings of Dale Carnegie, Levine and Crom outline human relations principles that can be applied to one's personal and business relationships. Communication is the key, note the authors, followed by a willingness to include others in the decision-making process and to make them feel that their contributions are important. Spelling out what the leader's job is, the tape offers sound advice on how to inspire and motivate others.

1 css 1½ hr Simon & Schuster Audio

Leadership Is An Art
Author: Max DePree
Reader: Joseph Campanella
★★

DePree, the chairman of furniture industry leader Herman Miller, puts forth his view of leadership based on civility, servitude, and trust. Seeing leadership more as an art than a science, DePree says that it begins with a belief in people and what they can accomplish. Putting relationships over structure, he advocates building "covenantal relationships" of people committed to a common purpose. Campanella's low-key reading reflects the tone of the book.

1 css 3 hr Dove Audio

Leadership Jazz
Author: Max DePree
Reader: Jay King
★★

DePree, chairman of the Herman Miller furniture company, likens leadership to playing jazz. According to him, the art of the leader's role is in bringing out the best individual and collective efforts of the group, encouraging communication and creativity, and, at times, stepping down and letting others lead (giving them their solo in the spotlight). Drawing on moral and theological principles as much as or more than management ones, DePree explains what's expected of a leader and what a leader must do. The program has much to commend it but rambles at times and could benefit from additional editing.

2 css 3 hr Bantam Audio

Learned Optimism
Author/Reader: Martin E. P. Seligman, Ph.D.
★★

The program focuses on the need to overcome pessimistic thinking habits. Utilizing cognitive psychology techniques, Seligman shows how to develop the ability to see oneself and situations in a more optimistic light. Rather than falling victim to self-defeating attitudes and behaviors, listeners will find themselves empowered, armed with the tools for bringing negative thoughts and feelings under control.

1 css 1½ hr Simon & Schuster Audio

The Magic of Thinking Big
Author/Reader: David J. Schwartz
★★

Motivation expert David Schwartz sets forth the theory that if you *think* big, you will *be* big. It's all a matter of believing in yourself and putting aside the excuses and fears that keep you from living up to your potential. Observing that more often than not people sell themselves short and are afraid to follow through on the things they really want to do, Schwartz shows how to become the person you want to be. The tape is well paced and includes interactive exercises to help enlarge your thinking.

1 css 1 hr Simon & Schuster Audio

Making People Talk
Author/Reader: Barry Farber
★★★

Farber, a syndicated radio-talk-show host, shares his techniques for getting people to talk in any and all situations. Peppering the program with numerous anecdotes and his own wealth of experience in drawing out shy, reluctant, and evasive subjects, Farber shows what it takes to get the conversation going. Whether it's meeting someone new at a social gathering, dealing with clients, or interacting with coworkers, Farber's tricks of the talk-show trade explain how to break the ice and heat up the conversation.

2 css 2 hr 45 min Dove/Morrow

Managing from the Heart
Authors: Hyler Bracey, Jack Rosenblum, Aubrey Sanford, and Roy Trueblood
★★★

There is much to be learned in this story of Harry Hartwell, an irascible, type-A manager who is transformed into a caring, compassionate leader. Just as Ebenezer Scrooge sees the light before it's too late, Harry learns how to manage from his heart rather than his spleen, and to appreciate and inspire his subordinates. In Harry the authors have found the perfect standard-bearer to advocate their kinder, gentler approach to management.

2 css 2 hr Bantam Audio

Masterthinker
Author: Dr. Edward de Bono
Readers: Dr. Edward de Bono and Alice Rosengard
★★

Utilizing a concept known as "body frame thinking," de Bono's "Masterthinker" system likens the various thought processes in problem-solving to the parts of the body—bones, muscles, nerves, fat, skin. Although the analogy is strained at times, the program offers some innovative ideas and alternative ways of looking at things.

1 css 50 min Simon & Schuster Audio

Maximum Achievement
Author/Reader: Brian Tracy
★★★

Setting forth Tracy's system for unlocking personal potential and removing barriers to success, the program explains how to become the architect of your future. Stressing the need to be an active participant in your own evolution, Tracy highlights the importance of goals, directions, and a sense of purpose. Rather than waiting for events to happen, you must *make* them happen. The tape contains numerous examples, which add to the program, as does Tracy's perceptive and persuasive reading.

2 css 2 hr Simon & Schuster Audio

Megatrends for Women
Authors: Patricia Aburdene and John Naisbitt
Readers: Jane Altman and Agnes Herrmann
★★★

Carrying on in the tradition of *Megatrends* and *Megatrends 2000,* this focuses on the changes occurring in society as a result of the new roles played by women and their increasing power in business, government, and education. Although it doesn't break new ground the way the original book did, with its portrayal of a "high-tech–high-touch" world, it does provide a broad compendium of information on women's issues and the ways that women are effecting change.

2 css 3 hr Random House AudioBooks

***Money* Magazine's Guide to Personal Finance in the '90s**
Authors: The Editors of *Money* Magazine
Readers: Annie Bergen and Bill Jerome
★★★

This provides a good overview of personal finance for individuals and families. In addition to discussing the various investment alternatives, it includes information on insurance, retirement and estate planning, college tuition funds, etc. The approach is basic, starting with an analysis of your current income and expenses and building from there to chart your financial future.

1 css 1 hr Random House AudioBooks

Napoleon Hill's "A Year of Growing Rich"
Author: Napoleon Hill
Readers: Rick Adamson and Deborah Allison
★★★

Based on the works of the world-renowned author and motivator Napoleon Hill, this provides a year's worth of advice to live by. Covering a wide range of topics from goal-setting to overcoming obstacles to finding peace of mind, the tape is designed to give a week-by-week boost in your efforts to achieve personal and financial success. The reading is well done and the fifty-two meditations—one for each week—are timely and thought provoking.

1 css 1½ Penguin HighBridge Audio

Negotiating the Game
Author/Reader: Herb Cohen
★★★

Cohen, the author of *You Can Negotiate Anything,* explains how to use a negotiation technique based on "conscious inattention" (caring, but not that much) that enables you to achieve your objective. As Cohen puts it, the point is to see the negotiation process as a game, rather than a life-or-death, personal confrontation. The better you are at separating your emotions from the outcome, the more effective you will be. Sounding much like a put-upon Walter Matthau, Cohen's asides and self-deprecating humor add to the presentation.

1 css 1 hr Harper Audio

NLP: The New Technology of Achievement
Authors/Readers: Charles Faulkner, Robert McDonald, Tim Hallbom, and Suzi Smith
★★

The authors outline the steps involved in using Neuro-Linguistic Programming—a self-motivation technique that channels thought into action. Utilizing examples and exercises (e.g., visualizing positive thoughts in sharp focus and negative ones in blurred focus), the tape explains how to enhance performance by altering your perceptions. The program provides a thorough overview of NLP, but what it has to say is undercut by its infomerciallike presentation style.

2 css 2 hr Simon & Schuster Audio

On Power
Author/Reader: Robert L. Dilenschneider
★★

Public relations expert Dilenschneider discusses the various aspects of power—its sources and uses and the emotions it arouses. Citing numerous examples, such as Ross Perot's bid for the presidency, to make his points, Dilenschneider's reading is slow-paced and scholarly.

2 css 3 hr Dove Audio

The One Minute Manager

Authors/Readers: Kenneth Blanchard, Ph.D., and Spencer Johnson, M.D.

★★★★

This rendition of Blanchard and Johnson's best-selling book sets forth the three steps to becoming a successful manager. Told in the form of a parable, it chronicles a young man's search for the perfect manager and his discovery of a very special person indeed—the "One Minute Manager." Capable of getting big results from people in very little time, the One Minute Manager shows the young man how the proper use of goal-setting, praise, and reprimands can spur one's team and oneself to greatness.

1 css 1 hr Random House AudioBooks

The One Minute Manager Meets the Monkey

Authors/Readers: Kenneth Blanchard, Ph.D., and William Oncken, Jr.

★★★★

Blanchard, coauthor of *The One Minute Manager* (above), teams with management consultant and author Oncken to explain how to keep subordinates' problems and responsibilities ("monkeys") from becoming yours, in effect getting monkeys off your back and putting them where they belong. Oncken tackles the task with common sense and humor worthy of a stand-up comic. Blanchard, with no less flair, offers "one minute management techniques" that get subordinates to take responsibility. The authors are a great team and should take their act not only into the executive boardroom, but on the road.

2 css 2 hr Simon & Schuster Audio

One Up on Wall Street

Author/Reader: Peter Lynch

★★★★

Wall Street wizard Peter Lynch, the former manager of the $9 billion Fidelity Magellan Fund, tells what it takes to be a successful investor in the stock market. In the parlance of Wall Street, the tape is a definite "ten-bagger" (a stock that increases in value ten times). Lynch's delivery is excellent. In clear, everyday language, he explains how the average investor can make outstanding returns just by doing some basic research and being alert to the environment.

2 css 2 hr Simon & Schuster Audio

The Organized Executive

Author/Reader: Stephanie Winston

★★★

Winston shows how to take control of your environment and add hours to your day. Sharing her TRAFfic system ("toss, refer, act, file") for dealing with paperwork, she explains ways to prioritize your activities and eliminate time wasters. The tape is loaded with examples, and Winston's obvious delight in combating clutter and chaos comes through.

1 css 45 min Simon & Schuster Audio

The Perfect Sales Presentation
Author/Reader: Robert L. Shook
★★

Consisting of two parts, the tape begins by showing a typical day in the life of fictional men's clothing salesman Michael Baker as he goes through the steps in the selling process with a potential customer. In the second part, five top sales professionals, including Mary Kay Cosmetics founder Mary Kay Ash and IBM supersalesman Buck Rodgers, analyze Baker's performance. The experts' insight and advice are excellent, but Baker's high-pressure sales approach falls short of perfection.

1 css 1 hr Bantam Audio

Phone Power
Author/Reader: George Walther
★★

Offering straightforward techniques for turning the telephone into one of your most profitable business tools, telecommunications expert Walther shows how to make positive connections when placing or receiving calls. Focused and upbeat, Walther outlines ways to get on the same wavelength ("power talking"), make your points, and polish your language.

1 css 1 hr Simon & Schuster Audio

The Popcorn Report
Author/Reader: Faith Popcorn
★★★

Faith Popcorn, the trend-spotter who coined the word *cocooning* and has been dubbed the Nostradamus of Marketing, focuses her crystal ball and computer on the nineties and beyond. A self-created futurist with a knack for knowing what's happening even before everyone else does, Popcorn's predictions have meant big profits for those who have followed them. Delivering her thoughts with clarity and style, she outlines the ten important trends that are shaping our lives and our world.

1 css 1½ hr Simon & Schuster Audio

Positive Attitude Training
Author/Reader: Michael Broder, Ph.D.
★★

Operating on the assumption that one's attitude is a choice, not dictated by circumstance, the program focuses on strategies for maintaining a positive attitude. Drawing on research from the field of cognitive-behavioral psychology, the training techniques described on the tapes are designed to reduce negative thoughts and behaviors and supplant them with positive ones. Broder articulates his points, but the pacing of the narrative lags in spots.

2 css 2 hr Simon & Schuster Audio

The Power of Positive Thinking
Author/Reader: Dr. Norman Vincent Peale
★★★★

Based on the watershed book that virtually created the self-help/self-improvement genre, this program puts into words the teachings of Dr. Norman Vincent Peale. Demonstrating that the biggest obstacle to achieving success is often our own insecurities and negative thoughts, Dr. Peale shows how to master the problems of everyday living through the "power of positive thinking." Inspiring and uplifting, the program shows how to link a belief in God with a belief in yourself, drawing strength from God's support and your own abilities.

4 css 4 hr Simon & Schuster Audio

Principle-Centered Leadership
Author/Reader: Stephen R. Covey
★★

Leadership expert Covey makes his case for a leadership style based on principles rather than priorities. Instead of ranking and assigning the tasks to be done, Covey notes that the leader must get group members to feel a sense of commitment to a common goal. The reading is even-paced and methodical.

1 css 1½ hr Simon & Schuster Audio

Pumping Ions
Author: Tom Wujec
★★★

Consisting of games and exercises to "flex your mind," this is designed to give you a mental workout, sharpening your powers of attention, memory, and decision-making. Utilizing listening, visualization, and recitation exercises, the program is divided into eight sections ("workout stations") that focus on building different mental muscles. Informative and fun, the tape lets you go at your own pace, spending as much time on each exercise as you choose.

1 css 1 hr Bantam Audio

Raise Your Self-esteem
Author/Reader: Dr. Nathaniel Branden
★★★

Dr. Branden outlines specific daily behaviors you can practice to raise your self-esteem and overcome feelings of guilt, self-doubt, and defeat. Utilizing dramatized case histories and exercises, he shows how to break negative, self-defeating patterns. Branden's supportive, nonjudgmental approach and speaking style help him to make his points about the need for self-acceptance and the acceptance of reality.

1 css 1 hr Bantam Audio

Reengineering the Corporation
Authors/Readers: Michael Hammer and James Champy
★★

Detailing the authors' radical approach to organizing and managing businesses, this explains how to strengthen an organization by removing its underpinnings and totally rebuilding it from the bottom up. "Reengineering," as they define it, doesn't just call for retooling or modifying existing systems, but for *reinventing* them.

1 css 1½ hr Harper Audio

Sales Effectiveness Training
Authors: Carl D. Zaiss and Thomas Gordon, Ph.D.
Readers: Eric Conger and Gayle Humphrey
★★★

A step-by-step guide to selling, this puts the emphasis on building customer relationships and working together as partners rather than adversaries. Dubbed "synergistic selling," the authors' approach focuses on customer satisfaction and creating mutually beneficial transactions, not just on making sales. Numerous examples of both constructive and destructive behaviors are provided, along with suggestions for improved sales organizations, training programs, and procedures.

1 css 1½ hr Penguin HighBridge Audio

Sam Walton: Made in America
Authors: Sam Walton with John Huey
Reader: Kevin O'Morrison
★★★

This offers an inside look at retailing giant Wal-Mart told from the horse's mouth by Mr. Sam himself. Getting into the mood, reader Kevin O'Morrison adopts a folksy style to tell Walton's story that adds to the authenticity. Detailing Walton's constant search for new products, suppliers, and markets, the tape captures his vitality and stick-to-itiveness. Buying a plane and learning to fly so he could open up stores faster, Walton maintained 30 to 70 percent annual sales growth over a thirty-year period . . . but never forgot his small-town roots or the need to make one sale at a time.

1 css 2 hr Bantam Audio

The Science of Personal Achievement
Author/Reader: Napoleon Hill
★★★★

Assembled from live recordings and radio broadcasts done by Napoleon Hill, the program shares his principles for achieving success. Hill, the author of the best-selling *Think and Grow Rich* (see page 63) and a contemporary of Andrew Carnegie, Edison, and Ford, combines equal parts of business savvy and folksy charm to make his points. A masterful storyteller with anecdotes to spare, Hill's success principles are as timely today as when he first made them.

2 css 2 hr Simon & Schuster Audio

The 7 Habits of Highly Effective People
Author/Reader: Stephen R. Covey
★★★

Calling for a "paradigm shift" in the way we perceive the world and behave, Covey outlines the seven habits of a successful life. Stressing the needs for short- and long-term goals and a proactive, cooperative approach that brings people together, Covey's reading and examples are on target. Each step, or habit to develop, flows into the next.

1 css 1½ hr Simon & Schuster Audio

Silva Mind Control for Super Memory and Speed Learning
Author/Reader: Hans de Jong
★★

The program, which employs the techniques taught in Silva Mind Control seminars, shows how to improve your memory by performing word association and visualization exercises. Recorded live, the tape demonstrates ways to expand your mind's potential to store and retrieve information. The ultimate goal is to be able to operate at the alpha brainwave frequency, which is the level most conducive to learning.

2 css 2 hr Audio Renaissance Tapes

The Soul of a Business
Author/Reader: Tom Chappell
★★

This provides a glimpse into the counterculture approach to building a business employed by Tom's of Maine, an environmentally conscious manufacturer of toothpaste and other hygiene products. Describing how he uses theological principles to formulate business guidelines, founder Tom Chappell explains how he taps employees' "inner sense of obligation and human connection" to develop a winning team. Chappell's sense of commitment and conviction comes through on the tape, but his low-key delivery doesn't convey the excitement inherent in conceiving and building a business.

2 css 3 hr BDD Audio

The Sound of Your Voice
Author/Reader: Dr. Carol Fleming
★★★

Speech consultant Dr. Carol Fleming does an excellent job of showing how to develop a vocal tone and speaking style that present the kind of image you want to convey. Using numerous examples and exercises to illustrate her points, she demonstrates ways to speak with ease, clarity, and confidence. Fleming's blend of humor and humanity serves her well and helps to make the material more accessible.

1 css 1 hr Newman

Success Mastery with NLP
Authors/Readers: Charles Faulkner and Robert McDonald
★★

The tape focuses on ways to reproduce high-level performance on a regular basis by utilizing Neuro-Linguistic Programming. The readers explain that, linking thoughts to action, NLP relies on such methods as visualization and positive association (called "anchoring") to bring about desired results. Though repetitive at times, the material is presented clearly.

2 css 2 hr Simon & Schuster Audio

Superself
Author/Reader: Charles J. Givens
★★★

Givens, an expert on the subject of financial strategies, turns his attention to success strategies, designing a program for achieving greater control over one's life and developing positive attitudes and habits. He explains when to accept the rules and when to change them, how to focus on your objectives, prepare a "dream list" of the things you want, and create a blueprint for achieving them. Enthusiastic and upbeat, Givens keeps the tape moving along at a rapid clip.

1 css 1½ hr Simon & Schuster Audio

Sweaty Palms
Author/Reader: H. Anthony Medley
★★★

Medley, the founder of a videotape interview service used by law firms seeking good job candidates, outlines the do's and don'ts of interviewing. Utilizing dramatizations of typical interview situations, he points out common blunders to avoid (trick questions, loaded questions) and ways to establish a positive rapport with the interviewer. Showing the wrong way and the right way to handle such touchy situations, the program is realistic and informative.

2 css 3 hr Ten Speed Press

The Ten Natural Laws of Successful Time and Life Management
Author: Hyrum W. Smith
Reader: George Lee Andrews
★★★

Smith, one of the founders of the Franklin Quest Company, makers of the Franklin Day Planner, shares his "ten natural laws" for gaining control of your life, becoming more productive, and finding inner peace. Noting that many people are suffering from "time fatigue" and feel trapped by demands on them, Smith says it's essential to identify your core values and prioritize your activities to reflect them. The ideas on the tape are clear and constructive and well presented by the reader.

2 css 3 hr Time Warner AudioBooks

Think and Grow Rich
Author: Napoleon Hill
Readers: Napoleon Hill and Joe Slattery
★★★★

A step-by-step plan for achieving all manner of riches—friendship, harmony, peace of mind, money, and more—this program is based on the landmark work that made Napoleon Hill a household name. Noting that all great accomplishments start with an idea, Hill underscores the point that "anything your mind can conceive and believe, you can achieve." Applying concepts learned from his years as a protégé of Andrew Carnegie, confidant to America's captains of industry and adviser to presidents, Hill's principles are straightforward and sensible. The program moves quickly, and the thirty-two page self-help booklet included with the tape makes it easy to put the principles into action.

2 css 2 hr Audio Renaissance Tapes

Thriving on Chaos
Author/Reader: Tom Peters
★★★

Peters offers his forty-five prescriptions for surviving, and even thriving, in a constantly changing business environment. Underscoring the point that successful organizations must be fleet and flexible, Peters tackles lumbering bureaucracies, outmoded practices, and rigid managers. In his no-nonsense, accept-no-excuses style, Peters calls for managers to learn to love change and to seek out new market niches and ways to better serve their customers.

1 css 1½ hr Random House AudioBooks

The Tom Peters Seminar
Author/Reader: Tom Peters
★★★★

Calling for nothing less than a management revolution, Peters puts forth the idea that "in an insane world, sane organizations make no sense." The way to succeed is by tapping into the power of imagination and the ability to behave and act in an unorthodox manner. Brain power is in; muscle power is out. Dispersed, ad hoc work groups are replacing fixed payrolls. Delivered in the trademark, high-energy style that Peters uses in his presentations, the tape is peppered with information, anecdotes, and advice.

2 css 3 hr Random House AudioBooks

Total Customer Service
Authors: William H. Davidow and Bro Uttal
Reader: Bro Uttal
★★★

This presents a six-point plan for providing superior customer service. Asserting that a customer service "crisis" is at hand, Davidow and Uttal point out that many businesses are not only incapable of providing good customer service, they can't even define it. Showing how to remedy this situation, Uttal does a good job of explaining the authors' plan for getting the whole company involved in customer service and redesigning products, procedures, and infrastructures to better meet customers' needs.

1 css 1½ hr Harper Audio

Total Quality Management
Authors: Stephen George and Arnold Weimerskirch
Reader: Lloyd Bochner
★★

Everybody talks about quality, but not everyone is willing to do what it takes to consistently deliver it. For those who are willing to make a commitment to excellence, the authors provide strategies and tips for effectively utilizing "total quality management" techniques. Citing examples of businesses using TQM in both the manufacturing and service sectors, they profile such companies as Motorola (with its "five initiatives") and the Ritz-Carlton Hotel chain (and its "Gold Standard").

1 css 1½ hr Dove Audio

The Twenty-two Immutable Laws of Marketing
Authors/Readers: Al Ries and Jack Trout
★★★

Combining more than forty years of marketing experience, Ries and Trout expound on their "twenty-two immutable laws of marketing," warning you to violate them at your own risk. Emphasizing that consumers' perceptions are even more important than companies' products, the authors provide techniques for creating the image that you want and generating positive perceptions. Citing numerous examples of successful products and marketing campaigns, they explain what works and why.

1 css 1½ hr Harper Audio

Unlimited Power
Author/Reader: Anthony Robbins
★★

Anthony Robbins, known for his "Firewalk" exhibitions in which he convinces people to walk barefoot on burning coals, recorded this in front of a live audience. The main focus of his message is that, through Neuro-Linguistic Programming, people can change their thought patterns of behavior and switch from a failure mode to a success mode. Emphasizing the need to set goals and communicate them to others (the basis of NLP), Robbins is energetic in his delivery, but doesn't connect as well with the audience outside the arena as he does with the one inside.

1 css 50 min Simon & Schuster Audio

Victory Secrets of Attila the Hun
Author: Wess Roberts
Readers: Wess Roberts and Ernest Abuba
★★★

Roberts applies the wisdom of Attila the Hun to the corporate battleground and shows how the warrior's methods can be used to win customers and beat back competitors. Lauding Attila's single-handed determination and concern for his followers, Roberts portrays him as a leader for the ages who has much to teach modern managers. Presented in the form of fictional lectures from Attila to his troops, the tape is as entertaining as it is instructive, with advice on "cultivating allies," "dodging arrows," and other key management skills.

2 css 3 hr Bantam Audio

Volume I Webster's New World Power Vocabulary
Authors/Readers: Elizabeth Morse-Cluley and Richard Read
★★★

Emphasizing the relationship between professional success and good language skills, the tape shows how to build a power vocabulary and communicate more effectively. Going beyond memorization, the authors explain how such techniques as identifying words from context and using visualization and clustering methods can help you to expand your vocabulary. Opting for language that is clear and concise rather than ornate and embellished, they point out the need to find your own voice and express yourself in a way that reaches people. Informative and well presented, the tape does a good job of showing you how to put words to work for you.

1 css 1 hr Simon & Schuster Audio

The West Point of Leadership
Author/Reader: Colonel Larry R. Donnithorne (Ret.)
★★

Donnithorne, a former teacher of leader development at West Point, outlines the academy's philosophy of leadership and shows how it can be applied in a business setting. Noting that West Pointers call the philosophy "white phosphorous," or "WP," he says that it burns with the white-hot intensity of a phosphorous artillery shell and can't be smothered. The insider's descriptions of the academy and its regimen of repetitive training and personal deprivation are intriguing, although the leadership techniques themselves may be difficult to apply in the less structured world of business.

2 css 3 hr BDD Audio

What They Still Don't Teach You at Harvard Business School
Author/Reader: Mark H. McCormack
★★★

Picking up where he left off with his best-selling book *What They Don't Teach You at Harvard Business School,* McCormack offers hard-hitting tips and strategies on building a career and succeeding in business. Whether it's getting a job, winning a promotion, negotiating a higher salary, or working with difficult people, McCormack tells what moves to make to accomplish one's goals. The pace never lags and McCormack never fails to deliver.

1 css 1 hr Bantam Audio

The Whiz Kids
Author: John A. Byrne
Reader: Paul Soles
★★★

This story of "The Whiz Kids," ten U.S. Army Air Corps officers who sold themselves in a package deal to Henry Ford II after World War II, is filled with drama and intrigue. Sounding more like fiction than fact, it tells how these friends and fellow officers rescued Ford Motor Company from debt and then went on to apply their management techniques to reshaping American business. Along the way the "Kids"—including Litton Industries founder Tex Thornton and former secretary of defense Robert McNamara—face personal moments of jubilation and despair while following an agenda that puts financial control and an allegiance to the "numbers" over everything else.

2 css 3 hr BDD Audio

The Winner Within
Author/Reader: Pat Riley
★★★

Riley, an NBA Coach of the Year, outlines the teamwork strategy he's used to get the best out of the Los Angeles Lakers and New York Knicks. Emphasizing that, just like in basketball, we're all part of a team, he shows how to develop a winning attitude and make the most of your skills. Balancing your territorial instincts (the desire to protect your turf and make your mark) with the needs of the team, Riley points out the importance of finding ways to contribute that let you *and* the team win. The program is fast moving and positive, using Riley's powers of motivation to good effect.

2 css 3 hr Simon & Schuster Audio

Winning the Fight Between You and Your Desk
Author: Jeffrey J. Mayer
Reader: Eric Conger
★★

This details the various procedures and products available to organize and computerize your office. Mayer, an executive efficiency expert and the author of

If You Haven't Got the Time to Do It Right, When Will You Find the Time to Do It Over? (page 52), explains the various computer software programs on the market and how and when to use them.

1 css   1½ hr   Harper Audio

The Wisdom of Teams
Authors: Jon R. Katzenbach and Douglas K. Smith
Reader: Martin Bookspan
★★

The beginning of the tape is devoted to making a case for teams. When it gets into the specifics of using them, examples, such as Burlington-Northern's use of a task force to develop its intermodal railroad-truck shipping unit, are included. Although the tape has a considerable amount of information to convey, the narrator's professorial reading lacks enthusiasm.

1 css   1½ hr   Harper Audio

Yes or No: The Guide to Better Decisions
Author: Spencer Johnson, M.D.
Reader: Edward Herrmann
★★★

Johnson, a coauthor of the best-selling *The One Minute Manager* (page 57), has a different story to tell here. Featuring another young man with a lesson to learn, this one centers on how to become a better decision-maker. On a mountain-climbing trip with a guide whose knowledge isn't limited to the terrain they're climbing, the young man is shown the steps he must take to develop a systematic approach to decision-making. Johnson's "Yes/No" method, which involves both the head and the heart, is well told by narrator Edward Herrmann.

2 css   3 hr   Harper Audio

You Can If You Think You Can
Author/Reader: Dr. Norman Vincent Peale
★★★

Dr. Norman Vincent Peale, the world-acclaimed speaker and author of *The Power of Positive Thinking* (page 59), directs his efforts here to overcoming adversity. Drawing on numerous examples of how others have turned their lives around and found success and happiness, he shows how to use the art of "creative anticipation" to achieve your life goals.

1 css   50 min   Simon & Schuster Audio

Zig Ziglar's Secrets of Closing the Sale
Author/Reader: Zig Ziglar
★★★★

Ziglar, the best-selling author of *See You at the Top,* grabs hold of his audience and doesn't let go in this fast-paced program on developing effective sales techniques. The tape is packed with ideas, anecdotes, and strategies that can help one to be a better salesperson. Pointing out the need to believe in your product and the benefits it has to offer, Ziglar shows how to overcome objections and turn reluctant prospects into satisfied customers.

4 css 4 hr Simon & Schuster Audio

The Academy of Master Closes
A/R: Tom Hopkins
HARP

Accidental Empires
A/R: Robert X. Cringeley
HARP

Age Wave: A Guide to Business Survival and the Options That Lie Ahead
A/R: Ken Dychtwald, Ph.D.
ART

Agents of Influence
A/R: Pat Choate
RH

The Art of Closing Any Deal
A/R: James W. Pickens
ART

The Art of Worldly Wisdom
A: Baltasar Gracian; translated by Christopher Maurer
R: Victor Garber
BDD

Bankruptcy 1995: The Coming Collapse of America and How to Stop It
A: Harry E. Figgie, Jr., with Gerald J. Swanson, Ph.D.
R: Joseph Campanella
DOVE

Barbarians at the Gate
A/R: Bryan Burrough and John Helyar
HARP

Beating the Dow: A High-Return, Low-Risk Method for Investing in the Dow Jones
A: Michael O'Higgins and John Downes
R: Michael O'Higgins
HARP

Believe and Achieve
A: W. Clement Stone
R: W. Clement Stone and Napoleon Hill
ART

Beyond the Reengineering: How the 21st Century Corporation Will Reshape Our Lives
A/R: Michael Hammer
HARP

A Book of Five Rings: Samurai Strategies for Modern Business Success
A: Miyamoto Musashi
R: Stanley Ralph Ross
ART

Can't Lose Sales Tips from the World's Greatest Salesman
A/R: Joe Girard
HARP

Closing the Sale
A Salenger Management Training Program
DOVE

Como Motivar a la Gente, (How to Motivate People) (Spanish)
A Salenger Management Training Program
DOVE

The Complete Negotiator
A/R: Gerald I. Nierenberg
S&S

The Confident Decision Maker
A/R: Roger Dawson
S&S

Conversation Power: Communication Skills for Business and Personal Success
A/R: James K. Van Fleet
S&S

Coping with Difficult Bosses
A/R: Robert M. Bramson, Ph.D.
S&S

The Do's and Don'ts of Delegation
A/R: Dr. Gary Fellows
S&S

Dr. Robert Anthony's Advanced Formula for Total Success
A/R: Dr. Robert Anthony
DOVE

Dr. Robert Anthony's Magic Power of Super Persuasion
A/R: Dr. Robert Anthony
DOVE

Double Your Profits . . . in Six Months or Less
A: Bob Fifer
HARP

Earl Nightingale's Greatest Discovery
A/R: Earl Nightingale
ART

El Cierre de la Venta (Closing the Sale) (Spanish)
A Salenger Management Training Program
DOVE

The Entrepreneur's Audio Handbook
A: Richard H. Buskirk, Ph.D.
R: Richard H. Buskirk, Ph.D. and Mack Davis
ART

The Fifth Discipline
A: Peter M. Senge
BDD

Financial Self-Defense
A/R: Charles J. Givens
S&S

Flight of the Buffalo
A/R: James A. Belasco
DOVE

The Force: They Sell for a Living, and What Drives Them to the Top Can Push Them over the Edge
A: David Dorsey
R: Robert O'Keefe
RH

Fortune Cookies: Management Wit and Wisdom from *Fortune* Magazine
A: Edited by Alan Deutschman
RH

Frontiers of Management
A: Peter F. Drucker
R: Introduction and commentary by Peter F. Drucker
S&S

Getting Organized
A/R: Stephanie Winston
S&S

Getting Through: Cold Calling Techniques to Get Your Foot in the Door
A/R: Stephan Schiffman
S&S

Giant Steps
A: Anthony Robbins
R: Various; introduction by Anthony Robbins
S&S

The Goal: A Process of Ongoing Improvement
A/R: Eliyahu M. Goldratt
PENG

The Great Boom Ahead
A/R: Harry S. Dent, Jr.
ART

The Great Game of Business
A: Jack Stack
BDD

Growing a Business
A/R: Paul Hawken
S&S

Guerrilla P.R.: Waging an Effective Publicity Campaign without Going Broke
A/R: Michael Levine
DOVE

The Heart and Soul of Excellence
A/R: Tom Peters
RH

Heroz: Empower Yourself, Your Coworkers, Your Company
A: William C. Byham and Jeff Cox
R: Rick Adamson, Agnes Herrmann, and James Lurie
RH

Hit the Ground Running
A/R: Mark McCormack
DOVE

How to Be a Winner
A/R: Zig Ziglar
S&S

How to Close Every Sale
A: Joe Girard and Robert L. Shook
R: Joe Girard
HARP

How to Get Out of Debt, Stay Out of Debt, and Live Prosperously
A/R: Jerrold Mundis
HARP

How to Get Your Point Across in Thirty Seconds or Less
A/R: Milo O. Frank
S&S

How to Handle Conflict and Manage Anger
A/R: Denis Waitley
S&S

How to Manage Time and Set Priorities
A: Stephen Young
RH

How to Motivate People: Especially in the Work Place
A Salenger Management Training Program
DOVE

How to Run a Successful Meeting in Half the Time
A/R: Milo O. Frank
S&S

How to Sell Yourself
A/R: Joe Girard
HARP

How to Think Like a Boss
A/R: Barry Eigen
ART

How to Turn an Interview into a Job
A/R: Jeffrey G. Allen, J.D., C.P.C.
S&S

How to Work a Room: Networking Strategies and Beyond
A/R: Susan RoAne
ART

The HP Way: How Bill Hewlett and I Built Our Company
A: David Packard
HARP

Job Shock
A/R: Harry S. Dent, Jr.
ART

A Journey into the Heroic Environment: A Parable about Creating a Quality Working Environment
A/R: Rob Lebow
ART

Leadership When the Heat's On
A/R: Danny Cox
PART

Liberation Management: Necessary Disorganization for the Nanosecond Nineties
A/R: Tom Peters
RH

The Light Touch
A/R: Malcolm Kushner
S&S

Los Siete Habitos de las Personas Altamente Eficaces (The Seven Habits of Highly Effective People) (Spanish)
A: Stephen R. Covey
R: Peter Gil and Maria Siccardi
S&S

Making the Most of Your Money
A/R: Jane Bryant Quinn
S&S

Managing for the Future: The 1990s and Beyond
A: Peter F. Drucker
R: Joseph Campanella
DOVE

Managing the Nonprofit Organization
A: Peter F. Drucker
R: Peter F. Drucker and others
HARP

Managing Your Goals
A/R: Alec Mackenzie and Mel Mackenzie Brown
S&S

Mastering Your Way to the Top
A: Joe Girard with Robert Casemore
R: Joe Girard
TW

Megatrends 2000
A: Patricia Aburdene and John Naisbitt
R: Martin Bookspan
HARP

More Can't Lose Sales Tips from the World's Greatest Salesman
A/R: Joe Girard
HARP

Motivation in the Real World
A/R: Saul W. Gellerman, Ph.D.
PENG

The New Money Masters: The Winning Investment Strategies of Lynch, Steinhardt, Rogers, Carret, and Many Wealthy Families
A: John Train
R: Steve Post
HARP

The 110% Solution
A/R: Mark McCormack
RH

One Minute for Myself
A: Dr. Spencer Johnson
RH

The One Minute Manager Audio Workshop
A/R: Kenneth Blanchard, Ph.D.
S&S

The One Minute Salesperson
A: Spencer Johnson and Larry Wilson
RH

A Passion for Excellence
A: Tom Peters and Nancy Austin
R: Robert O'Keefe
RH

Personal Excellence: Where Achievement and Fulfillment Meet
A/R: Kenneth Blanchard, Ph.D.
S&S

Positive Imaging
A/R: Dr. Norman Vincent Peale
HARP

Power and Influence
A/R: Robert L. Dilenschneider
DOVE

The Power of Ethical Persuasion
A: Tom Rusk, M.D., with D. Patrick Miller
R: Tom Rusk, M.D.
PENG

The Power of Optimism
A/R: Alan Loy McGinnis
HARP

The Power of the Plus Factor
A/R: Dr. Norman Vincent Peale
HARP

Powertalk!: The Decision That Ensures Your Success
A: Anthony Robbins with Coach John Wooden
ART

Powertalk!: Learn to Use the Power of Question
A: Anthony Robbins with Dr. Barbara de Angelis
ART

Powertalk!: The Master Key to Personal Transformation
A: Anthony Robbins with Dr. Wayne Dyer
ART

Powertalk!: The Power of Anticipation
A: Anthony Robbins with Dr. Stephen R. Covey
ART

Powertalk!: The Power of the Human Paradox
A: Anthony Robbins with Deepak Chopra
ART

Powertalk!: The Power to Create, the Power to Destroy
A: Anthony Robbins with Paul Zane Pilzer
ART

Powertalk!: The Six Master Steps to Change
A: Anthony Robbins with Mark McCormack
ART

Powertalk!: Where Love Begins
A: Anthony Robbins with Dr. Leo Buscaglia
ART

The Practice of Management
A: Peter F. Drucker
R: Martin Bookspan
HARP

The Predators' Ball
A: Connie Bruck
R: Michael Jackson
DOVE

Profiting from the Bank and Savings and Loan Crisis
A: Stephen Pizzo and Paul Muolo
R: Paul Muolo
HARP

The Psychology of Achievement
A/R: Brian Tracy
S&S

The Psychology of Selling: The Art of Closing Sales
A/R: Brian Tracy
S&S

Raving Fans: A Revolutionary Approach to Customer Service
A: Kenneth Blanchard and Sheldon Bowles
RH

Reengineering Management: The Mandate for New Leadership
A: James Champy
HARP

Sales Magic: Revolutionary New Techniques That Will Double Your Sales Volume
A/R: Kerry L. Johnson
S&S

Sales Power
A: Jose Silva with Ed Bernd, Jr.
R: Anthony Fusco
HARP

Say It Right: How to Talk in Any Business Situation
A/R: Lillian Glass, Ph.D.
HARP

Say It Right: How to Talk in Any Social Situation
A/R: Lillian Glass, Ph.D.
HARP

Secrets of Closing the Sale
A/R: Zig Ziglar
HARP

Self-made in America
A: John McCormack with David R. Legge
R: John McCormack
HARP

Sell Your Way to the Top
A/R: Zig Ziglar
S&S

Selling You!
A: Napoleon Hill
R: Napoleon Hill and Joe Slattery
ART

Seven Steps to Master the Interview and Get the Job
A/R: Stephen Young
RH

Sharkproof
A/R: Harvey Mackay
HARP

Smart Negotiating
A/R: James Freund
S&S

Straight A's Never Made Anyone Rich
A/R: Wess Roberts, Ph.D.
HARP

Straight Talk for Monday Morning
A/R: Allan Cox
DOVE

Straight Talk on Money: Ken and Daria Dolan's Guide to Family Money Management
A/R: Ken and Daria Dolan
S&S

The Strategy of Meetings
A/R: George David Kieffer
S&S

Succeeding Against the Odds
A: John H. Johnson with Lerone Bennett, Jr.
R: John H. Johnson
DOVE

The Success System That Never Fails
A/R: W. Clement Stone
ART

Swim with the Sharks
A/R: Harvey Mackay
RH

Talk Your Way to Success
A/R: Lilyan Wilder
S&S

The Tao of Leadership
A: John Heider
R: Ralph Blum; commentary by Denis Waitley
ART

The Tao of Management
A: Bob Messing
R: Ralph Blum; commentary by Ken Blanchard
ART

Teaching the Elephant to Dance
A/R: James A. Belasco
DOVE

Technotrends
A: Daniel Burrus and Roger Gittines
R: Daniel Burrus
HARP

Terry Savage: Understanding Insurance and Planning for the Future
A/R: Terry Savage
HARP

Terry Savage: Understanding Investments
A/R: Terry Savage
HARP

Terry Savage: Understanding Your Money
A/R: Terry Savage
HARP

Think and Grow Rich: A Black Choice
A: Dennis Kimbro, Ph.D., and Napoleon Hill
R: Dennis Kimbro, Ph.D.
HARP

Top Performance
A/R: Zig Ziglar
HARP

The Ultimate Secrets of Total Self-confidence
A/R: Dr. Robert Anthony
DOVE

The Unconventional Tom Peters
A/R: Tom Peters
RH

Upward Nobility: How to Succeed in Business Without Losing Your Soul
A: Owen Edwards
R: Joseph Campanella
DOVE

Visionary Companies
A: James C. Collins and Jerry J. Porras
HARP

What A Great Idea!: Key Steps Creative People Take
A/R: Chic Thompson
HARP

Winnie-The-Pooh on Management
A: Roger E. Allen
PENG

Working with Jerks
A: Ron Zemke
R: Liane Hansen
S&S

You Can Negotiate Anything
A/R: Herb Cohen
ART

You've Got to Be Believed to Be Heard
A/R: Bert Decker
ART

Zapp!: The Lightning of Empowerment
A: William C. Byham, Ph.D., with Jeff Cox
R: Don Batcher
RH

CHILDREN

There is a tremendous versatility and virtuosity in spoken-word children's recordings.

Classic fairy tales have had many renditions with mixed results. Likewise, some of the classic Twain and Dickens. Some children's recordings seem to blossom on their own to become evergreens, even if the original source material is not as famous as *Alice's Adventures in Wonderland* or *The Wizard of Oz.* For instance, Patricia MacLachlan's *Sarah Plain and Tall,* sensitively read by Glenn Close, and Maurice Sendak's *Where the Wild Things Are,* with a lively performance by Tammy Grimes and music by Mozart, have sustained interest and won new listeners since their releases. A new recording that might have a long life is the wonderful anthology of poetry by Robert Louis Stevenson, *A Child's Garden of Verses.*

There is much to choose from and I hope the following selection will make you aware of the numerous choices you and your children have in discovering audio tapes.

HIGHLY RECOMMENDED(★★★★)

The Adventures of Huckleberry Finn*
Black Beauty**
A Child's Christmas in Wales
A Child's Garden of Verses
Matilda
Sarah Plain and Tall
The Secret Garden***
Where the Wild Things Are

The Adventures of Huckleberry Finn
Author: Mark Twain
Reader: Dick Cavett
★★

Huckleberry Finn, one of literature's best-loved characters, can stand no longer the restrictions of life with the widow Douglas, or with his drunken Pap, so he fakes his own death and escapes to the freedom of the Mississippi River. Dick Cavett reads with a wry, tongue-in-cheek style, taking character voices with ease. Unfortunately, he is too mature a narrator to convey the sense of boyish wonder and adventure that the story demands. Still, there is a liveliness that makes for an easy river voyage with Jim and Huck.

2 css 2hr Durkin Hayes Audio

The Adventures of Huckleberry Finn
Author: Mark Twain
Performer: Wil Wheaton
★★★★

Wil Wheaton is the perfect choice to capture the flavor of Huck and friends. His performance is remarkable in that his dialects seem authentic and his lively narration transports you directly to Twain's world.

2 css 3 hr Dove Audio

The Adventures of Tom Sawyer
Author: Mark Twain
Reader: Robby Benson
★★

Twain's story of boyhood and the adventures of Tom Sawyer and his friends Huck Finn and Becky in the lazy town of St. Petersburg on the banks of the Mississippi River continue to entertain. Though Robby Benson has a pleasant, evocative voice, it's a bit too soft and laid back to convey the spirited goings-on in Twain country. However, this is a serviceable introduction to this great piece of Americana.

2 css 2 hr Durkin Hayes Audio

* Dove Audio
** TW Kids
*** Penguin HighBridge Audio

Alice's Adventures in Wonderland
Author: Lewis Carroll
Told by Kathleen Turner
★

Kathleen Turner is the wrong choice to bring the complexities and ingenuity of Carroll's masterpiece to life. With no attempt at either humor or a British accent, Turner can't seem to find a key to the witty and imaginative characters that weave through the fantasy. An overwrought sound track that sounds like a film score destroys any vestiges of atmosphere left.

1 css 1 hr Everyman's Library Children's Classics

Alice in Wonderland
Author: Lewis Carroll
Reader: Catherine O'Hara
★

In this version of *Alice's Adventures in Wonderland,* Catherine O'Hara reads at such a fast clip that you can hardly follow the sense of Carroll's complex conundrum. A talented comedienne, O'Hara nails some comic characters, but her flat, nasal narration unfortunately overpowers.

1 css 1 hr Paperback Audio

Anne of Green Gables
Author: L. M. Montgomery
Performer: Megan Fellows
★

Though Megan Fellows seems the appropriate choice for this material, since she appeared in the film version of *Anne of Green Gables,* she is not adept at reading at the microphone. This is a case in which coming from another medium to audio is not a smooth transition. This is read too quickly, with no sense of pace, and with some garbled pronunciations. The program is not well recorded, with some distortion to the voice.

2 css 2½ hr Bantam Audio

Audrey Hepburn's Enchanted Tales
Stories Adapted by Mary Sheldon
Performer: Audrey Hepburn
★★

Fantastic characters and their magical adventures are the basis of this retelling of such treasured fairy tales as *Sleeping Beauty, Tom Thumb, Beauty and the Beast,* and *Laidronette, Empress of the Pagodes.* Highlighting the musical score of this collection are selections from Maurice Ravel's celebrated *Mother Goose Suite.* Audrey Hepburn reads in an evocative, clean voice. But the voice is quiet and sometimes overwhelmed by the insistent classical score.

1 css 1 hr Dove Kids

The Baby-sitters Club: The Baby-sitters Remember
Author: Ann M. Martin
Performers: Multiple Cast
★★★

Stacey, Dawn, Mary Anne, Claudia, and Kristy share firsthand their most vivid memories as members of the Baby-sitters Club. (Included in this package is a special charm bracelet.) The author makes a somewhat awkward introduction, then lets the girls tell their stories. They read in a winsome manner, sharing memories any young baby-sitter could identify with.

1 css 1 hr TW Kids

The Baby-sitters Club: Stacey and the Mystery at the Empty House
Author: Ann M. Martin
Performers: Multiple Cast
★★★

America's favorite baby-sitters are detectives, too. While the Johanssens are away, Stacey is in charge of walking their dog and watching their house. Before long, strange things start happening. Stacey is sure someone is in the house. Who could it be? This charming production is really a full-cast radio play with all the right ingredients—a clever script, creative sound effects, catchy music, and a very nicely cast group of seven "baby-sitters" and supporting players, both children and adults. This takes place around Christmas, with sleigh rides and snow, so it is enjoyable holiday fare as well. (Official Stacey charm included.)

1 css 1 hr TW Kids

The Big Book for Peace
Authors: Various
Narrators: Jane Alexander, Milton Berle, Gregory Harrison, Juliet Mills, Peter Strauss, and Blair Underwood
★★★

Based on the book, here are thirteen stories and poems thoughtfully selected to bring an awareness and help promote the cause of peace. A portion of the proceeds of this recording are being donated to the following organizations: Amnesty International, The Carter Center's Conflict Resolution Program, Greenpeace, The Lion and the Lamb Peace Center, and SANE/FREEZE. These selections are well presented, and Gregory Harrison is especially effective reading "The Two Brothers" and "Enemies."

1 css 1½ hr The Publishing Mills AudioBooks

Black Beauty
Author: Anna Sewell (Based on the Caroline Thompson Film)
Performers: Multiple Cast
★★★★

This beautiful production features the Danny Elfman score from the Warner Bros. movie; tasteful, well-placed sound effects; and a handsome thirty-two-page companion storybook with color photographs from the motion picture. The cast here is simply wonderful. Young Joe, his uncle John, Farmer Grey, Squire Gorden and his family, and the narrator, Black Beauty himself, all come together in a seamless ensemble that represents a high point in children's audio production.

1 css 25 min TW Kids

Black Beauty
Author: Anna Sewell
Reader: Frances Sternhagen
★

In this fairly complete version of *Black Beauty,* Frances Sternhagen, known for many fine theatrical portrayals, fails to bring this timeless story to life. This is read too quickly and breathlessly, with no time to contemplate the evocative passages that fill the book. In fact, the reading is not fluidly edited and the breathiness is annoying.

2 css 3 hr Durkin Hayes Audio

Buck's Ducks: Classic Christmas Songs
Author: Buck Peterson
Performers: Buck's Ducks and the Big Babe Lake Brass and Bong Ensemble
Unrated

It's the Christmas season, the best and jolliest time of year, and "Buck" Peterson, master-guide-to-all-that-is-wild, breaks open and calls his feathered friends home for the holidays. On this novel Christmas album, Bucksters are invited to enjoy the songs of the season by Buck's alpha ducks, Biff and Eddie, and the Big Babe Lake Brass and Bong Ensemble. Wild quacking ensues through such selections as *Quacking of the Bells, Silent but Deadly Night, O Little Town of Bedlam* and *Blown Away from the Manger.* I'd like to give this recording one or two quacks, but it's best left unrated. It may just be the thing you've been looking for—either for hours of listening enjoyment or to torment a friend. Great for telephone messages, too.

1 css ½ hr Ten Speed Press

Bunnicula: A Rabbit-Tale of Mystery
(Parents' Choice Award/An ALA Notable Children's Recording)
Authors: Deborah and James Howe
Performer: Lou Jacobi
★★★

It's really cute! The bunny looks ordinary to Harold, the dog. But Chester, his friend and housemate, is a very well read cat and *he* is convinced there is something strange about Bunnicula. When white vegetables—drained of their juices—start turning up, Chester becomes convinced Bunnicula is a vampire. James Howe began his writing career in 1979 with *Bunnicula: A Rabbit-Tale of Mystery,* which introduced readers to the infamous vampire rabbit and his friends.

Bunnicula and follow-ups *The Celery Stalks at Midnight* and *Nighty-Nightmare* work particularly well on audio and this trilogy of terror (each story is sold separately) is witty, suspenseful, and a lot of fun for an actor to (pardon the pun) sink his teeth into. Lou Jacobi's comic whine scores here.

1 css 40 min Caedmon Audio

The Butterfly Jar
Author: Jeff Moss
Performers: Jane Curtin and Mandy Patinkin
★

From Jeff Moss, one of the original creators and head writers for *Sesame Street,* comes *The Butterfly Jar,* a collection of short poems. . . . Maybe you can't stand crumbs in bed or you secretly dream of being a rock 'n' roll star. Maybe you've even noticed that your floor is somebody's ceiling and that your ceiling is somebody's floor. These wacky poems cry out for a spirited reading and while Curtin breathes some life into them, Patinkin seems uninvolved and the production itself is minimal and low on creativity.

1 css 50 min Bantam Audio

Carly Simon's Bells, Bears, and Fishermen
Author/Performer: Carly Simon
★★

Carly performs three of her stories, accompanied by an original musical score. In *Amy and the Dancing Bear,* a young bear tries to convince her mother that it's just too early to go to bed one golden summer evening. *The Boy of the Bells* shows just what a boy can do on Christmas Eve when he gets advice from a jolly man in a red suit. And in *The Fisherman's Song,* Carly tells and sings a timeless story of enduring love. Carly musicalizes these tales in a sweet and earnest way, but it's almost too much saccharine and not enough sugar.

1 css ½ hr Bantam Audio

The Children's Aesop
Author: Aesop
Retold by Stephanie Calmenson
Reader: Dudley Moore
★★★

These morals are as true today as they ever were. That is why, for generations, Aesop's fables have been treasured by readers of all ages. Now in twenty-eight fresh retellings for young children, Stephanie Calmenson introduces us to old friends (and foes) such as Hare and Tortoise, Fox and Crow, and Lion and Mouse. Dudley Moore gives a spirited, focused, and delightful performance, keeping Aesop fresh and accessible. A portion of the proceeds from this tape is being donated to pediatric AIDS research.

1 css 1 hr Soundelux Audio

Children's Letters to God
Authors/Performers: The Students of Boys Harbor Performing Arts Center
★

Children's Letters to God is a presentation of kids pondering the world around them. Letters that are serious and funny, knowing and naive, are all addressed to God in a spirit of hope and trust. Sadly, many of the children are hard to understand. Syrupy musical underscoring further complicates intelligibility. Long musical interludes between letters bring whatever pace there is to a grinding halt.

1 css 20 min Harper Audio

A Child's Christmas in Wales
Author/Reader: Dylan Thomas
★★★★

In this classic recording from 1952, Dylan Thomas's reading recalls all of the sights, smells, and sounds of a long-ago Christmas. The author's voice is haunting and compelling. Thomas's wonderful recollection of his holiday in the seaside town of his youth is captured in this vivid performance. Also included are five other selected poems read by Dylan Thomas, including his well-known "Do Not Go Gentle into That Good Night." Whether sharing his wistful memory of a holiday spent with people long past, or addressing the perennial problem of our mortality, Thomas gives us great pleasure in our personal and common memories while affirming life with a resounding "Yes!" Highly recommended to young and old alike.

1 css 45 min Caedmon Audio
1 CD 45 min Caedmon Audio

A Child's Garden of Verses
Author: Robert Louis Stevenson
Readers: Ethan Hawke, Ben Kingsley, Elizabeth McGovern, Roger Moore, Cathy Moriarty, Priscilla Presley, Deborah Raffin, Carl Reiner, John Ritter, Mary Sheldon, Cybill Shepherd, Susan Sontag, Dick Van Patten, Ben Vereen, Betty White, B. D. Wong, and Michael York
★★★★

No collection of children's poetry has left such an indelible mark on so many generations as this Robert Louis Stevenson classic. First published in 1885, Stevenson's sentimental tribute to the joys of childhood has stood the test of time. A star-studded cast of renowned celebrities has gathered together to breathe new life into these magical verses. This is a must-hear experience. On the face of it, these poems, which have their own musicality, would not seem best served to be underscored. But somehow the music interweaving helps give this a unified, connected feeling, and it is discreetly lowered during the verses themselves. The men win the day here. Ethan Hawke, Michael York, Ben Vereen, and B. D. Wong read beautifully, finding the magic of Stevenson's verse in an effortless way. For their performances alone, this is given a high rating. The women are more erratic. Cybill Shepherd and Cathy Moriarty are weak, but surprisingly Priscilla Presley recites poetry with ease and Susan Sontag brings out some of the darker aspects of

Victorian values, especially in "Good and Bad Children." But the standouts remain "Travel" (Michael York), "My Ship and I" (Ethan Hawke), and "Night and Day" (B. D. Wong).

1 css 1 hr Dove Audio
1 CD 1 hr Dove Audio

Dancing Animals
Author/Performer: David Spangler
★★★

A one-of-a-kind recording that electronically integrates actual animal sounds into the up-to-the-minute rhythms of David Spangler's irresistible story-songs about the animal kingdom. You'll have to listen very closely to identify all the different animals present and accounted for here! Their sounds become as melodious as musical instruments, and you'll find yourself getting to know and appreciate animal friends in an endlessly fun and fascinating way. David Spangler has written music that jumps as well as enchants in a New Age style. And his introduction of such exotic animals as a zoomie, and a gazorbablop, as well as various gibbons, fruit bats, and wildebeests, is inspired.

1 css 40 min Caedmon Audio

Day at the Zoo, Day at the Aquarium, Day at the Library, and Day at the Farm
Author: Mary Sheldon
Performer: Betty White
★★★

In this attractively packaged set, Betty White's engaging and warm personality pervades the proceedings and makes for enjoyable company. Lizzy, Eric, and Lizzy's dog, Petunia, share in the fun and so will everyone listening to the sounds of zoo animals and sea creatures. You will discover exciting activities at the local library, and learn about cow milking, hayrides, and the environment.

4 css 3 hr Dove Kids

General Moustache and White Storm and The Long Journey of the Little Seed
Author: Annie Reiner
Performer: Anne Bancroft
★★

General Moustache and White Storm shows how the power of imagination can transform the world around you, making believers out of even the biggest skeptics. When a young girl's imagination brings to life a 100-year-old statue of a general and his horse, the girl and a young boy are transported back in time. In *The Long Journey of the Little Seed* a small seed goes on a marvelous adventure of discovery. This coming-of-age tale follows the magical journey of a young seedling searching for her identity. Anne Bancroft whispers her way along, is overpowered by the musical score, and, sadly, great actress though she is, is a bit of a disappointment here.

1 css 40 min Dove Kids

The Golden Key
Author: George MacDonald
Reader: Michael Zebulon
★★★

This program presents the most famous fairy tale by master of fantasy George MacDonald. *The Golden Key* satisfies on many levels, reawakening and entertaining the imagination and the senses. Here is a spiritual coming-of-age tale, a story of love, nature, and triumph over adversity. Michael Zebulon seems to have an affinity for reading this imaginative tale; his dark dulcet tones and easy pace are a pleasure to the ear.

1 css 1 hr Audio Literature

Jack and the Beanstock and The Frog Prince
Traditional English Tales
Performer: John Ritter
★★

Daring feats, magical spells, and high adventure combine in these two familiar children's stories that share the common themes of responsibility, commitment, and just rewards for kind deeds. John Ritter comes through with a good mellow reading. But the mood he sets is disturbed by the frenetic underscoring.

1 css ½ hr Dove Kids

Jerusalem, Shining Still
(An ALA Notable Children's Recording)
Author: Karla Kuskin
Performer: Theodore Bikel
★★

Author Karla Kuskin describes the vivid sights and sounds of peace and war in the streets of Jerusalem. Theodore Bikel's deep, resonant voice guides us through the swirling masses of pilgrims, settlers, invaders, and conquerors. A vital musical score is a plus, but frankly the book is a bit lightweight. Side Two features a read-along version, but you must purchase the book separately.

1 css 40 min Caedmon Audio

The Lemming Condition
Author/Reader: Alan Arkin
★

The Lemming Condition is about a young lemming who calls into question the blind urge of his fellow lemmings to drown themselves in the sea. It is a parable of the spiritual crisis of our time and of the courage each of us hopes to find within ourselves. Alan Arkin reads his own story in a dull, spiritless voice. You can hardly follow what he is saying, he seems so disinterested. This is a *lemming,* indeed.

1 css 55 min Audio Literature

Little Bear's Thirty-fifth Anniversary Collection
Author: Else Holmelund Minarik
Reader: Sigourney Weaver
★★

Little Bear has been a friend to generations of young readers, and celebrates his thirty-fifth birthday in these five tales: *Little Bear, Little Bear's Visit, A Kiss for Little Bear, Father Bear Comes Home,* and *Little Bear's Friend.* Sigourney Weaver reads nicely and there is a pleasant musical accompaniment. However, without the Maurice Sendak illustrations to peruse, the stories are just too bare bones to work well alone on audio. In fact, the constant repetition of the words "Little Bear" begins to grate.

1 css 1 hr Caedmon Audio

The Little Princess
Author: Frances Hodgson Burnett
Reader: Julie Harris
★★

Sara Crew, a spoiled little rich girl, loses her father and money and faces the misery of existing on charity. This piece of Victoriana is less engrossing than the same author's *The Secret Garden.* Julie Harris scores with the cold headmistress, but is less adept at portraying young Sara's vulnerability.

2 css 3 hr Durkin Hayes Audio

Little Women
Author: Louisa May Alcott
Reader: Jean Smart
★★★

Here is the story of Meg, Jo, Beth, and Amy, their happy hours and their trials; the story of their plays, of the Pickwick Club, of Laurie and Jo, of Meg and John Brooke, of Marmee and Mr. March. Jean Smart is especially good at all the wonderful characterizations and her differentiations of the March sisters makes for wonderful dramatic interchanges.

2 css 3 hr Durkin Hayes Audio

The Magic Locket
Author/Reader: Elizabeth Koda-Callan
★★

She's a little girl who can't seem to do anything right, no matter how hard she tries, until one day she receives a golden locket (just like the one packaged with this tape) that teaches her the magical power of believing in herself. The story is read by its author, who talks afterward about how she deals with the issue of self-confidence and how she became a best-selling children's book author and artist. Koda-Callan sounds like, well, an author reading. This sweet tale of dreams and the gaining of self-confidence would have been much better served read by an actress who could bring out the best in the writing.

1 css 40 min Caedmon Audio

The Magic School Bus: Fun with Sound
Author: Scholastic
Performer: Lily Tomlin and Cast
Sixteen-page activity pamphlet included
★★★

Visit the Sound Museum, a.k.a. a creaky old haunted house, with the Friz, Arnold, and the rest of the class, and discover how sound travels, how vibrations affect sound, and what's making those eerie noises inside the Sound Museum. This is great on audio; we get to hear all the spooky, sonorous sounds and vibrations and learn as we have a great time with Lily Tomlin and the kids. An energized theme song performed by Little Richard gets the bus rolling. A sixteen-page activity pamphlet offers puzzles, games, and at-home experiments, all related to sound.

1 css ½ hr TW Kids

Matilda
Author: Roald Dahl
Performer: Jean Marsh
★★★★

Bright, imaginative, and misunderstood, poor Matilda is the family doormat. With an oily used-car salesman for a father and a bingo junkie for a mother, she fights back against an unappreciative world through a hidden talent: Matilda is the world's greatest practical joker! Roald Dahl (*Charlie and the Chocolate Factory, James and the Giant Peach*) scores again to conspire with children against adults. Jean Marsh, best known for her role of Rose in the much-loved television series *Upstairs, Downstairs,* is quite wonderful here—she has a natural ability to communicate in the audio medium and takes full advantage of Dahl's wit and humor.

1 css 1½ hr Caedmon Audio

Mighty Morphin Power Rangers: Day of the Dumpster
3-D Read-Along
Author: Saban's Cool Kids Records
Performers: Multiple Cast
★★★

Hear the remarkable history of the Power Rangers and read along as five teenagers "morph" into superheroes and fight to save Earth from the evil forces of Rita Repulsa. The TV series that thrills kids is also a hit on tape. Featuring the popular theme song "Go, Go Power Rangers" and the rockin' "I Will Win," this recording scores as we follow the Rangers on their first mission. And the 3-D read-along book (with glasses included) leads to an extra cool adventure as the pictures in the book literally jump out at you. Realistic sound effects and a pulsing musical score should have kids saying, "Go, go Power Rangers."

1 css ½ hr TW Kids

Misty of Chincoteague
Author: Marguerite Henry
Performer: Daisy Eagan
Bomb

Author Marguerite Henry (*King of the Wind* and *Brighty of Grand Canyon*) deserves better for her popular horse tale. Daisy Eagan (Tony Award winner for *The Secret Garden*) reads in a wobbly, rushed, confused manner that makes it impossible to concentrate on the story. It's too bad her deep intakes of breath weren't edited out. Add to this some ill-placed sound effects that drop in out of nowhere (the storm sounds like radio interference) and you have an unpleasant piece of audio production all around. Let them eat oats!

1 css 1½ hr Caedmon Audio

The Moose Tales
Author/Reader: Daniel M. Pinkwater
★★★

What happens when a blue moose wanders into a small restaurant from the snowy winter woods and becomes the headwaiter? Things become topsy-turvy and nothing is ever the same again. And when the Blue Moose turns author, watch out! Finally, there is the legend of the Moosepire, a monster moose that lurks at the edge of town, a riddle that only the Blue Moose can unravel. These three Blue Moose stories are a children's delight, and the reading by Daniel Pinkwater is a special treat.

1 css 1½ hr Dove Kids

Music Is a Miracle
(Sing-a-Song Booklet and Cassette)
Music by Patrick Hyde/Lyrics by Cary L. Moore
Performer: Patrick Hyde
★★

Many of the catchy songs here tell the story and demonstrate the sound of a particular musical instrument or family of instruments. Several songs offer an added message of friendship, sharing, and family. Clarinets, violins, pianos, tubas—they all sound off so you'll know the score. Patrick Hyde, formerly of the Charlie Midnight Band, manages to find an entertaining way to tune kids in to learning about musical instruments and the joyful pop sounds he calls the miracle of music. He has a pleasant, light voice, too.

1 css 35 min Caedmon Audio

The Paddington Audio Collection
Author/Performer: Michael Bond
★★

In these stories, England's most cherished export is brought to life through the voice of his creator, Michael Bond. The collection begins with Paddington's arrival in London in *A Bear Called Paddington*. Also included are *Paddington and the Disappearing Trick and Other Stories, Paddington Turns Detective,* and *Paddington for Christmas.* These are truly delightful stories. But would the talented author were as good a reader as he is a writer! In a dry, rather colorless voice, Bond makes us wish a talented actor had done Paddington justice.

4 css 4 hr Caedmon Audio

Peter Pan
(Parent's Choice Award)
Author: J. M. Barrie
Reader: Sandy Duncan
★★

Sandy Duncan, who starred as Peter Pan in Broadway's musical revival, was a hit on stage, but hits and misses here. There is a spritely charm about her, but she reads a bit quickly in a down-home style that seems at odds with the stately Barrie fantasy. In fact, when she mentions the Darling family, it comes out sounding like "the Darlin's." Still, her perkiness is admirable.

1 css 1 hr 35 min Dove Audio

Piggins and Picnic with Piggins
Author: Jane Yolen
Performer: Roddy McDowall
★★★

In this delightful recording, music, mystery, mayhem, and plenty of fun surprises are in store when Piggins, the very proper butler-sleuth of *47 The Meadows,* takes on two interesting cases. The menagerie of captivating suspects include Lord and Lady Ratsby, Professor T. Ortoise, madcap rabbit explorer Pierre Lapin, and even Piggins's own employers, the elegant fox couple, Mr. and Mrs. Reynard. It's *Upstairs, Downstairs* animal-style—fast, clever, and full of exciting wordplay. Roddy McDowall shines brightly as he creates these witty animal characterizations. The musical underscoring is original, effective, and light as a feather. The only drawback is the absence of the wonderful book illustrations. Even though this is a word-for-word recording of the books, you have to get them separately. Still, this is heads and tails above the crowd.

1 css 25 min Caedmon Audio

Robin Hood
Author: Roger Lancelyn Green
Reader: Anthony Hyde
★★★

Robin Hood is everyone's hero and takes his place alongside the immortals of English folklore. Joining Robin Hood are his famous companions Little John, Maid Marion, Will Scarlett, and Friar Tuck, all battling against Prince John and the Sheriff of Nottingham. British thespian Anthony Hyde is perfectly suited to this exciting material and reads in an energetic, well-paced, easy-to-follow style.

The recording could stand to be longer than its hour time, with additional adventures.

1 css 1 hr Paperback Audio

Sarah Plain and Tall
(Parents' Choice Award)
Author: Patricia MacLachlan
Performer: Glenn Close
★★★★

This is the story of Anna and Caleb, two children who live with their widowed father on the prairie and whose whole world is turned upside down one day when Papa advertises for a mail-order bride. This is a special recording. From the first soft notes of the piano and the opening characterizations by Glenn Close, who played the role of Sarah in a highly-acclaimed television production of the story, we know we are about to be swept up in this drama of fragile family relationships struggling for permanency. Glenn Close seems to care about the nuances of the characters and turns this into a touching drama.

1 css 1 hr Caedmon Audio

Scary Stories to Tell in the Dark
Stories from American Folklore
(An ALA Notable Children's Recording)
Author: Alvin Schwartz
Performer: George S. Irving
★★★

Every boy and girl has heard and most likely knows by heart some old story to make the flesh crawl . . . the kind of weird, wild, and wonderful yarn breathlessly passed around the campfire or at slumber parties, told slowly and softly . . . as if letting the listener in on a deep, dark secret. Folklore scholar Alvin Schwartz has collected what he considers the scariest stories *ever*—but among these eighteen stories, some are scarier than others and a few are complete throwaways. No matter. Performed by Tony Award winner George S. Irving, probably the most talented comic reader in the books-on-tape field, this is a well-produced and entertaining event. It's tongue-in-cheek fun all the way!

1 css 40 min Caedmon Audio

The Secret Garden
(An ALA Notable Children's Recording)
Author: Frances Hodgson Burnett
Performer: Claire Bloom
★

This is the earliest version of *The Secret Garden* and does not stand the test of time. Heavily truncated, the material is presented in selections that are not cohesive. Hearing excerpts is not as effective as listening to a fluid abridgement. It is hard to tell what the talented Claire Bloom might have done with a more complete version. Here she struggles against appalling sound quality and an electronic buzz that underscores this remastered recording, originally produced in 1976.

1 css 1 hr Caedmon Audio

The Secret Garden
Author: Frances Hodgson Burnett
Reader: Helena Bonham Carter
★★★★

Since its original publication in 1911, *The Secret Garden* has captivated children and adults alike with its luminous tale of enigmas and revelations, growth and renewal, and the transforming power of love. This is read in a gracious and lively manner by Helena Bonham Carter, who manages to breathe the spirit of late Victorian England into this enchanting story. Once some incidental music that threatens to overwhelm the voice is dispensed with, this high-quality recording in both sound and performance works its magic.

2 css 3 hr Penguin HighBridge Audio

The Secret Garden
(Unabridged)
Author: Frances Hodgson Burnett
Reader: Susan Fitzgerald
★★★

The inspiring story of how Mary, unloved and selfish, finds friendship and happiness helping her neurotic, invalid cousin become strong and healthy continues to form the basis for recordings, movies, and a recent award-winning Broadway musical. Susan Fitzgerald, a leading actress in Dublin theater, reveals a great versatility in bringing all the story's characters to life using both educated British and broad Yorkshire accents. She has a sprightly quality to her narrative voice as well, which never flags through this complete version. Add to this an appropriate piano score and you have very good entertainment value indeed.

6 css 7 hr 55 min Audio Editions

The Secret Garden
Author: Frances Hodgson Burnett
Reader: Juliet Stevenson
★★

An associate artist of the Royal Shakespeare Company, Juliet Stevenson manages to find the key to unleash a magical reading, infused with warmth and wit. See other entries, above, for other audio versions of this classic story.

2 css 3 hr Durkin Hayes Audio

Shiloh
Author: Phyllis Reynolds Naylor
Performer: Peter MacNicol
★★

What do you do when a dog you suspect is being mistreated runs away and comes to you? When the man who owns the dog has a gun? That is Marty Preston's problem, and it is one he will have to face alone. Peter MacNicol does character voices well—both male and female—and creates a folksy atmosphere appropriate to the material. At times the musical score overwhelms.

2 css 3 hr 5 min Bantam Audio

Stuart Little
Author: E. B. White
Reader: Julie Harris
★★

Stuart Little is a shy, philosophical little mouse with a big heart and a taste for adventure. But Stuart's greatest adventure begins when he decides to find his best friend, Margalo, a pretty little bird who once lived in a Boston fern in the Littles' house in New York City. Climbing into his tiny car, Stuart hits the open road only to find himself in for a big surprise. Unfortunately, Julie Harris lacks the warmth, humor, and wryness to make this classic book into a classic recording.

2 css 1 hr 55 min Bantam Audio

There Is a Carrot in My Ear and Other Stories
Author: Alvin Schwartz
Performer: George S. Irving
★★★

This is a fun-filled collection of tales, tongue twisters, riddles, and folksy rhymes that have engaged children for generations. George S. Irving moves swiftly over tongue twisters (you try to say "busy buzzing bumblebees" as fast as he can), asks the greatest riddles of all time (what is as big as an elephant, but weighs nothing at all?), and regales you with "Noodle Tales" (about silly people who say and do silly things). Sprightly music adds to the teasing humor.

1 css 1 hr Caedmon Audio

Thumbelina and The Princess and the Pea
Author: Hans Christian Andersen
Performer: Jaclyn Smith
★★

These beloved stories feature as their heroines two young ladies who must rise to the occasion and prove their nobility in the face of hardship. Jaclyn Smith gives a winning, breezy performance, easy for kids to follow. But the music and sound effects are overwhelming and not chosen with much discretion, taking away from Smith's efforts.

1 css ½ hr Dove Kids

Treasure Island
Author: Robert Louis Stevenson
Reader: Keir Dullea
★★★

Fifteen men on a dead man's chest. Yo-ho-ho and a bottle of rum! Keir Dullea, best known for his role as Commander David Bowman in *2001: A Space Odyssey*, gives an exciting reading in Stevenson's colorful tale of Jim Hawkins's search for buried treasure. It's a bit disconcerting that Dullea doesn't read the narrative in a British accent, but he handles all the character voices with assurance and aplomb.

2 css 3 hr Durkin Hayes Audio

Treasure Island
Author: Robert Louis Stevenson
Performers: Multiple Cast
★★★

Aye, me hearties! Step aboard the *Hispaniola* for an unforgettable adventure in search of buried treasure. This version of the penultimate pirate story is heavily dramatized with sound effects galore. The dramatics are a little over the edge at times, but children won't mind and should easily get into the fun. Very nice music, too.

2 css 2 hr 10 min The Mind's Eye

The Trumpet of the Swan
Author/Reader: E. B. White
★

Here is the story of Louis, a trumpeter swan who has no voice. Author E. B. White, reading in a dry, monotone voice, fails to engage the listener. This is a wonderful book, but this audio is another case of an author who fails to bring his own work to life.

4 css 4 hr 20 min Bantam Audio

Where the Red Fern Grows
Author: Wilson Rawls
Performer: Richard Thomas
★★★

A loving threesome, Billy and his two dogs range the dark hills and river bottoms of Cherokee country. Old Dan has the brawn, Little Ann has the brains—and Billy has the will to train them to be the finest hunting team in the valley. Soon their skills will be put to the test as they brave the dangers of the wilds for the ultimate glory in this classic adventure story. Richard Thomas brings this to life in a well-paced, dramatic performance that conjures up the spirit of country manners and mores.

2 css 3 hr Bantam Audio

Where the Wild Things Are
(An ALA Notable Children's Recording)
Author: Maurice Sendak
Performer: Tammy Grimes
★★★★

Young Max, the hero of *Where the Wild Things Are,* is sent to bed for misbehaving, and sails off to a land where huge, bizarre creatures make him their king. In the haunting and mysterious *Outside over There,* Ida rescues her baby sister from goblins by charming them with a captivating tune on her wonder horn. Also included are *In the Night Kitchen, The Nutshell Library, The Sign on Rosie's Door,* and *Very Far Away.* This wonderful recording features a stately score by Mozart and a passionate performance by Tammy Grimes, who gets the most out of Sendak's celebrated characters and their ability to master the frightening aspects of life by their own imagination and invention.

1 css 45 min Caedmon Audio

The Wind in the Willows
Author: Kenneth Graham
Performers: Multiple Cast
★★★

This is probably one of the greatest "animal" stories ever written. But then Mole, Water Rat, Toad, and Badger are not so much "animals" as people. This is a dramatized, multi-cast performance, with plenty of music and sound effects, and while purists may object to some dramatic high jinks, kids are bound to have fun.

2 css 2 hr 25 min The Mind's Eye

Winnie-the-Pooh
Author: A. A. Milne
Performer: Carol Channing
★★★

The best of all bears—the one-and-only, ever-endearing Winnie-the-Pooh—shares adventures with Christopher Robin and the gang in a captivating retelling of the famous story with special songs by Pooh's creator A. A. Milne. Carol Channing reads in her usual zany voice without much attempt at British accents. However, if you can get past that, and realize this is Pooh à la Channing, it's fun to enter into her specialized interpretation. Channing has a voice that young listeners will find easy to follow and her characters are drawn with humor and well differentiated. The songs are catchy.

1 css 1 hr Caedmon Audio

The Wonderful Wizard of Oz
Author: L. Frank Baum
Told by Rebecca De Mornay
Bomb

Despite beautiful packaging, this selection from Everyman's Library Children's Classics is a dud. It is hard to believe we are listening to the much beloved *Wonderful Wizard of Oz.* Rebecca De Mornay reads this timeless tale in an inappropriately sexy, breathless manner. She meanders in a slow, soft voice, losing the sense of the material sentence by sentence. To make matters worse, heavily orchestrated and intrusive musical passages make it hard to hear her.

1 css 1 hr Everyman's Library Children's Classics

World of Stories
Authors: Brothers Grimm
Reader: Katharine Hepburn
★★

Six fairy tales are read here with vitality by Katharine Hepburn, though her famous tremolo may not be the best vehicle for all the stories. Hepburn hits her stride with fanciful interpretations of *The Emperor's New Clothes* and *The Nightingale.* Less successful is *Jack and the Beanstalk,* with many of the characters sounding alike. However, Hepburn's energetic performance and good-natured introductions should appeal to children. But it may well be their parents and grandparents who will most enjoy listening to this legend weave her spell. Musical interludes separate each tale. Also included: *Beauty and the Beast, Tattercoats,* and *The Musicians of Bremen.*

1 css 1 hr 20 min Caedmon Audio

Zlateh the Goat and Other Stories
(An ALA Notable Children's Recording)
Author: Isaac Bashevis Singer
Performer: Theodore Bikel
★★★

This collection includes seven whimsical folktales: *Fool's Paradise, Grandmother's Tale, The Snow in Chelm, The Mixed Up Feet and the Silly Bridegroom, The First Schlemiel, The Devil's Trick,* and *Zlateh the Goat.* Set in the village of Chelm, where many a fool dwells, the stories range from the silly to the superb as Singer writes of devils, innocents, and schlemiels. In this collection, we meet an heroic goat, an irresponsible bridegroom, four sisters who mix up their feet in bed, and a young man who imagines himself dead. Theodore Bikel reads well in mellifluous tones, yet some of the stories are more effective than others.

1 css 1½ hr Caedmon Audio

The Adventures of Huckleberry Finn
A: Mark Twain
R: Ed Begley
HARP

The Adventures of Robin Hood: How Robin Became an Outlaw
A: Paul Creswick
R: Anthony Quayle
HARP

The Adventures of Robin Hood: Robin and His Merry Men
A: Paul Creswick
R: Anthony Quayle
HARP

The Adventures of Robin Hood Audio Collection
A: Paul Creswick
R: Anthony Quayle
HARP

The Adventures of Tom Sawyer
A: Mark Twain
R: Ed Begley
HARP

Aesop's Fables
A: Aesop
R: Boris Karloff
HARP

Air Is All Around You
A: Franklyn M. Branley
HARP

Aladdin and His Lamp
A: Amabel Williams-Ellis
R: Anthony Quayle
HARP

Aladdin's Lamp
From *Tales of the Arabian Nights* (Revised)
R: Lou Diamond Phillips
DOVE

Alexander and the Terrible, Horrible, No Good, Very Bad Day and Other Stories
A: Judith Viorst
R: Blythe Danner
HARP

Ali Baba and the Forty Thieves
A: Amabel Williams-Ellis
R: Anthony Quayle
HARP

Alice in Wonderland
A: Lewis Carroll
R: Joan Greenwood and Stanley Holloway
HARP

Alice in Wonderland
A: Lewis Carroll
R: Cybill Shepherd
DOVE

Alice through the Looking Glass
A: Lewis Carroll
DOVE

All the Little Toot Stories
A: Hardie Gramatky
R: Hans Conried
HARP

Alvin and the Chipmunks: Alvin's Christmas Carol
Read-Along
TW

Alvin and the Chipmunks: A Chipmunk Celebration
Read-Along
TW

Alvin and the Chipmunks: The Easter Chipmunk
Read-Along
TW

Amelia Bedelia
A: Peggy Parish
HARP

Amelia Bedelia and the Surprise Shower
A: Peggy Parish
HARP

American Tall Tales Audio Collection
A: Adrian Stoutenberg
R: Ed Begley
HARP

And I Mean It, Stanley
A: Crosby Bonsall
HARP

Angelina Ballerina and Other Stories
A: Katharine Holabird
R: Sally Struthers
HARP

Animal Songs A–Z
A/R: David Polansky
HARP

Arthur's Christmas Cookies
A: Lillian Hoban
HARP

Arthur's Funny Money
A: Lillian Hoban
HARP

Arthur's Honey Bear
A: Lillian Hoban
HARP

Arthur's Pen Pal
A: Lillian Hoban
HARP

Arthur's Prize Reader
A: Lillian Hoban
HARP

Aspire to the Heavens
A/R: Mary Higgins Clark
DOVE

Aunt Eater Loves a Mystery
A: Doug Cushman
HARP

Babar Audio Collection
A: Jean de Brunhoff
R: Louis Jourdan
HARP

Babar the King and Babar and Zephir
A: Jean de Brunhoff
R: Louis Jourdan
HARP

Babar's Mystery and Babar and the Wully-Nully
A: Laurent de Brunhoff
R: Louis Jourdan
HARP

Baby
A: Patricia MacLachlan
R: Blythe Danner
BDD

Bambi
A: Felix Salten
R: Glynis Johns
HARP

A Bargain for Frances
A: Russell Hoban
R: Glynis Johns
HARP

Beach Bunnies
A/R: Jane Burbank and Robert Stecko
HARP

A Bear Called Paddington
A/R: Michael Bond
HARP

Bears' Christmas and Other Stories
A/R: The Berenstains
HARP

Bears' Picnic and Other Stories
A/R: The Berenstains
HARP

Beatrix Potter Audio Collection
A: Beatrix Potter
R: Claire Bloom
HARP

Beauty and the Beast and Other Stories
Fortieth Anniversary Edition
A: A. Lang
R: Douglas Fairbanks, Jr.
HARP

Beauty and the Beast and Puss in Boots
A: Jan Brett and Traditional Version
R: Bess Armstrong and Robby Benson
DOVE

The Beginner's Bible
Old Testament
R: Richard Thomas and Jodi Benson
DOVE

The Best Christmas Pageant Ever
A: Barbara Robinson
R: Elaine Stritch
HARP

The Big Balloon Race
A: Eleanor Coerr
HARP

The Big Book for Our Planet
A: Edited by Ann Durell, Jean Craighead George, and Katherine Paterson
R: Ed Begley, Jr., Robby Benson, Shelley Hack, Deborah Raffin, Mark Rolston, Laura San Giacomo, and Marina Sirtis
MILLS

Big Max
A: Kin Platt
HARP

The Biggest Pumpkin Ever and Other Stories
A: Steven Kroll
R: Hal Linden
HARP

Billy and Blaze Stories
A: C. W. Anderson
R: David Cassidy
HARP

Binky Brothers, Detectives
A: James Lawrence
HARP

Black Beauty
A: Anna Sewell
R: Claire Bloom
HARP

Black Beauty
A: Anna Sewell
R: Lynn Redgrave
RH

The Borrowers
A: Mary Norton
R: Claire Bloom
HARP

The Boy Who Lived with the Bears and Other Iroquois Stories
A/R: Joe Bruchac
HARP

Bump in the Night
Song Album
TW

Bury Me Deep
A: Christopher Pike
R: Kelly Ripa
HARP

Captain History
A: Michael Viner and Allan Katz
R: Mel Blanc and Gary Owens
DOVE

Carnival of the Animals
A: Ogden Nash; music by Camille Saint-Saens
R: Charlton Heston, Walter Matthau, Lily Tomlin, and Audrey Hepburn
DOVE

The Case of the Hungry Stranger
A: Crosby Bonsall
HARP

The Case of the Scaredy Cats
A: Crosby Bonsall
HARP

The Cay
A: Theodore Taylor
R: LeVar Burton
BDD

The Celery Stalks at Midnight
A: James Howe
R: George S. Irving
HARP

Charlie and the Chocolate Factory
A/R: Roald Dahl
HARP

Charlie and the Great Glass Elevator
A: Roald Dahl
R: Robert Powell
HARP

Charlotte's Web
A/R: E. B. White
BDD

Cheaper by the Dozen
A: Frank B. Gilbreth, Jr., and Ernestine Gilbreth Carey
BDD

A Child's Garden of Verses
A: Robert Louis Stevenson
R: Dame Judith Anderson
HARP

Chinese Fairy Tales
A: Isabelle C. Chang
R: Siobhan McKenna
HARP

Chitty Chitty Bang Bang
A: Ian Fleming
R: Hermione Gingold
HARP

The Chronicles of Narnia: The Complete Collection
A: C. S. Lewis
R: Claire Bloom, Anthony Quayle, Ian Richardson, and Michael York
HARP

The Chronicles of Narnia Audio Collection
A: C. S. Lewis
R: Claire Bloom, Anthony Quayle, and Ian Richardson
HARP

The Chronicles of Narnia: Horse and His Boy
A: C. S. Lewis
R: Anthony Quayle
HARP

The Chronicles of Narnia: The Last Battle
A: C. S. Lewis
R: Michael York
HARP

The Chronicles of Narnia: The Lion, the Witch and the Wardrobe
A: C. S. Lewis
R: Ian Richardson
HARP

The Chronicles of Narnia: The Magician's Nephew
A: C. S. Lewis
R: Claire Bloom
HARP

The Chronicles of Narnia: Prince Caspian
A: C. S. Lewis
R: Claire Bloom
HARP

The Chronicles of Narnia: The Silver Chair
A: C. S. Lewis
R: Ian Richardson
HARP

The Chronicles of Narnia: The Voyage of the "Dawn Treader"
A: C. S. Lewis
R: Anthony Quayle
HARP

Cinderella and Yeh-Shen
A: The Brothers Grimm and Ai-Ling Louie
R: Stefanie Zimbalist and Joan Chen
DOVE

The Classics Collection: Beauty and the Beast and Puss in Boots; The Happy Prince and the Steadfast Tin Soldier; The Ugly Duckling and The Emperor's New Clothes; Aladdin's Lamp
A: Traditional Versions
R: Bess Armstrong, Robby Benson, David Dukes, Dudley Moore, Lou Diamond Phillips, and Michael York
DOVE

Come Back, Amelia Bedelia
A: Peggy Parish
HARP

Comets
A: Franklin M. Branley
HARP

The Complete Alice in Wonderland Audio Collection
A: Lewis Carroll
R: Christopher Plummer
HARP

The Complete Winnie-the-Pooh and the House at Pooh Corner
A: A. A. Milne
R: Carol Channing
HARP

Coyote and Rock and Other Lushootseed Stories
A: Translated by Vi Hilbert
R: Vi Hilbert
HARP

Curious George
A: H. A. Rey
R: Julie Harris
HARP

Curious George Learns the Alphabet and Other Stories
A: Margaret and H. A. Rey
R: Julie Harris
HARP

The Dancing Granny and Other African Stories
A/R: Ashley Bryan
HARP

Danny and the Dinosaur
A: Sid Hoff
HARP

Danny, The Champion of the World
A: Roald Dahl
R: Robert Powell
HARP

Day at Santa's Workshop
A: Mary Sheldon
R: Betty White
DOVE

Day in the City
A: Mary Sheldon
R: Betty White
DOVE

A Day in the Lives of Dina and Darren Dinosaur
A: Tony Haynes
R: Solomon Burke and Freda Payne
DOVE

The Day Jimmy's Boa Ate the Wash and Other Stories
A: Trinka Hakes Noble
R. Sandy Duncan
HARP

Day with Dad at the County Fair
A: Mary Sheldon
R: Betty White
DOVE

Days with Frog and Toad
A: Arnold Lobel
HARP

Digging Up Dinosaurs
A: Aliki
HARP

Dinosaur Rock
A/R: Michele Valeri and Michael Stein
HARP

Dinosaur Time
A: Peggy Parish
HARP

Dinosaurs Are Different
A: Aliki
HARP

Doctor De Soto and Other Stories
A: William Steig
R: Pat Carroll
HARP

The Drinking Gourd
A: F. N. Monjo
HARP

Emily
A: Michael Bedard
R: Christine Lahti
BDD

The Emperor's New Clothes and Other Tales
A: Hans Christian Andersen
R: Sir Michael Redgrave
HARP

The Enormous Crocodile and the Magic Finger
A/R: Roald Dahl
HARP

Fall into Darkness
A: Christopher Pike
R: Kelly Ripa
HARP

Fantastic Mr. Fox
A/R: Roald Dahl
HARP

The First Dog and Other Chippewa-Cree Stories
A: Translated by Ron Evans
HARP

Flash, Crash, Rumble, and Roll
A: Franklyn M. Branley
HARP

The Flood and Other Lakota Stories
A/R: Kevin Locke
HARP

Frances
A: Russell Hoban
R: Glynis Johns
HARP

Freaky Friday
A: Mary Rodgers
R: Mary-Louis Parker
HARP

The Friendly Snowflake
A/R: M. Scott Peck
HARP

Frog and Toad All Year
A/R: Arnold Lobel
HARP

Frog and Toad Are Friends
A/R: Arnold Lobel
HARP

Frog and Toad Audio Collection
A/R: Arnold Lobel
HARP

Frog and Toad Together
A: Arnold Lobel
HARP

Further Adventures of Tweedle Dum and Tweedle Dee and The Shoes That Were Danced to Pieces
A: Nicholas Ball and The Brothers Grimm
R: Nicholas Ball and Cathy Moriarty
DOVE

Germs Make Me Sick
A: Melvin Berger
HARP

The Gift of the Magi and The Little Match Girl
A: O. Henry and Traditional Version
R: Dudley Moore and Robby Benson
DOVE

Goblin Tales: Spectacles
A/R: Ann Beattie
HARP

Goblin Tales: The Temptation of Wilfred Malachey
A/R: William F. Buckley, Jr.
HARP

Golden Slumbers Lullabies from Far and Near
R: Oscar Brand, Pete Seeger, and others
HARP

The Good Luck Pony
A: Elizabeth Koda-Callan
R: Julie Krone
HARP

Goodnight Moon
A: Margaret Wise Brown
R: Cathy Fink, Si Kahn, and Marcy Marxer
HARP

Grandmother Remembers Songbook: Heirloom Songs for My Grandchild
A: Judith Levy and Judy Pelikan
HARP

Grasshopper on the Road
A: Arnold Lobel
HARP

A Graveyard of Ghost Tales
R: Vincent Price
HARP

Hans Brinker: Or, the Silver Skates
A: Mary M. Dodge
R: Claire Bloom
HARP

Hansel and Gretel
A: The Brothers Grimm
R: Claire Bloom
HARP

Happy Birthday to You! and Other Dr. Seuss Stories
A: Dr. Seuss
R: Hans Conried
HARP

The Happy Prince and The Steadfast Tin Soldier
A: Oscar Wilde and Hans Christian Andersen
R: Dudley Moore and David Dukes
DOVE

Heidi
A: Johanna Spyri
R: Claire Bloom
HARP

Here Comes the Strikeout
A: Leonard Kessler
HARP

Higglety Pigglety Pop! or There Must Be More to Life
A: Maurice Sendak
R: Tammy Grimes
HARP

Hill of Fire
A: Thomas Lewis
HARP

A Hornbook for Witches: Stories and Poems for Halloween
R: Vincent Price
HARP

The House at Pooh Corner
R: A. A. Milne
R: Carol Channing
HARP

How Rabbit Tricked Otter and Other Cherokee Animal Stories
A/R: Gayle Ross
HARP

How the Leopard Got His Spots and Other Stories
A: Rudyard Kipling
R: Arte Johnson
DOVE

How the Rhinoceros Got His Skin and Other Stories
A: Rudyard Kipling
R: Arte Johnson
DOVE

How the Whale Got His Throat and Other Stories
A: Rudyard Kipling
R: Arte Johnson
DOVE

Howliday Inn
A: James Howe
R: Lou Jacobi, Larry Robinson, and the Caedmon Players
HARP

Hug Me and Other Stories
A: Patti Stren
R: Blythe Danner
HARP

In a Dark, Dark Room and Other Scary Stories
A: Alvin Schwartz
HARP

Jacob Have I Loved
A: Katherine Paterson
R: Moira Kelly
HARP

Jacob Two-Two and the Dinosaur
A: Mordecai Richler
R: Christopher Plummer
HARP

Jacob Two-Two Meets the Hooded Fang
A: Mordecai Richler
R: Christopher Plummer
HARP

James and the Giant Peach
A/R: Roald Dahl
HARP

Jolly Postman
A: Janet and Allan Ahlbert
R: Tim Curry and Andrea Martin
HARP

Journey
A: Patricia MacLachlan
R: Lucas Haas
BDD

Joyful Noise and I Am Phoenix
A: Paul Fleischman
R: John Bedford and Lloyd Anne Twomey
HARP

Julie of the Wolves
A: Jean Craighead George
R: Irene Worth
HARP

The Jungle Book
A: Rudyard Kipling
R: Tony Roberts
DURK

Just Plain Fancy
A/R: Patricia Polacco
BDD

Kenny's Window
A: Maurice Sendak
R: Tammy Grimes
HARP

King Arthur Audio Collection
A: Howard Pyle
R: Ian Richardson
HARP

Lassie Come Home
A: Eric Knight
R: David McCallum
HARP

The Last of the Mohicans
A: James Fennimore Cooper
R: James Mason and full cast
HARP

Let's Listen Stories
A: Rex Parkin
R: Julie Harris and Boris Karloff
HARP

The Light in the Forest
A: Conrad Richter
R: Robert Sean Leonard
BDD

Little Bear
A: Else Holmelund Minarik
R: Sigourney Weaver
HARP

The Little Grey Men
A: B. B.
R: Julie Andrews
DOVE

Little Hans and Meg and The Princess on the Glass Hill
A: The Brothers Grimm and Abjorsen and Moe
R: Cathy Moriarty and Dudley Moore
DOVE

The Little Lame Prince
A: Dinah M. Mulock
R: Cathleen Nesbitt
HARP

The Little Prince
A: Antoine de Saint Exupery
R: Louis Jourdan
HARP

The Little Princess
A: Frances Hodgson Burnett
R: Wanda McCaddon
PART

Little Women
A: Louisa May Alcott
R: Julie Harris
HARP

Little Women
A: Louise May Alcott
R: Joanne Woodward
DOVE

The Littlest Angel and The Bells of Christmas
A: Charles Tazewell
R: Dame Judith Anderson
HARP

The Long Way to a New Land
A: Joan Sandin
HARP

Lullabies and Night Songs
A: Compiled by Alec Wilder and Maurice Sendak
R: Jan DeGaetani
HARP

Lyle, Lyle, Crocodile and Other Adventures of Lyle
A: Bernard Waber
R: Gwen Verdon
HARP

Madeline and Other Bemelmans
A: Ludwig Bemelmans
R: Carol Channing
HARP

Mandy
A/R: Julie Andrews
DOVE

Mary Poppins
Fortieth Anniversary Edition
A: P. L. Travers
R: Maggie Smith
HARP

Mary Poppins Audio Collection
A: P. L. Travers
R: Maggie Smith
HARP

The Maurice Sendak Audio Collection
A: Maurice Sendak
R: Tammy Grimes
HARP

Mi Casa Es Su Casa: A Latin American Journey
A/R: Michele Valeri
HARP

Mighty Morphin Power Rangers: The Album: A Rock Adventure
Song Album
TW

Mighty Morphin Power Rangers: Christmas Read-Along
Read-Along
TW

Mighty Morphin Power Rangers: Island of Illusion
3-D Audio Power Pack
TW

Mighty Morphin Power Rangers: On Fins and Needles
3-D Audio Power Pack
TW

Mrs. Katz and Tush
A: Patricia Polacco
R: Patricia Polacco and Omar Sharif Scroggins
BDD

The Moon Lady
A/R: Amy Tan
DOVE

Moose Tales
A/R: Daniel Pinkwater
DOVE

More Scary Stories to Tell in the Dark
A: Alvin Schwartz
R: George S. Irving
HARP

Mother Goose
R: Celeste Holm, Boris Karloff, and Cyril Richard
HARP

The Mouse and His Child
A: Russell Hoban
R: Peter Ustinov
HARP

My Family Tree
A/R: Robin Moore
HARP

The Napping House and Other Stories
A: Audrey Wood
R: Lynn Redgrave
HARP

Nightmares and The Headless Horseman Rides Tonight: Poems to Trouble Your Sleep
A/R: Jack Prelutsky
HARP

Nighty Nightmare
A: James Howe
R: George S. Irving
HARP

Nutcracker
A: E.T.A. Hoffman
R: Christopher Plummer
HARP

Once upon a Forest
A: Novelization by Mark Young and Kelly Ward
R: Ben Vereen
DOVE

The Oz Audio Collection
A: L. Frank Baum
R: Ray Bolger
HARP

Paddington for Christmas
A/R: Michael Bond
HARP

Parabola Boxed Audio Collection
A: Roald Dahl
HARP

Peter and the Wolf
Read-Along
R: Kirstie Alley, Lloyd Bridges, and Ross Malinger
TW

Peter and the Wolf and Tubby the Tuba
A: Serge Prokofiev, Paul Tripp, and George Kleinsinger
R: Carol Channing
HARP

Peter Pan
A: J. M. Barrie
R: Tom Conti
RH

The Phantom Tollbooth
A: Norton Juster
R: Pat Carroll
HARP

The Pied Piper and Other Stories
A: Hans Christian Andersen
R: Keith Baxter
HARP

Play Ball, Amelia Bedelia
A: Peggy Parish
HARP

The Pony Engine and Other Stories
A: Doris Garn
R: Julie Harris, Boris Karloff, and Davis Wayne
HARP

The Pooh Song Book
A: A. A. Milne; music by H. Fraser-Simson
R: Carol Channing
HARP

The Prince and the Pauper
A: Mark Twain
R: Ian Richardson
HARP

The Princess and the Goblin
A: George MacDonald
R: Glenda Jackson
DOVE

Rap, Rap, Rap, Rapunzel and Little Red Ride 'n the Hood
A: Taro Meyer
R: Patti Austin
DOVE

The Reading Rainbow Songs
A: Steve Horelick
R: Steve Horelick, Ben Vereen, and others
HARP

Really Rosie
A: Maurie Sendak; music by Carole King
HARP

The Red Pony
A: John Steinbeck
R: Eli Wallach
HARP

Return to Howliday Inn
A: James Howe
R: George Irving
HARP

Ride through the Solar System
A: Michael Stein and Bryan Smith
R: Michael Stein
HARP

The Roald Dahl Audio Collection
A/R: Roald Dahl
HARP

Robinson Crusoe: Extracts from His Journal
A: Daniel Defoe
R: Ian Richardson
HARP

Roland the Minstrel Pig and Other Stories
A: William Steig
R: Carol Channing
HARP

Rolling Harvey Down the Hill and Other Rhyme Stories
A/R: Jack Prelutsky
HARP

The Rudyard Kipling Audio Collection
A: Rudyard Kipling
R: Boris Karloff
HARP

Rumpelstiltskin and Rapunzel
A: The Brothers Grimm
R: Dudley Moore and Robby Benson
DOVE

The Runaway Bunny
A: Margaret Wise Brown
R: Cathy Fink, Si Kahn, and Marcy Marxer
HARP

Russian Fairy Tales
A: Translated by Moura Budberg and Amabel Williams-Ellis
R: Morris Carnovsky
HARP

Saban's VR Troopers
Read-Along
TW

Saban's VR Troopers
3-D Audio
TW

Sacred Twins and Spider Woman
A: Translated by Geri Keams
R: Geri Keams
HARP

Sam the Minuteman
A: Nathaniel Benchley
HARP

Santasaurus
A: Mary Sheldon
R: Jonathan Winters
DOVE

Scary Stories 3: More Tales to Chill Your Bones
A: Alvin Schwartz
R: George S. Irving
HARP

The Secret Garden
A: Frances Hodgson Burnett
R: Geraldine James
RH

The Silver Slippers
A: Elizabeth Koda-Callan
R: Marianna Tcherkassky
HARP

Skylark
A: Patricia MacLachlan
HARP

The Snow Queen
A: Hans Christian Andersen
R: Cathleen Nesbitt
HARP

Snow White and Rose Red and Brier Rose
A: The Brothers Grimm
R: Dudley Moore and Robby Benson
DOVE

Sounder
A: William Armstrong
R: Avery Brooks
HARP

The Star of Melvin and Waldo, Tell Me about Christmas
A: Zimelman and Hans Wilhelm
R: Ralph Waite and Dudley Moore
DOVE

Star Wars Adventures: The Empire Strikes Back
Read-Along
TW

Star Wars Adventures: A New Hope
Read-Along
TW

Star Wars Adventures: Return of the Jedi
Read-Along
TW

The Story of Babar and Babar and Father Christmas
Fortieth Anniversary Edition
A: Jean de Brunhoff
R: Louis Jourdan
HARP

The Story of Babar, and The Travels of Babar
A: Jean de Brunhoff
R: Louis Jourdan
HARP

A Story of Hanukkah
A: Daniel Bloom
R: Pat Carroll and Jackie Cytrynbaum
HARP

The Story of Peter Pan
A: J. M. Barrie
R: Glynis Johns
HARP

The Story of Sleeping Beauty
A: Peter Ilyitch Tchaikovsky
R: Claire Bloom
HARP

The Story of Swan Lake
A: Peter Ilyitch Tchaikovsky
R: Claire Bloom
HARP

The Story of the Nutcracker
A: E.T.A. Hoffman
R: Claire Bloom
HARP

The Story of the Three Kings
A: Margaret B. Freeman
R: George Rose
HARP

Strega Nona's Magic Lessons and Other Stories
A: Tomie De Paola
R: Tammy Grimes
HARP

The Summer Friend
A: Mary Sheldon
R: Mary Sheldon, Julie Andrews, Elliott Gould, and Michael York
DOVE

Sunshine Makes the Seasons
A: Franklyn M. Branley
HARP

The Swiss Family Robinson
A: Johann David Wyss
RH

The Tale of Peter Rabbit and Other Stories
A: Beatrix Potter
R: Claire Bloom
HARP

The Tale of Squirrel Nutkin and Other Stories
A: Beatrix Potter
R: Claire Bloom
HARP

The Thirteen Clocks
A: James Thurber
R: Peter Ustinov
HARP

The Three Little Pigs and Other Fairy Tales
A: Traditional Versions
R: Boris Karloff
HARP

Thumbelina
Read-Along
TW

To Space and Back
A: Sally Ride and Susan Okie
R: Carrie Snodgress
DOVE

Tom Sawyer—Adventures with Injun Joe
A: Mark Twain
R: Ed Begley
HARP

Tongue Twisters
A: Alvin Schwartz
R: George S. Irving
HARP

Treasure Island
A: Robert Louis Stevenson
R: Charles Dance
RH

Treasure Island
A: Robert Louis Stevenson
R: Ian Richardson
HARP

Trick or Treat: Halloween Celebrated in Story and Song
A/R: Oscar Brand
HARP

The Ugly Duckling and The Emperor's New Clothes
A: Hans Christian Andersen
R: Michael York
DOVE

The Velveteen Rabbit
A: Margery Williams
R: Gwen Verdon
HARP

Waldo, Tell Me about Christ and Waldo, Tell Me about Me
A: Hans Wilhelm
R: Ralph Waite
DOVE

Waldo, Tell Me about God and Waldo Tell Me about Guardian Angels
A: Hans Wilhelm
R: Ralph Waite
DOVE

What the Moon Is Like
A: Franklyn M. Branley
HARP

When We Were Very Young and Now We Are Six
A: A. A. Milne
R: Dame Judith Anderson
HARP

Why Mosquitoes Buzz in People's Ears and Other Tales
A: Verna Aardema
R: Ossie Davis and Ruby Dee
HARP

The Wild Swans and The Elves and the Shoemaker
A: Hans Christian Andersen and the Brothers Grimm
R: Michael York
DOVE

The Wind in the Willows
A: Kenneth Grahame
R: David McCallum
HARP

Winnie-the-Pooh: Kanga and Roo
A: A. A. Milne
R: Carol Channing
HARP

Winnie-the-Pooh and Eeyore
A: A. A. Milne
R: Carol Channing
HARP

Winnie-the-Pooh and Tigger
A: A. A. Milne
R: Carol Channing
HARP

Witch
A: Christopher Pike
R: Kristy Swanson
HARP

The Witches
A: Roald Dahl
HARP

The Wizard of Oz
A: L. Frank Baum
R: Ray Bolger
HARP

The Wolves of Willoughby Chase
A: Joan Aiken
R: Lynn Redgrave
BDD

The Year without a Santa Claus and Other Stories
A: Phyllis McGinley and Clement Moore
R: Carol Channing
HARP

The Yearling
A: Marjorie Kinnan Rawlings
R: Eileen Heckart, David Wayne, and Luke Yankee
HARP

FICTION

"Fiction" is divided into two sections—"Classic" and "Contemporary." Frankly, the classic fiction on tape is stronger than the contemporary. This may well have something to do with the proven worth of the material, as opposed to choice of readers or production values. On the other hand, those actors chosen to read the classics are generally trained theater professionals with dynamic storytelling abilities. The contemporary fiction is sometimes undertaken by TV or movie stars who don't have quite the range or vocal training to bring it off. Also, the quality of the writing may be mediocre, the audiotape brought out to coincide with the release of a new book that may or may not be a hit. Still, there are some fine moments: Lee Horsley's magnetic interpretation of Larry McMurtry's *Lonesome Dove,* Tonya Pinkins's theatrical turn with Gloria Naylor's *The Women of Brewster Place,* and Jean Marsh's fluid, smooth-as-silk reading of Daphne du Maurier's *Rebecca.*

Classics are well represented more often than not; skilled actors ensure they have a dramatic life of their own. My favorites include Juliet Stevenson's inspired reading of the Brontë sisters' *Jane Eyre* and *Wuthering Heights,* John Lynch's haunting rendition of James Joyce's *A Portrait of the Artist as a Young Man,* and Derek Jacobi's perceptive illumination of the poetry of Homer's *The Iliad.*

There's a lot of pure fun here, too, from Jackie Collins to Danielle Steel to

Armistead Maupin—even some high-voltage erotica in *The Edge of the Bed: Cyborgasm 2.* So whatever your tastes, relax, listen, and enjoy.

CLASSIC

HIGHLY RECOMMENDED (★★★★)

A Christmas Carol*
The Great Gatsby
The Iliad
The Last of the Mohicans
O Pioneers!
A Portrait of the Artist as a Young Man
Wuthering Heights

The Age of Innocence
Author: Edith Wharton
Reader: Kate Nelligan
★★

Set in gaslit 1870s New York, this delicate drama of society people is considered Wharton's masterpiece. Newland Archer's overwhelming passion for the bizarre and challenging Countess Ellen Olenska pits him against the conventions of his time and the superficial values of the elite. Kate Nelligan reads passably, if not engagingly, but unfortunately has to vie for attention at times with a pompous musical accompaniment.

2 css 3 hr Random House AudioBooks

Another Country
Author: James Baldwin
Reader: Howard Rollins
★★

Baldwin's *Another Country* is the author's masterpiece as well as a classic of contemporary American fiction. The characters—homosexual, heterosexual, black, white—are poignantly drawn and interact in the pressure cooker of 1950s New York City as well as in the romantic south of France. Howard Rollins gives us a sense of how blue Baldwin's world is. The problem is, the book is too long to be effectively abridged and many key scenes are missing.

2 css Listen for Pleasure

* Simon & Schuster Audio

Billy Budd
Author: Herman Melville
Reader: Simon Jones
★★

Billy Budd, a paragon of simple goodness and virile beauty, is press-ganged into the crew of H.M.S. *Indomitable* in 1797. Billy is popular with everyone on board except Claggart, the master-at-arms. Life on board a warship of Nelson's time is vividly described in this drama of the sea. Simon Jones has made a number of fine recordings and it is with some surprise that this tale, seemingly suited to him, is not among his best. There is a distance from the material that eventually does this one in.

2 css 3 hr Listen for Pleasure

The Brothers Karamazov
Author: Fyodor Dostoyevsky
Reader: Debra Winger
Bomb

In the book version of *The Brothers Karamazov,* murder, betrayal, sacrifice, tragedy, and glory all combine with astonishing force. Debra Winger seems lost in Russia here. Her delivery is straight out of *Terms of Endearment,* and any sense of Dostoyevsky's power is missing.

4 css 6 hr Audio Literature

Call of the Wild
Author: Jack London
Reader: Theodore Bikel
★★★

From the harsh and frozen Yukon comes Buck, a dog born to luxury but stolen and sold as a sledge dog. But the spirited Buck escapes captivity and rises to face his enemies. Theodore Bikel has a deeply resonant, evocative voice, which he uses to great effect here and in the companion piece, *White Fang* (see page 114). Bikel actively journeys with the listener from the first minute to the last.

2 css 3 hr Durkin Hayes Audio

Charles Dickens Gift Set
Author: Charles Dickens
Reader: Multiple Narrators
★★

Includes *David Copperfield, Great Expectations,* and *Oliver Twist,* plus a special bonus cassette containing *A Christmas Carol.* This is actually better than the Twain gift set (see page 111). While the narration is a bit hollow, there are some nice performances in the dramatization. Seven tapes are packaged in a little wooden crate.

7 css 7 hr The Mind's Eye

A Christmas Carol
Author: Charles Dickens
Performer: Sir John Gielgud
★★★

Ever since the first publication of *A Christmas Carol* in 1843, the tale of stingy Ebenezer Scrooge, humble Bob Crachit, and beloved Tiny Tim has been a special part of our Christmas tradition. Sir John Gielgud's dramatic reading of this holiday classic brings Dickens's memorable characters to life. However, the story cries out for more than sixty minutes' playing time, and the production values themselves are a bit austere.

1 css   1 hr   Bantam Audio

A Christmas Carol
Author: Charles Dickens
Performer: Patrick Stewart
★★★★

Dickens's characters come to marvelous life in Patrick Stewart's (*Star Trek: The Next Generation* and the Royal Shakespeare Company) critically acclaimed solo interpretation of *A Christmas Carol,* which he has performed to sold-out audiences in New York and Los Angeles. Now in this studio recording, Stewart invites listeners to rediscover the timeless story at its source: Dickens's own, classic words, presented in a soaring, virtuoso solo performance in which Stewart plays all parts. No sound effects, no gimmicks, just a great voice of the contemporary classical stage creating as vivid a cast of characters as Dickens imagined.

2 css   1 hr 50 min   Simon & Schuster Audio
1 CD   1 hr 50 min   Simon & Schuster Audio

A Connecticut Yankee in King Arthur's Court
Author: Mark Twain
Reader: Richard Kiley
★★

In the course of describing our practical Yankee hero's adventures, Twain takes the opportunity to make objects of mirth out of the ways of the Old World, the chivalry of knights, and the pomposity of kings. Richard Kiley illuminates much of the wit of Twain's fantasy, if not providing much variety.

2 css   3 hr   Durkin Hayes Audio

Daisy Miller
Author: Henry James
Reader: Tammy Grimes
Bomb

Daisy Miller, a young American traveling abroad for the first time, openly ignores the rigid European social code of the day and earns the disapproval of her fellow Americans. Tammy Grimes is miscast, unable to convey the rigidity of the

European social code that Daisy ignores. Nor is she able to portray Daisy's innocence, as her voice is awash with world-weariness and irony.

2 css 3 hr Listen for Pleasure

David Copperfield
Author: Charles Dickens
Reader: Simon Callow
★

Much of this novel is based on Dickens's own life, with David's harsh and unhappy childhood, which we see from the boy's point of view, closely mirroring the author's own. Simon Callow narrates in a rather haughty, pompous manner, which goes against the humanity of Dickens's point of view.

2 css 3 hr Listen for Pleasure

Day of the Locust
Author: Nathaniel West
Reader: William Atherton
★★

The Hollywood that set designer Tod Hackett discovered was full of monstrous architecture and bizarre people turning to the dream factory for excitement and an answer to their dreary lives. William Atherton tells this tale of Tinseltown in too self-conscious a manner to be truly effective.

2 css 3 hr Listen for Pleasure

Ethan Frome
Author: Edith Wharton
Reader: Irene Worth
★★

The suspenseful writing and the vivid characterizations make this popular novel like no other Wharton ever wrote. One of America's leading stage actresses, Irene Worth gives a rather quirky interpretation. I found myself concentrating more on her prodigious technique (she makes doubly sure the tone is all terse, repressed New England) than on the intimacies of the tragic triangle of Ethan, Mattie, and Zeena.

2 css 3 hr Durkin Hayes Audio

Far from the Madding Crowd
Author: Thomas Hardy
Reader: Julie Christie
★★

Hardy's novel revolves around the beautiful and willful Bathsheba Everdene, mistress of Weatherbury Upper Farm, and the three men who love her. Hardy combines outstanding description of West Country rural life with a deep knowledge of romantic passion. Julie Christie played Bathsheba in the 1967 film version and reprises her role with a high-spirited delivery that generally serves Hardy well. She is less effective in the story's tragic moments.

2 css 3 hr Listen for Pleasure

Great Expectations
Author: Charles Dickens
Reader: Tom Baker
★★★

This is the story of Pip and his mysterious rise from ill-used orphan to gentleman. Magwitch, the brutal convict, withered Miss Havisham, still wearing her yellowed wedding gown, and the heartless and beautiful Estella are all drawn with typical Dickensian warmth and humor. As in *A Tale of Two Cities* (see page 113), Tom Baker (TV's *Dr. Who*) proves to be a fine interpreter of Dickens. Character voices involve the listener.

2 css 3 hr Durkin Hayes Audio

The Great Gatsby
Author: F. Scott Fitzgerald
Reader: Christopher Reeve
★★★★

An American classic, Fitzgerald's depiction of the Jazz Age and the power of myth set on New York's Long Island tells of wealthy Jay Gatsby and his ill-fated love for Daisy Buchanan. Christopher Reeve gives an amazing reading, full of insight into the disparate but frail characters he tackles. He breathes the spirit of Fitzgerald's writing and presents the author's vision in a seamless flow, with a strong narrative skill.

2 css 3 hr Durkin Hayes Audio

The House of Mirth
Author: Edith Wharton
Reader: Joanna Cassidy
★

There has been a recent renaissance for this tragic story of Lily Bart, a beautiful young lady caught up in the shallow and corrupt, yet glittering, world of New York society at the turn of the century. Joanna Cassidy is unable to sustain the power of Wharton's prose or convincingly portray the subtleties of it.

2 css 3 hr Listen for Pleasure

The Iliad
Author: Homer
Translated by Robert Fagles
Reader: Derek Jacobi
★★★★

In this new translation, Robert Fagles brings the vigor of contemporary language to Homer's 2,700-year-old story of the Trojan War. The result is an accessible *Iliad* that preserves every nuance of Homer's poetry and imagination. This is a rather mammoth undertaking and Derek Jacobi (*Masterpiece Theatre's* "I, Claudius") rises to the occasion. By never taking an actor's turn or trying to upstage the material, he allows the listener to appreciate the magnificence and clarity of Homer's great prose-poem. Thankfully, the sound quality is sterling, which allows us to concentrate fully on the text. Maria Tucci pleasingly presents the introductory material.

6 css 9 hr Penguin HighBridge Audio

The Isak Dinesen Collection
Author: Isak Dinesen
Readers: Colleen Dewhurst ("Babette's Feast" and "Sorrow Acre"), Isak Dinesen ("The King's Letter" and "The Wine of the Tetrarch"), and Julie Harris (*Out of Africa*)
★★★

This is a collection of some of the most treasured stories by Dinesen, full of soul-searching fantasies and autobiographical tales. The sensibilities of Julie Harris and Colleen Dewhurst complement Dinesen's stories. But the real treat here is hearing Baroness Blixen-Finecke herself, in her stately voice fragile with age, read live before an appreciative audience, presumably in America, since she thanks the United States for publishing *Seven Gothic Tales,* which her native country, Denmark, as well as England declined to do.

5 css 6 hr 40 min Audio Editions

Jane Eyre
Author: Charlotte Brontë
Reader: Juliet Stevenson
★★★

In this masterpiece of Victorian literature that has an impact even today, Brontë tells the story of Jane Eyre from her unhappy childhood as an orphan to her adult life as a governess and her eventual serenity. This is a love story of great magnitude as well as a hard-hitting social commentary on the powerful and powerless. Juliet Stevenson (of the Royal Shakespeare Company) is a wonderful reader, but she is a bit less successful here than in her reading of *Wuthering Heights* (see page 115) only because she is better at interpreting its wild, passionate qualities than she is at conveying the equally passionate but subtler, more introspective *Jane Eyre.*

2 css 3 hr 5 min Durkin Hayes Audio

The Last of the Mohicans
Author: James Fenimore Cooper
Reader: Theodore Bikel
★★★★

A small party of colonial Americans flee before the British and their Indian allies during the French and Indian wars. The tragic encounter between Magwa, the treacherous fox, and Uncas, the last Mohican chief, is one of the great climaxes in American literature. Theodore Bikel brings drama and excitement to this sweeping epic. The excellent abridgement weaves skillfully among scenes of terrifying massacres, love trysts, and moving funeral ceremonies.

2 css 3 hr Durkin Hayes Audio

Mark Twain Gift Set
Author: Mark Twain
Performers: Multiple Cast
★★

Includes *The Adventures of Huckleberry Finn* and *A Connecticut Yankee in King Arthur's Court,* plus a bonus cassette with "The Celebrated Jumping Frog of Calaveras County," "The Bride Comes to Yellow Sky" by Stephen Crane, and "The Luck of Roaring Camp" by Bret Harte. These are part dramatized, with music, and run the gamut from the amusing to the amateurish.

7 css 7 hr The Mind's Eye

Middlemarch
Author: George Eliot
Reader: Harriet Walter
★★★

Full of intricate plots, subplots, and decisive character portraits, Eliot's epic is a sweeping portrayal of nineteenth-century morals and social issues that explores the whole range of human nature. Harriet Walter's perky read succeeds only partly; she keeps the plot twists clear, but sometimes loses focus on characterizations.

4 css 6 hr Penguin HighBridge Audio

Moby Dick
Author: Herman Melville
Reader: George Kennedy
★

Few authors have created one mythological character, but Melville created two in one work: Captain Ahab, the Hunter, and Moby Dick, the Hunted. Epic adventure and psychological drama weave an inevitable course toward a final tragic confrontation between man and nature. George Kennedy lacks the classic requisite style necessary to convey the intricacies of Melville's early American treasure.

2 css 2 hr Durkin Hayes Audio

Northanger Abbey
Author: Jane Austen
Reader: Joanna Lumley
★★★

This is Austen's satirization of the melodramatic gothic novels of her time, with their exaggerated heroes and heroines who indulged in facile displays of emotion. The heroine Catherine Morland is by contrast cheerful and straightforward. Joanna Lumley paints a realistic picture of the social mores of early Victorian society.

2 css 3 hr Listen for Pleasure

O Pioneers!
Author: Willa Cather
Reader: Dana Ivey
★★★★

In this novel, first published in 1913, Cather tells of Alexander Bergson, who assumes responsibility for her family of Swedish immigrants and their farm. Dana Ivey, in a beautifully modulated tone, gets the most from Cather's alternately plain and poetic prose. This is a tasteful production all the way around, with a sensitive reader, fine sound quality, and beautiful packaging.

2 css 3 hr Penguin HighBridge Audio

Oliver Twist
Author: Charles Dickens
Reader: Dick Cavett
★

Oliver struggles with the burden of being a child and of being poor in industrial England, where poverty breeds crime and the road from the workhouse to Fagin's gang is a short and straight one. Why have Dick Cavett read this British story and with an American accent to boot? The match just doesn't work.

2 css 3 hr Durkin Hayes Audio

The Pearl
Author: John Steinbeck
Reader: Hector Elizondo
★★

In this famous parable, Kino finds a great pearl worth a fortune, but it brings only tragedy and evil to his family. Hector Elizondo has deep dulcet tones but reads each sentence in a softly conspiratorial, meaningful manner, which gives an uneven sense of import to the words in Steinbeck's naturalistic tale.

2 css 3 hr Penguin HighBridge Audio

A Portrait of the Artist as a Young Man
Author: James Joyce
Reader: John Lynch
★★★★

The richness of Joyce's language permeates the story of the Dedalus family, young Stephen's education by the Jesuits, his sexual awakening, intellectual development, and eventual revolt against the religion in which he has been raised. John Lynch reads with a dynamism that brings this book immediately to life. To my mind, Lynch becomes Stephen Dedalus, and that's no mean feat.

2 css 3 hr Durkin Hayes Audio

Pride and Prejudice
Author: Jane Austen
Reader: Jane Lapotaire
★★

In this finely etched satire, the scatterbrained Mrs. Bennett is determined to see her five daughters married. Austen's characters are rich and varied. Tony Award winner Jane Lapotaire is effective with her dark, husky tones, but there is an almost direct, contemporary feminist strength about her characterizations that comes across without the wry subtleness that would have been necessary in Austen's world.

2 css 3 hr Durkin Hayes Audio

The Red Badge of Courage
Author: Stephen Crane
Reader: Richard Crenna
★★

A young private in the Union army gives way to increasing worry that when he comes to be tested in his first encounter with the enemy, he will be found wanting in courage. Richard Crenna, if not a great reader, is enthusiastic and his dialogue sparkles most of the time.

2 css 2hr Listen for Pleasure

Spotted Horses and Other Stories
Author: William Faulkner
Selected and Read by Wendell Berry
★★

Writer Berry's reading of these stories testifies to his admiration of Faulkner's work. A small farmer in Kentucky as well as an author, Berry calls the stories collected here "damn good yarns." Included are "Spotted Horses," "The Old People," and the funny, poignant story about reroofing a church, "Shingles for the Lord." Berry underplays here, but it doesn't do much harm and lets Faulkner's prose take center stage.

2 css 3 hr Audio Literature

A Tale of Two Cities
Author: Charles Dickens
Reader: Tom Baker
★★★

A Tale of Two Cities, set against the bloody background of the French Revolution, is possibly Dickens's most famous work. Tom Baker is wonderfully skilled at getting to the heart of the humanity or inhumanity in Dickens's unforgettable characters.

2 css 3 hr Durkin Hayes Audio

The Three Musketeers
Author: Alexandre Dumas
Reader: Louis Jourdan
★★★

In this classic story of the young Gascon D'Artagnan at the court of King Louis XIII of France, the Three Musketeers weave their spells of chivalry, adventure, and love. France's Louis Jourdan is oh-so-appropriately French and propels Dumas's adventure with a finely honed sense of pace and style.

2 css 3 hr Listen for Pleasure

Tropic of Cancer
Author: Henry Miller
Reader: Martin Balsam
Bomb

Not quite fiction, not quite autobiography, Henry Miller's first book chronicles the extremes of experience in the life of a poverty-stricken artist living in Paris before the war. Martin Balsam drifts like a somnambulist through this noisy recording that includes scraping chairs and constant lip smacks. The worst problem, though, is that this classic book should have had a rich and sensual interpretation.

2 css 2 hr Listen for Pleasure

Under the Volcano
Author: Malcolm Lowry
Reader: Christopher Cazenove
★★

The horrors of alcoholism are vividly presented—equally vivid is the setting of the magnificent, uncaring Mexican mountains under which the consul examines his disastrous life. This tragic novel is read by Christopher Cazenove, who, though coming up with some harrowing moments, would have been even more effective if his narration had been better modulated and not delivered with such overpowering intensity.

2 css 3 hr Listen for Pleasure

White Fang
Author: Jack London
Reader: Theodore Bikel
★★★

White Fang is forced to accept a way of life innate to his kind—kill or be killed. No man can tame him, until one recognizes his nobility and intelligence. Theodore Bikel is a born storyteller and a good choice to interpret this heartwarming story for all ages.

2 css 3 hr Durkin Hayes Audio

Wuthering Heights
Author: Emily Brontë
Reader: Juliet Stevenson
★★★★

Here is Emily Brontë's classic novel of love and revenge on the moors. Juliet Stevenson, who also reads *Jane Eyre* (see page 110), takes a definite and appropriate point of view with her characters, giving them the nuances needed to make this a moving experience.

2 css 3 hr Durkin Hayes Audio

CONTEMPORARY

HIGHLY RECOMMENDED (★★★★)

Lonesome Dove
Rebecca
The Women of Brewster Place

The Accidental Tourist
Author: Anne Tyler
Reader: John Malkovich
★★

John Malkovich gives a rather perfunctory reading of this Tyler story of a travel-hating writer of travel books. Macon Leary systematically avoids adventure until he meets the frizzy-haired, stiletto-heeled Muriel, who upends Macon's world and thrusts him into engagement with life.

2 css 2 hr 55 min Random House AudioBooks

Adam's Fall
Author: Sandra Brown
Performer: Michael Zaslow
★★★

Her new patient, Adam, challenges physical therapist Lilah Mason's methods and authority at every turn. What she can't see is that while she's winning Adam's battle, she's losing her heart. This standard romance benefits from a lively interpretation by Michael Zaslow (of television's *One Life to Live*), who has an ability to deliver sharp dialogue.

2 css 3 hr BDD Audio

Alaska
Author: James A. Michener
Reader: Peter Graves
★★

Alaska is the story of America's last great frontier land. We hear about the first humans to settle in this vast land, specifically following the fortunes of two families drawn to the territory seeking gold. Peter Graves is a fine narrator and brings to Michener a commanding presence that fits the scope of this story.

2 css 3 hr Random House AudioBooks

All the Pretty Horses
Author: Cormac McCarthy
Reader: Brad Pitt
★★★

To escape a society moving in the wrong directions, John Grady Cole and two companions decide to seek their fortune in Mexico. But what begins as an idyllic, sometimes comic adventure leads to a place where dreams are paid for in blood. Brad Pitt manages to keep this story of revenge and survival interesting and suspenseful.

2 css 3 hr Random House AudioBooks

Angel
Author: Barbara Taylor Bradford
Reader: Christine Baranski
★

Here is pure Bradford fluff about four friends, who, as teenage orphans, vow to remain united forever. Unbelievably, as adults, they are all part of the glamorous world of show business. Baranski is up against it here and in her smoky voice attempts to wring some passion out of the messy proceedings, but to no avail. The story just doesn't ring true and the tacky music score that literally tries to mirror the action only means double trouble.

2 css 3 hr Random House AudioBooks

At Play in the Fields of the Lord
Author: Peter Matthiessen
Reader: John Lithgow
★★★

In backwater malarial South America, two missionary couples attempt to convert the Indians to their brand of Christianity, a corrupt army official schemes to destroy the tribe and clear the land, while an American-Indian mercenary, hired to kill the Indians, instead goes to live among them, hoping to regain his lost heritage. John Lithgow, who appeared in the film version, is a good match for material he is obviously familiar with, and brings the author's mystic vision alive with his well-paced narrative flow. Some characterizations are more skillfully done than others, however.

2 css 3 hr Random House AudioBooks

Belinda
Author: Anne Rice
Reader: Al Mohrmann
★★★

To Jeremy Walker, a handsome and famous forty-four-year-old illustrator of children's books, Belinda is a forbidden passion. She's sweet sixteen and the most seductive woman he's ever known. Al Mohrmann scores with *Belinda*! He puts a lot of oomph in his confident, quiet reading of this erotic morality tale.

2 css 2 hr Random House AudioBooks

The Bellarosa Connection
Author: Saul Bellow
Reader: Jerry Orbach
★★★

Harry Fonstein, an immigrant rescued from Nazi-occupied Europe, arrives in America and is denied final passage to his adopted homeland by the man who rescued him. Jerry Orbach fuels this story in an engaging delivery well suited to Bellow's wry machinations.

2 css 3 hr Durkin Hayes Audio

The Bluest Eye
Author: Toni Morrison
Readers: Toni Morrison and Ruby Dee
★★

This is the story of a black girl whose admiration for blond, blue-eyed children is devastating—who prays for her eyes to turn blue so that she will be beautiful, so that her world will be different. Morrison, winner of the Nobel Prize in literature is, unfortunately, a much better writer than reader. Her reading seems vacant of feeling, unlike Ruby Dee, who sweeps you away with her magnetism, technique, and characterizations.

2 css 3 hr Random House AudioBooks

The Boy Who Made Dragonfly
Zuni Myth as Told by Tony Hillerman
Reader: Debra Winger
★★

First told over five hundred years ago, this Zuni Indian myth about a boy who saves his people from an ecological disaster is retold by mystery writer Hillerman. "In our society it would be called a 'Bible story,' " Hillerman explains. Winger lends appropriate gentleness and simplicity to this morality tale.

1 css 1 hr 25 min Audio Literature

The Bridges of Madison County
Author/Reader: Robert James Waller
★★

This is the story of Robert Kincaid, a world-class photographer, and Francesca Johnson, an Iowa farm wife. When Kincaid drives through the heat and dust of an Iowa summer, looking for directions, the two of them are joined in an experience that will haunt them forever. Robert James Waller happens to read his own material very well and keeps interest up throughout.

2 css 3 hr Dove Audio

Buffalo Girls
Author: Larry McMurtry
Reader: Betty Buckley
★★★

When her old friend and rival Buffalo Bill Cody sweeps her into his ragtag band of legends and half legends on a Wild West tour of Europe, Calamity Jane begins her last bittersweet adventure. Betty Buckley impresses here in this unabridged saga, keeping a strong sense of time, place, and characterization through the entire venture, a difficult task in that the material is not McMurtry's best. She is best at wringing pathos out of the novel's tough, uncompromising sections.

8 css 12 hr Simon & Schuster Audio

Catch-22
Author: Joseph Heller
Reader: Alan Arkin
★★

Yossarian has a problem. The war is driving him crazy. Catch-22 says if Yossarian were crazy, he wouldn't have to fly any more missions, but since he is sane enough to know he'd be crazy to keep flying, then he isn't crazy and will have to continue. Alan Arkin reads in a brisk style, bringing to the fore some of Heller's trademark irony, but this version seems too truncated and we need to feel more involved.

2 css 2 hr Listen for Pleasure

The Celestine Prophecy: An Adventure
Author: James Redfield
Presented by Jesse Corti
★★★

An ancient manuscript has been found amid ruins in Peru. It reveals nine key insights critical to the evolution of the human race. It contains secrets that are changing our world—and tells you how to make connections between the events happening in your own life right now. Jesse Corti reads this Redfield phenomenon with conviction and a sense of wonder at discovering the road to an enlightened destiny.

2 css 3 hr Time Warner AudioBooks

Centennial
Author: James A. Michener
Reader: David Dukes
★★★

Centennial celebrates what used to be called "the winning of the West"—the story of the land and the Indians who inhabited it and of the people of many nations who came to drive them out. David Dukes gives a fluid reading with good characterizations. The abridgment flows, too.

4 css 6 hr The Publishing Mills AudioBooks

Charade
Author: Sandra Brown
Performer: Constance Towers
★★★

This story—part romance, part suspense— is about a woman who receives a heart transplant and reevaluates her life, is stalked by a mysterious figure, and falls in love with an ex-cop. This is a lively recording, due to the animated and on-the-mark performance by Constance Towers, who should be reading more audio books—she shines at the microphone.

2 css 3 hr Dove Audio

The Copper Beech
Author: Maeve Binchy
Performer: Fionnula Flanagan
★★★

Carved on the trunk of the mighty copper beech tree that embraces the school yard in Shancarrig are declarations of love, hope, and identity—the youthful dreams of eight children who studied there. Now grown, yet shaped by their years in the schoolhouse, they lead different lives. This recording benefits from a spirited, effortless performance by Fionnula Flanagan and crisp production values.

2 css 3 hr Bantam Audio

The Covenant
Author: James A. Michener
Reader: Simon Jones
★★★

This is a story of struggle and adventure, peopled with missionaries, tribesmen, adventurers, and scoundrels who play an important part in the development of the flourishing empire of South Africa. Simon Jones impresses as usual with his stately acumen and ability to hone in on the finer dynamics of a scene.

2 css 3 hr Random House AudioBooks

Cowboys Are My Weakness
Author/Reader: Pam Houston
Bomb

Yet another example of an author unable to read adequately. Pam Houston's stories about women who follow their cowboys, shoot rapids, and hunt contain some shrewd, funny observations about the relationships between the sexes. But Houston's reading is very slow going, with no sense of the rhythm or dramatic irony that is needed to let the stories blossom.

2 css 3 hr The Publishing Mills AudioBooks

Crazy in Alabama
Author/Reader: Mark Childress
★

Lucille Vinson has always dreamed of being a Hollywood star, but she's ended up in Alabama with six kids and an abusive husband who doesn't understand her. Everything goes a little crazy in this tale of a hot, restless summer in Alabama and a woman who looks for salvation in Hollywood. Author Childress reads in a distant, poetic trance, missing much of the hilarity inherent in his writing.

2 css 3 hr Harper Audio

Creatures of the Kingdom
Stories of Animals and Nature
Author: James A. Michener
Reader: John Cullum
★

Animals and nature have figured prominently in Michener's oeuvre. Here are some tales about the natural world—a woolly mammoth (*Alaska*), a wily gander who outwits his hunters (*Chesapeake*), and the awesome birth of the Hawaiian islands (*Hawaii*). Frankly, this collection seems a bit of a conceit, and the stories represented are lightweight. This is read in a detached style by John Cullum.

2 css 2 hr Random House AudioBooks

Crossing to Safety
Author: Wallace Stegner
Reader: John Randolph Jones
★★★

From Pulitzer Prize–winning author Wallace Stegner comes the story of a lifelong friendship between two couples, the Morgans and the Langs. Stegner evokes the dense web of feeling and experience that binds these four people together. John Randolph Jones brings his usual strong interpretive sense and mellow voice to many haunting descriptive passages. Nicely done. The packaging is beautiful, too, with an inside spread of a late autumnal landscape.

4 css 6 hr Penguin HighBridge Audio

Daybreak
Author: Belva Plain
Performer: Sada Thompson
★★★

Plain creates a living, breathing portrait of two families, joined by a childhood illness, yet divided by the politics of hatred and the sons they love. Sada Thompson has the range and depth to create believable dramatic confrontations among the family members and imbue them with pathos and dignity.

2 css 3 hr Bantam Audio

Deliverance
Author/Reader: James Dickey
★★

This is quite a curio. Author Dickey himself reads his own story—a penultimate macho fantasy. Four businessmen decide to get away from their dull suburban lives for a weekend of canoeing down a wild and remote Georgia river. This turns out to be quite a test. Dickey has the most down-home, backwoods voice I've ever heard from either author or actor, and somehow flavors these escapades with the right stuff.

2 css 2 hr Listen for Pleasure

The Edge of the Bed: Cyborgasm 2
Erotica in 3-D Sound
Performers: Multiple Cast
★★★

This collection of erotic stories and music with 3-D sound is best listened to using headphones, but you'll feel the impact with or without. The scenarios are diverse and the sound quality and production values are great. Definitely triple X.

1 CD Time Warner AudioBooks

The Enchanted April
Author: Elizabeth Von Arnim
Reader: Josie Lawrence
★★

High above the bay on the Italian Riviera stands a medieval castle into which Mrs. Wilkins, Mrs. Arbuthnot, Mrs. Fisher, and Lady Caroline Dexter are beckoned. Here they gradually shed their public skins and discover a harmony each of them has longed for. Josie Lawrence, who appeared in the film version, is a bit mannered here in a story that calls out for breathing room and a bit of abandonment.

2 css 3 hr Durkin Hayes Audio

Exit to Eden
Author: Anne Rice
Readers: Gillian Anderson and Gil Bellows
★

This piece of fluffy erotica transports us to The Club, a vacation paradise where no aspect of sexual pleasure is taboo. Read in a terribly obvious, breathy manner, presumably meant to represent sexual tension, this misses the mark with its lack of naturalness. Gillian Anderson does not do well with characters—the dominant master she depicts sounds like a croaking old frog rather than a sensual epicure. Gil Bellows does better with the female voices, but if the two actors had appeared in each other's sequences (in appropriate male and female roles), there would have been more than a few sparks.

2 css 2 hr Random House AudioBooks

The Feast of All Saints
Author: Anne Rice
Reader: Courtney B. Vance
★★★

Courtney B. Vance is the perfect choice for this tale of half-castes in pre–Civil War New Orleans, who form their own aristocracy and spread their talents beyond the limits of their small world. In soft-spoken, dramatic accents, Vance, who has an affinity for this material, propels us quickly into the unfolding events. Luckily the abridgment here is cohesive, and this recording misses a top rating only because the story itself is not top-notch.

2 css 3 hr Random House AudioBooks

Forrest Gump
Author/Reader: Winston Groom
★

"Bein' a idiot is no box of chocolates," but "at least I ain't led no hum-drum life," says Forrest Gump, the lovable, surprisingly savvy hero of this comic tale, which is also a hit movie starring Tom Hanks. But with a lackluster reading by the author, this recording is far removed from the movie and is a good remedy for insomnia.

2 css 3 hr Simon & Schuster Audio

Fried Green Tomatoes
Author/Reader: Fannie Flagg
★★★

The Whistle Stop Cafe feeds the hungry, the heartbroken, the righteous, and the garrulous. The movie was a hit and so is this. Author Flagg is very comfortable at the helm, reading many long monologues very convincingly. This has all the fun, laughter, and pathos we would hope for in this audio version.

2 css 2 hr Random House AudioBooks

The Golden Mean: In Which the Extraordinary Correspondence of Griffin and Sabine Concludes
Author: Nick Bantock
Performers: Maxwell Caulfield, Ben Kingsley, and Marina Sirtis
★★★

In this third part of *The Griffin and Sabine Trilogy,* which also includes *Griffin and Sabine* and *Sabine's Notebook,* Caulfield, Kingsley and Sirtis skillfully weave their voices in a unified narrative in which the mystery of the two artists deepens, and a sinister intruder tests the tenacity of their passion. An interesting audio project in that this material is more literary and esoteric than most.

1 css   40 min   The Publishing Mills AudioBooks

Grand Passion
Author: Jayne Ann Krentz
Reader: Susan Gibney
★

Passion and suspense collide at the Robbins' Nest Inn when art collector Max Fortune meets Cleopatra Robbins, the inn's owner. Susan Gibney (of TV's *L.A. Law*) seems as bland as the material and the passion here is in the title only.

2 css   3 hr   Simon & Schuster Audio

Harlot's Ghost
Part I
Author/Reader: Norman Mailer
★

Harlot is the code name for Hugh Tremont Montague, one of the grand old men of the CIA. He is linked to narrator Hubbard, whose father was the founder of the CIA and is in love with Harlot's wife. I groaned when the narrator ended his clear, involving, and easy-on-the-ear introduction and Mailer began reading quickly in monotone, with seemingly little emotional involvement. But I listened, and I admit I got confused pretty quickly.

2 css   2 hr 15 min   Random House AudioBooks

Hawaii
Author: James A. Michener
Reader: Philip Bosco
★★

Philip Bosco is a more than competent narrator, but you have to wonder what the purpose was in recording such a small portion of Michener's epic drama and calling it *Hawaii,* as if something fairly complete were in the works. This story of the clash between the Polynesians and the American missionaries was much better served in the motion picture version, to say nothing of the novel.

2 css   3 hr   Random House AudioBooks

Heaven and Hell
Volume III in the *North and South Trilogy*
Author: John Jakes
Reader: George Grizzard
★★

In the conclusion of the *North and South Trilogy,* the Mains and the Hazards struggle against fear and despair as they work to restore peace to their families, homes, and hearts. Overwhelming music sets the pace for a rather overwhelming reading by George Grizzard, who seems to be anxious to get through with the proceedings at hand. His unedited breaths quickly annoy.

2 css 3 hr Random House AudioBooks

Hill Towns
Author: Anne Rivers Siddons
Performer: Marcia Gay Harden
★★

Something so traumatic happened to Catherine when she was a small child that for thirty years she couldn't bring herself to leave the cloistered mountaintop town in Tennessee where she grew up. When she and her husband Joe venture out of their haven into Italy to attend a wedding of their friends, change is in the air. Joe turns away from Cat and she turns to Sam, a celebrated American painter. The story is slight, but Marcia Gay Harden casts a soft spell with appropriately subtle interpretations.

2 css 3 hr Harper Audio

The Joy Luck Club
Author/Reader: Amy Tan
★

Amy Tan may have had luck with the novel and the movie, but there is little joy in finding her unable to bring the dramatic and ironic moments the work is known for to fruition. Another author who would have benefited from the talents of a seasoned performer. Still, if you want to hear this story on tape. . . .

2 css 3 hr Dove Audio

Lady Boss
Author/Reader: Jackie Collins
★★★

Lucky, daughter of Mafia boss Gino, buys her own Hollywood studio so that her actor lover can have the plum parts he craves. In addition, Lucky can pay back all her Tinseltown enemies in spades. Here is all the greed, sleaze, and sparkle Collins fans expect. There's even a Madonna character to keep the sizzle current. The only trouble is that Collins's own reading is flat. She can't get the zing out of the nasty one-liners she's famous for. But if you want an exciting, sinful story that never flags, *Lady Boss* delivers.

2 css 3 hr Simon & Schuster Audio

Last Go Round
Authors: Ken Kesey with Ken Babbs
Reader: Ken Kesey
Bomb

The last go round should have have happened before this was recorded. This is a yarn of the old Northwest set in 1910 at the first Pendleton Round-Up, where three good friends are pitted against one another in fierce competition for the bronc-busting title. Author Kesey just doesn't cut it as a reader, making slow going of an interesting tale. Sound quality and editing are not up to par.

2 css 3 hr Time Warner AudioBooks

Last Tango in Brooklyn
Author/Reader: Kirk Douglas
★★★

This May-September romance has been told before, and probably better, yet there are enough twists and turns (a terrible accident and murder) in this story of Ben and his love for the younger Ellen that keep interest up. And Kirk Douglas is a very good reader. His voice, fragile with age, is still wonderfully recognizable from the over eighty movies he has made . . . and, not surprisingly, he cares enough about his own story to imbue it with a spirited charm.

3 css 4 hr Time Warner AudioBooks

Legacy
Author: James A. Michener
Reader: Stephen Collins
★★★

Army Major Norman Starr has been called before the Senate Investigating Committee on the Iran Contra Affair. He has forty-eight hours before he must announce his decision: Will he testify? This is the premise of this provocative Michener tome, which is read admirably by Stephen Collins in a straightforward, clear voice. Collins is also very good at presenting believable characters.

2 css 2 hr Random House AudioBooks

The Light in the Forest
Author: Conrad Richter
Performer: Robert Sean Leonard
★★

True Son, born John Butler in a little frontier town, is captured by the Indians when he is four. They rear him as their own. But by the time the Indians make a treaty and agree to return all white captives, True Son has learned to dislike white people. Robert Sean Leonard comes through with a sensitive, intelligent interpretation that is constantly bulldozed by an insensitive musical score that intrudes at all the wrong moments.

2 css 3 hr Bantam Audio

Lonesome Dove
Author: Larry McMurtry
Reader: Lee Horsley
★★★★

Set in the late nineteenth century, *Lonesome Dove* is an adventurous American epic of a cattle drive from Texas to Montana. It is also the name of a dusty little Texas town, where heroes, outlaws, whores, ladies, Indians, and settlers embody the spirit of the last wilderness. This is one of audio's best-kept secrets. Lee Horsley does a terrific job bringing this daring adventure to life. . . . His smooth, charismatic voice is the perfect vehicle to unite and ignite McMurtry's wild bunch.

(*Note:* Lonesome Dove *is sold in two volumes, each 12 cassettes and 18 hours in length. Only Volume II was reviewed for* The Listener's Guide to Audio Books.)
Dove Audio

The Lords of Discipline
Author: Pat Conroy
Performer: Randy Quaid
★★★

At an elite military institute steeped in southern tradition, outsider Will McClean is swept up into a world of hazing, heartbreak, pride, and betrayal. And while immersed in a love affair with a South Carolina beauty, Will discovers a terrible secret that reaches into the history of the institute and the dark past of one of Charleston's finest families. Read with a mesmerizing intensity, Randy Quaid keeps our ears on edge through this rite of passage.

2 css 3 hr Bantam Audio

Lovers
Author: Judith Krantz
Reader: Christine Baranski
Bomb

Gigi Orsini begins her first day on the job as a copywriter at an advertising agency in Los Angeles. She encounters enough professional challenges and passionate entanglements to keep her on a roller-coaster ride. This is about as silly as they come, with cardboard characters being manipulated through sexy-cum-ludicrous situations. In petulant tones, reader Baranski dives into the fray but manages to be only either serviceable or embarrassing.

2 css 3 hr Random House AudioBooks

Mama
Author: Terry McMillan
Reader: Hattie Winston
★★★

Mildred Peacock is a survivor and in her world men come and go as quickly as her paychecks. But she faces poverty as best she can with five kids in tow. Hattie

Winston gives a gutsy read. . . . She is both funny and poignant and was a great choice for this saga of survival.

2 css 3 hr Penguin HighBridge Audio

Mistress
Author: Amanda Quick
Performer: Harriet Walter
★★

Iphiginia Bright lost no time in closing down her academy for young ladies to set off on a life of adventure touring the classical ruins of Italy and Greece. Now, upon her return to England, she discovers her aunt has fallen victim to a sinister blackmailer and only she can hope to stop the culprit! If this is your cup of tea, Harriet Walter (a member of the Royal Shakespeare Company) is just what the doctor ordered to convey all this wicked humor and intrigue.

2 css 3 hr BDD Audio

Mrs. De Winter
Author: Susan Hill
Reader: Jean Marsh
★★★

In this sequel to the evergreen *Rebecca* (see page 130), author Susan Hill tries to re-create the gothic splendor of du Maurier's original. Unfortunately, this is a self-conscious attempt to ape de Maurier's style with little attention paid to the substance. Still, Jean Marsh is such a good reader that she makes even mediocre material pleasurable to hear.

4 css 6 hr Audio Renaissance Tapes

Morning Glory
Author: LaVyrle Spencer
Performer: Deborah Raffin
★★

An outsider all her life, labeled "crazy" by the town, Elly has never known the true meaning of love—until she runs a newspaper ad for a husband and Will Parker walks across her shabby yard. This is given an earnest, pleasing performance from Deborah Raffin, who appeared in the film version, but my tape was unfortunately marred by print-through (the effect is similar to having a phone conversation and hearing other voices talking distantly in the background).

2 css 3 hr Dove Audio

Natural Causes
Author: Michael Palmer
Performer: Natasha Richardson
★

Here is another Robin Cookesque medical tale of treachery and terror. Author Palmer is a practicing physician, but his story seems weak. Dr. Sarah Baldwin discovers that healthy young women in the Medical Center of Boston have hemorrhaged to death during labor—and that they had all taken Sarah's mix of prenatal herbal vitamins. She must save her career as well as other women who are at risk. Natasha Richardson's strong film career (*Patty Hearst*) has propelled the Redgrave family into a new generation. But here she races through the material, without building suspense or creating effective characterizations. Her male voices are particularly weak.

2 css 3 hr BDD Audio

Now You See Her
Author: Whitney Otto
Presented by Blair Brown
★★

In *Now You See Her,* Otto illuminates the lives of five seemingly ordinary women. She draws their dreams, their disappointments, and their passions until they are transformed into five remarkable heroines. Blair Brown makes more than a few telling points about familial webs that have the power to trap.

2 css 3 hr Time Warner AudioBooks

Oldest Living Confederate Widow Tells All
Author: Allan Gurganus
Reader: Judith Ivey
★

From a novel about the Civil War and its aftermath in our own time, told in the voice of a ninety-nine-year-old woman who lived through it all. The talented Judith Ivey, who is in the forefront of audio performers, goes a little bit over the top here and the intensity of her feisty narrative becomes a casualty of its own by the time three hours pass.

2 css 3 hr Random House AudioBooks

One Flew Over the Cuckoo's Nest
Author/Reader: Ken Kesey
Bomb

Set in the bleak confines of a state mental hospital, this is the story of a titanic battle of wills between Big Nurse and Patrick McMurphy, a lustful, brawling inmate. The movie had a lot of kick, but Kesey fizzles with a disjointed, strangely paced read that brings the fabled confrontations to a grinding halt.

2 css 3 hr Penguin HighBridge Audio

Paradise Junction
Author: Philip Finch
Reader: Peter Bergman
★★

Rich, bored, and reckless, Caitlin Hames and Hays Teale are catalysts for the combustion of five unlikely lives when they talk ex-con Sonny Naull into giving them an apprenticeship in theft. Peter Bergman brings as much excitement to this fairly undistinguished light thriller as possible, but it needs more than his enthusiasm to ignite this tape.

2 css 3 hr Durkin Hayes Audio

Pigs in Heaven
Author/Reader: Barbara Kingsolver
★

After seeing Taylor and Turtle on television, an idealistic young attorney for Oklahoma's Cherokee nation challenges Taylor's claim to her adopted child. Author Kingsolver (*The Bean Trees*) is gaining a reputation as a writer of sensitivity and perception, but she would have been better off with her material read by an actress. Her reading is stilted, with few dramatic dynamics put into play, and it's not long before her little-girl whine begins to grate.

2 css 3 hr Harper Audio

Possessing the Secret of Joy
Author: Alice Walker
Readers: Alice Walker and Joe Morton
★★★

Tashi Johnson, a tribal African woman, is genitally mutilated in a misguided act of loyalty to her customs, and spends the rest of her life battling madness. It is only with the help of an unlikely ally that she begins to understand the reasons invented for what was done to her. Author Walker reads her own words with sincerity and serenity, though there is a sacrifice of dramatic involvement in her monotone delivery. Yet if an actress had read the material, we would have been denied hearing Walker's obviously deep connection to her material. The toss of a coin?

4 css 5½ hr Simon & Schuster Audio

The Prince of Tides
Author: Pat Conroy
Performer: Richard Thomas
★★★

Tom Wingo's life in the low country of South Carolina is shaken by the news of a suicide attempt by his twin sister. This tale sweeps from Tom's childhood during World War II through the Vietnam War and into the present day. Richard Thomas presents us with a dreamy, southern-voiced Tom Wingo, and it works. The tide is high during this bittersweet three hours.

2 css 3 hr Bantam Audio

Rebecca
Author: Daphne de Maurier
Reader: Jean Marsh
★★★★

This is a handsome presentation from the inviting packaging to the original source material to the tasteful production and the sensitive, engrossing reading by Jean Marsh. This is a rave, and to be able to hear Jean Marsh tell so beautifully this rich story of romantic suspense (which includes scenes not in the famous movie) is a very rare treat indeed.

4 css 6 hr Audio Renaissance Tapes

The River
Author: Gary Paulsen
Performer: Peter Coyote
★★★

In Paulsen's sequel to *Hatchet,* a boy named Brian is asked to go back into the wilderness so astronauts and the military can learn the survival techniques that saved his life two years earlier. During a freak storm, Brian's companion is injured, and Brian is left on his own—with no supplies and only his wits between him and death. Peter Coyote plunges the listener headfirst into this exciting adventure of boy versus nature.

2 css 2 hr 45 min BDD Audio

Scarlett
Author: Alexandra Ripley
Reader: Dixie Carter
★★

In this bland but authorized sequel to *Gone With the Wind,* Dixie Carter tries to breathe life into this sagging saga as she reintroduces us to Rhett, Ashley, Mammy, and Scarlett. Truth be told, she presents a nice panoply of Irish and southern voices. The problem is her Scarlett, which is wan, pale, and sounds more like Melanie than the spunky savior of Tara herself. Musical accents are provided by a listless piano rendition of the famous Steiner score.

4 css 6 hr Simon & Schuster Audio

Schindler's List
Author: Thomas Keneally
Reader: Ben Kingsley
★★★

A remarkable narrative of the Holocaust, *Schindler's List* re-creates the daring exploits of Oskar Schindler, who used his enormous fortune to build a factory near a concentration camp and saved the lives of over 1,300 Jews. Fans of the motion picture should not be disappointed here, especially as there are scenes that were not included in the film and Ben Kingsley smoothly ushers the listener through many effective moments.

4 css 4 hr Simon & Schuster Audio

Shoeless Joe
Author: W. P. Kinsella
Reader: John Heard
★★

John Heard reads this book about baseball, love, and the power of dreams with a laid-back, folksy feel, but this is one occasion that an abridgment of the repetitive material would have been welcome. (The movie *Field of Dreams* was based on this book.)

4 css 5½ hr Durkin Hayes Audio

Simple Prayers
Author: Michael Golding
Presented by Frank Muller
★★★

Simple Prayers transports us into the world of fourteenth-century Italy. Among the villagers is Albertino, a vendor of fruits and vegetables, who delights in his collection of ornate boxes. Miriam, an enchanting stranger, wanders into the village one day carrying a secret and igniting the lust of two men with dangerous results. This is not your standard audio material. Its quality of old worldliness has fairy tale allusions and sets it apart in a charming way. It benefits from a fine, thoughtful interpretation by Frank Muller (of TV's *All My Children*).

2 css 3 hr Time Warner AudioBooks

Sin
Author: Josephine Hart
Reader: Lynn Redgrave
★★

The deadliest of sins is envy, at least according to author Hart, who tells of a woman obsessed with destroying another woman's life—only to destroy her own in the process. The problem is that this story holds few surprises and lacks a deft delineation of characters. Moreover, Lynn Redgrave approaches the proceedings with an almost breathy somberness, though she is adept at conveying psychological suspense.

2 css 3 hr Random House AudioBooks

Sins
Author: Judith Gould
Reader: Juliet Mills
★★★

A star of the fashion world, Helene Junot nonetheless still suffers from the brutality of her childhood in France during the Nazi reign, and the indignities visited upon her family. This is her story of revenge and Juliet Mills convincingly portrays Helene on her quest to repay the sins of the past.

2 css 3 hr The Publishing Mills AudioBooks

Stories from Flowers in the Rain
Author: Rosamunde Pilcher
Performer: Lynn Redgrave
★★★

This is a recording of some of Pilcher's (*The Shell Seekers*) unabridged stories from *Flowers in the Rain.* Redgrave is an inspired choice to read these sensitive and beguiling tales. With her soft yet magnetic voice, she describes ordinary events that become extraordinary. Perhaps the most moving story concerns a widow who learns in the course of arranging a wedding that she's stronger than she thinks.

2 css 3 hr Bantam Audio

Streets of Laredo
Author: Larry McMurtry
Reader: Daniel von Bargen
★★★

In this sequel to *Lonesome Dove,* McMurtry brings back Captain Woodrow Call, the legendary Texas Ranger, to track down and kill Mexican bandit Joey Garaza. Call leads a chase into northern Mexico to an outlaw community where killing is a fact of life. This western epic is a delight to hear unabridged and actor Daniel von Bargen does a more than serviceable job bringing McMurtry's characters to life.

14 css 21 hr Simon & Schuster Audio

Tales of the City
Volume I in the *Tales of the City* Series
Author/Performer: Armistead Maupin
★★

Through the lovelorn tenants of a San Francisco apartment house, Maupin takes us into a new world of laundromat Lotharios, cutthroat debutantes, and Jockey shorts dance contests. This gay extravaganza calls for a multi-cast dramatization. Author Maupin has a twangy, brittle voice that would have been great for a western, but it's too one-note to do his own comic dialogue much good.

2 css 3 hr Harper Audio

Their Eyes Were Watching God
Author: Zora Neal Hurston
Reader: Ruby Dee
★★★

Ruby Dee is an inspired choice to read this classic from the thirties by underrated author Hurston. Dee makes us feel Jamie Crawford's independent spirit as she sets out to be her own person—no mean feat for a black woman in the thirties. Hurston's unique rhythmic and idiosyncratic style seems effortlessly negotiated by Dee.

2 css 3 hr Caedmon Audio

The Trial of Abigail Goodman
Author: Howard Fast
Reader: Diane Ladd
★

Fast has set his tale of a woman's legal battle over a recent abortion in the not-so-distant future when abortion is a crime punishable by death. With so much chance to deliver a hard-hitting punch with his material, it is hard to understand why Diane Ladd fails to rise to the occasion. Her reading is stilted, missing important nuances, and her southern drawl weaves in and out at will. Some choppy edits as well.

4 css 6 hr Durkin Hayes Audio

Vanished
Author: Danielle Steel
Performer: Boyd Gaines
★★

Vanished tells the story of a man and woman faced with an unthinkable tragedy—the abduction of their young son. This is a tale of guilt, desire, suspense—and of people drawn together, seeking the child. Soft-spoken Boyd Gaines plays with what nuances there are in this rather plain, mediocre tale.

2 css 3 hr BDD Audio

Where or When
Author: Anita Shreve
Readers: Gregory Harrison and Judith Ivey
★★★

Charles Callahan is reading the Sunday paper when an alluring photo catches his eye—it is of his first love and he's compelled to make contact with her again. The two lovers struggle against formidable odds to reclaim what they once lost. This is nicely read by both Gregory Harrison and Judith Ivey, two actors who seem to be adept interpreters in this medium.

2 css 3 hr The Publishing Mills AudioBooks

The Women of Brewster Place
Author: Gloria Naylor
Reader: Tonya Pinkins
★★★★

Brewster Place is a blind alley feeding into a dead end. Seven women have made their way there. From a variety of backgrounds, with individual goals and dreams, they experience, battle, and sometimes transcend the fate of black women in America today. This "novel in seven stories" is performed with dramatic impact by Tony Award-winner Tonya Pinkins, who helps create a listening experience of theatricality and electricity.

2 css 3 hr Penguin HighBridge Audio

A Yellow Raft in Blue Water
Author: Michael Dorris
Performer: Colleen Dewhurst
★★

Stage actress Colleen Dewhurst gives a somewhat harsh monotone performance as three Indian women (spanning three generations) beset by hardship and torn by angry secrets. Dewhurst does have some effective moments in angry confrontations. But there is little feeling of poignancy or new beginnings, essential to the lyrical aspects of Dorris's writing.

2 css 3 hr Caedmon Audio

Yuppie Scum
Author: Sean Breckenridge
Reader: Eric Douglas
★★

A young executive bankrupts four of his college friends and runs off with one of their wives. In hot pursuit, the friends race to catch the couple, only to discover a devious double cross. Eric Douglas (*Delta Force III*) has some effective moments in Yuppie bashing, but overall his delivery is too slow and scenes that should be sharp are more often than not a yawn.

2 css 3 hr The Publishing Mills AudioBooks

Acceptable Risk
A: Robin Cook
ART

Accident
A: Danielle Steel
BDD

Acts of Faith
A/R: Erich Segal
S&S

African Village Folktales Audio Collection
A: Edna Mason Kaula
R: Brock Peters and Diana Sands
HARP

After All These Years
A: Susan Isaacs
R: Christine Baranski
HARP

The Afterlife and Other Stories
A/R: John Updike
RH

Ain't That Good News
A: Garrison Keillor
R: Garrison Keillor and Emmylou Harris
PENG

Albert Camus Reading from His Novels and Essays (in French)
A/R: Albert Camus
HARP

Alex Haley's *Queen*
A: Alex Haley and David Stevens
R: Lonette McKee
S&S

All Our Tomorrows
A: Ted Allbeury
R: Nigel Davenport
DURK

All Our Yesterdays
A: Robert B. Parker
BDD

An American Dream
A: Norman Mailer
R: Macdonald Carey
DURK

American Hero
A: Larry Beinhart
R: Peter Onorati
RH

American Star
A/R: Jackie Collins
S&S

The Anastasia Syndrome
A: Mary Higgins Clark
R: Lynn Redgrave
S&S

Angie, I Says
A: Avra Wing
R: Theresa Saldana
MILLS

Anne of Avonlea
A: L. M. Montgomery
R: Megan Fellows
BDD

Anne of Lantern Hill
A: L. M. Montgomery
R: Mairon Bennett
BDD

Anne of the Island
A: L. M. Montgomery
R: Megan Fellows
BDD

Another View
A. Rosamunde Pilcher
R: Lynn Redgrave
BDD

The Assassini
A: Thomas Gifford
R: Will Patton
BDD

At Risk
A: Alice Hoffman
R: Barbara Hershey
S&S

At Weddings and Wakes
A/R: Alice McDermott
DOVE

Avalanche
A: Zane Grey
R: Michael Rider
ART

The Aviators
A: W.E.B. Griffin
R: Gerald McRaney
S&S

Babycakes
A/R: Armistead Maupin
HARP

Bad Desire
A: Gary Devon
R: Jennette Goldstein and Mark Ralston
ART

The Ballad of Robin Hood
R: Anthony Quayle
HARP

The Basketball Diaries
A/R: Jim Carrol
AUDLIT

Bastard out of Carolina
A/R: Dorothy Allison
PENG

Beach Music
A: Pat Conroy
BDD

Beaches
A/R: Iris Rainer Dart
DOVE

Beauty's Punishment
A: Anne Rice
Elizabeth Montgomery
S&S

Beauty's Release
A: Anne Rice
Elizabeth Montgomery
S&S

Because It Is Bitter, and Because It Is My Heart
A: Joyce Carol Oates
R: Constance Towers
DOVE

A Bed by the Window
A/R: M. Scott Peck
BDD

The Beet Queen
A: Louise Erdrich
R: Louise Erdrich and Michael Dorris
HARP

Before and After
A: Rosellen Brown
R: Dennis Boutsikaris and Kate Nelligan
S&S

The Berlin Stories
A: Christopher Isherwood
R: Michael York
DOVE

The Best Cat Ever
A/R: Cleveland Amory
TW

The Beverly Hillbillies
Novelization based on the motion picture
R: Henry Gibson
DOVE

Big Blonde and Other Stories
A: Dorothy Parker
R: Lauren Bacall
DURK

Billy Phelan's Greatest Game
A: William Kennedy
R: Jason Robards
PART

Bittersweet
A: LaVyrle Spencer
R: Nancy Dussault
DOVE

Bittersweet, the Gamble and Vows
A: LaVyrle Spencer
R: Mary Crosby, Nancy Dussault, and Constance Towers
DOVE

Black Boy
A: Richard Wright
R: Brock Peters
HARP

Black Money
A: Michael M. Thomas
R: Theodore Bikel
ART

Black Water
A: Joyce Carol Oates
R: Amanda Plummer
DOVE

The Blackberry Day and Other Stories from Flowers in the Rain
A: Rosamunde Pilcher
R: Lynn Redgrave
BDD

Bleak House
A: Charles Dickens
R: Paul Scofield
DOVE

Bloodline
A: Sidney Sheldon
R: Jenny Agutter
DOVE

The Blue Bedroom
A: Rosamunde Pilcher
R: Lynn Redgrave
BDD

The Blue Deep
A: Layne Heath
R: James Naughton
S&S

Bodies Electric
A: Colin Harrison
R: Cotter Smith
DOVE

Body and Soul
A: Frank Conroy
R: Rene Auberjonois
RH

The Body Farm
A: Patricia Cornwell
S&S

Body of Truth
A: David L. Lindsey
R: Keith Szarabajka
BDD

Bondage
A: Patti Davis
R: Sally Kirkland
S&S

The Bonfire of the Vanities
A: Tom Wolfe
R: John Lithgow
RH

The Book of Guys
A/R: Garrison Keillor
PENG

Border Music
A/R: Robert James Walker
TW

Borderliners
A: Peter Hoeg
S&S

Borgel
A/R: Daniel Pinkwater
DOVE

The Boy, the Devil and Divorce
A: Richard Frede
R: Richard Dysart
ART

Boy's Life
A: Robert R. McCammon
R: Richard Thomas
S&S

Brazil
A/R: John Updike
RH

Breathing Lessons
A: Anne Tyler
R: Jill Eikenberry
RH

Bright Captivity
A: Eugenia Price
R: Linda Purl
BDD

Brightness Falls
A: Jay McInerney
R: Victor Garber
RH

Brothers and Sisters
A/R: Bebe Moore Campbell
ART

The Brothers K
A: David James Duncan
R: Will Patton
BDD

The Buccaneers
A: Edith Wharton; completed by Marion Mainwaring
R: Dana Ivey
PENG

Buffy, the Vampire Slayer
A: Novelization by Richie Tankersley Cusick
R: Kristy Swanson
DOVE

The Bull from the Sea
A: Mary Renault
R: Michael York
DOVE

But Where Is Love?
A/R: Abbe Lane
DOVE

The Butcher Boy
A/R: Patrick McCabe
S&S

By the Rivers of Babylon
A: Nelson DeMille
R: Len Cariou
RH

Bygones
A: LaVyrle Spencer
R: Susan Ruttan
DOVE

Bygones, Forgiving and Morning Glory
A: LaVyrle Spencer
R: Susan Ruttan, Constance Towers, and Deborah Raffin
DOVE

Caedmon 1951–1992: An Anthology
A/R: Various
HARP

California Gold
A: John Jakes
R: Richard Dysart
RH

The Call of the Wild
A: Jack London
R: Ed Begley, Jr.
HARP

The Call of the Wild
A: Jack London
R: Ethan Hawke
DOVE

The Canterbury Tales
A: Geoffrey Chaucer
R: Martin Starkie
DURK

The Canterbury Tales: The Miller's Tale and The Pardoner's Tale
A: Geoffrey Chaucer
R: Michael MacLiammoir and Stanley Holloway
HARP

The Canterbury Tales: The Wife of Bath
A: Geoffrey Chaucer; translated by J. U. Nicholson
R: Dame Peggy Ashcroft
HARP

The Canterbury Tales (In Middle English)
A: Geoffrey Chaucer
R: J. B. Bessinger, Jr.
HARP

Canyons
A: Gary Paulsen
R: Peter Coyote
BDD

Cape Cod
A: William Martin
R: David Birney
DOVE

Capital Crimes
A: Lawrence Sanders
R: Chris Sarandon
RH

The Cardinal of the Kremlin
A: Tom Clancy
R: David Ogden Stiers
S&S

The Cardinal Virtues
A: Andrew M. Greeley
R: Philip Bosco
HARP

Caribbean
A: James A. Michener
R: Roscoe Lee Browne
RH

Carnival of the Animals
A: Ogden Nash; music by Camille Saint-Saens
R: Audrey Hepburn, Charlton Heston, Walter Matthau, and Lily Tomlin
DOVE

The Carousel
A: Belva Plain
R: Blair Brown
BDD

The Cat Who Came in From the Cold
A/R: Deric Longden
BDD

Cathedral
A: Nelson DeMille
R: Michael Murphy
RH

Cat's Eye
A: Margaret Atwood
R: Kate Nelligan
BDD

Cauldron
A: Larry Bond
R: Edward Herrmann
S&S

A Celebration of Christmas Classics: The Story of the Nutcracker, A Child's Christmas in Wales, A Christmas Carol
A: E.T.A. Hoffman, Dylan Thomas, and Charles Dickens
R: Clair Bloom, Dylan Thomas, Sir Ralph Richardson, and Paul Scofield
HARP

A Celebration of Hanukkah: A Holiday Collection of Stories and Legends for the Festival of Lights
R: Hal Linden
BDD

Chances Part I: Gino's Story
A/R: Jackie Collins
S&S

Chances Part II: Lucky's Story
A/R: Jackie Collins
S&S

Charleston
A: Alexandra Ripley
R: Diane Ladd
DOVE

The Charm School
A: Nelson DeMille
R: James Naughton
RH

Charms for the Easy Life
A/R: Kaye Gibbons
S&S

Chesapeake
A: James A. Michener
R: George Grizzard
RH

The Cheshire Moon
A: Robert Ferrigno
R: Barry Bostwick
ART

China Boy
A: Gus Lee
R: B. D. Wong
RH

China Lake
A: Anthony Hyde
R: David McCallum
S&S

A Christmas Carol
A: Charles Dickens
R: Paul Scofield
DOVE

Christy
A: Catherine Marshall
R: Kellie Martin
ART

Circle of Friends
A: Maeve Binchy
R: Fionnula Flanagan
BDD

The Claiming of Sleeping Beauty
A: Anne Rice
S&S

The Class
A/R: Erich Segal
DOVE

Cleopatra Gold
A: William J. Caunitz
R: Joe Mantegna
RH

The Clock Winder
A: Anne Tyler
R: Blair Brown
RH

Closing Time: The Sequel to *Catch-22*
A: Joseph Heller
S&S

Cold Cold Heart
A: James Elliot
R: Stephen Lang
BDD

Cold Sassy Tree
A: Olive Ann Burns
R: Richard Thomas
BDD

Collected Stories of Katherine Anne Porter
A: Katherine Anne Porter
R: Siobhan McKenna
PART

Colony
A: Anne Rivers Siddons
R: Judith Ivey
HARP

Como Agua Para Chocolate (Like Water For Chocolate) (Spanish)
A: Laura Esquivel
R: Yareli Arizmendi
BDD

Compelling Evidence
A: Steve Martini
R: Joe Mantegna
DOVE

A Confederacy of Dunces
A: John Kennedy Toole
R: Arte Johnson
DOVE

A Connecticut Yankee in King Arthur's Court
A: Mark Twain
R: Carl Reiner
DOVE

Corelli's Mandolin
A: Louis de Bernieres
RH

Corsican Honor
A: William Heffernan
R: Harry Hamlin
ART

Crime and Punishment
A: Fyodor Dostoyevsky; translated by David McDuff
R: Alex Jennings
PENG

Crimes of the Heart
A: Screenplay by Beth Henley; novelization by Claudia Reilly
R: Amy Irving; performed by Diane Keaton, Jessica Lange, and Sissy Spacek
DOVE

Crimson
A: Shirley Conran
R: Stephanie Beacham
S&S

The Crossing
A: Cormac McCarthy
R: Brad Pitt
RH

The Crossing Guard
A: David Rabe
BRILL

Cry to Heaven
A: Anne Rice
R: Tim Curry
RH

Curtain
A: Michael Korda
R: Simon Jones
S&S

Cyborgasm 1
R: Full cast production
TW

Daddy
A: Danielle Steel
R: Richard Thomas
BDD

Daisy Fay and the Miracle Man
A/R: Fannie Flagg
RH

Damage
A: Josephine Hart
R: Edward Petherbridge
RH

Dance with the Devil
A/R: Kirk Douglas
DOVE

Dangerous to Know
A: Barbara Taylor Bradford
HARP

David Copperfield
A: Charles Dickens
R: Paul Scofield
DOVE

Dazzle
A: Judith Krantz
R: Virginia Madsen
RH

Dazzle
A: Judith Gould
R: Theresa Saldana
MILLS

The Dead and Other Stories from Dubliners
A: James Joyce
R: Danny Huston and Kate Mulgrew
PART

Death Is Forever
A: John Gardner
R: Simon Jones
RH

Deceptions
A: Michael Weaver
R: Joe Mantegna
TW

Deep Six
A: Clive Cussler
R: Tom Wopat
S&S

Degree of Guilt
A: Richard North Patterson
R: Ken Howard
RH

Delusions of Grandma
A/R: Carrie Fisher
S&S

Designs of Life
A: Elizabeth Ferrars
DURK

Dessa Rose
A: Sherley Anne Williams
R: Ruby Lee
DOVE

The Deus Machine
A: Pierre Ouellette
R: Robert Vaughn
RH

Devil's Juggler
A: Murray Smith
R: David McCallum
S&S

The Dharma Bums
A: Jack Kerouac
R: Allen Ginsberg
AUDLIT

The Diary of Jack the Ripper: The Discovery, the Investigation, the Debate
R: Nicholas Ball
DOVE

Dinner at the Homesick Restaurant
A: Anne Tyler
R: Pamela Reed
RH

Dirty White Boys
A: Stephen Hunter
R: Will Patton
TW

Disappearing Acts
A: Terry McMillan
R: Terry McMillan and Avery Brooks
PENG

The Distinguished Guest
A: Sue Miller
R: Blair Brown
HARP

Doctors
A/R: Erich Segal
DOVE

Does She or Doesn't She?
A: Sidney Sheldon
DOVE

Dorothy Parker Stories
A: Dorothy Parker
R: Shirley Booth
HARP

Double Vision
A: Mary Higgins Clark
R: Mary-Louise Parker
S&S

Downtown
A: Anne Rivers Siddons
R: Kate Burton
HARP

Dragonfly in Amber
A: Diana Gabaldon
R: Geraldine James
BDD

Dubliners
A: James Joyce
R: Gerald McSorley
PENG

The Duchess
A: Jude Deveraux
R: Nicol Williamson
S&S

The Eagle and the Raven
A: James A. Michener
R: Michael Rider
ART

18mm Blues
A: Gerald A. Browne
R: Barry Bostwick
ART

Einstein's Dreams
A: Alan Lightman
R: Michael York
DOVE

El Amo Del Juego (Master of the Game) (Spanish)
A: Sidney Sheldon
R: Rogelio Guerra
DOVE

El Capricho de los Dioses (Windmills of the Gods) (Spanish)
A: Sidney Sheldon
R: Adriana Roel
DOVE

Empire of the Sun
A: J. G. Ballard
R: Jeremy Irons
S&S

The Empty House
A: Rosamunde Pilcher
R: Lynn Redgrave
BDD

The End of Summer
A: Rosamunde Pilcher
R: Geraldine James
BDD

The Endearment
A: LaVyrle Spencer
R: Constance Towers
DOVE

The English Patient
A: Michael Ondaatje
R: Michael York
RH

Ernest Hemingway Reads
A/R: Ernest Hemingway
HARP

Erotica: Women on Women
R: Meryl Streep and Others
DOVE

***Esquire* Readings Gift Collection**
A: Various
R: Ed Asner, Len Cariou, Ossie Davis, Julie Harris, and Sam Waterston
PART

Et Tu Babe
A/R: Mark Leyner
DOVE

Ethan Frome
A: Edith Wharton
R: Richard Thomas
DOVE

Eudora Welty Reading "Why I Live at the P.O."
A/R: Eudora Welty
HARP

Eudora Welty Reads
A/R: Eudora Welty
HARP

The Evening News
A: Arthur Hailey
R: Fritz Weaver
BDD

Evening Star
A: Larry McMurtry
R: Dana Ivey
S&S

Everything to Gain
A: Barbara Taylor Bradford
R: Kate Mulgrew
HARP

Exceptional Clearance
A: William J. Caunitz
R: Kevin Spacey
RH

Extraordinary Powers
A: Joseph Finder
R: David Rasche
RH

Extreme Measures
A: Michael Palmer
R: John Pankow
BDD

Fade the Heat
A: Jay Brandon
R: Robert Foxworth
S&S

A Faint Cold Fear
A: Robert Daley
R: Michael McConnohie
ART

A Fall from Grace
A: Andrew M. Greeley
R: Philip Bosco
HARP

False Dawn
A: Paul Levine
R: Jay Sanders
RH

Family Blessings
A: LaVyrle Spencer
R: Barbara Rush
DOVE

Family Pictures
A: Sue Miller
R: Pam Dawber
HARP

Fanta C
A: Sandra Brown
R: Sally Kirkland
DOVE

Far and Away
A: Sonja Massie
R: Charles Durning
ART

Farewell to My Concubine
A: Lilian Lee
R: Nancy Kwan
DOVE

Fashionably Late
A/R: Olivia Goldsmith
HARP

Fatherland
A: Robert Harris
R: Werner Klemperer
RH

Fearless: A Novel
A: Rafael Yglesias
R: Jamey Sheridan
S&S

Femmes Fatal
A: Dorothy Cannell
R: Amanda Donohoe
BDD

The Fermata
A: Nicholson Baker
R: Will Patton
RH

Final Argument
A: Clifford Irving
R: Harry Hamlin
S&S

Fine Things
A: Danielle Steel
R: Richard Thomas
BDD

Fires in the Mirror
A/R: Anna Deavere Smith
BDD

The First Man in Rome
A: Colleen McCullough
R: David Ogden Stiers
S&S

The First Sacrifice
A: Thomas Gifford
R: Ron Rifkin
BDD

The First Wives Club
A: Olivia Goldsmith
R: Christine Baranski
RH

Flight of the Old Dog
A: Dale Brown
R: Peter Waldren
S&S

The Flying Dutchman and Other Ghost Ship Tales
A: Edgar Allan Poe, Richard Wagner, Thomas Moore, and Wilhelm Hauff
R: Douglas Fairbanks, Jr.
HARP

For Love
A: Sue Miller
R: Blair Brown
HARP

For Love Alone
A: Ivana Trump
R: Morgan Fairchild
S&S

For My Daughters
A: Barbara Delinsky
HARP

Forever
A: Mildred Cram
R: Deborah Raffin
DOVE

Forever
A: Judith Gould
R: Natalie West
MILLS

Forgiving
A: LaVyrle Spencer
R: Constance Towers
DOVE

Fortune's Favorites
A: Colleen McCullough
R: Michael York
S&S

The Fountainhead
A: Ayn Rand
PENG

The Fourteen Sisters of Emilio Montez O'Brien
A: Oscar Hijuelos
R: Cathy Moriarty
DOVE

Foxfire: Confessions of a Girl Gang
A: Joyce Carol Oates
PENG

Free to Love
A: Ivana Trump
R: Morgan Fairchild
S&S

The French Lieutenant's Woman
A: John Fowles
R: Jeremy Irons
PART

French Silk
A: Sandra Brown
R: Loretta Swit
DOVE

Friend of My Youth
A/R: Alice Munro
RH

From Fields of Gold
A: Alexandra Ripley
R: Lindsay Crouse
S&S

From Time to Time
A: Jack Finney
R: Campbell Scott
S&S

Further Tales of the City
A/R: Armistead Maupin
HARP

The Gamble
A: LaVyrle Spencer
R: Constance Towers
DOVE

The Gift
A: Danielle Steel
R: Tim Curry
BDD

The Gift
A/R: Kirk Douglas
DOVE

Gimpel the Fool and Other Stories
A: Isaac Bashevis Singer
R: Theodore Bikel
PART

The Girls
A/R: Elaine Kagan
RH

The Glass Lake
A: Maeve Binchy
R: Fionnula Flanagan
BDD

The Glimpses of the Moon
A: Edith Wharton
ART

The Golden Notebook
A/R: Doris Lessing
HARP

Goldman's Anatomy
A: Glenn Savan
R: Barry Williams
MILLS

Gone, but Not Forgotten
A: Phillip Margolin
R: Margaret Whitton
BDD

Gone South
A: Robert R. McCammon
R: Will Patton
S&S

Gone Wild
A: James W. Hall
R: Gates McFadden
BDD

The Good Husband
A: Gail Godwin
RH

Gospel
A/R: Wilton Barnhardt
ART

The Grapes of Wrath
A: John Steinbeck
R: Henry Fonda
HARP

The Grass Crown
A: Colleen McCullough
R: F. Murray Abraham
S&S

The Great Alone
A: Janet Dailey
R: Lloyd Bochner
DOVE

Great American Short Stories
A: Mark Twain, Ambrose Bierce, Stephen Crane, and Jack London
R: Joe McHugh, Bruce Robertson, Patrick Hagan, and Russ Holcomb
PART

A Great Deliverance
A: Elizabeth George
R: Derek Jacobi
BDD

Great Expectations
A: Charles Dickens
R: Paul Scofield
DOVE

Great Expectations
A: Charles Dickens
R: Hugh Laurie
PENG

The Great Gatsby
A: F. Scott Fitzgerald
R: Alexander Scourby
PART

Great Plains
A/R: Ian Frazier
HARP

The Great Switcheroo
A: Roald Dahl
R: Patricia Neal
HARP

Griffin and Sabine
A: Nick Bantock
MILLS

Griffin and Sabine Trilogy
A: Nick Bantock
R: Maxwell Caulfield, Ben Kingsley, and Marina Sirtis
MILLS

H . . . the Story of Healthcliff's Journey Back to Wuthering Heights
A: Lin-Haire Sargeant
R: Roger Rees
S&S

Half Asleep in Frog Pajamas
A: Tom Robbins
DOVE

Hard Aground
A: James W. Hall
R: Jameson Parker
BDD

Hard Fall
A: Ridley Pearson
R: David Rasche
BDD

Hard Times
A: Charles Dickens
R: Paul Scofield
DOVE

Hardware
A: Linda Barnes
R: Margaret Whitton
BDD

Harmful Intent
A: Robin Cook
R: John Rubinstein
S&S

Harvest
A: Belva Plain
R: Len Cariou
BDD

Hatchet
A: Gary Paulsen
R: Peter Coyote
BDD

Havana
A: Novelization by Paul Monette
R: Gregory Harrison
MILLS

The Haymeadow
A: Gary Paulsen
R: Richard Thomas
BDD

Heart of Darkness
A: Joseph Conrad
R: Anthony Quayle
HARP

Heart of Darkness
A: Joseph Conrad
R: Richard Thomas
DOVE

Heart of Darkness
A: Joseph Conrad
R: David Threlfall
PENG

Heartbreak Hotel
A: Anne Rivers Siddons
R: Jane Alexander
HARP

Heaven's Price
A: Sandra Brown
BDD

Heaven's Prisoners
A: James Lee Burke
R: Will Patton
S&S

Heir Apparent
A: Kate Coscarelli
DURK

The Heiress Bride
A: Catherine Coulter
R: Emma Samms
MILLS

The Hellion
A: LaVyrle Spencer
R: Bruce Boxlietner
DOVE

The Hellion Bride
A: Catherine Coulter
R: Juliet Mills
MILLS

Henderson the Rain King
A: Saul Bellow
R: Tom Skerritt
DURK

Hollywood Husbands
A/R: Jackie Collins
DOVE

Hollywood Kids
A/R: Jackie Collins
S&S

Hollywood Wives
A/R: Jackie Collins
DOVE

Home Fires
A: Luanne Rice
BDD

Homeland
A: John Jakes
R: Edward Herrmann
BDD

Homesung
A/R: LaVyrle Spencer
DOVE

Honor and Duty
A: Gus Lee
R: B. D. Wong
RH

The Hope
A: Herman Wouk
R: Theodore Bikel
ART

The Horse Latitudes
A: Robert Ferrigno
R: Robert Culp
DOVE

Hostile Witness
A: William Lashner
R: Eric Roberts
HARP

Hotel Pastis: A Novel of Provence
A: Peter Mayle
R: Tim Pigott-Smith
RH

How to Make an American Quilt: A Novel
A: Whitney Otto
R: Judith Ivey
RH

Howards End
A: E. M. Forster
R: Emma Thompson
PENG

I Smell Esther Williams
A/R: Mark Leyner
DOVE

Iberia
A: James A. Michener
R: Philip Bosco
RH

The Iliad
A: Homer
R: Anthony Quayle
HARP

I'll Be Seeing You
A: Mary Higgins Clark
R: Ellen Parker
S&S

I'll Be There
A/R: Iris Rainer Dart
DOVE

Illusions: The Adventures of a Reluctant Messiah
A/R: Richard Bach
ART

The Immortals
A: Michael Korda
R: Jerry Orbach
S&S

Impulse
A: Michael Weaver
R: Stacy Keach
TW

In Pursuit of the Green Lion
A: Judith Merkle Riley
R: Juliet Mills
MILLS

Inadmissable Evidence
A: Philip Friedman
R: Dennis Boutsikaris
S&S

An Inconvenient Woman
A: Dominick Dunne
R: Robert Morse
RH

Indecent Proposal
A: Jack Engelhard
R: William H. Macy
S&S

Independence Day
A: Richard Ford
RH

Intracom and Gwilan's Harp
A/R: Ursula K. Le Guin
HARP

The Intruders
A: Stephen Coonts
R: Jay O. Sanders
S&S

Ironweed
A: William Kennedy
R: Jason Robards
PART

Irreparable Harm
A: Lee Gruenfeld
R: Angie Dickinson
MILLS

Isaac Bashevis Singer Reads in Yiddish
A/R: Isaac Bashevis Singer
HARP

Isak Dinesen Herself
A/R: Isak Dinesen (Karen Blixen-Finecke)
PART

James Joyce Audio Collection
A: James Joyce
R: James Joyce and Cyril Cusack
HARP

James Joyce Reads
A: James Joyce
R: James Joyce and Cyril Cusack
HARP

Jane Eyre
A: Charlotte Brontë
R: Claire Bloom, Anthony Quayle, and full cast
HARP

Jazz
A/R: Toni Morrison
RH

Jesus and the Sweet Pilgrim Baptist Church
A: Clayton Sulliva
R: Earle Hyman
BDD

Jewels
A: Danielle Steel
R: Tim Curry
BDD

John Cheever Reads "The Swimmer" and "The Death of Justina"
A/R: John Cheever
HARP

John Irving Reads
A/R: John Irving
PART

John Updike Reads from "Couples" and "Pigeon Feathers"
A/R: John Updike
HARP

Jonathan Livingston Seagull
A/R: Richard Bach
ART

Journey
A: James A. Michener
R: David McCallum
RH

The Juror
A: George Dawes Green
R: Lolita Davidovich, Jim Ward, John Heard
TW

Kane and Abel
A: Jeffrey Archer
R: Ken Howard
HARP

Kidnapped
A: Robert Louis Stevenson
R: Robbie Coltrane
PENG

Kinflicks
A: Lisa Alther
R: Jo Beth Williams
DURK

The King Must Die
A: Mary Renault
R: Michael York
DOVE

King of the Hill
A: A. E. Hotchner
R: Hal Linden
ART

King's Oak
A: Anne Rivers Siddons
R: Tandy Cronyn
HARP

The Kitchen God's Wife
A/R: Amy Tan
DOVE

A Knight in Shining Armor
A: Jude Deveraux
R: Stephanie Zimbalist
S&S

Kurt Vonnegut, Jr., Reads *Slaughterhouse Five*
A/R: Kurt Vonnegut, Jr.
HARP

Kwanzaa
A: Gordon Lewis
R: Multicast
TW

Ladder of Years
A: Anne Tyler
R: Barbara Barrie
RH

Lady Chatterly's Lover
A: D. H. Lawrence
R: Pamela Brown
HARP

Lake Wobegon Days
A/R: Garrison Keillor
PENG

Lake Wobegon Loyalty Days
A/R: Garrison Keillor
PENG

Las Arenas del Tiempo (The Sands of Time) (Spanish)
A: Sidney Sheldon
R: Rogelio Guerra
DOVE

Lasher
A: Anne Rice
R: Joe Morton
RH

Lassie
A: Sheila Black
PENG

The Last of the Mohicans
A: James Fenimore Cooper
R: Lou Diamond Phillips
DOVE

The Last Princess of Manchuria
A: Lilian Lee
R: Joan Chen
DOVE

The Last Unicorn
A/R: Peter S. Beagle
PENG

The Last Voyage of Somebody the Sailor
A: John Barth
R: Arte Johnson
DOVE

Leaving Cold Sassy
A: Olive Ann Burns
R: Olive Ann Burns, Joanne Camp, and Peter MacNicol; excerpts by the author
BDD

The Legend of the Baal Shem
A: Martin Buber
R: Theodore Bikel
AUDLIT

Legendary Tales of Mighty Men (Soundbook)
A: Various; retold by Eleanor Farjeon
R: Ian Richardson
HARP

Legs
A: William Kennedy
R: Jason Robards
PART

Les Misérables
A: Victor Hugo
R: Christopher Cazenove
DOVE

Les Misérables
A: Victor Hugo; translated by Lee Fahnestock and Norman MacAfee
R: Mark McKerracher
PENG

A Lesson Before Dying
A: Ernest J. Gaines
R: Denzel Washington and Blair Underwood
TW

Let 'Em Eat Cake
A: Susan Jedren
R: Pamela Hensley Vincent
DOVE

Life After God
A/R: Douglas Coupland
S&S

The Light in the Forest
A: Conrad Richter
R: E. G. Marshall, Mandy Patinkin, and full cast
HARP

Like Water for Chocolate
A: Laura Esquivel
R: Yareli Arizmendi
BDD

Lila: An Inquiry into Morals
A: Robert M. Pirsig
R: Will Patton
BDD

Lincoln
A/R: Gore Vidal
RH

Little John
A: Howard Owen
MILLS

Live from Golgotha
A: Gore Vidal
R: B. D. Wong
RH

The Living
A: Annie Dillard
R: Lawrence Luckinbill
HARP

Local Man Moves to the City
A/R: Garrison Keillor
PENG

Local Rules
A: Jay Brandon
R: Jay O. Sanders
BDD

Lolita
A: Vladimir Nabokov
R: James Mason
HARP

London Fields
A: Martin Amis
R: David McCallum
DOVE

Loose Woman
A/R: Sandra Cisneros
RH

Lord Jim
A: Joseph Conrad
R: Simon MacCorkindale
DURK

Lord of Hawkfell Island
A: Catherine Coulter
R: Shelley Hack
MILLS

The Lost Angel
A: Mary Higgins Clark
R: Mary-Louise Parker
S&S

Lost Boys
A: Orson Scott Card
R: Robby Benson
ART

The Lost Father
A: Mona Simpson
R: Blair Brown
RH

The Lottery and Other Stories
A: Shirley Jackson
R: Maureen Stapleton
HARP

The Lottery Winner
A: Mary Higgins Clark
S&S

Love and War
A: John Jakes
R: George Grizzard
RH

Love Medicine
A: Louise Erdrich
R: Louise Erdrich and Michael Dorris
HARP

Love-Makers
A: Judith Gould
R: Katey Sagal
MILLS

The Lover
A: Marguerite Duras
R: Leslie Caron
S&S

Loves Music, Loves to Dance
A: Mary Higgins Clark
R: Kate Burton
S&S

Lucia in London
A: E. F. Benson
R: Geraldine McEwan
HARP

Lucky
A/R: Jackie Collins
S&S

Lucky Day
A: Mary Higgins Clark
R: Greer Allison
S&S

Lust for Life
A: Irving Stone
R: Sam Waterston
DURK

Madame Bovary
A: Gustave Flaubert
R: Glenda Jackson
DOVE

Madame Bovary
A: Gustave Flaubert; translated by Mildred Marmur
R: Claire Bloom
PENG

The Magic Christian
A/R: Terry Southern
DOVE

Magic Hour
A: Susan Isaacs
R: Ken Howard
HARP

The Magician of Lublin
A: Isaac Bashevis Singer
R: Eli Wallach
DURK

The Mambo Kings Play Songs of Love
A: Oscar Hijuelos
R: E. G. Marshall
DOVE

The Manchurian Candidate
A: Richard Condon
R: Robert Vaughn
DURK

Martin Chuzzlewit
A: Charles Dickens
R: Martin Jarvis
DURK

The Mary Higgins Clark Double Feature: While My Pretty One Sleeps and Weep No More, My Lady
A: Mary Higgins Clark
R: Jessica Walter and Elizabeth Ashley
S&S

Masterclass
A: Morris West
R: Mark Rolston
ART

The Masters Collection: The Dead and Other Stories, Gimpel the Fool and Other Stories and Collected Stories of Katherine Anne Porter
R: Danny Huston and Kate Mulgrew, Theodore Bikel and Siobhan McKenna
PART

The Masterworks and Science Fiction of Edgar Allan Poe
A: Edgar Allan Poe
R: Paul Scofield
DOVE

Maybe the Moon
A/R: Armistead Maupin
HARP

Mean High Tide
A: James W. Hall
R: Will Patton
BDD

Member of the Wedding
A: Carson McCullers
R: Tammy Grimes
DURK

Memoirs of an Invisible Man
A: H. F. Saint
R: Jeff Daniels
S&S

Mercy
A: David L. Lindsey
R: Judith Ivey
BDD

Message from Nam
A: Danielle Steel
R: Richard Thomas
BDD

Mexico
A: James A. Michener
R: Tony Roberts
RH

Miami
A: Pat Booth
R: Morgan Fairchild
MILLS

The Milagro Beanfield War
A: John Nichols
R: Cheech Marin
PART

Miss Lonelyhearts
A: Nathaniel West
R: Keir Dullea
PART

Missing Joseph
A: Elizabeth George
R: Derek Jacobi
BDD

Mr. and Mrs. Bridge
A: Evan S. Connell
R: Paul Newman and Joanne Woodward
DOVE

Moby Dick
A: Herman Melville
R: Keir Dullea, Charlton Heston, and George Rose
HARP

Moll Flanders
A: Daniel Defoe
R: Siobhan McKenna
HARP

The Monkey Handlers
A/R: G. Gordon Liddy
ART

Montana 1948
A: Larry Watson
S&S

The Monument
A: Gary Paulsen
R: Daisy Eagan
BDD

More Dylan Thomas Reads
A/R: Dylan Thomas
HARP

More News from Lake Wobegon
A/R: Garrison Keillor
PENG

More News from Lake Wobegon: Faith
A/R: Garrison Keillor
PENG

More News from Lake Wobegon: Hope
A/R: Garrison Keillor
PENG

More News from Lake Wogegon: Humor
A/R: Garrison Keillor
PENG

More News from Lake Wobegon: Love
A/R: Garrison Keillor
PENG

More Tales of the City
A/R: Armistead Maupin
HARP

Morgan's Passing
A: Anne Tyler
R: Tony Roberts
RH

Mortal Fear
A: Robin Cook
R: Anthony Zerbe
S&S

Mountain Laurel
A: Jude Deveraux
R: Judith Light
S&S

Mules and Men
A: Zora Neale Hurston
R: Ruby Dee
HARP

The Music Room
A: Dennis McFarland
R: Peter MacNicol
HARP

Mutation
A: Robin Cook
R: Kelsey Grammer
S&S

My Cousin, My Gastroenterologist
A/R: Mark Leyner
DOVE

My Cousin Rachel
A: Daphne du Maurier
R: Mel Gibson
HARP

My Sister's Keeper
A/R: Shirley Lord
DOVE

The Mystery of Edwin Drood
A: Charles Dickens
R: Paul Scofield
DOVE

Mystique
A: Amanda Quick
R: Suzanne Bertish
BDD

Native Son
A: Richard Wright
R: James Earl Jones
HARP

Native Tongue
A: Carl Hiaasen
R: Tony Roberts
RH

The Natural
A: Bernard Malamud
R: Ken Howard
DURK

Never Cry Wolf
A/R: Farley Mowat
BDD

Never Send Flowers
A: John Gardner
R: Simon Jones
RH

New Orleans Legacy
A: Alexandra Ripley
R: Diane Ladd
DOVE

News from Lake Wobegon
A/R: Garrison Keillor
PENG

News from Lake Wobegon: Fall
A/R: Garrison Keillor
PENG

News from Lake Wobegon: Spring
A/R: Garrison Keillor
PENG

News from Lake Wobegon: Summer
A/R: Garrison Keillor
PENG

News from Lake Wobegon: Winter
A/R: Garrison Keillor
PENG

Nicholas Nickleby
A: Charles Dickens
R: Roger Rees
HARP

Nicholas Nickleby
A: Charles Dickens
R: Paul Scofield
DOVE

Night Magic
A: Tom Tryon
R: Anthony Heald
S&S

Night Woman
A: Nancy Price
R: Wendy Phillips
S&S

The Nightingale Legacy
A: Catherine Coulter
BRILL

No Witnesses
A: Ridley Pearson
R: Keith Szarabajka
BDD

Nobody's Fool
A: Richard Russo
RH

None to Accompany Me
A: Nadine Gordimer
BRILL

North
A: Alan Zweibel
R: Rob Reiner
RH

North of Montana
A: April Smith
RH

Notes from the Country Club
A: Kim Wozencraft
R: Morgan Fairchild
ART

The Novel
A: James A. Michener
R: Len Cariou
RH

November of the Heart
A: LaVyrle Spencer
R: Barbara Rush
DOVE

The Obstacle Course
A: J. F. Freedman
R: Tobias Jelinek
PENG

An Occasion of Sin
A: Andrew M. Greeley
R: Philip Bosco
HARP

Of Mice and Men
A: John Steinbeck
R: Gary Sinise
PENG

The Old Man and the Sea
A: Ernest Hemingway
R: Charlton Heston
HARP

Oliver Twist
A: Charles Dickens
R: Paul Scofield
DOVE

On Leaving Charleston
A: Alexandra Ripley
R: Diane Ladd
DOVE

On the Road
A: Jack Kerouac
R: David Carradine
PENG

Once Is Not Enough
A: Jacqueline Susann
R: Genie Francis
DOVE

One
A: Richard Bach
R: Richard Bach and Leslie Parrish-Bach
ART

One on One
A: Tabitha King
R: Stephen King
PENG

One True Thing
A: Anna Quindlen
S&S

Open Secrets
A: Alice Munro
R: Jackie Burroughs
DURK

The Optimist's Daughter
A/R: Eudora Welty
RH

Our Mutual Friend
A: Charles Dickens
R: Paul Scofield
DOVE

Out of Africa
A: Isak Dinesen (Karen Blixen-Finecke)
R: Julie Harris
PART

Outer Banks
A: Anne Rivers Siddons
R: Kate Nelligan
HARP

Outerbridge Reach
A: Robert Stone
R: Tom Skerritt
ART

Pacific Beat
A: T. Jefferson Parker
R: Harry Hamlin
ART

Paddy Clark HA HA HA
A: Roddy Doyle
R: Aiden Gillen
PENG

Paradise
A: Judith McNaught
R: Lisa Eichorn
S&S

The Pardon
A: James Grippando
R: John Rubenstein
HARP

Paris Trout
A: Pete Dexter
R: Charles S. Dutton
HARP

Peachtree Road
A: Anne Rivers Siddons
R: Peter MacNicol
RH

Perfect
A: Judith McNaught
R: Kim Cattrall
S&S

The Pickwick Papers
A: Charles Dickens
R: Paul Scofield
DOVE

The Picture of Dorian Gray
A: Oscar Wilde
R: Hurd Hatfield
HARP

Picturing Will
A/R: Ann Beattie
DOVE

The Pillars of the Earth
A: Ken Follett
R: Tim Pigott-Smith
S&S

The Player
A: Michael Tolkin
R: Mark Linn-Baker
RH

Playing for the Ashes
A: Elizabeth George
R: Derek Jacobi
BDD

Point of Impact
A: Stephen Hunter
R: Beau Bridges
BDD

Poland
A: James A. Michener
R: Robert Vaughn
RH

Possession
A: A. S. Byatt
R: Alan Howard
RH

Postcards from the Edge
A/R: Carrie Fisher
DOVE

Pot of Gold
A: Judith Michael
R: Margaret Whitton
S&S

Powerhouse and Petrified Man
A/R: Eudora Welty
HARP

Praetorian
A: Thomas Gifford
R: Kenneth Welsh
BDD

The President's Lady
A: Irving Stone
R: Madeleine Potter
DURK

Pride and Prejudice
A: Jane Austen
R: Claire Bloom
HARP

Primal Fear
A: William Diehl
R: Will Patton
RH

The Prime of Miss Jean Brodie
A: Muriel Spark
R: Geraldine McEwan
PART

Prime Witness
A: Steve Martini
R: Joe Mantegna
DOVE

The Prince
A: Niccolo Machiavelli; translated by George Bull
R: Fritz Weaver
PENG

Prince Charming
A: Julie Garwood
R: Harriet Walter
S&S

The Princess Bride
A: William Goldman
R: Rob Reiner
DOVE

Princess Daisy
A: Judith Krantz
PENG

Private Lies
A: Warren Adler
R: David Dukes
DOVE

Private Pleasures
A: Lawrence Sanders
R: Maryann Plunkett and Jay O. Sanders
S&S

Private Screening
A: Richard North Patterson
R: Christopher Reeve
RH

The Prize
A: Irving Wallace
R: Joseph Campanella
DOVE

Prizzi's Honor
A: Richard Condon
R: Paul Sorvino
DURK

Probable Cause
A: Ridley Pearson
R: John Shea
RH

Pronto
A: Elmore Leonard
R: Joe Mantegna
BDD

Proud & Free
A: Janet Dailey
DOVE

Putting on the Ritz
A: Joe Keenan
R: Stephen Bogardus
PENG

Rabbit at Rest
A/R: John Updike
RH

The Raiders
A: Harold Robbins
R: James Naughton
S&S

The Rainmaker
A: John Grisham
R: Michael Beck
BDD

Recessional
A: James A. Michener
RH

The Rector's Wife
A: Joanna Trollope
R: Patricia Hodge
DURK

Red Army
A: Ralph Peters
R: David Ogden Stiers
S&S

Red Dragon
A: Thomas Harris
R: Chris Sarandon
S&S

The Red Fox
A: Anthony Hyde
R: Donald Sutherland
S&S

The Red Horseman
A: Stephen Coonts
R: Joe Morton
S&S

Red Phoenix
A: Larry Bond
R: David Purdham
S&S

Redemption
A: Leon Uris
R: Charles Keating
HARP

The Remains of the Day
A: Kazuo Ishiguro
R: Michael York
RH

Remember
A: Barbara Taylor Bradford
R: Mary Beth Hurt
RH

Remember Me
A: Mary Higgins Clark
R: Megan Gallagher
S&S

Remembrance
A: Jude Deveraux
S&S

Remembrance of Things Past
A: Marcel Proust; translated by C. K. Scott Moncrieff
R: Sir Ralph Richardson
HARP

Return Journey to Swansea
A/R: Dylan Thomas
HARP

Rich in Love
A/R: Josephine Humphreys
PENG

Rivals
A: Janet Dailey
R: Stephanie Zimbalist
RH

River of Hidden Dreams
A: Connie Mae Fowler
R: Pamela Reed and Reni Santoni
TW

A River Sutra
A/R: Gita Mehta
RH

The Road to Wellville
A/R: T. Coraghessan Boyle
PENG

The Robber Bride
A: Margaret Atwood
R: Blythe Danner
BDD

The Roman Spring of Mrs. Stone
A: Tennessee Williams
R: Shirley Knight
DURK

A Room of One's Own
A: Virginia Woolf
R: Claire Bloom
HARP

Rosamunde Pilcher
A: Rosamunde Pilcher
R: Lynn Redgrave
BDD

A Ruling Passion
A: Judith Michael
R: Morgan Fairchild
S&S

Rum Punch
A: Elmore Leonard
R: Joe Mantegna
BDD

Rumble Fish
A: S. E. Hinton
R: Christopher Atkins
DURK

Runaway
A: Heather Graham
MILLS

Running from Safety and Other Adventures of the Spirit
A: Richard Bach
R: Richard Bach and Leslie Parrish-Bach
ART

Russka
A: Edward Rutherford
R: Denis Quilley
RH

S.
A: John Updike
R: Kathryn Walker
RH

Saint Croix Notes
A/R: Noah Adams
PENG

Saint Maybe
A: Anne Tyler
R: John Lithgow
RH

Saving Grace
A: Julie Garwood
R: Emma Samms
S&S

The Scarlet Letter
A: Nathaniel Hawthorne
R: Michael Learned
PART

The Scarlet Letter
A: Nathaniel Hawthorne
DOVE

The Scarlet Pimpernel
A: Baroness Emmuska Orczy
R: Roddy McDowall
DOVE

The Scarlet Pimpernel
A: Baroness Emmuska Orczy
R: Simon Williams
DURK

The Scout
A: Harry Combs
BDD

The Screwtape Letters
A: C. S. Lewis
R: John Cleese
AUDLIT

Scruples
A: Judith Krantz
R: Dana Delany
RH

Scruples Two
A: Judith Krantz
R: Dana Delany
RH

The Sea Wolf
A: Jack London
R: Theodore Bikel
DURK

The Sea Wolf
A: Jack London
R: Stuart Whitman
PART

A Season in Purgatory
A: Dominick Dunne
R: Campbell Scott
RH

Second Nature
A: Alice Hoffman
R: Kate Nelligan
S&S

The Secret History
A: Donna Tartt
R: Robert Sean Leonard
RH

The Secret Oceans
A: Betty Ballantine
BDD

The Secret of Villa Mimosa
A: Elizabeth Adler
R: Monica Buckley
BRILL

The Select
A: F. Paul Wilson
R: Elizabeth Shue
S&S

Selected Stories
A/R: John Updike
RH

A Separate Peace
A: John Knowles
R: Matthew Modine
BDD

September
A: Rosamunde Pilcher
R: Lynn Redgrave
BDD

The Shell Seekers
A: Rosamunde Pilcher
R: Lynn Redgrave
BDD

The Sherbrooke Bride
A: Catherine Coulter
R: Juliet Mills
MILLS

Sherwood: A Novel of Robin Hood
A/R: Parke Godwin
PART

Shining Through
A: Susan Isaacs
R: Stockard Channing
RH

Siddhartha
A: Hermann Hesse
R: Derek Jacobi
PART

Significant Others
A/R: Armistead Maupin
HARP

Silent Treatment
A: Michael Palmer
R: Adam Arkin
BDD

The Silken Web
A: Sandra Brown
R: Brooke Adams
DOVE

A Simple Plan
A: Scott Smith
R: Griffin Dunne
S&S

Simple Stories
A: Langston Hughes
R: Ossie Davis
HARP

Sing to Me of Dreams
A: Kathryn Lynn Davis
R: Cynthia Nixon
S&S

Sioux Dawn
A: Terry C. Johnson
R: Ed Asner
DOVE

Sisters and Lovers
A: Connie Briscoe
HARP

Skin Tight
A: Carl Hiaasen
R: Edward Asner
RH

Slaughterhouse Five
A: Kurt Vonnegut
R: Jose Ferrer
DURK

Slaves of Spiegel: The Best of Daniel Pinkwater
A/R: Daniel Pinkwater
DOVE

Sleeping Beauty
A: Judith Michael
R: Kate Burton
S&S

Sleeping Tiger
A: Rosamunde Pilcher
R: Lynn Redgrave
BDD

Slow Waltz in Cedar Bend
A/R: Robert James Waller
DOVE

The Snake and Johnny Bear
A/R: John Steinbeck
HARP

Snapshot
A: Linda Barnes
R: Kate Nelligan
BDD

Snarkout Boys & Avocado Death
A/R: Daniel Pinkwater
DOVE

Snow in April
A: Rosamunde Pilcher
R: Lynn Redgrave
BDD

The Snows of Kilimanjaro
A: Ernest Hemingway
R: Charlton Heston
HARP

Someone Is Killing the Great Chiefs of America
A: Nan and Ivan Lyons
R: George Segal
ART

Someone Is Killing the Great Chiefs of Europe
A: Nan and Ivan Lyons
R: George Segal
ART

Song of Solomon
A/R: Toni Morrison
RH

Songs of the Cat
A: Garrison Keillor
R: Garrison Keillor with Frederica von Stade
PENG

Sophie's Choice
A: William Styron
R: Norman Snow
RH

The Source
A: James A. Michener
R: Norman Lloyd
RH

A Southern Family
A: Gail Godwin
R: Nina Foch
DOVE

Space
A: James A. Michener
R: Darren McGavin
RH

Spencerville
A: Nelson DeMille
R: Boyd Gaines
RH

Spring Fancy
A: LaVyrle Spencer
R: Loryn Locklin
DOVE

The Stalkers
A/R: Terry C. Johnston
ART

The Stand-Off
A: Chuck Hogan
R: Stacy Keach
BDD

Star Quality
A: Noel Coward
R: Denholm Elliott
PART

The Stark Truth
A: Peter Freeborn
R: David Ogden Stiers
S&S

Stars
A: Kathryn Harvey
R: Paula Prentiss
MILLS

The Stars Shine Down
A: Sidney Sheldon
R: Roddy McDowall
DOVE

Staying On
A: Paul Scott
R: Geraldine James
DURK

Stealth
A: Guy Durham
R: Ken Howard
DURK

Stitches in Time
A: Barbara Michaels
R: Barbara Rosenblat
HARP

Stolen Blessings
A: Lawrence Sanders
R: Jerry Orbach
S&S

Stories
A/R: Garrison Keillor
PENG

Stories and Humorous Essays of Dylan Thomas
A/R: Dylan Thomas
HARP

The Stories of Eva Luna
A: Isabel Allende
R: Elizabeth Pena
DOVE

The Stories of John Cheever
A: John Cheever
R: Mason Adams
DURK

The Stories of John Cheever
A: John Cheever
R: Maria Tucci
RH

The Stormy Petrel
A: Mary Stewart
R: Jenny Seagrove
DOVE

Strip Tease
A: Carl Hiaasen
R: Edward Asner
RH

Such Devoted Sisters
A: Eileen Goudge
R: Stephanie Zimbalist
RH

Summer of Fear
A: T. Jefferson Parker
R: Barry Bostwick
ART

Sure of You
A/R: Armistead Maupin
HARP

Surrender the Pink
A/R: Carrie Fisher
DOVE

Sweet Liar
R: Jude Deveraux
R: Mel Harris
S&S

Sweet Memories
A: LaVyrle Spencer
R: Constance Towers
DOVE

The Swiss Account
A: Paul Erdman
R: Edward Woodward
ART

Taboo
A: Elizabeth Gage
R: Kate Mulgrew
DOVE

The Talbot Odyssey
A: Nelson DeMille
R: George Grizzard
RH

The Tale of the Body Thief
A: Anne Rice
R: Richard E. Grant
RH

A Tale of Two Cities
A: Charles Dickens
R: James Mason
HARP

A Tale of Two Cities
A: Charles Dickens
R: Paul Scofield
DOVE

Taltos: Lives of the Mayfair Witches
A: Anne Rice
R: Tim Curry
RH

Tangled Vines
A: Janet Dailey
R: Adrienne Barbeau
DOVE

Tangled Web: The Sequel to *Deceptions*
A: Judith Michael
S&S

Team Yankee
A: Harold Coyle
R: Charles Durning
S&S

The Temple of My Familiar
A/R: Alice Walker
S&S

Terminal
A: Robin Cook
R: Jon Tenney
S&S

Texas
A: James A. Michener
R: Peter Graves
RH

Texas! Lucky, Texas! Sage and Texas! Chase
A: Sandra Brown
R: Judith Light
DOVE

The Thin Woman
A: Dorothy Cannell
R: Amanda Donohoe
BDD

The 13th Juror
A: John Lescroat
R: Chris Noth
BDD

This Boy's Life
A: Tobias Wolff
R: Campbell Scott
HARP

This Calder Range and Stands a Calder Man
A: Janet Dailey
R: Michael Nouri
DOVE

This Calder Sky and Calder Born, Calder Bred
A: Janet Dailey
R: Michael Nouri
DOVE

The Three Musketeers
A: Alexandre Dumas
R: Michael York
DOVE

Time and Again
A: Jack Finney
R: Campbell Scott
S&S

A Time of War
A: Michael Peterson
R: Joe Spano
S&S

Tracks
A: Louise Erdrich
R: Louise Erdrich and Michael Dorris
HARP

Travels with Charley: In Search of America
A: John Steinbeck
R: Gary Sinise
PENG

Treasures
A: Belva Plain
R: Joanne Gleason
BDD

A Treasury of Christmas Stories and Poems
R: Jane Alexander
BDD

True Women
A: Janice Woods Windle
R: Judith Ivey
HARP

Trust Me
A: Jayne Ann Krentz
R: Marcia Strassman
S&S

Trust Me
A/R: John Updike
RH

Tully
A: Paulina Simons
R: Karen Allen
TW

Twenty Jataka Tales
A: Noor Inayat Khan
R: Ellen Burstyn; musical accompaniment by Alauddin Mathieu
AUDLIT

The Two Mrs. Grenvilles
A: Dominick Dunne
R: F. Murray Abraham
S&S

Under Gemini
A: Rosamunde Pilcher
R: Kate Burton
BDD

Under the Garden
A: Graham Greene
R: Derek Jacobi
PART

Undue Influence
A: Steve Martini
S&S

The Unicorn in the Garden and Other Fables for Our Time
A: James Thurber
R: Peter Ustinov
HARP

Until You
A: Judith McNaught
S&S

Valley of the Dolls
A: Jacqueline Susann
R: Juliet Mills
DOVE

Venganza de Angeles (Rage of Angels) (Spanish)
A: Sidney Sheldon
R: Jacqueline Andere
DOVE

Villette
A: Charlotte Brontë
R: Juliet Stevenson
PENG

Virtual Light
A: William Gibson
R: Peter Weller
BDD

Vital Signs
A: Robin Cook
R: Bebe Neuwirth
S&S

The Volcano Lover
A/R: Susan Sontag
DOVE

Vortex
A: Larry Bond
R: David Purdham
S&S

Vows
A: LaVyrle Spencer
R: Mary Crosby
DOVE

Wages of Sin
A: Andrew M. Greeley
R: Fritz Weaver
HARP

Waiting to Exhale
A/R: Terry McMillan
PENG

Walden
A: Henry David Thoreau
R: Archibald MacLeish
HARP

Walter de la Mare Speaking and Reading
A/R: Walter de la Mare
HARP

The War in 2020
A: Ralph Peters
R: David Purdham
S&S

The Waterworks
A: E. L. Doctorow
RH

Way Past Cool
A: Jess Mowry
R: Giancarlo Esposito
HARP

What I Lived For
A: Joyce Carol Oates
PENG

Wheels
A: Arthur Hailey
R: Victor Garber
BDD

Where I'm Calling From
A: Raymond Carver
R: Peter Riegert
RH

Where Shadows Go
A: Eugenia Price
R: Linda Purl
BDD

Where There's Smoke
A: Sandra Brown
R: Lynda Carter
DOVE

Whispers
A: Belva Plain
R: Kate Burton
BDD

The White Birds and Other Stories from the Blue Bedroom
A: Rosamunde Pilcher
R: Lynn Redgrave
BDD

The White Deer
A: James Thurber
R: George Rose
DURK

White Fang
A: Jack London
R: John Ritter
DOVE

White Jazz
A: James Ellroy
R: Jerry Orbach
RH

White People
A/R: Allan Gurganus
RH

The Wicked Day
A: Mary Stewart
R: Theodore Bikel
DOVE

Wild Mountain Thyme
A: Rosamunde Pilcher
R: Kate Burton
BDD

Wilderness Tips
A: Margaret Atwood
R: Helen Shaver
BDD

William Faulkner Reads
A/R: William Faulkner
HARP

William Kennedy's Albany Cycle: Ironweed, Legs, and Billy Phelan's Greatest Game
A: William Kennedy
R: Jason Robards
PART

The Wind Chill Factor
A: Thomas Gifford
R: Ron Vawter
BDD

Wiseguy
A/R: Nicholas Pileggi
S&S

WLT: A Radio Romance
A/R: Garrison Keillor
PENG

Woman Hollering Creek and The House on Mango Street
A/R: Sandra Cisneros
RH

The Woman in White
A: Wilke Collins
R: Nigel Anthony
PENG

A Woman of Independent Means
A: Elizabeth Forsythe Hailey
R: Barbara Rush
DOVE

The Women in His Life
A: Barbara Taylor Bradford
R: Lynn Redgrave
RH

Wuthering Heights
A: Emily Brontë
R: F. Murray Abraham
PENG

Wuthering Heights
A: Emily Brontë
R: Claire Bloom
HARP

Wuthering Heights
A: Emily Brontë
R: Martin Shaw
DOVE

Your Blues Ain't Like Mine
A: Bebe Moore Campbell
R: Alfre Woodard with Allison Smith
TW

Zero Coupon
A: Paul Erdman
R: Michael McConnohie
ART

HORROR

Horror stories make for great listening. Think of the first scary story you ever heard and chances are that's exactly the way you discovered this genre of shivers and screams: Somebody *told* you something scary. Sound is more important to horror stories than to any other kind of storytelling. Even in print, these are stories of things that go bump in the night. Shhhh! Something's breathing under the bed.

Old-time radio proved the shudder value of telling horror stories out loud. Radio's golden age—forty, fifty, sixty years ago—made household visitors of such creeps as *The Mysterious Traveler.* And, of course, thousands of people panicked over Orson Welles's Mercury Theatre production of *The War of the Worlds* in 1938, believing the show's Martian attack was for real.

Because sound is so integral to the horror genre, some of the scariest horror stories are those on tape. Cassette choices range from old-timers (*Dracula, Frankenstein*) to the latest tombstone-sized novel from Stephen King. Just as this guide went to the publisher, Penguin HighBridge released King's long night of *Insomnia* on tape. The excellent actor Eli Wallach risks lung collapse by reading all 787 pages word for word for a total of twenty-one tapes, running twenty-six hours: the perfect audio package for that drive to Florida.

King dominates the horror tape section the same as he does all the rest of the modern horror genre, from books to movies. But he's not the only monster in the closet. Other horror writers haunting the tape shelves include Dean

R. Koontz (*Lightning*), John Saul (*Shadows*), Anne Rice (*Interview with the Vampire*), Peter Straub (*Ghost Story*), and Michael Crichton (*Jurassic Park*). Not to mention Shakespeare. If *Hamlet* isn't a ghost story, what is?

Here are three clammy handfuls of general advice about listening to horror books on tape:

- Don't be afraid of the classics. *Dracula* and *Frankenstein* were the popular literature of their time. They can be hard to read now simply because times have changed and the language is old fashioned. But the stories endure for the best of all reasons: They're great stuff. Hearing them well read is like hearing them brand new.
- Whether to look for books abridged or unabridged is a matter of taste, but horror is a special case. Poe contended the short story was the only right length for horror. Trying to sustain a creepy mood can be like trying to freeze-dry a soap bubble. Some unabridged horror books run from ten to fifteen hours or more on tape, but longer isn't always better.
- Horror depends on mood. The more you settle into the icy mood of a horror story, the more it will get to you. The creepiest way is to listen alone at night in a dark room.

In general, these tapes aren't so good for in-town car listening. Driving takes too much attention, and traffic is too distracting. Dracula is a one-on-one sorta guy.

Go ahead, now. Get a grip.

Try to be comfortable.

And tell yourself, "It's only a tape. It's only a tape."

HIGHLY RECOMMENDED (★★★★)

Dragon Tears
Frankenstein
Interview with the Vampire
The Phantom of the Opera
Psycho
The Twilight Zone Six: "The Lonely"
The Wolfen

The Burning
Author: Graham Masterson
Reader: David Dukes
★★

A spark of originality ignites the start of this novel by Graham Masterson, an author best known for his *The Manitou.* It seems people are burning alive by choice, embracing the flames, cursing their rescuers. The rest of the book never quite catches fire, though. Masterson loads on an evil cult, rituals set to Richard

Wagner's music, a would-be world conqueror, and the threat of a fearsome Fourth Reich. *Now,* how much would you believe?

2 css 3 hr Dove Audio

Classic Tales of Horror
Authors: Bram Stoker and Robert Louis Stevenson
Readers: Donald Pickering and John Hurt
★★★

Donald Pickering reads Bram Stoker's *Dracula,* and John Hurt reads Robert Louis Stevenson's *Dr. Jekyll and Mr. Hyde.* (See the review of *Dracula* on page 162 for Pickering's reading, which is also available on single cassette.) These two make a fitting match: Both stories have endured since the late 1800s, and both are about a man's discovery of absolute evil. Instead of finding a vampire in a coffin, though, Stevenson's good Dr. Jekyll finds the monster inside himself. And if ever a film were made of Stevenson's life, Hurt would be fine in the role of this writer: a quiet, modest man inspired by his nightmares to write about Jekyll and Hyde.

2 css 3 hr Durkin Hayes Audio

Creature
Author: John Saul
Reader: Robert Englund
★★

Here's a team-up that would mean bad news for any novel's cast of young people. Saul has made a career of books about menaced and evil children. Englund is best known for his recurring role as bogeyman Freddy Krueger, stalking the dreams of troubled teenagers in the *Nightmare on Elm Street* movies. Sure enough, they make things rough on the small town of Silverdale, where the high school football jocks seem to be changing into mindless brutes (wow!—what a transformation). Saul's horrific hokum is complete with evil goings-on in a mad scientist's lab, thinly disguised as a sports clinic. Englund brings little conviction to the reading, but then, who would?

2 css 3 hr BDD Audio

The Damnation Game
Author: Clive Barker
Performers: Colin Fox, Merwin Goldsmith, and Graeme Malcolm
★★

Clive Barker followed the phenomenal success of his six-volume short-story collection, *Books of Blood,* with this first novel (1985). It found him so-so as a novelist. One problem is the utter lack of any redeemable characters to care about in this group of hell-raisers. Bad guy Marty Strauss becomes the hero by default, sprung from prison to guard a rich, reclusive industrialist, who has struck a bad deal with the devil. Faust and Mephistopheles played it better, but Barker's fans will find this tape worth hearing for its gruesome effects and twists of black humor.

2 css 2½ hr Random House AudioBooks

Darkness
Author: John Saul
Reader: Anthony Zerbe
★★

A mean old man is doing something awful to stolen babies in his secret lab. As for subtlety, this one is the horror equivalent of a pie in the face. Saul's typically traumatized teenagers are off to find out why they share the same bad dreams—if not from watching *Nightmare on Elm Street.* The story is nothing to scream home about, but it gains considerable life from Zerbe's performance. Zerbe (the worst of the hooded creeps in *The Omega Man*) has a voice made for scare stories: like a malted milk laced with needles.

2 css 3 hr BDD Audio

Dracula
Author: Bram Stoker
Reader: Donald Pickering
★★★

A class performance. Pickering reads Stoker's vampire masterpiece with fire and reverence. He is properly British in reading poor Jonathan Harker's account of his visit to Castle Dracula, and sounds genuinely horror-struck at Harker's discovery that his host is a monster. ("It seemed as if the whole awful creature were simply gorged with blood; he lay like a filthy leech. . . .") But it's Pickering's rendition of the vampire-hunter Dr. Van Helsing that brings fresh blood to the telling. Pickering's Van Helsing is a man obsessed. You could sharpen a wooden stake on the doctor's hard edges.

1 css 1½ hr Durkin Hayes Audio

Dracula
Author: Bram Stocker
Performers: Multiple Cast
★★★

Rather than confining himself to his journal, a traumatized Jonathan Harker steps up to the mike to talk about his bad time in Transylvania. "Whenever I take up a letter from poor Lucy, a note from Professor Van Helsing . . . it all comes back to life," he testifies. Here is a different but all the while generally faithful approach to Stoker's tale of the undead. Cue the howling wolves.

2 css 3 hr The Mind's Eye

Dracula's Guest
Author: Bram Stoker
Reader: Victor Garber
★★★

Here's an interesting tape for listeners who know the history of what they are getting (unfortunately, the package doesn't say). Garber reads two stories that Stoker wrote in the decade before he published *Dracula* (1897). "Dracula's Guest"—more atmosphere than story—was nipped out of the novel, but it finds Stoker at work with the same ideas that pulse in his vampire classics, though the character of Dracula does not appear in this story or the other one on the tape, "The Secret of the Growing Gold," Stoker's take on Edgar Allan Poe's "The Tell-Tale Heart." The stories are from *Dracula's Guest,* a collection published after Stoker's death.

1 css   1½ hr   Durkin Hayes Audio

Dragon Tears
Author: Dean Koontz
Reader: Jay O. Sanders
★★★★

Dean Koontz seems to have gathered up all he's learned about writing thrillers and horror stories (*Phantom, Cold Fire*), somehow added to the total, and come up with *Dragon Tears,* easily among the high marks in his prolific career. The first sentence sums up the story's tone: "Tuesday was a fine California day, full of sunshine and promise, until Harry Lyons had to shoot someone at lunch." Lyons is a no-nonsense detective who longs for a "better world," only to find he is stuck in a bad one about to get worse. Koontz takes and wins risks that lift *Dragon Tears* well above being just another killer-on-the-loose story. Among them—incredibly—is his narration of key parts of the story from a dog's viewpoint. Jay O. Sanders reads with just the right edge of tough-guy grit.

8 css   13 hr   Simon & Schuster Audio

Frankenstein
Author: Mary Shelley
Reader: Julie Harris
★★★★

Frankenstein is not only a classic, it is undoubtedly the world's best-known, least-read horror novel. For most people, Frankenstein's monster is Boris Karloff with bolts in his neck. But here's the original: a sensitive, well-spoken wretch, tortured by rejection. *Frankenstein* is rightly told in a woman's voice, even though the story's narrator is a man. Mary Shelley was only eighteen years old when she wrote her more laboriously titled *Frankenstein: Or, the Modern Prometheus* (1818). It was published anonymously, so most critics of Shelley's time imagined a man wrote it. Like the monster himself, they had a shock coming. Harris is Shelley's voice in this reading, sparking new life into the old story. Horror fans know Harris for her role in *The Haunting.*

2 css   3 hr   Dove Audio

Graveyard Shift and Other Stories from *Night Shift*
Author: Stephen King
Reader: John Glover
★★★

Of the two collections from King's *Night Shift* (see *Gray Matter* below), this one has the strongest stories. "Graveyard Shift" stands as the ultimate rats-and-slime-in-the-dark tale. "Jerusalem's Lot" is an effective homage to H. P. Lovecraft, complete with purple ranting. The surprise in this package is "The Last Rung on the Ladder," a touching story about failed trust. It proves what the venerable John D. McDonald wrote in his introduction to *Night Shift:* that King could be writing whatever he likes. Other stories on the tape include "The Man Who Loved Flowers" and "Night Surf."

3 css 3½ hr BDD Audio

Gray Matter and Other Stories from *Night Shift*
Author: Stephen King
Reader: John Glover
★★★

Night Shift (1978) was King's first short-story collection—stories written before or shortly after his breakthrough novel, *Carrie* (1974). It can be argued these stories still represent King at his leanest, meanest best, back when he was scaring people for fun and not (much) profit. Glover reads in the clipped tone of a dentist promising that it won't hurt. The title story, "Gray Matter," is a black comedy—make that an oozing gray comedy—about a man who pops the top on a colossally bad can of beer. Other stories on the tape include "The Bogeyman," "I Know What You Need," "Strawberry Spring," "The Woman in the Room," and "Battleground."

3 css 3½ hr BDD Audio

Interview with the Vampire
Author: Anne Rice
Reader: F. Murray Abraham
★★★★

If ever a book seemed written for a performance on tape, it is this one, the first of Anne Rice's *Vampire Chronicles.* After all, the story begins with switching on a tape recorder. Asking if the tape is long enough for the story of a life, the vampire Louis proceeds to recount his two hundred years of blood-sucking debauchery. Meantime, like the skeptical "boy" who has come to interview Louis, the listener is made privy to the everyday life of the vampire, as well as terrible secrets. F. Murray Abraham reads with the same relish Louis might have for his listener's neck.

2 css 3 hr Random House AudioBooks

Lasher
Author: Anne Rice
Reader: Joe Morton
★★

Be warned: This is not the place to start the saga of Rice's Mayfair witches. *Lasher* is a sequel to *The Witching Hour* (see page 170)—a slow-going 600 pages in print and not much snappier on tape—and the story casts an evil spell on those who try to pick it up in the middle. Basically, queen witch Rowan Mayfair is on the run from the demon Lasher. It's hard not to imagine Joe Morton scratching his head in puzzlement as he nonetheless gamely plows into the book's opening. It's a malevolent muddle of preestablished characters and relationships.

2 css 3hr Random House AudioBooks

The Mist
Author: Stephen King
Performers: Multiple Cast
★★★

Break out the headphones. The gimmick here is "Kunstkopf" biaural sound, a three-dimensional effect that really works. Thunder cracks in the distance, rain hammers the roof; disembodied voices seem to come from over here, over there, sometimes in back of you. It's a weird feeling—like being surrounded by ghosts—and then these merciless sound *meisters* at Simon & Schuster Audio go and apply it to Stephen King's story of giant bugs and squishy, tentacled things in the misty-moisty morning, when rowdy was the weather.

1 css 1½ hr Simon & Schuster Audio
1 CD 1½ hr Simon & Schuster Audio

The Monkey's Paw and Other Tales of Terror
Authors: W. W. Jacobs, Edgar Allan Poe, and others
Reader: Victor Garber
★★★

William Wymark Jacobs wrote more humor than horror stories. But at the turn of the century, he penned one of the horror genre's most indelible tales, "The Monkey's Paw." Imitated and parodied to the point of cliché (even *The Simpsons* had a go at it), Jacobs's story still bears hearing. Beware of the dried-out monkey's paw that will grant three wishes, each with some terrible consequence. Garber lends a crisp, cultured reading to five other, more obscure old short stories, including Edgar Allan Poe's "The Oval Portrait."

1 css 1½ hr Durkin Hayes Audio

The Phantom of the Opera
Author: Gaston Leroux
Reader: F. Murray Abraham
★★★★

This is the classic novel, not the musical, even though the cover represents the famous mask-and-rose logo from the hit play. What an actor like F. Murray

Abraham can do with Leroux's wildly evocative scenes and his elaborate prose is astonishing. With a voice that alternately soothes and excites, Abraham provides some of the most electrifying moments I've heard on tape. His phantom is both terrifying and pitiful, not unlike Lon Chaney's, and Abraham's interpretation is just as enduring and ensures that this audio is a classic of the genre. Tasteful musical underscoring adds to the drama.

2css 3 hr Caedmon Audio

Praying for Sleep
Author: Jeffrey Deaver
Reader: Anthony Heald
★★

This one has all the right elements for a chase thriller, but it winds up answering the title prayer: It's mostly a snooze. Convicted murderer Michael Hrubek escapes from the insane asylum, seemingly bent on killing schoolteacher Liz Atcheson, the witness who put him away. But Hrubek is no Hannibal Lecter—hardly much crazier than the assortment of nuts who are trying to catch him, all for their own twisted reasons. Heald delivers a taut reading, but the story goes slack, many tangled motives need explaining, and the ending is improbable.

2 css 3 hr Penguin HighBridge Audio

Psycho
Author: Robert Bloch
Reader: Kevin McCarthy
★★★★

Thirty-five years after Bloch published his psychological horror novel—thirty-four years after it became the most notorious of director Alfred Hitchcock's movies—surely everyone who ever took a shower knows the story. But how many know the book? Even though Hitchcock followed Bloch's novel like a blueprint, the book is full of knife-edged little surprises. Hitchcock cast lean, handsome Anthony Perkins as the troubled motel keeper Norman Bates, but Bloch had a much different Bates in mind: a pudgy, balding Bates. And the book allowed its author to delve into the creepiest corners of Bates's mind—parts that McCarthy reads with particular dementia. McCarthy's creepy performance is among the best of his career (including his starring role in 1956's *Invasion of the Body Snatchers*). Check in for the night.

2 css 2 hr Listen for Pleasure

Queen of the Damned
Author: Anne Rice
Readers: Kate Nelligan and David Purdham
★★★

Having drained New Orleans dry of decadence, Anne Rice turns to the nasty possibilities of ancient Egypt, land of sharp-pointed pyramids that arise from the desert like vampire teeth. Learn how the first vampire, Akasha, Queen of the Damned, came to be 6,000 years ago. David Purdham reads the vampire Lestat's more-and-more lengthy monologues, while Kate Nelligan sinks her teeth into the rest of the narration: an effective tag team.

2 css 3 hr Random House AudioBooks

Scanners Two: The New Order
Author: Professor Janus Kimball
Reader: Roddy McDowall
★★

Another case of splitting headaches. This is a novelization (based on B. J. Nelson's screenplay) of an eagerly unawaited sequel to the movie *Scanners* (1981). Fast thinkers with superbrains use their enhanced noggins to read other people's minds, and to make other people's heads explode. The premise is a grabber, since haven't we all felt like somebody was trying to work this trick on us, one time or another? But enough is enough already, in spite of a good reading by Roddy McDowall (aside from calling Janus Kimball "Joseph").

2 css 3 hr Dove Audio

Second Child
Author: John Saul
Reader: Lee Meriwether
★

The last thing a miserable, thirteen-year-old misfit like Melissa needs is more trouble, so, naturally, Saul heaps it on. In addition to her mother-from-hell, Melissa is beset with the arrival of her horrendously popular fifteen-year-old half-sister-from-hell, Teri, and bedeviled by an imaginary playmate, D'Arcy, who just might be an evil ghost. The story is tedious, but like most of Saul's books, this 1990 outing was an almost immediate best-seller, so what do the critics know?

2 css 3 hr BDD Audio

Shadows
Author: John Saul
Reader: Lee Meriwether
★★

Ten-year-old Josh MacCallum is too smart for his own good, and unable to get along with other kids in regular school. The Academy, a stately school for gifted children, seems to be the answer for Josh. At least, his mother thinks so, since she is unaware they are characters in a John Saul novel, where evil is bound to befall any boy as sensitive as Josh. Saul engenders genuine sympathy for Josh and the lonely boy's schoolmate, Amy. Despite a somewhat silly ending, Meriwether's schoolteacherlike reading is a perfect fit to the school setting.

2 css 3 hr BDD Audio

The Tale of the Body Thief
Author: Anne Rice
Reader: Richard E. Grant
★★★

Lestat bites again. This time, the 200-year-old vampire hero so longs to be human, he swaps bodies with a mortal. By now, Lestat is much changed from the insatiable nuzzler 'n' guzzler that he was in *Interview with the Vampire* (see page 164). He not only speaks well (as does Richard E. Grant), but is also blithely aware that people have been following his story through the *Vampire Chronicles.* "If you read *Interview with the Vampire,* then you know all about this," he remarks on his sordid past. "If you read my autobiographical books, *The Vampire Lestat* [page 169] and *Queen of the Damned* [page 166], you know all about me, also." And if not, snap up the tapes.

2 css 3 hr Random House AudioBooks

The Thief of Always
Author: Clive Barker
Reader: John Glover
★★

Here's a tough call. *The Thief of Always* is something different from Barker—a children's fable, but still the unrepentant fright-master at work. Ten-year-old Harvey is saved from unbearable boredom when a mysterious little man named Rictus comes calling, whisking him away to a land of magic and treats. The tough call is that Barker's creepy black-and-white illustrations are integral to the book's mood in print, and, of course, missing on tape. In this unique case, our advice is, skip the tape, even though it sounds fine; get the illustrated book instead.

2 css 3 hr Harper Audio

Thinner
Author: Stephen King (writing as Richard Bachman)
Reader: Paul Sorvino
★★★

Thinner (1984) is the book that blew the cover off Stephen King's pseudonym Richard Bachman. King's fans made it a best-seller, even though sales had been "thin" before. Curiously, King had chosen to attach his Bachman pseudonym to a better book than those he was publishing under his own name at about the same time—*Christine* and *The Talisman.* The story is pure King, that of a good man who falls victim to a Gypsy curse that makes him lose weight until he is thinner, and thinner, and . . . thinner. The excellent actor Paul Sorvino makes a poisonous snake's hiss of that word, "Thiiiinnnnnnnnnnnnnner."

2 css 2½ hr Durkin Hayes Audio

The Twilight Zone Four: "The Midnight Sun"
Author: Rod Serling
Reader: Lois Nettleton
★★

As a 1961 episode of Serling's *The Twilight Zone* TV series, "The Midnight Sun" starred Lois Nettleton as a woman on a doomed and increasingly insane planet earth. Every day, the broiling earth is moving closer to the sun. Here, Nettleton reads Serling's prose version of the story, and she makes it hard to listen without sweating. But the half-hour TV episode takes twice as long to tell on tape, meaning the twist ending is twice as easy to guess. Nettleton's character—Norma—suffers just too much, and too long past making the point that, whew! it's hot. Worthwhile listening for fans of the TV series, but don't try it in a stuffy car.

1 css 1 hr Harper Audio

The Twilight Zone Six: "The Lonely"
Author: Red Serling
Reader: Jean Marsh
★★★★

First aired in November 1959, "The Lonely" is one of the most poignant and memorable episodes of Serling's *The Twilight Zone* TV series. This recording is from Serling's prose version. Convicted of a murder that anyone might have committed under the same circumstances, James Corry is serving his fifty-year sentence in solitary confinement on an asteroid. The captain of a supply ship takes pity on him, bringing Corry a robot in the form of a woman, named Alicia. The story is impeccably well read by Jean Marsh, who played Alicia in the TV episode, and the tape concludes with her memories of filming "The Lonely" in Death Valley. Oddly, the tape's packaging says nothing about Marsh's role as Alicia or the bonus of a charming chat with her. But as Serling himself might have said, here it is: presented for your (definite) approval.

1 css 1½ hr Harper Audio

The Vampire Lestat
Author: Anne Rice
Reader: Michael York
★★★

Lestat becomes a rock superstar. While *Interview with the Vampire* (see page 164) remains Anne Rice's best-known novel, this is the one that gave vampires a whole new image. Gone are the capes and cobwebs of Bela Lugosi's time; enter the vampire as superstar—sleek creature of leather and lust, yet strangely vulnerable. Maybe he just wants your understanding—and, of course, your blood. Michael York's intelligent reading makes him perfectly well cast, and suggests how well he might have played Lestat on screen.

2 css 3 hr Random House AudioBooks

The Witching Hour
Author: Anne Rice
Reader: Lindsay Crouse
★★★

Bubble, bubble, toil and . . . forget all that. Just as Anne Rice crafted a new mythos from the old trappings of the vampire, she does much the same for witches. *The Witching Hour* begins her saga of Rowan Mayfair, queen of the coven, and the demon called Lasher (see *Lasher*, the sequel, on page 165). It was overlong in print, but the abridged book casts a leaner, meaner spell. Lindsay Crouse reads with an unsettling calm that sometimes drops to a whisper, as if to keep witches from hearing.

2 css 3 hr Random House AudioBooks

The Wolfen
Author: Whitley Strieber
Reader: Roddy McDowall
★★★★

The Wolfen (1978) is the innovative, big-city werewolf story that launched Strieber's horror-writing career. And it still bites. The story pits a couple of increasingly scared detectives—Becky Neff and George Wilson—against a long-hidden breed of canine predators, the Wolfen. Strieber not only makes the detectives real, vulnerable, and sympathetic, but also does the same for the Wolfen. Take it as a man-against-monster story, or—from the Wolfen's side, equally valid—a story of man as the monster. It works either way, thanks as well to McDowall's reading. McDowall is a versatile film actor with a knack for horror (*Fright Night*). Here, he contributes the breathless and sometimes whispery delivery of telling age-old, deep, dark secrets.

2 css 3 hr Dove Audio

Anne Rice's Vampire Chronicles: Interview with the Vampire, The Vampire Lestat, and the Queen of the Damned
A: Anne Rice
R: F. Murray Abraham, Michael York, Kate Nelligan, and David Pardham
RH

Billy
A. Whitley Strieber
R: Roddy McDowall
DOVE

Black Lightning
A: John Saul
RH

The Body Politic in 3-D Sound from the Inhuman Condition
A: Clive Barker
R: Kevin Conway
S&S

Cabal: Nightbreed
A: Clive Barker
R: David Purdham
S&S

Dark Rivers of the Heart
A: Dean Koontz
RH

Dr. Jekyll and Mr. Hyde
A: Robert Louis Stevenson
DOVE

Dolores Claiborne
A: Stephen King
R: Frances Sternhagen
PENG

Donovan's Brain
A: Curt Siodmak
R: Michael Murphy
DURK

Dracula
A: Bram Stoker
R: Richard E. Grant
PENG

Dracula
A: Bram Stoker
R: David McCallum and Carole Shelley
HARP

Dracula
A: Bram Stoker
R: Edward Woodward
DOVE

The Drawing of the Three (The Dark Tower, Part II)
A/R: Stephen King
PENG

Edgar Allan Poe Stories
A: Edgar Allan Poe
R: Basil Rathbone
HARP

Everville
A: Clive Barker
HARP

Fall of the House of Usher and other Poems and Tales
A: Edgar Allan Poe
R: Basil Rathbone
HARP

Floating Dragon
A: Peter Straub
R: Fritz Weaver
DURK

Flowers in the Attic
A: V. C. Andrews
R: Dorothy Lyman
S&S

Four Past Midnight: The Sun Dog
A: Stephen King
R: Tim Sample
PENG

Frankenstein
A: Mary Shelley
R: Kenneth Branagh
S&S

Frankenstein
A: Mary Shelly
R: James Mason
HARP

Frankenstein
A: Mary Shelley
PENG

Gerald's Game
A: Stephen King
R: Lindsay Crouse
PENG

Ghost Stories of Charles Dickens Volume I
A: Charles Dickens
R: Paul Scofield
DOVE

Ghost Stories of Charles Dickens Volume II
A: Charles Dickens
R: Paul Scofield
DOVE

Ghost Story
A: Peter Straub
R: William Windom
S&S

The Great and Secret Show: The First Book of the Art
A: Clive Barker
R: Stephen Lang
HARP

The Gripping Hand
A: Larry Niven and Jerry Pournelle
R: Jay O. Sanders
S&S

Guardian
A: John Saul
R: Lee Meriwether
RH

The Gunslinger (The Dark Tower, Part I)
A/R: Stephen King
PENG

The Hellbound Heart
A/R: Clive Barker
S&S

The Homing
A: John Saul
RH

Houses without Doors
A: Peter Straub
R: Will Patton
S&S

If You Could See Me Now
A: Peter Straub
R: Keir Dullea
DURK

Imajica
A: Clive Barker
R: Peter MacNicol
HARP

The Inhuman Condition
A: Clive Barker
R: Full cast
S&S

Insomnia
A: Stephen King
PENG

The Invisible Man
A: H. G. Wells
R: Ben Kingsley
DOVE

Koko
A: Peter Straub
R: James Woods
S&S

Lightning
A: Dean Koontz
R: Peter Marinker
S&S

The Masque of the Red Death and Other Poems and Tales
A: Edgar Allan Poe
R: Basil Rathbone
HARP

The Memoirs of Elizabeth Frankenstein
A: Theodore Roszak
S&S

Mr. Murder
A: Dean Koontz
R: Jay O. Sanders
S&S

Mrs. God
A: Peter Straub
R: Kevin Spacey
S&S

The Mummy: or Ramses the Damned
A: Anne Rice
R: Michael York
RH

Mystery
A: Peter Straub
R: James Woods
S&S

The Narrative of Arthur Gordon Pym of Nantucket
A: Edgar Allan Poe
R: Christopher Plummer
DURK

Needful Things: The Last Castle Rock Story
A/R: Stephen King
PENG

Nightcrawlers: Stories from *Blue World*
A: Robert R. McCammon
R: William Windom
S&S

Nightmares and Dreamscapes Volume I
A: Stephen King
R: Various
PENG

Nightmares and Dreamscapes Volume II
A: Stephen King
R: Various
PENG

Nightmares and Dreamscapes Volume III
A: Stephen King
R: Various
PENG

One Past Midnight: The Langoliers
A: Stephen King
R: Willem Dafoe
PENG

Petals on the Wind
A: V. C. Andrews
R: Leslie Charleson
S&S

The Phantom of the Opera
A: Gaston Leroux
R: Christopher Casenove
DOVE

The Pit and the Pendulum and Other Works
A: Edgar Allan Poe
R: Basil Rathbone
HARP

Prime Evil I: A Taste for Blood
A: Douglas Winter
R: Ed Begley, Jr.
S&S

Prime Evil II: Secrets and Shadows
A: Douglas Winter
R: James Sikking
S&S

Prime Evil III: Into the Darkness
A: Douglas Winter
R: Michael Murphy
S&S

The Purloined Letter and Poems
A: Edgar Allan Poe
R: Anthony Quayle
HARP

Rose Madder
A: Stephen King
PENG

The Secret Life of Laszlo, Count Dracula
A: Roderick Anscombe
HARP

Selections from *Skeleton Crew*
A: Stephen King
R: Stephen King, Matthew Broderick, Dana Ivey, and Frances Sternhagen
PENG

Something Passed By: Stories from *Blue World*
A: Robert R. McCammon
R: Michael O'Keefe
S&S

The Strange Case of Dr. Jekyll and Mr. Hyde
A: Robert Louis Stevenson
R: Anthony Quayle
HARP

Taltos: Lives of the Mayfair Witches
A: Anne Rice
R: Tim Curry
RH

Three Past Midnight: The Library Policeman
A: Stephen King
R: Ken Howard
PENG

The Throat
A: Peter Straub
R: William H. Macy
S&S

Twilight Zone #1: The Mighty Casey
A: Rod Serling
R: Fritz Weaver
HARP

Twilight Zone #2: Walking Distance
A: Rod Serling
R: Cliff Robertson
HARP

Twilight Zone #3: The Odyssey of Flight 33
A: Rod Serling
R: Roddy McDowall
HARP

Twilight Zone #5: The Monsters Are Due on Maple Street
A: Rod Serling
R: Theodore Bikel
HARP

Two Past Midnight: Secret Window, Secret Garden
A: Stephen King
R: James Woods
PENG

The Waste Lands, (The Dark Tower, Part III)
A/R: Stephen King
PENG

HUMOR

Radio was the original mass medium for comedy, and the great comedic voices that filled American airwaves in the 1920s and beyond are still legendary today. Audiotapes are a modern extension of that radio tradition, an exceptional showcase for humor, both old and new.

Many of the funniest voices from the golden age of radio are available again in compilations like the Milton Berle collection, which features golden age greats like W. C. Fields, Fibber McGee and Molly, and, of course, Berle, the master himself, whose career spanned vaudeville, radio, movies, and television.

Dave Barry, whom *The New York Times* called "America's funniest man," has a career that's like Berle's without the vaudeville. With a newspaper column and a TV show based on his life, Barry has brought his best-selling books to cassettes in a major way, with six entries. Barry's work moves seamlessly from the page to tape, and he's at his funniest when reading his own work. It's somewhat less funny when read by stand-in Arte Johnson, who made his major humor mark on the 1960s TV hit *Laugh-In.* Johnson is in fact the voice on many of the humor tapes, reading everything from Barry to Art Buchwald.

The works of Tom Bodett and Garrison Keillor define a genre of their own. Rich, humorous storytelling unlike anything else available, Bodett's and Keillor's stands above and apart from the rest. For a warm, comfortable laugh, there's nothing like these two.

The range of humor available on tape is so broad that everyone will find something that appeals to them—from young mothers to grandmothers to fans of established talents like Lewis Grizzard and Larry King. And the great part is, when you find a good one, you can rewind it and laugh all over again.

HIGHLY RECOMMENDED (★★★★)

All Things Wise and Wonderful
As Far as You Can Go Without a Passport
The Best of Jonathan Winters
The Book of Guys
Cats and Dogs
Catskills on Broadway
Dave Barry Slept Here
Dog Stories
Growing Up, Growing Old and Going Fishing at the End of the Road
Jeeves
The Last Decent Parking Place in North America
A Marriage Made in Heaven or Too Tired for an Affair
Milton Berle's Mad, Mad World of Comedy
More Dog Stories
Old Fools and Young Hearts
Those Grand Occasions at the End of the Road
When You Look Like Your Passport Photo, It's Time to Go Home

All Things Wise and Wonderful
Author: James Herriot
Reader: Christopher Timothy
★★★★

In *All Things Wise and Wonderful,* instead of pets, Herriot employs his skills on farm animals, showing a different side of the world's best-loved vet. Herriot's many fans will be more than happy with this tape, which shows the tremendous range of Christopher Timothy's wonderful English voice characterizations.

2 css   3½   Durkin Hayes Audio

As Far As You Can Go Without A Passport: The View from the End of the Road
Author/Reader: Tom Bodett
★★★★

Tom Bodett's charming Alaskan hamlet, the End of the Road, has become an important part of many people's lives. Bodett takes aim at some easy targets here, like grocery shopping, lost socks, and living in a small house. This book is more about small-town life in general than the particulars of End of the Road that so many came to love. Bodett's voice, as always, is superb. Bob Elliott, of Bob and Ray, said that this is "one of those all-too-few gems that really make you laugh out loud."

2 css   2 hr   Bantam Audio

The Best Cat Ever
Author/Reader: Cleveland Amory
★★★

This is Amory's third book centering on Polar Bear, written just after Polar Bear's death. No one is better suited to reading Amory's work than himself. Amory apologizes for the book's title, knowing that every cat lover thinks his cat is the best cat ever, and allowing that we're all entitled to think that. This is Amory's best book, his wittiest and most poignant, and, sadly, the final entry in the Polar Bear series.

2 css 3 hr Time Warner AudioBooks

The Best of Jonathan Winters
Author/Reader: Jonathan Winters
★★★★

From the mind and mouth of one of America's most peculiar and funniest talents comes a solo collection featuring the most off-the-wall humor anywhere. Almost unbelievably versatile, Winters unleashes his limitless hoard of voices and his colorful asylum of characters, as well as fully functional outgoing messages for your answering machine. Antics, impressions, improvisions, and visits from old-standby Winters characters make this tape a real gem.

1 css 35 min Dove Audio

The Book of Guys
Author/Reader: Garrison Keillor
★★★★

This is Garrison Keillor at the top of his form, which is lofty indeed. Eight new stories are included here: "The Midlife Crisis of Dionysis," "Herb Johnson, the God of Canton," "Casey at the Bat (Road Game Version)," "Lonesome Shorty," "Don Giovanni," "Marooned," "Buddy the Leper," and "The Country Mouse and the City Mouse." Keillor puts that famous passion into his voice even when covering the mundane—of which there is very little in *The Book of Guys.* You just can't go wrong with Garrison Keillor, and this tape is more evidence of why that is.

2 css 3 hr Penguin HighBridge Audio

Cats and Dogs
Author: James Herriot
Reader: Christopher Timothy
★★★★

The celebrated veterinarian James Herriot is back with another collection of stories, focusing this time on those most popular of domesticated creatures, cats and dogs. Mixed by the skilled hand of Herriot, the pets and their owners combine to bring listeners a rare and joyful smorgasbord of animal tales unlike those found anywhere else. Once again, actor Christopher Timothy brings an astonishing array of rich English accents to his readings, the better to illuminate these already brilliant stories.

2 css 2½ hr Durkin Hayes Audio

Catskills on Broadway
Authors: Kenneth D. Greenblatt and Stephen D. Fish
Performers: Dick Capri, Louise Dart, Mal Z. Lawrence, and Freddie Roman
★★★★

In live production, *Catskills on Broadway* received the Outer Critics Circle Award for Comedy in 1992. It faithfully and hilariously re-creates the ambience of the legendary Catskill resorts where so many of America's most beloved comics got their starts. The resorts and famed hotels—Grossinger's, the Concord, the Nevele—were the arenas that helped hone the acts of stars like Joan Rivers, Milton Berle, Danny Kaye, Woody Allen, and Mel Brooks. The cast is flawless, and the laughs come fast and furious. Between laughs are reminiscences of the sights on old Route 17, the Red Apple Restaurant, and the foundations of Borscht Belt humor.

1 css 1 hr 10 min Dove Audio

Dates From Hell: True Stories from the Front
Author: Katherine Ann Samon
Performers: Margaret Klenck, Elizabeth Roby, Greg Schaffert, and Robert Sevra
Bomb

You'll hear story after story of bad dating experiences, like the woman who suffered through dinner with a klutz. Not much to laugh at here. The box says, "If you've ever been on a date from hell . . . you'll appreciate this hilarious audio." If only it were true.

1 css 1½ hr Penguin HighBridge Audio

Dave Barry Does Japan
Author: Dave Barry
Reader: Arte Johnson
★★

Barry now turns his mighty thunderbolts of humor in the direction of the Pacific Rim. Japanese culture, dining, sports, and industry all suffer broadside attacks from the S.S. *Barry.* Arte Johnson reads this unabridged work, and doesn't do justice to it like Barry himself would have.

4 css 6 hr Dove Audio

Dave Barry Is Not Making This Up
Author: Dave Barry
Reader: Arte Johnson
★★★

Many of his fans feel that Dave Barry is at his funniest when he just looks at the oddballs and curveballs and screwballs in the world around him and explains them in his own way—a way that has earned him the title "the funniest man in America." For Dave Barry fans these tapes may well be the ultimate Barry audio fare. Only the introduction is read by the man himself—the rest is read by Arte Johnson, and the tape lacks some punch because of that.

2 css 3 hr Dove Audio

Dave Barry Slept Here
Author/Reader: Dave Barry
★★★★

One of America's favorite humorists gleefully tackles a serious national shortfall: the widespread lack of coherent knowledge about the history of our great nation. Barry brings his special brand of wisdom to the entire range of American history, from the colonial days ("England Starts Some Fun Colonies") to the Reagan/Bush years ("Napping towards Glory"). Events are wildly scrambled and convoluted into a delightful hash that only Dave Barry could serve up. Only problem: The book was released in 1989, and we're out of the Reagan/Bush years.

1 css 1 hr Random House AudioBooks

Dave Barry Talks Back
Author/Reader: Dave Barry
Reader: Arte Johnson
★★

All across the nation lurk millions of loyal Barry fans, Alert Readers who stand ever ready to send him stories of mismanagement, misdirected animal husbandry, and general oddness. Now the absolute best of Barry is available, complete with many Alert Reader items, and, more important, Dave talking back. He talks back to traffic cops, dentists, doctors, Congress, and his own dynamic duo of very stupid dogs. But as for Arte Johnson, Barry should do his own talking back, not hire it out.

2 css 3 hr Dove Audio

Dave Barry Turns Forty
Author/Reader: Dave Barry
★★★

Growing old, as Barry points out, is "a major lifestyle trend." Among those who are breathing, it's quite common. But what happens when you turn forty? In an attempt to act like a responsible grown-up and offer up something with redeeming social value, Barry places himself square in middle age: too young for the nursing home but too old to be a rock star. Dave Barry reads his own work with a special delight that comes through clearly to listeners—even if he is over the hill.

1 css 1 hr Random House AudioBooks

Dave Barry's Only Travel Guide You'll Ever Need
Author/Reader: Dave Barry
★★★

Barry starts his travelogue with tender childhood reminiscences about riding in the backseat of his parents' car and fighting bitterly with his sister, a tradition that continues today in families with more than one child. Going international, Barry examines mysterious foreign cuisine, menus in unfamiliar languages, tipping, and travel agents; staying stateside, he makes a visit to Walt Disney World ("You *will* have fun"). This is the first, last, and definitely funniest word on travel today.

1 css 1 hr Random House AudioBooks

Delusions of Grandma
Author/Reader: Carrie Fisher
★★

The actress Carrie Fisher turned to writing with *Postcards from the Edge* and *Surrender the Pink.* Opening with the Chinese curse "May you live in interesting times," this new novel leads a pregnant young screenwriter through a fight-or-flight confrontation with maturity. Spiritedly read by Fisher, this is an unrepentantly L.A. book. You can smell the suntans, though Fisher tries to make this book sound less autobiographical than it most certainly is. Unfortunately, this book is not her best.

2 css 3 hr Simon & Schuster Audio

Dog Stories
Author: James Herriot
Reader: Christopher Timothy
★★★★

James Herriot, thoughtful and dedicated English veterinarian, is not only a prolific author on the subject of his beloved animals, but also the inspiration for the long-running British TV series, *All Creatures Great and Small.* Few writers bring such love and understanding to the sometimes sad, sometimes hilarious world of the four-footed. Herriot has the unique perspective of being their vet, maintaining a delicate balance at the place where humans and their pets interact. Of them all, dogs are Herriot's favorite pets, and he brings to their stories a special magic. Actor Christopher Timothy plays Herriot in the television series, and does a sparkling job as a storyteller.

2 css 2½ hr Durkin Hayes Audio

Don't Bend Over in the Garden, Granny, You Know Them Taters Got Eyes
Author: Lewis Grizzard
Reader: Peter Waldren
★★

The subject this time is sex, and according to humorist Lewis Grizzard, sex not only makes the world go around, but also leads to marriage, fun, jokes, and everything else. Fault here: The book was written while Richard Nixon was alive, and jokes pertaining to his sex life—or lack thereof—are not as amusing now that he's the late Richard Nixon. That said, Waldren gives a terrific reading to some terrific material.

1css 1 hr Random House AudioBooks

Elvis is Dead and I Don't Feel So Good Myself
Author/Reader: Lewis Grizzard
★★

Lewis Grizzard was lying on the beach drinking beer the day Elvis Presley died. The passing of the man who had been a symbol of everything that riled parents in the 1950s cast Grizzard into some serious and not-so-serious reminiscing and introspection. "At his best," *Atlanta* magazine said, "Grizzard is a comic genius. He is at his best here." Only fault: References to people like Boy George make it sound slightly dated.

1 css 1 hr Random House AudioBooks

A Fine and Pleasant Misery
Author: Patrick F. McManus
Reader: George S. Irving
★★★

Modern technology has taken all the rustic can-do spirit out of modern camping—so says Patrick McManus. Camping ain't what it used to be and McManus will tell you all about it—how tough the food was to get, how fires were different then, the agonies of sleeping in a bedroll, and even worse, a primitive sleeping bag—providing laughs all the way.

2 css 3 hr Durkin Hayes Audio

Funny, You Don't Look Like A Grandma
Author/Reader: Lois Wyse
★

There are more grandmothers alive today than at any other time in the history of the world. No longer is Grandma the blue-haired lady with the cane. Today Grandma is running marathons, flying airplanes, and driving red convertibles with overhead cams. Being a grandmother herself—and thus an expert on the ever-changing subject of being a grandma in the 1990s—Lois Wyse presents readings of her own stories, poems, theories, and observations on this delicate, joyful subject. Funny, though, she does sound like a grandma.

2 css 2 hr 5 min The Publishing Mills AudioBooks

The Good Samaritan Strikes Again
Author: Patrick F. McManus
Reader: George S. Irving
★★★

Away from the wilderness for once (which no doubt gives the wilderness a great sigh of relief), McManus finds himself in the office, suffering the stresses of the workaday world and then discovering that escape from work is even more difficult. In emergencies, he is probably not the first guy you'd want on the scene, unless you're looking for a laugh instead of first aid—but then, they say laughter is the best medicine.

2 css 3½ hr Durkin Hayes Audio

The Grasshopper Trap and Other Stories
Author: Patrick F. McManus
Reader: George S. Irving
★★★

If you've never heard McManus's humorous tales of man against nature, this sixth audio release in the McManus series is a good place to start. As his many fans have discovered, you don't have to be a nature lover to enjoy these zany spoofs and McManus's skewed wisdom. If you thought hunters actually went into the woods to hunt, or that there are no rules to getting lost in the woods, think again. And find out the answer to that age-old debate: Is a hunker a squat? Or not?

2 css 2½ hr Durkin Hayes Audio

Groucho Marx and Other Short Stories and Tall Tales: Selected Writings of Groucho Marx
Author: Groucho Marx
Reader: Carl Reiner
★★★

Groucho Marx was one of the funniest men who ever walked, and in his long career he conquered the vaudeville stage, films, radio, and finally television. Surprising to many, Groucho was also a prolific author. He wrote about himself, the trials and glories of show business, his brothers, family life, anything that caught his eye. Robert S. Bader, a Marx Brothers fanatic since childhood, edited this tape, and the reading by comedian Carl Reiner breathes vibrant life into these remembrances of the early days of show business. It's full-blown nostalgia, Groucho-style.

2 css 3 hr Dove Audio

Growing Up, Growing Old and Going Fishing at the End of the Road
Author/Reader: Tom Bodett
★★★★

The old friends are back—Argus Winslow, Tamara Dupree, Bud Koenig, the Flannigans, Doug McDoogan, and the rest—and this time the bigger world has intruded on the End of the Road in the form of the Alaskan oil spill. Bodett is a master at hanging very intimate, universal human experiences on the sharp hook of vast world events. You also don't want to miss the tale of how Alaska's ugliest lamp made friends.

2 css 2 hr 5 min Bantam Audio

How to Speak Southern
Authors: Steve Mitchell and Sam C. Rawls
Reader: Charlie Dell
Bomb

This is the kind of thing that was prevalent during the Carter Administration, the sort of alleged witticism that treated southerners as if they were zoo animals being trotted out to speak their near-incomprehensible lingo for the amusement of "normal" people—Yankees: "Fo' a dollah ah'll say sumpum." Obviously the authors got their reference material from Andy of Mayberry and Gomer Pyle, and they can't tell the difference between Southern and Hick.

1 css 40 min Bantam Audio

Humor on Wry
Authors: James Thurber, Art Buchwald, and Robert Benchley
Readers: Henry Morgan and Mark Russell
★★★

Three cassettes, three world-class humorists, expertly delivered by first-rate readers—it all adds up to a feast for the discerning ear. Thurber's humor helped define the early *New Yorker*, and many favorites are read here. "The Best of Art Buchwald" tape lets Washington's resident jester snipe at modern horrors like computers, the phone company, the sexual revolution, and college football. Buchwald says he hates to read his own material, but the two pieces he does read are terrific. And his friend Mark Russell also does a good job. "Benchley's Best," the last tape, offers a generous eleven essays that clearly showcase his unique wit, humanity, and wisdom.

3 css 4 hr Audio Editions

I Don't Remember Dropping the Skunk But I Do Remember Trying to Breathe
Survival Skills for Teenagers
Author/Reader: Ken Davis
★★★

Ken Davis, conference speaker, communications consultant, and stand-up comic addresses himself to the problems of teens today. Some of the advice falls into that shadow world of blended myth and reality. Other advice, like practicing your smooth date moves in front of a mirror, has been a joke at least since the 1940s and certainly had good exposure on the *Happy Days* TV show. Cornball city. Though also recorded live, sound quality here is somewhat less muddy than on Super Sheep (see page 187).

1 css 1½ Zondervan

Jeeves
Author: P. G. Wodehouse
Performers: Roger Livesey, Terry-Thomas, and others
★★★★

Jeeves is the gentleman's gentleman, an unflappable character who has steered his befuddled employer Bertie Wooster through countless scrapes. This brilliant dramatized tape casts the great Terry-Thomas as Bertie and Roger Livesey as Jeeves in two vintage stories: "Jeeves Takes Charge," in which Jeeves helps save Bertie from marriage to an icily highbrow woman; and "Indian Summer," which finds Jeeves doing the same thing for Bertie's uncle, who has become entangled with a silly young girl. Wodehouse's sparkling prose was meant to be read out loud, and Terry-Thomas's voice is one of the most expressive ever recorded.

1 css 50 min Caedmon Audio

Larry King Laughs
Volume I of *The Best of the Larry King Show*
Author/Reader: Larry King
★★

Larry King's CNN television program and Mutual Radio's *Larry King Show* have made King one of the most listened-to men in America. His shows have brought him into contact with hundreds of movers and shakers and top comics. This tape is not, as one might hope, excerpts from his long-running shows, but rather a special made-for-audio original program. Guests include Billy Crystal, Jay Leno, Richard Pryor, Lily Tomlin, Jonathan Winters, Bob Hope, and Albert Brooks.

1 css 1 hr Simon & Schuster Audio

The Last Decent Parking Place in North America
Author/Reader: Tom Bodett
★★★★

Homer, Alaska—otherwise known as the End of the Road—is where the land ends and the sea begins. Through his incomparable storytelling, Tom Bodett has made it one of the most familiar and enjoyable spots in North America. You don't even have to physically arrive to pay a visit to Homer's residents—Argus Winslow, Bud Koenig, Doug McDoogan, Tamara Dupree, and the rest—or to have a cuppa baked-boot joe at Clara's Coffee Cup, home of the worst, and only, cup of coffee in town. Join the rest of Bodett's fans and park your car at the End of the Road and relax. Something will happen soon enough, trust Tom Bodett for that.

2 css 2½ Bantam Audio

Legends, Lies and Cherished Myths of Southern History
Author: Richard Shenkman
Reader: Arte Johnson
★★

Shenkman, an award-winning investigative reporter, devoted the entirety of this *New York Times* best-seller to skewering the nonsense and misconceptions about the world's heros, revolutions, religions, and inventors that have been woven into our history. Think Cleopatra was beautiful? Think Robin Hood was a nice guy? "Everyone who wrote history was full of it," Shenkman says, while firing live ammunition at history's sacred cows. Shenkman has a way of draining the grandeur out of history and showing it for what it is—humans doing human things. Reader Arte Johnson does a fine job of bringing this unabridged text to audio mode.

4 css 6 hr Dove Audio

A Marriage Made In Heaven or Too Tired For an Affair
Author/Reader: Erma Bombeck
★★★★

Over the course of her career, Erma Bombeck has sold over 17 million books, and her fans just can't get enough. Her writing career has repeatedly gotten her named as one of the twenty-five most influential women in America. She married her husband in 1949, and since then, their marriage and home life have been the mainstay of her immensely popular column. Aside from "We have lift-off" and "This country is at war," Bombeck says there is no more sobering phrase than "I now pronounce you man and wife." And from that beginning, she is off and running on subjects of dogs, neighbors, in-laws and outlaws—and, of course, marriage itself. Her work translates marvelously into audio, and she gives her own material a terrific read.

2 css 3 hr Harper Audio

Milton Berle's Mad, Mad World of Comedy
Author: Paul Werth
Reader: Milton Berle
★★★★

Uncle Miltie is an icon spanning seventy years of American comedy, with solid careers in vaudeville, nightclubs, radio, TV, and movies. Over his lifetime in show biz he's worked with all the best, so who better to host this tribute to the great ones? Here are bits of acts and interviews with giants like Jimmy Durante, W. C. Fields, Burns and Allen, Jack Benny, Will Rogers, Pat Buttram, Fibber McGee and Molly, Fred Allen, Eddie Cantor, Martin and Lewis, Fanny Brice, Phyllis Diller, and a host of others. The program concludes with a special tribute to Groucho Marx.

1 css 1½ hr The Publishing Mills AudioBooks

More Dog Stories
Author: James Herriot
Reader: Christopher Timothy
★★★★

Herriot explains in his very British way, "I am as soppy over my dogs as any old lady. . . . So many people are embarrassed when they have to reveal to the vet their affection for their pets, their worries over their welfare, the anguish when their too-short lives come to an end. . . . They don't have to tell me, I know." Reveling in the performances of man's best friend without shying away from the pains involved, Herriot's dog stories are warm and enthralling, made even better by Christopher Timothy's readings.

2 css 2½ hr Durkin Hayes Audio

More of the 776 Stupidest Things Ever Said
Authors: Ross and Kathryn Petras
Readers: Arte Johnson, Jayne Meadows, Bruce Vilanch, and others
★

Funny, yes, but eventually you need a high tolerance for pain when you realize that most of these incredibly stupid statements come from people we elected to public office and paid lavishly for their services. This one-hour tape, including stupid statements from entertainers, broadcasters, and others in the public eye, will leave you laughing, but also drained. Maybe stupidity is a transmissible disease, and you can catch it from hearing too much. It's something to worry about. Guest voice appearances by Ed Asner, Ed Begley, Jr., Ben Kingsley, and Michael York spice up the proceedings.

1 css 1 hr Dove Audio

Motherhood Stress
Author: Deborah Shaw Lewis
Readers: Deborah Shaw Lewis and Gregg Lewis
★

Motherhood is a job—most mothers call it a job and a half. And with every job comes stress. In fact, *Redbook* magazine has called motherhood the most stressful job in the world. "Deborah Shaw Lewis's advice," *Redbook* wrote, "is to treat parenting like the profession it is. She encourages the use of tried-and-true stress management techniques to feel better and be a better mom." On this tape, Lewis gives you the causes and effects of motherhood stress, ways to take care of yourself, tips for relieving motherhood stress, and advice on what fathers can do, but the sound quality is not the best. Another reviewer wrote, "This book sparkles with humor, joy, and some of the best advice you'll ever get in your life."

1 css 1 hr Zondervan

Never Sniff a Gift Fish and Other Stories
Author: Patrick F. McManus
Reader: George S. Irving
★★★

Patrick McManus presents the theory that eventually all fishermen turn into philosophers, and that the worse the fisherman, the better the philosopher. Judging from the breadth of McManus's philosophical musings, that doesn't say much for his abilities as an angler. But you never need to have held a rifle, strapped on a backpack, or even considered sticking a squirming worm on a hook to appreciate McManus's country-straight, cracker-barrel insights and humor. George S. Irving brings McManus's words into sparkling audio life.

2 css 2½ hr Durkin Hayes Audio

The Night the Bear Ate Goombaw and Other Stories
Author: Patrick F. McManus
Reader: George S. Irving
★★★

McManus further stakes out his claim to the funny side of the streambed. In *The Night the Bear Ate Goombaw . . .*, flawlessly read by George S. Irving, McManus unreels one unforgettable story after another. Fishings fans will take special delight in the logical—or illogical—discourse on the theory of sequences, and the practical aspects of how to avoid the chores that get in the way of quality fishing.

2 css 2½ hr Durkin Hayes Audio

Old Fools and Young Hearts
Author/Reader: Tom Bodett
★★★★

Even the most mossbacked and cantankerous residents of the End of the Road harbor their tender passions and sweet secrets, and somewhere in the hearts of all of us, young or old, it is always springtime. In *Old Fools and Young Hearts,* Tom Bodett shows us the cast of America's favorite small town as unlikely neighbors bond in the midst of a blizzard. The oil spill, far from cleaned up, again becomes an important part of local lives (See *Growing Up, Growing Old and Going Fishing at the End of the Road* on page 181).

2 css 2 hr 10 min Bantam Audio

Real Ponies Don't Go Oink
Author: Patrick F. McManus
Reader: George S. Irving
★★★

Another volume of Patrick McManus's brand of outdoor adventures that bring his unique brand of wit to questions like: How do you make a man on crutches break land speed records? How do you make blood sausage—and, more important, how do you avoid having to eat it? and, of course, How do you ride a pony that goes "oink"? Again, George S. Irving gives a good read to these folksy goings-on.

2 css 2½ hr Durkin Hayes Audio

Rubber Legs and White Tail-Hairs
Author: Patrick F. McManus
Reader: George S. Irving
★★★

McManus is back with another two-cassette collection, including the essays "Pigs," "Nude, with Other Wildlife," "Cry Wolf," "Claw of the Sea Puss," "Summer Reading," "Rubber Legs and White Tail-Hairs," "Throwing Stuff," "To Filet or Not Filet," and "The Cabin at Spooky Lake."

2 css 2½ hr Durkin Hayes Audio

Russell Baker's Book of American Humor
Author: Edited by Russell Baker
Reader: Tony Randall
★★★

A very funny writer himself, Baker recognizes the best of that quality in others. His *Book of American Humor* is a virtual hall of fame of American humor writers. This four-cassette selection brings together a range of humorists from classics like Ambrose Bierce to modern curmudgeons and cynics like Mike Royko and P. J. O'Rourke. In between, Baker serves up Art Buchwald, Fran Lebowitz, Erma Bombeck, Mark Twain, Abe Lincoln, Ring Lardner, O. Henry, Tom Wolfe, Nora Ephron, and others. For humor lovers, this is a gold mine. Tony Randall does a very good job with the classic material, but falls somewhat short when dealing with more modern items like Lebowitz or O'Rourke—however, this is far from a fatal flaw.

4 css 4 hr The Mind's Eye

A Southern Belle Primer or Why Princess Margaret Will Never Be a Kappa Kappa Gamma
Author: Maryln Schwartz
Performer: Dixie Carter
★

Think Southern Belledom is gone with the wind? Think again. It's alive and well below the Mason-Dixon line, costumes and all. Adapted from the *New York Times* best-selling guide to propriety, protocol, and survival in the gossamer world of the Southern Belle, this tape, featuring Dixie Carter of television's *Designing Women,* airs out hitherto unexplained mysteries of the Deep South. Discover "A Southern Belle's Ten Golden Rules," "The Twelve Patterns of the Southern Silver Zodiac," and much more. Dixie Carter's delivery is a delight.

1 css 1 hr Bantam Audio

Stories from the Herriot Collection
Author: James Herriot
Reader: Christopher Timothy
★★★

James Herriot's books about his career as a veterinary surgeon in the Yorkshire Dales are international best-sellers. In this collection of stories not previously recorded from the first four Herriot books, Christopher Timothy, who plays Herriot on the television series, gives a focused, entertaining read and makes this tape a pleasure to listen to.

2 css 2½ hr Listen for Pleasure

Super Sheep
Author/Reader: Ken Davis
★

Inspirational and amusing, Ken Davis's stand-up scripture focuses here on why sheep are not such great images when it comes to animals and the Bible.

Davis's powers as an author and communicator are muddied badly by the terrible quality of the sound. The tape was recorded live at a gathering in 1992, and much of the message is just plain lost in the poor reproduction.

1 css 1 hr Zondervan

Those Grand Occasions at the End of the Road
Author/Reader: Tom Bodett
★★★★

You never know what the people from the End of the Road will do when they get together for a special event. But one thing is for sure—whether it's Christmas in a new downtown park, New Year's Eve in a pea-soup fog, the Rod and Gun League's Easter Egg Stalk, or any of a number of other group high jinks in America's favorite hometown—it won't be boring. Tom Bodett is one of America's best-loved storytellers, and these unforgettable tales showcase his considerable abilities in marvelous style.

2 css 2 hr 10 min Bantam Audio

A Twisted Mind: A Comedy Concert
Author/Reader: Ken Davis
★

Davis's anecdotal approach often becomes so long winded and mundane that any underlying message is sunk far beneath the surface. A story about his panicked wife, pointing a 12-gauge shotgun at a tiny mouse, takes many minutes and leaves its message on perspective deep out of sight. If comedy is timing, Davis needs a better watch. As with Davis's other tapes, this one was recorded live, and this time, the recording quality is good.

1 css 1 hr Zondervan

When You Look Like Your Passport Photo, It's Time to Go Home
Author/Reader: Erma Bombeck
★★★★

Join Erma Bombeck as her husband sleeps peacefully through the gunfire of a tribal war somewhere in New Guinea. She would like to crawl to the bathroom for water, but there is no water. As people will in wartime, Erma demands a bedtime story—and her husband tells her the one about the housewife (Bombeck) who decided one day that she was no longer going to house-sit while her friends traveled, but that she herself would travel, see the world, really taste life. A purely Bombeckian journey.

2 css 3 hr Harper Audio

All I Really Need to Know I Learned from Watching Star Trek
A: Dave Marinaccio
R: Rick Adamson
RH

All the Trouble in the World
A: P. J. O'Rourke
RH

America . . . There's Still Hope!: A Revolutionary History with Bob Hope and The All-Star Patriots
R: Bob Hope, Jim Backus, Phyllis Diller, Arte Johnson, Judy Kaye, Gordon MacRae, Karl Malden, Dudley Moore, Demond Wilson, and others
PART

Ask Marilyn: The Best of "Ask Marilyn" Letters
A/R: Marilyn vos Savant
HARP

Babies and Other Hazards of Sex
A: Dave Barry
R: Arte Johnson
DOVE

The Bachelor Home Companion: A Practical Guide to Keeping House like a Pig
A: P. J. O'Rourke
R: Adam Arkin
RH

Bailey White: An Interesting Life (An NPR Presentation)
A/R: Bailey White
DOVE

Benchley's Best
A: Robert Benchley
R: Henry Morgan
PART

The Best of Benchley
A: Robert Benchley
R: Bob Elliot
HARP

The Best of News of the Weird
A: Chuck Sheperd, John J. Kohut, and Roland Sweet
R: Full cast
PENG

The Best of Russell Baker: The Rescue of Miss Yaskell and Other Pipe Dreams
A: Russell Baker
R: Arte Johnson
DOVE

The Best of the 776 Stupidest Things Ever Said
A: Ross and Kathryn Petras
R: Arte Johnson, Jayne Meadows, and Bruce Vilanch
DOVE

The Better Part of the End of the Road
A: Tom Bodett
R: Tom Bodett; music by Johnny B.
BDD

The Big Garage on Clear Shot
A: Tom Bodett
R: Tom Bodett; music by Johnny B.
BDD

Chili Dawgs Always Bark at Night
A: Lewis Grizzard
R: Dion Anderson
RH

Claw Your Way to the Top
A: Dave Barry
R: Arte Johnson
DOVE

Dave Barry's Audio Guide to Marriage and/or Sex
A: Dave Barry
R: Ed Begley, Jr.
ART

Do Penguins Have Knees? And Even More Imponderables
A/R: David Feldman
HARP

The Encyclopedia of Bad Jokes: Jokes and Humor to Offend Everyone
A: Robert Hollenbach
R: Jack Carter, Shirley McNight, Art Metrano, and Bruce Vilanch
DOVE

The End of the Road
A: Tom Bodett
R: Tom Bodett; music by Johnny B.
BDD

The End of the Road Audio Boxed Set
A: Tom Bodett
R: Tom Bodett; music by Johnny B.
BDD

An Evening with Garrison Keillor, Maya Angelou, Laurie Colwin and Tom Wolfe
R: Hosted by Calvin Trillin
DOVE

An Evening with George Burns
R: George Burns; introduction by Jack Benny
DOVE

Extraordinary Origins of Everyday Things
A/R: Charles Panati
HARP

Fathers
A: Compiled and edited by Jon Winokur
R: Full cast
PENG

Freda Payne Sings the (Unauthorized) I Hate Barney Songbook: A Parody
R: Freda Payne
DOVE

Funny People
A/R: Steve Allen
DOVE

Give War a Chance: Eyewitness Accounts of Mankind's Struggle against Tyranny, Injustice and Alcohol-Free Beer
A: P. J. O'Rourke
R: Willian Macy
RH

Guys Versus Men
A: Dave Barry
DOVE

Haunted Halloween—Spooky Sounds to Chill Your Bones
DOVE

High Spirits
A: Robertson Davies
R: Christopher Plummer
PART

Holidays in Hell
A: P. J. O'Rourke
RH

Hollywood Anecdotes
A: Paul F. Boller, Jr., and Ronald L. Davis
R: Debbie Reynolds
DOVE

How Does Aspirin Find a Headache?
A: David Feldman
R: David Feldman and full cast
HARP

How to Be Hap Hap Happy like Me
A/R: Merrill Markoe
PENG

How to Save the Earth with Laughter
A/R: Joey Adams
DOVE

How to Talk Minnesotan
A/R: Howard Mohr
PENG

I Haven't Understood Anything Since 1962
A/R: Lewis Grizzard
RH

I Know More than You Do!
A/R: Dr. Science (Dan Coffey)
PENG

I Took a Lickin' and Kept on Tickin'
A/R: Lewis Grizzard
RH

Ian Shoales' Perfect World
A/R: Merle Kessler
PENG

If I Ever Get Back to Georgia I'm Gonna Nail My Feet to the Ground
A: Lewis Grizzard
R: Dion Anderson
RH

If Life is a Bowl of Cherries, What Am I Doing in the Pits?
A/R: Erma Bombeck
HARP

If Love Were Oil, I'd Be About a Quart Low
A/R: Lewis Grizzard
RH

James Herriot's Cat Stories
A: James Herriot
R: Christopher Timothy
ART

The Jeopardy! Audio Book
A/R: Alex Trebek
HARP

The Jeopardy! Challenge: The Toughest Games from America's Greatest Quiz Show
A: Alex Trebek and Merv Griffin
R: Alex Trebek
HARP

Jewish as a Second Language
A: Molly Katz
R: Carol Leifer
DOVE

Jonathan Winters Answers Your Telephone
A/R: Jonathan Winters
DOVE

Jonathan Winters, Finally Captured
A/R: Jonathan Winters
DOVE

Jonathan Winters into the '90s
A/R: Jonathan Winters
DOVE

Jonathan Winters Is Terminator 3
A/R: Jonathan Winters
DOVE

Kid You Sing My Songs
A/R: Lois Wyse
MILLS

Lamb Chop's Nutcracker Suite
R: Shari Lewis and Lamb Chop
ART

Leslie Nielsen's Stupid Little Golf Book
A: Leslie Nielsen and Henry Beard
R: Leslie Nielsen
BDD

Life's Little Destruction Book
A: Charles Sherwood Dane
R: Bruce Vilanch
DOVE

Molly Ivins Can't Say That, Can She?
A/R: Molly Ivins
RH

My Daddy Was a Pistol and I'm a Son of a Gun
A/R: Lewis Grizzard
RH

My Gorgeous Life
A/R: Dame Edna Everage
DOVE

Naked Beneath My Clothes: Tales of a Revealing Nature
A/R: Rita Rudner
PENG

The New! Improved! Bob and Ray Book
A/R: Bob Elliott and Ray Goulding
PART

New Times in the Old South (Or Why Scarlett's in Therapy and Tara's Going Condo)
A: Maryln Schwartz
R: Blair Brown
RH

Not Exactly What I Had in Mind
A/R: Roy Blount, Jr.
PART

Not that You Asked
A/R: Andy Rooney
RH

Nothin' but Good Times Ahead
A/R: Molly Ivins
RH

Official Sexually Correct Dictionary
A/R: Christopher Cerf
DOVE

Once Upon a More Enlightened Time: More Politically Correct Bedtime Stories
A/R: James Finn Garner
S&S

Parliament of Whores: A Lone Humorist Attempts to Explain the U.S. Government
A: P. J. O'Rourke
R: William Macy
RH

The Politically Correct Dictionary and Handbook
A: Henry Beard and Christopher Cerf
R: Christopher Cerf
DOVE

The Portable Curmudgeon
A: Compiled by Jon Winokur
R: Full cast
PENG

P.S. I Love You
A: Compiled by H. Jackson Brown, Jr.
R: Sada Thompson
HARP

Russel Baker's Book of American Humor
R: Tony Randall
MIND

Small Comforts
A: Tom Bodett
R: Tom Bodett; music by Johnny B.
BDD

Steven Spielberg, Give Me Some of Your Money: Greatest Satirical Hits of Moe Moskowitz and the Punsters
R: Moe Moskowitz and the Punsters
DOVE

Stories from the Herriot Collection
A: James Herriot
R: Christopher Timothy
DURK

Sweet and Sour
A/R: Andy Rooney
DOVE

Thank You for Smoking
A: Christopher Buckley
R: John Glover
BDD

There's a Country in My Cellar
A: Russell Baker
DOVE

Wedding Nightmares
As Told to the Editors of *Bride's* Magazine
R: Full cast
PENG

When Did Wild Poodles Roam the Earth?
A: David Feldman
R: David Feldman and full cast
HARP

When Do Fish Sleep? And Other Imponderables
A: David Feldman
R: David Feldman and full cast
HARP

When My Love Returns from the Ladies Room, Will I Be Too Old to Care?
A: Lewis Grizzard
R: Peter Waldren
RH

Who Put the Butter in Butterfly?
A: David Feldman
R: David Feldman and full cast
HARP

Why Do Dogs Have Wet Noses? And Other Imponderables
A/R: David Feldman
HARP

Winters' Tales
A/R: Jonathan Winters
RH

Wisdom of the 90s
A: George Burns with Hal Goldman
R: George Burns and Harvey Korman
HARP

The World of James Thurber
A: James Thurber
R: Henry Morgan
PART

The World's Worst Jokes
R: Henny Youngman
DOVE

You Can't Put No Boogie-Woogie on the King of Rock and Roll
A/R: Lewis Grizzard
RH

You're Good Enough, You're Smart Enough, and Doggone It, People Like You!
A: Al Franken
R: Stuart Smalley
BDD

MYSTERY AND SUSPENSE

Mysteries are especially suited to audio. Just as in the golden age of radio, when families sat spellbound listening to programs like *The Shadow,* waiting for the creaking door to open, listening for footsteps on the stairs or the scream in the night, today's mystery lover has the opportunity to experience similar chills and also to discover much more sophisticated and varied fare.

Mysteries are well represented as a genre on audio . . . from classic Christie and durable Doyle to the new purveyors of suspense like Scott Turow, Elmore Leonard, and mystery *meisters* Tony Hillerman and Ruth Rendell.

There's something about following clues, the whole deductive process, that final revelation, that works better perhaps in books—and hence with a single reader or listener—than on a movie or TV screen. There's an intimacy, a privacy, to the puzzle . . . creations that, full of wonderful characters as they may be, always provide a solitary thrill as you say (with no modest pride) I figured that one out!

It's no accident then that there are so many highly recommended recordings in this category. They range from classic Sir Arthur Conan Doyle (with his Holmes mysteries performed by British acting greats Sir John Gielgud, Sir Ralph Richardson, and Tony Britton, among others) and Agatha Christie (her *Poirot Investigates* read by David Suchet), to American noirists like Jim Thompson (ably represented with *The Grifters* read by Tony Goldwyn), to contemporary hard-boiled suspensers (James Lee Burke's *Black Cherry Blues* read by Will Patton) and witty charmers (Lawrence Sanders's *McNally's Caper* and *McNally's Risk* read by Boyd Gaines.

I have heard few duds here and have reveled in the well-presented variety available. There is definitely something here for every mystery and suspense aficionado.

HIGHLY RECOMMENDED (★★★★)

Black Cherry Blues
Corporate Bodies
The Grifters
The Hound of the Baskervilles
In the Electric Mist with Confederate Dead
Kissing the Gunner's Daughter
McNally's Caper
McNally's Risk
The Old Contemptibles
The Perfect Murder
Poirot Investigates
Presumed Innocent
A Red Death
Sherlock Holmes

After Dark, My Sweet
Author: Jim Thompson
Reader: Joe Mantegna
★★

William Collins has broken out of his fourth mental institution. He meets up with a con man and a run-down beauty whose plans for him include kidnapping and murder. This should be right up Mantegna's alley, but the dark webs Thompson spins are a bit thrown away by the usually talented reader. He also has to contend with an intrusive music score.

2 css   3 hr   Random House AudioBooks

The Alienist
Author: Caleb Carr
Reader: Edward Herrmann
★★★

In 1896, a serial killer is on the loose in New York City. *Times* reporter John Moore and Dr. Laszlo Kreizler embark on a revolutionary attempt to identify the killer by assembling his psychological profile. Edward Herrmann gives a studied, very careful read that evokes the atmosphere and terrible goings-on in this best-selling psychological thriller.

4 css   4½ hr   Simon & Schuster Audio

The Anastasia Syndrome
Author: Mary Higgins Clark
Reader: Lynn Redgrave
★★★

In a search for her childhood, Judith Chase becomes involved in a daring psychological experiment and finds herself leading a terrifying double life. Lynn Redgrave beautifully captures the bizarre nature of Clark's unraveling mystery in a voice that is both compelling and sensitive.

2 css 3 hr Simon & Schuster Audio

The Angel Maker
Author: Ridley Pearson
Performer: John Glover
★★★

Seattle police psychologist Daphne Matthews encounters a grisly series of murders at a shelter for women in which human organs are being harvested for the black market. She turns for help to the best cop she knows, Lou Boldt, who also happens to be her ex-lover. John Glover turns in a sterling performance and is unusually expert with the female voices. Suspense abounds but so do some annoying breaths that hinder the listener's pleasure.

2 css 3 hr BDD Audio

Bad Love
Author: Jonathan Kellerman
Performer: John Rubenstein
★★

With the help of L.A.P.D. detective Milo Sturgis, Alex Delaware discovers that a seemingly random series of violent deaths may be related to a celebrated child psychologist. If Alex fails to decipher the twisted logic of the stalker's mind games, he will be the next to die. This story never reaches its potential due in part to a lackadaisical read by John Rubenstein.

2 css 3 hr BDD Audio

Black Cherry Blues
Author: James Lee Burke
Reader: Will Patton
★★★★

When ex–New Orleans cop Dave Robicheaux's old friend makes a surprise appearance, Dave finds himself thrust back into the violent world of Mafia goons and wily federal agents. Will Patton brings Cajun detective Robicheaux to life with his intense southern drawl. You really get the sense this man is running from the bottle, a homicide rap, and a killer, as well as demons from his own past.

2 css 3 hr Simon & Schuster Audio

Blindsight
Author: Robin Cook
Reader: Lindsay Crouse
★★

Forensic pathologist Dr. Laurie Engler searches to prove that the victims of unrelated Yuppie cocaine overdoses were never involved with drugs and finds a medical nightmare that involves the Mafia. This is an exciting story, but Lindsay Crouse is the wrong choice for this thriller. She has a soft, pleasant delivery that is particularly unsuited for this twisted tale of gruesomely described murders and aftermaths in the morgue.

2 css 3 hr Simon & Schuster Audio

The Blue Geranium and Other Stories
Author: Agatha Christie
Reader: Joan Hickson
★★★

Joan Hickson, TV's Miss Marple, is back to observing human nature in the sleepy village of St. Mary Mead. Using her soft voice that we recognize from TV, Joan Hickson has the ability behind the gentility to unravel even the most obscure mystery. Included here are "The Blue Geranium," "The Four Suspects," "The Companion," and "The Christmas Tragedy."

2 css 3 hr Listen for Pleasure

The Burden of Proof
Author: Scott Turow
Reader: Len Cariou
★★

While Sandy Stern—the defense lawyer from *Presumed Innocent* (see page 207)—hunts for answers to his wife's suicide, he is caught up in the threatened federal prosecution of his most powerful and troublesome client, his own brother-in-law. Len Cariou gives a serviceable read, but he is too slow too much of the time and the thriller starts to drag. Not nearly as good as the tape of *Presumed Innocent.*

2 css 3 hr Simon & Schuster Audio

Burn Marks
Author: Sara Paretsky
Performer: Kathy Bates
★

When ne'er-do-well Aunt Elena vanishes and one of her cohorts is found dead, V. I. Warshawski gets moving—straight into a wall of surly police and campaigning politicians. Kathy Bates gets some of Paretsky's exaggerated characters down, but she reads like a speeding train anxious to be up and out of the studio.

2 css 3 hr Bantam Audio

"C" Is for Corpse
Author: Sue Grafton
Reader: Judy Kaye
★★★

After surviving a near-fatal car accident, Bobby Callahan asks Kinsey to help him find clues about his past and catch the stalker responsible for his fate. But three days later Bobby is dead and Kinsey must capture a killer. This is one of a series of well-done Grafton alphabet mysteries. The light plots and writing style are well matched by Judy Kaye's breezy yet focused performance.

2 css 3 hr Random House AudioBooks

The Case of the Curious Bride
A Perry Mason Mystery
Author: Erle Stanley Gardner
Reader: William Hootkins
★

He'd charm women into marriage, then disappear with everything they had. But Gregory Moxley's been found dead in his apartment and the only clue left for Perry Mason is a set of keys dropped at the scene. This is a typical Perry Mason mystery . . . simple and somehow solvable and better left on TV. Actor Hootkins brings little intensity to the proceedings.

2 css 3 hr Durkin Hayes Audio

Clockers
Author: Richard Price
Reader: Joe Mantegna
★★★

When Victor Dunham, who's never been in trouble, confesses to a drug killing, Detective Rocco Klein becomes convinced that he is innocent and that his half brother Strike is the real killer. Price is a cult writer of some status and Mantegna scores with all the evil nuances of the complex characters.

2 css 3 hr Random House AudioBooks

Corporate Bodies
Author: Simon Brett
Reader: Simon Jones
★★★★

Often out-of-work actor Charles Paris has a star gig as a forklift driver in a corporate video. But jealousy and lust are pervasive at this company and soon Charles discovers a forklift can be a potent murder weapon. This is a hilarious romp through the corporate echelons of suburban Britain with wonderfully drawn characterizations in every statum of the corporate structure. Simon Jones has a field day with this material, wringing pathos and laughter out of every preposterous yet real clash of personalities. Good twists and turns of plot that will keep you guessing.

2 css 2½ hr Durkin Hayes Audio

Decked
A Regan Reilly Mystery
Author: Carol Higgins Clark
Reader: Mary Higgins Clark
Bomb

Ten years after disappearing from college, Athena Poplous's body is found in an excavation. Private investigator Regan Reilly is determined to track down her friend's killer. Mary Higgins Clark reading her daughter's book may have been a promoter's dream, but it's a listener's nightmare, as Clark has absolutely no sense of natural pacing or any ability to portray characters . . . what few there are in daughter Clark's humdrum conundrum.

2 css 3 hr Dove Audio

The Devil Knows You're Dead
Author: Lawrence Block
Performer: Stephen Lang
★★★

Glenn Holtzmann and his wife were affluent Manhattanites, sitting on the top of the world until Glenn was found dead on the pavement at an Eleventh Avenue pay phone. Ugly secrets set Matthew Scudder searching the twisted alleys of Hell's Kitchen to catch the killer. Stephen Lang is skilled at navigating the listener through a rogues' gallery of hard-boiled characters that writer Block can create so believably. Not for the sensitive or weak of heart, as we journey to some pretty dark regions.

2 css 3 hr Harper Audio

Devil's Waltz
Author: Jonathan Kellerman
Performer: John Rubenstein
★★

Someone is deliberately attempting to make Cassie Jones ill, and heading up the list of suspects are her own parents. But Dr. Alex Delware at Western Pediatric Medical Center begins to realize that something very disturbing is going on in the hospital itself and it's not long before a staff physician is brutally murdered. Rubenstein does his best to keep things clear in this complicated, overwrought tale that probably would have benefited from including more of the book. The use of music is curious . . . it just drops off after trying to establish mood.

2 css 3 hr BDD Audio

Divine Inspiration
Author: Jane Langton
Reader: Perry King
★★

As a new organ is being installed at the First Church of the Commonwealth, a lost baby boy toddles up the steps. Master organist Alan Starr teams with Homer

Kelly to find the child's mother and learns someone is willing to kill for the job of organist at First Church. Perry King is generally effective in presenting this rather low-key mystery. Production values and sound quality are very good.

2 css 3 hr Penguin HighBridge Audio

Double Indemnity
Author: James M. Cain
Performer: Barry Bostwick
★★

Two lovers plot to commit the perfect murder and cash in on an insurance policy that pays double indemnity. Barry Bostwick has some effective moments as sexy, obsessed Walter Neff, but this is a case where an actress playing Phyllis would have raised the intensity of the lovers' passion. Musical underscoring is exciting, especially in the famous train sequence. But it's hard to forget the classic Wilder movie.

2 css 3 hr Caedmon Audio

The End of the Pier
Author: Martha Grimes
Reader: Anne Meara
★★

Sam DeGheyn, the sheriff of a sleepy American town, turns his attentions to a waitress at the Rainbow Cafe as well as to the murders of three local women. His suspicion is that the wrong man has been convicted and the right man may kill again. Anne Meara doesn't do much with the special lyricism that haunts Grimes's writing. In fact, sometimes her very distinctive voice has a distancing effect from the naturalness of the narrative.

2 css 3 hr Random House AudioBooks

The Fallen Curtain
Author: Ruth Rendell
Reader: Simon Jones
★★

Includes "The Fallen Curtain," "A Bad Heart," "People Don't Do Such Things," "You Can't be Too Careful," and "Almost Human." In these stories of psychological suspense by the master of the genre, the disturbances of the human mind are portrayed with conviction and a sense of irony. Simon Jones can't quite deliver the chills inherent in Rendell's writing. He sounds too chipper, especially in the story "The Fallen Curtain," a tale of a man who was molested as a child destined to repeat history by molesting a young boy.

2 css 3 hr Listen for Pleasure

Fatal Cure
Author: Robin Cook
Reader: Barry Bostwick
★★

Drs. David and Angela Wilson's dream of bliss in a state-of-the-art medical facility in Bartlet, Vermont, becomes a nightmare when they discover a number of people in Bartlet have died under suspicious circumstances. Barry Bostwick is a bit rushed and therefore a lot of the horror is undermined. Not one of Cook's best, anyway.

4 css 6 hr Audio Renaissance Tapes

Female Sleuths
Author: Various
Performers: Various
★

A collection of eight unabridged stories by eight female mystery writers: "Settled Score" by Sarah Paretsky, "Full Circle" by Sue Grafton, "Getting to Know You" by Antonia Frazer, "Death and Diamonds" by Susan Dunlap, "Lucky Dip" by Liza Cody, "Ghost Station" by Carolyn Wheat, "Her Good Name" by Carolyn Hart, and "The Scar" by Nancy Pickard. Performed by various artists, these recordings range from nice attempts to dismal failures. For the most part, the characterizations are amateurish and overdone. Unfortunately, this is one of those cases where you can actually hear the actors acting.

4 css 6 hr The Mind's Eye

The First Deadly Sin
Author: Lawrence Sanders
Reader: John Lithgow
★★★

Daniel Blank is introduced to a mysterious seductress who incites him to the heights of ecstasy and the depths of evil, including the thrill of ruthless murder. Captain Edward X. Delaney, a veteran cop with an unfailing nose and eye for truth, vows to track down the killer. John Lithgow manages to tie all the loose ends together. Production values are good, with some carefully placed, if unnecessary, sound effects.

2 css 2 hr Random House AudioBooks

For the Sake of Elena
Author: Elizabeth George
Performer: Derek Jacobi
★★

When a young student is found brutally murdered on an isolated jogging path, the university calls in New Scotland Yard, and Lynley and his partner Hayes enter the world of Cambridge University to solve the mystery. Derek Jacobi is a seasoned reader of audio books, but he seems a bit too seasoned here, reading by rote and not from the heart.

2 css 3 hr Bantam Audio

Gaudy Night
Author: Dorothy L. Sayers
Reader: Edward Petherbridge
★

Obscene graffiti and poison-pen letters greet Harriet Vane on her return to Oxford. She turns to Lord Peter Wimsey for help, who pursues not only the criminal but also the girl. There is nothing much to recommend Petherbridge's succinct reading, and certainly this lengthy Sayers classic deserves more time to leisurely unfold than is afforded in this heavily abridged version.

2 css 3 hr Durkin Hayes Audio

Get Shorty
Author: Elmore Leonard
Performer: Joe Mantegna
★★

Miami loan shark Chili Palmer finds himself forming a partnership with horror-film producer Harry Zimm. All Chili has to do to reap the rewards is to stay one step ahead of a trigger-happy investor. Mantegna lends his usual macho talents to the proceedings at hand, but few sparks fly when all's told.

2 css 3 hr Bantam Audio

The Grifters
Author: Jim Thompson
Reader: Tony Goldwyn
★★★★

Jim Thompson's story of corruption and perverse love was made into a motion picture that has already gained cult status. Tony Goldwyn is another winner in the stable of audio performers and Thompson's down and dirty situations are a springboard that lets the talented Goldwyn dive into the fray with a no-holds-barred attitude in creating disturbed characters.

2 css 3 hr Random House AudioBooks

Happy Are the Peace Makers
Author: Andrew M. Greeley
Reader: Tom Bosley
★★

Nora McDonaugh's two previous husbands died under mysterious circumstances. Her latest, an Irish millionaire, changed his will in her favor a week before the bomb went off in his study. There are no surprises and no subtlety in Tom Bosley's characterization of Bishop Blackie Ryan, the only man who can resist the widow's charms and solve the crime.

2 css 3 hr Durkin Hayes Audio

Heat
Author: Stuart Woods
Reader: Tony Roberts
★★★

To earn his freedom from prison, Jesse Warden must infiltrate a dangerous religious cult in the mountains of the Idaho panhandle that makes prison seem like a romp in the woods. Tony Roberts breezes through the "heat" and comes out with a cool, unsentimental delivery that propels the suspense.

2 css 3 hr Harper Audio

Herb of Death and Other Stories
Author: Agatha Christie
Reader: Joan Hickson
★★★

Includes "Herb of Death," "The Thumbmark of St. Peter," "The Affair of the Bungalow," and "Death by Drowning." Here are stories told by TV's Miss Marple and her friends. Joan Hickson reads in her trademark frail yet controlled voice, which easily conjures up the elderly white-haired detective with the faded blue eyes and quiet nature.

2 css 2 hr 5 min Durkin Hayes Audio

The Holy Thief
A Mediaeval Whodunnit
Author: Ellis Peters
Reader: Paul Scofield
★★

In the spring of 1145, a precious reliquary is stolen from the Benedictine abbey at Shrewsbury. Brother Cadfael turns his mind to the problem—but before the answer is found, a young man is brutally murdered. Paul Scofield gives a curiously ponderous reading in a story that cries out for vigor and a keen sense of satire.

2 css 3 hr Durkin Hayes Audio

The Hound of the Baskervilles
Author: Sir Arthur Conan Doyle
Reader: Tony Britton
★★★★

After the death of Sir Charles Baskerville, what will happen to his heir, Sir Henry Baskerville, is a question that Sherlock Holmes and Watson must answer. Tony Britton transports us directly to the fog-shrouded moors and keeps our ears entranced through the whole tape. He is a consummate Holmes, a delightful Watson, and a sensitive narrator who evokes the spirit of this classic mystery.

2 css 3 hr Durkin Hayes Audio

In the Electric Mist with Confederate Dead
Author: James Lee Burke
Reader: Will Patton
★★★★

While confronting the gruesome present-day rape and murder of young prostitutes, detective Dave Robicheaux must also contend with a new partner from the FBI, and the local criminal gentry. This is another in the Robicheaux arsenal that is strongly interpreted by actor Will Patton. A native of South Carolina, Patton negotiates the southern landscape with complete believability and nails Burke's characters with equal ease, all the time propelling the narrative forward with a calm forcefulness.

2 css 3 hr Simon & Schuster Audio

The Jewel That Was Ours
An Inspector Morse Mystery
Author: Colin Dexter
Reader: Edward Woodward
★

An American tourist, Mrs. Laura Straton, is found dead at the Randolph Hotel less than a day after arriving in England. With only a naked, battered corpse and a jewel-encrusted antique as clues, Inspector Morse has a problem on his hands. In a relentlessly cheery voice that soon begins to grate, Edward Woodward keeps the proceedings all on one note. A lunatic-sounding harpsichord accompaniment tries to set a mood that doesn't need setting.

2 css 3 hr Durkin Hayes Audio

Kissing the Gunner's Daughter
Author: Ruth Rendell
Reader: Christopher Ravenscroft
★★★★

When three people are discovered shot at Trancred House and Sergeant Cleb Martin loses his life in a bank robbery, Chief Inspector Wexford comes to believe there is a connection between the crimes. From England's queen of crime comes an atypical bloodbath, but it is replete with all of the deft characterizations one expects from Rendell. This is very well read in nicely modulated tones by Christopher Ravenscroft, who played Wexford's conversative partner Mike Burden on BBC's *Ruth Rendell Mysteries.*

2 css 3 hr Durkin Hayes Audio

The Labors of Hercules
Volume II The Cretan Bull
Author: Agatha Christie
Reader: Daniel Massey
★★

In volume two of a three-part series, Hercule Poirot battles more modern monsters who prey on the human flesh, spirit, and mind. Daniel Massey reads adequately, but there is the sense that some of the fun and joie de vivre of Hercule himself has gone missing.

2 css 3 hr Durkin Hayes Audio

Lost and Found
Author/Reader: Jim Lehrer
★★

Speaker of the Oklahoma House of Representatives Luther Wallace disappears without a trace and his friend One-Eyed Mack sets out to find the lost Speaker. For an author reading his own work, Lehrer comes out alive, if not with shining marks. You can sense his pleasure with his own material, and the twinkling rural accents lend an air of authenticity, but some of his genuinely funny moments would have been better served by a comedic actor.

2 css 3 hr Durkin Hayes Audio

McNally's Caper
Author: Lawrence Sanders
Reader: Boyd Gaines
★★★★

When millionaire Griswald Forsythe II hires Archy McNally to find who's been pilfering high-priced objects from his estate, and Forsythe's sultry daughter-in-law is almost strangled to death, Archy knows there is more at stake than a few family heirlooms. Boyd Gaines has an easy delivery most suitable to Sanders's swank mysteries, and is the best interpreter of Sanders's audio oeuvre, which is well presented in general by actors such as Mark Linn-Baker, Nathan Lane, Victor Garber, and Jerry Orbach. A great romp.

2 css 3 hr Simon & Schuster Audio

McNally's Luck
Author: Lawrence Sanders
Reader: by Mark Linn-Baker
★★

Hired to locate a stolen cat, McNally is suddenly ignited by a tycoon's alluring wife and her stunning sister, a side trip into the occult, and a series of events that leads to murder. This is, as you might guess, a lot of fun, though Mark Linn-Baker's luck runs out on this one. He just doesn't get to the heart of the Palm Beach charm or the sophisticated suspense.

2 css 3 hr Simon & Schuster Audio

McNally's Risk
Author: Lawrence Sanders
Reader: Boyd Gaines
★★★★

When McNally starts to place together the puzzle surrounding a drop-dead gorgeous stranger in Palm Beach, bodies begin to appear. This is another Boyd Gaines triumph in which he brings to the fore all the blithe-spirited mysterious doings in fashionable Palm Beach while unraveling the mystery in clear ringing tones.

2 css 3 hr Simon & Schuster Audio

McNally's Secret
Author: Lawrence Sanders
Reader: Nathan Lane
★★

Archy McNally is called to retrieve a set of rare stamps from one of Palm Beach's wealthiest and most curvaceous matrons, but gets much more as he faces two murders and an all-too-real romance. The wonderful comedian Nathan Lane hits all the funny spots but delivers few chills and doesn't seem a very well rounded McNally.

2 css 3 hr Simon & Schuster Audio

Means of Evil
Author: Ruth Rendell
Reader: George Baker
★★

Here are two short stories featuring Rendell's popular Chief Inspector Wexford and his conservative Watsonesque partner Mike Burden. The first, "Means of Evil," concerns a poisoning by edible fungi and the second, "Ginger and the Kingsmarkham Chalk Circle," concerns the disappearance of a red-haired baby snatched from his carriage. (The color of his hair is, naturally, a clue). George Baker, the Wexford from the British TV series, gives a colorful reading, if a bit hurried.

2 css 2½ hr Listen for Pleasure

Miami, It's Murder
Author: Edna Buchanan
Performer: Kate Mulgrew
★

Crime reporter Britt Montero takes us through the dark side of the city as she investigates a series of bizarre deaths involving terminal sex, electrocution, and freshly poured concrete. Kate Mulgrew whines and frets and overacts as Britt Montero (presumably Buchanan's alter ego), sounding more like a streetwise waitress than a crime reporter.

2 css 3 hr Harper Audio

A Morbid Taste for Bones
A Mediaeval Whodunnit
Author: Ellis Peters
Reader: Glyn Houston
★★★

Brother Cadfael has settled down to a quiet life at the Benedictine Monastery of Shrewsbury. But when his prior determines to acquire the bones of a saint,

Cadfael's worldly experience becomes important, especially since murder is involved. Glyn Houston's cultured delivery is suitable for the intellectual, satiric flavor of Peters's writing.

2 css 3 hr Listen for Pleasure

Murder on the Potomac
A Capitol Crimes Mystery
Author: Margaret Truman
Reader: Dana Ivey
★

When a weed-covered body is discovered on the banks of the Potomac, ex-lawyer Mac Smith is called in on the case and drawn into several overlapping circles, which include a theatrical group that reenacts murders from Washington's history, sometimes at the risk of murdering one another. Dana Ivey overkills all the character parts with stereotypical accents and can't quite find the key to make a mountain out of this molehill. Canned music intrudes now and again.

2 css 3 hr Random House AudioBooks

Night Prey
Author: John Sanford
Reader: Jay O. Sanders
★★

A torn body turns up in the snow at a game reserve, another in a Dumpster. Still recovering from near-fatal wounds and trying to settle down with one woman, Deputy Police Chief Lucas Davenport finds this political hot potato of a case is the last thing he needs. Jay O. Sanders is appealing, yet he is a slow reader given to long pauses, just what this thriller doesn't need.

2 css 3 hr Simon & Schuster Audio

The Old Contemptibles
Author: Martha Grimes
Reader: Tim Curry
★★★★

While detained in London under suspicion in the death of his fiancée, Richard Jury sends his old friend Melrose Plant to find some answers. Plant discovers a family history of too many fatal accidents. He and Jury seek to uncover the link between these unsolved mysteries and today's tragedy. Tim Curry is a rare treat to hear, his voice full of charm and deep, mellifluous tones, using an upper-crust British accent to convey the flavor of Grimes's sophisticated whodunnit.

2 css 3 hr Simon & Schuster Audio

The Perfect Murder
Authors: Jack Hitt, Lawrence Block, Sarah Caudwell, Tony Hillerman, Peter Lovesey, and Donald E. Westlake
Readers: Michael Patrick McGrath, Lynn Redgrave, John Randolph Jones, George S. Irving, and Josef Sommer
Narrator: Victor Garber
★★★★

In *The Perfect Murder,* five masters of suspense provide editor Jack Hitt with their blueprints for the ideal crime. All built on the diabolical premises that Hitt sets forth, their scenarios—from exotic jellyfish to a mass murder—are as diverse and representative as their talents. This is a true delight, with the mystery writers critiquing one another's nefarious murder methods. The actors enter into the spirit of the fun with a relish that is lacking in all too many audio books. There is no standout performance here, with all of their interpretations on the mark, blending into a fine piece of ensemble acting. I must note that John Randolph Jones is a dead ringer for the voice of the Southwest's Tony Hillerman.

2 css 3 hr Durkin Hayes Audio

Poirot Investigates
Author: Agatha Christie
Reader: David Suchet
★★★★

Here Poirot pits his agile mind against murderers, impostors, espionage, and even the curse of Men-her-Ra. What a delight to hear the superb David Suchet (TV's *Poirot*) weave his magic spell through these stories. He *is* Poirot . . . and a terrific narrator, too, who never lets the interest flag.

2 css 3 hr Listen for Pleasure

Presumed Innocent
Author: Scott Turow
Reader: John Heard
★★★★

Chief deputy prosecuting attorney Rusty Sabich is handling the investigation of the brutal murder of fellow prosecuting attorney, Carolyn Polhemus. A political enemy's private investigation reveals Rusty's illicit affair with Carolyn, and charges Rusty with murder. John Heard gives a powerhouse performance that keeps you riveted from the first sentence to the last. The tape is as effective as the movie or the book.

2 css 3 hr Simon & Schuster Audio

Proof
Author: Dick Francis
Reader: Charles Dance
★★★

Tony Beach, wine merchant, knows his scotch. So when he is asked to give his opinion on one particular bottle it seems harmless enough. But the bottle contains firewater of a highly explosive nature, and Tony finds himself on a one-way route to danger. Even before I listened to this tape, I guessed that Francis and Dance would make a good match. With *Proof* I was proved correct. A jolly romp.

2 css 2½ hr Durkin Hayes Audio

A Red Death
An Easy Rawlins Mystery
Author: Walter Mosley
Reader: Paul Winfield
★★★★

To keep a corrupt IRS agent off his back, Easy Rawlins cuts a deal to spy on a World War II resistance fighter suspected of stealing top secret government plans, but when killings begin Easy finds himself the prime suspect. Paul Winfield is perfectly wonderful as Easy Rawlins, and adept at creating diverse characters whose dialogue with one another is so natural that a real mood and sense of setting is created along with believable interactions.

2 css 3 hr Audio Renaissance Tapes

Remember Me
Author: Mary Higgins Clark
Reader: Megan Gallagher
★★

Adam Nichols moves his family to Cape Cod for a late-summer respite, and as mysterious incidents amass, his wife Menly must confront the past and her fear for her daughter's life. Megan Gallagher gives an appropriate mellow read, but the story itself doesn't give you much to remember.

2 css 3 hr Simon & Schuster Audio

Rumpole for the Prosecution
Author: John Mortimer
Reader: Leo McKern
★★★

Leo McKern played Rumpole in the celebrated British TV series and here he delights his fans with his same quirky yet sharp personality. This is one of a series of Rumpole tapes read by McKern, short on production values but long on entertainment thanks to McKern's wit.

2 css 3 hr Durkin Hayes Audio

Sherlock Holmes
Author: Sir Arthur Conan Doyle
Performers: Sir John Gielgud, Sir Ralph Richardson, Orson Welles, and others
★★★★

The twelve multi-cast dramatizations that comprise this set are "The Blue Carbuncle," "The Yoxley Case," "The Norwood Builder," "The Solitary Bicyclist," "The Final Problem, "A Case of Identity," "The Blackmailer," "A Scandal in Bohemia," "Six Napoleons," "Rare Disease," "The Speckled Band," and "The Mystery of the Second Stain." If you are a fan of Sherlock Holmes and Watson, you'll definitely want this collection in your audio library. Sir John Gielgud plays supersleuth Sherlock Holmes beautifully—his characterization sounds just the way I would want Holmes to sound and he does a fine job of conveying Holmes's cleverness and wit. Sir Ralph Richardson's Watson is very appealing. Orson Welles as Professor Moriarty is the perfect choice to play Holmes's archenemy. The only drawback with this series is that some of the sound effects are a bit amateurish. For example, a storm that sounds like someone is actually emptying a bucket of water. But the acting here, with fine supporting casts, rises above this.

6 css 9 hr The Mind's Eye

Short List
Author/Reader: Jim Lehrer
★★

When the governor of Oklahoma is felled by a stroke, lieutenant governor One-Eyed Mack stumbles to the rescue and delivers a keynote address to the Democratic National Convention and receives instant stardom and candidacy for vice president of the United States. The hypocrisy of the powerful in our political system is displayed more as gentle foibles in Lehrer's tolerant world, but that's okay. There are many telling moments in this odyssey and Lehrer, if not the most dynamic reader, keeps it lively.

2 css 2½ hr Durkin Hayes Audio

The Silence of the Lambs
Author: Thomas Harris
Reader: Kathy Bates
Bomb

This story takes you from the tormenting words of homicidal maniac Dr. Hannibal Lecter and the flesh-rending depravity of an elusive killer to the courage of a young FBI novice who risks her life to track the killer down. The book and movie were great, but we'd like to have silenced reader Bates, who literally races (without feeling) through this important story, leaving the listener without a clue as to the power and horror of the piece.

2 css 3 hr Simon & Schuster Audio

Snagged
Author/Reader: Carol Higgins Clark
Bomb

When an executive is found murdered, a pair of fishnet stockings wrapped around his neck (do you believe it?) at a panty hose convention at the Palm Hotel in Naples, Florida, Regan Reilly finds herself searching out the killer. Maybe this is the ultimate party tape (the equivalent of such midnight movies as *Beyond the Valley of the Dolls* and *Plan 9 from Outer Space*), as Clark, in a nasal banter, recounts one wildly improbable incident after another with a seriousness that is sorely misplaced. The tasteless bedazzled cover adds to the kitsch.

2 css 3 hr Dove Audio

Strong Poison
Author: Dorothy L. Sayers
Reader: Edward Petherbridge
★

Detective-story writer Harriet Vane is on trial for the murder of her former lover. Lord Wimsey, who has fallen madly in love with her, hopes to prove she is innocent. Again, as in *Gaudy Night* (see page 201), Petherbridge fails to deliver Sayers's wit, and to cut such a large book to this time length is a crime in itself.

2 css 3 hr Durkin Hayes Audio

Talking God
Author/Reader: Tony Hillerman
★

Set in the Southwest, two seemingly unrelated cases reunite Lieutenant Joe Leaphorn and Office Jim Chee. One is about grave robbing to protest a museum's policy of not returning ancestral remains to Native Americans; the other concerns a murder victim whose body has been stripped of identification. Of course the two are related in a rather obvious way. It is of some value to hear Hillerman's voice, to get that sense of connectedness between the author and his work, but an actor he is not and three hours is a long time to be without a good dramatic interpreter.

2 css 3 hr Caedmon Audio

Ten Little Indians
Author: Agatha Christie
Reader: Norman Barrs
★★★

Ten house guests, trapped on an isolated island, are the prey of a killer. When they realize that every one of them is marked for murder, terror mounts as their number dwindles. It is nice indeed to have this unabridged edition of Christie's greatest work, and Norman Barrs gives an erudite performance full of suspense and descriptive characterizations.

4 css 6 hr Audio Editions

There Was a Little Girl
Author: Ed McBain
Reader: Stacy Keach
★★★

Hired to close a real estate deal for a small circus, Matthew Hope finds himself surrounded by circus freaks who share a society of amazing feats, kinky sex, and dark secrets. While Hope lies in a coma, his friends scramble for clues. Stacey

Keach is good at delivering the nitty-gritty and has a voice that is kind to the ear. Sound effects are imaginative and well integrated.

2 css 3 hr Time Warner AudioBooks

The Thin Man
Author: Dashiell Hammett
Performers: Lynne Lipton and Daniel J. Travanti
★★

In *The Thin Man,* petty gangsters, an eccentric inventor, his oddball family, and his beautiful mistress all have enough secrets to keep Nick and Nora Charles from unraveling the clues to a brutal murder. Both Travanti as Nick (and the narrator) and Lipton as Nora have fun with their witty repartees and there are some cute sound effects such as Asta barking with fervor, but the substance is uneven, both in the abridgment and in the reading itself.

2 css 2 hr 45 min Caedmon Audio

Tunnel Vision
Author: Sara Paretsky
Performer: Pamela Hensley Vincent
★★★

In her attempt to help a homeless family, V. I. Warshawski comes in contact with a homeless advocates' group. When one of their board members is found murdered, V. I. uncovers a trail of abuse and fraud. Vincent is a more effective Warshawski than Kathy Bates in *Burn Marks* (see page 196). She's spunky, funky, and hard-boiled enough to be credible in numerous dangerous situations.

4 css 6 hr Dove Audio

Valley of Fear
Author: Sir Arthur Conan Doyle
Reader: Christopher Lee
★★

A rich American is murdered in a manor house in Sussex, England, and Sherlock Holmes, accompanied by Dr. Watson, is invited to help the investigation. Oddly enough, Christopher Lee disappoints, seeming distanced from Doyle's clever and rarefied world.

2 css 3 hr Listen for Pleasure

Walking Shadow
Author: Robert P. Parker
Performer: Daniel Parker
★★

When an actor is gunned down during a performance of a politically controversial play, private investigator Spencer, and his cohort Hawk, plunge into a maze of motives that constitutes a master class in the difficulty of judging reality from appearances. Daniel Parker performs his father's work in a strangely somber, quiet voice that is more often than not at odds with the high anxiety described by the elder Parker.

4 css 6 hr Dove Audio

When Death Comes Stealing
A Tamara Hayle Mystery
Author: Valerie Wilson Wesley
Reader: Angela Bassett
★★★

Former cop Tamara Hayle must find out who's killing her ex-husband's sons before death comes stealing her only child. This is given a bold, effective rendition by actress Bassett. Be sure to catch the opening theme song, "When Death Comes Stealing," that begins the recording.

2 css 3 hr Time Warner AudioBooks

Winter Prey
Author: John Sanford
Performer: Ken Howard
★★★

Lucas Davenport, the hard-bitten detective from the Twin Cities, is up against his most determined foe—a serial killer driven to cover his brutal tracks with blood. Ken Howard builds the suspense nicely and makes you feel the cold and driving snow of the north country as he pursues the Iceman, hoping to stop his razor-sharp corn knife from striking again.

2 css 3 hr Harper Audio

The Witness for the Prosecution and Other Stories
Author: Agatha Christie
Reader: Sir Anthony Quayle
★★

Quayle reads Christie's most famous and popular short story as well as "Where There's a Will," "The Second Gong," and "SOS." He brings the tragic fate of Leonard Vole to life and seems thoroughly at ease with Christie's machinations. But there has been such an improvement in recording standards since this production that is hard not to fault Quayle's constant lip smacks and sniffs. Let's edit out all this noise and brighten the listening experience on rerelease.

2 css 3 hr Listen for Pleasure

"A" is for Alibi
A: Sue Grafton
R: Judy Kaye
RH

An Absence of Light
A: David Lindsey
BRILL

Against the Wind
A: J. E. Freedman
R: Joe Mantegna
PENG

Agatha Christie Mysteries
A: Agatha Christie
R: Tim Pigott-Smith
DURK

All Our Yesterdays
A: Robert B. Parker
BDD

All that Remains
A: Patricia D. Cornwell
R: Kate Burton
HARP

Along Came a Spider
A: James Patterson
R: Keith David
HARP

Anna's Book
A: Ruth Rendell writing as Barbara Vine
R: Wanda McCaddon
PART

The Anodyne Necklace
A: Martha Grimes
R: Tim Curry
S&S

"B" Is for Burglar
A: Sue Grafton
R: Judy Kaye
RH

Baby, Would I Lie
A: Donald E. Westlake
BRILL

Beastly Tales
A: Mystery Writers of America Anthology; edited by Gregory McDonald
R: Adrienne Barbeau, David Birney, Joseph Campanella, and Arte Johnson
DOVE

The Big Kill
A: Mickey Spillane
R: Stacy Keach
S&S

The Big Sleep
A: Raymond Chandler
R: Elliott Gould
DOVE

Bitter Medicine
A: Sara Paretsky
R: Christine Lahti
BDD

Black Betty
A: Walter Mosley
R: Paul Winfield
ART

Black for Remembrance
A: Carlene Thompson
R: Adrienne Barbeau
DOVE

Black Money
A: Michael Thomas
R: Theodore Bikel
ART

The Blessing Way
A/R: Tony Hillerman
HARP

Blood Shot
A: Sara Paretsky
R: Kathy Bates
BDD

Blood Test
A: Jonathan Kellerman
R: John Rubinstein
BDD

The Body in the Closet
A: Mary Higgins Clark
R: Carol Higgins Clark
DOVE

Body of Evidence
A: Patricia D. Cornwell
R: Lindsay Crouse
HARP

The Burglar Who Traded Ted Williams
A: Lawrence Block
R: Joe Mantegna
PENG

Burglars Can't Be Choosers: A Bernie Rhodenbarr Mystery
AR: Lawrence Block
PENG

The Butcher's Theater
A: Jonathan Kellerman
R: Ben Kingsley
BDD

By the Dawn's Early Light and Other Stories
A: Lawrence Block
DURK

The Case of the Beautiful Beggar
A: Erle Stanley Gardner
R: Perry King
DOVE

The Case of the Late Pig
A: Margery Allingham
R: Peter Davison
DURK

Cat Chaser
A: Elmore Leonard
R: Ken Howard
DURK

The Cat Who Came to Breakfast
A: Lillian Jackson Braun
R: Dick Van Patten
DOVE

The Cat Who Knew a Cardinal
A: Lillian Jackson Braun
R: Theodore Bikel
DOVE

The Cat Who Moved a Mountain
A: Lillian Jackson Braun
R: Theodore Bikel
DOVE

The Cat Who Wasn't There
A: Lillian Jackson Braun
R: Theodore Bikel
DOVE

The Cat Who Went into the Closet
A: Lillian Jackson Braun
R: Dick Van Patten
DOVE

The Cereal Murders
A: Diane Mott Davidson
MILLS

The Chamber
A: John Grisham
BDD

Cinderella
A: Ed McBain
R: Ken Howard
DOVE

Clouds of Witness
A: Dorothy L. Sayers
R: Edward Petherbridge
DURK

Comeback
A: Dick Francis
R: Simon Jones
HARP

Coyote Waits
A/R: Tony Hillerman
HARP

The Crackler
A: Agatha Christie
R: James Warwick
DURK

The Cradle Will Fall and Other Stories
A: Mary Higgins Clark
R: Carol Higgins Clark
DOVE

Crime's Leading ladies
A: Various
R: Sharon Gless
DURK

Criminal Conversation
A: Evan Hunter
BRILL

Crimson Joy
A: Robert B. Parker
R: Philip Bosco
S&S

The Crocodile Bird
A: Ruth Rendell
R: Lisanne Cole
ART

Cruel and Unusual
A: Patricia D. Cornwell
R: Kate Burton
HARP

A Cry in the Night
A: Mary Higgins Clark
R: Carol Higgins Clark
DOVE

The Curious Facts Preceding My Execution and Other Fictions
A: Donald E. Westlake
R: Arte Johnson
DOVE

"D" Is for Deadbeat
A: Sue Grafton
R: Judy Kaye
RH

A Dance at the Slaughterhouse
A: Lawrence Block
R: Stephen Lang
HARP

Dance Hall of the Dead
A: Tony Hillerman
R: Michael Ansara
PART

The Danger
A: Dick Francis
R: Tim Pigott-Smith
DURK

The Dark Wind
A: Tony Hillerman
R: Gil Silverbird
HARP

A Dark-Adapted Eye
A: Ruth Rendell (writing as Barbara Vine)
R: Sophie Ward
PART

Dead Cert
A: Dick Francis
R: James Fox
HARP

Dead Eyes
A: Stuart Woods
R: Joan Allen
HARP

Dead Man's Dance
A: Robert Ferrigno
RH

Dead Man's Mirror
A: Agatha Christie
R: Nigel Hawthorne
DURK

Deadly Allies
A: Private Eye Writers of America and Sisters of Crime
R: Bess Armstrong, David Dukes, Stephen Macht, and Loretta Swit
DOVE

Deadly Allies Two
A: Edited by Robert J. Randisi and Susan Dunlap
BRILL

Deadly Evidence
A: Harrison Arnston
R: Joe Mantegna
HARP

A Deadly Shade of Gold
A: John D. MacDonald
R: Darren McGavin
RH

Death at the Cape
A: Mary Higgins Clark
R: Carol Higgins Clark
DOVE

Deceptions
A: Michael Weaver
TW

Decider
A: Dick Francis
R: Simon Jones
S&S

Devil in a Blue Dress
A: Walter Mosley
R: Paul Winfield
ART

Dick Francis Audio Collection
A: Dick Francis
R: Simon MacCorkindale and Tim Pigott-Smith
HARP

The Dirty Duck
A: Martha Grimes
R: Tim Curry
S&S

Dixie City Jam
A: James Lee Burke
R: Will Patton
S&S

Don't Cry Now
A: Joy Fielding
BRILL

Double Deuce
A: Robert B. Parker
R: David Dukes
DOVE

Downtown
A: Ed McBain
R: Stephen Macht
DOVE

Driving Force
A: Dick Francis
R: Simon Jones
HARP

Drowned Hopes
A: Donald E. Westlake
R: Artie Johnson
DOVE

Dying for Chocolate
A: Diane Mott Davidson
MILLS

"E" Is for Evidence
A: Sue Grafton
R: Judy Kaye
RH

East Beach
A/R: Ron Ely
BRILL

The Edge
A: Dick Francis
R: Peter Marinker
DURK

Eyes of Prey
A: John Sandford
R: Ken Howard
HARP

"F" Is for Fugitive
A: Sue Grafton
R: Judy Kaye
RH

Farewell, My Lovely
A: Raymond Chandler
R: Elliott Gould
DOVE

Finessing the King
A: Agatha Christie
R: James Warwick
DURK

Finnegan's Week
A: Joseph Wambaugh
BRILL

First Offense
A: Nancy Taylor Rosenberg
R: Lindsay Crouse
PENG

Five Minute Mysteries
A: Ken Weber
BRILL

The Fly on the Wall
A/R: Tony Hillerman
HARP

Flying Finish
A: Dick Francis
R: Simon MacCorkindale
HARP

Four and Twenty Blackbirds
A: Agatha Christie
R: David Suchet
DURK

The Fourth Durango
A: Ross Thomas
R: Robert Culp
DOVE

Freaky Deaky
A: Elmore Leonard
R: Robert Lansing
DURK

"G" Is for Gumshoe
A: Sue Grafton
R: Judy Kaye
RH

The Ghostway
A: Tony Hillerman
R: Gil Silverbird
HARP

The Girl in the Plain Brown Wrapper
A: John D. MacDonald
R: Darren McGavin
RH

The Good Son
A: Ian McEwan
R: John Glover
HARP

Great Mysteries/Great Writers
A: Robert B. Parker, Mary Higgins Clark, Sara Paretsky, Dean R. Koontz, and Carol Higgins Clark
R: David Dukes, Carol Higgins Clark, Bess Armstrong, and Betsy Palmer
DOVE

The Great Taos Bank Robbery
A/R: Tony Hillerman
HARP

Guardian Angel
A: Sara Paretsky
R: Jane Kaczmarek
BDD

"H" Is for Homicide
A: Sue Grafton
R: Judy Kaye
RH

Hard-Boiled: The Best in Mystery Fiction
A: John Lutz, Bill Pronzini, and Stuart Kaminsky
DURK

Have His Carcase
A: Dorothy L. Sayers
R: Edward Petherbridge
DURK

Hidden Riches
A: Nora Roberts
BRILL

High Stakes
A: Dick Francis
R: James Bolam
DURK

The High Window
A: Raymond Chandler
R: Elliott Gould
DOVE

The Horse You Came In On
A: Martha Grimes
R: Tim Curry
S&S

Hot Money
A: Dick Francis
R: Christopher Cazenove
DURK

The Hound of the Baskervilles
A: Sir Arthur Conan Doyle
R: Gordon Gould, George Rose, Nicol Williamson, and full cast
HARP

"I" Is for Innocent
A: Sue Grafton
R: Judy Kaye
RH

I, The Jury
A: Mickey Spillane
R: Stacy Keach
S&S

If You Could See Me Now
A: Peter Straub
R: Keir Dullea
DURK

In the Frame
A: Dick Francis
R: Jim Dale
HARP

In the Presence of Enemies
A: William Coughlin
R: Len Cariou
DURK

Indemnity Only
A: Sara Paretsky
R: Kathy Bates
BDD

The Innocent
A: Ian McEwan
R: David Dukes
HARP

Inspector Wexford on Holiday
A: Ruth Rendell
R: George Baker
DURK

Interest of Justice
A: Nancy Taylor Rosenberg
R: Lindsay Crouse
PENG

"J" Is for Judgment
A: Sue Grafton
R: Judy Kaye
RH

James Bond: Seafire
A: John Gardner
R: Christopher Cazenove
DOVE

The Juror
A: George Dawes Green
TW

Just Cause
A: John Katzenbach
R: Burt Reynolds
S&S

Justice Denied
A: Robert K. Tanenbaum
PENG

"K" Is for Killer
A: Sue Grafton
R: Judy Kaye
RH

The Killer Inside Me
A: Jim Thompson
R: Will Patton
RH

The Killing Man
A: Mickey Spillane
R: Stacy Keach
S&S

Kiss
A: Ed McBain
R: Len Cariou
HARP

Kiss Me, Deadly
A: Mickey Spillane
R: Stacy Keach
S&S

Kiss the Girls
A: James Patterson
TW

Knockdown
A: Dick Francis
R: Tim Pigott-Smith
HARP

Kolymsky Heights
A: Lionel Davidson
R: Theodore Bikel
ART

L.A. Times
A: Stuart Woods
R: Tony Roberts
HARP

The Labor of Hercules Volume III Apples of the Hesperides
A: Agatha Christie
DURK

The Lady in the Lake
A: Raymond Chandler
R: Elliott Gould
DOVE

Las Aventuras De Sherlock Holmes (A Treasury of Sherlock Holmes) (Spanish)
A: Sir Arthur Conan Doyle
DOVE

Last Laughs
A: Mystery Writers of America Anthology; edited by Gregory McDonald
R: Marty Allen, David Birney, Joseph Campanella, Freda Payne, John Standing, and Bruce Weitz
DOVE

The Last Suppers
A: Diane Mott Davidson
MILLS

Let Me Call You Sweetheart
A: Mary Higgins Clark
S&S

Let Us Prey
A: Bill Branon
R: James Naughton
HARP

Libra
A: Don DeLillo
R: Stephen Lang
HARP

Lieberman's Choice
A: Stuart Kaminsky
DURK

Lieberman's Day
A: Stuart Kaminsky
R: Saul Rubinek
DURK

The List of Seven
A: Mark Frost
R: Rene Auberjonois
DOVE

The Little Sister
A: Raymond Chandler
R: Elliott Gould
DOVE

The Lonely Silver Rain
A: John D. MacDonald
R: Darren McGavin
RH

The Long Goodbye
A: Raymond Chandler
R: Elliott Gould
DOVE

Longshot
A: Dick Francis
R: Kenneth Branagh
HARP

Los Escritores de Misterior de Estados Unidos Antologica (Last Laughs) (Spanish)
A: Mystery Writers of America Anthology; edited by Gregory McDonald
DOVE

Lovejoy: Paid and Loving Eyes
A: Jonathan Gash
R: Ian McShane
DURK

Lullaby
A: Ed McBain
R: Len Cariou
HARP

Mallory's Oracle
A: Carol O'Connell
RH

The Man with a Load of Mischief
A: Martha Grimes
R: Tim Curry
S&S

Maximum Bob
A: Elmore Leonard
R: Brian Dennehy
BDD

Mean Streets
A: Various
R: Dennis Franz
ART

Mind Prey
A: John Sandford
S&S

Mischief
A: Ed McBain
R: Len Cariou
HARP

Miss Marple Investigates
A; Agatha Christie
R: Joan Hickson
DURK

Mrs. Pollifax and the Second Thief
A: Dorothy Gilman
BRILL

Mrs. Pollifax Pursued
A: Dorothy Gilman
BRILL

Mitigating Circumstances
A: Nancy Taylor Rosenberg
R: Lindsay Crouse
PENG

A Morning for Flamingos
A: James Lee Burke
R: Will Patton
S&S

Mother's Day
A: Patricia MacDonald
BRILL

Ms. Murder
A: Agatha Christie, Mignon G. Eberhart, Dorothy L. Sayers, Gladys Mitchell, Phylis Bentley, Ruth Rendell, Patricia McGeer, and Amanda Cross; edited by Marie Smith
R: Juliet Mills
MILLS

Murder at the National Gallery
A: Margaret Truman
RH

Murder in a Distant Land
A: Mystery Writers of America Anthology; edited by Gregory McDonald
R: Nancy Dussault, Arte Johnson, Peter Marshall, Roddy McDowall, and Andrew Stevens
DOVE

Murder in Hollywood
A: Various
R: Morgan Fairchild and Roddy McDowall
ART

Murder in Los Angeles
A: M. R. Henderson, Jon A. Breen, and William F. Nolan
R: Roddy McDowall, James Stacy, and Perry King
DOVE

Murder in Manhattan
A: Mary Higgins Clark, Whitley Strieber, Dorothy Salisbury Davis, and Thomas Chastain
R: Betsy Palmer, Roddy McDowall, Juliet Mills, and Peter Graves
DOVE

Murder in the CIA
A: Margaret Truman
R: Joanna Cassidy
RH

Murder in the Mews
A: Agatha Christie
R: Nigel Hawthorne
DURK

Murder on the Aisle
A: Mystery Writers of America Anthology; edited by Gregory McDonald
R: David Birney, Arte Johnson, Perry King, and Joan Rivers
DOVE

Murder on the Glitter Box
A: Steve Allen
DOVE

Murder, She Wrote: Manhattans and Murder
A: Jessica Fletcher and Donald Bain
PENG

Murder to Go
A: Sharyn McCrumb, Wendy Hornsby, Barbara Michaels, Marcia Muller, Barbara Paul, Bill Pronzini, Loren D. Estleman, Joan Hess, Sara Paretsky, and Nancy Pickard
R: Barbara Bain, Diane Baker, Ed McMahon Henry Polic II, and Paula Prentiss
DOVE

Murder with a Twist
A: Various
R: Morgan Fairchild and Roddy McDowall
ART

My Gun is Quick
A: Mickey Spillane
R: Stacy Keach
S&S

Natural Causes
A: Michael Palmer
BDD

The New Adventures of Sherlock Holmes
A: Anthony Bocher and Denis Green
R: Nigel Bruce and Basil Rathbone
S&S

Volume 1: "The Unfortunate Tobacconist" and "The Paradol Chamber"

Volume 2: "The Viennese Strangler" and "The Notorious Canary Trainer

Volume 3: "The April Fool's Day Adventure" and "The Stranger Adventurc of the Uneasy Easy Chair"

Volume 4: "The Strange Case of the Demon Barber" and "The Mystery of the Headless Monk"

Volume 5: "The Amateur Mendicant Society" and "The Case of the Vanishing White Elephant"

Volume 6: "The Case of the Limping Ghost" and "The Girl with the Gazelle"

Volume 7: "The Case of the Out of Date Murder" and "The Waltz of Death"

Volume 8: "Colonel Warburton's Madness" and "The Iron Box"

Volume 9: "A Scandal in Bohemia" and "The Second Generation"

Volume 10: "In Flanders Fields" and "The Eyes of Mr. Leyton"

Volume 11: "The Tell Tale Pigeon Feathers" and "The Indiscretion of Mr. Edwards"

Volume 12: "The Problem of Thor Bridge" and "The Double Zero"

Volume 13: "Murder in the Casbah" and "The Tankerville Club"

Volume 14: "The Strange Case of the Murderer in Wax" and "The Man with the Twisted Lip"

Volume 15: "The Guileless Gypsy" and "The Camberwell Poisoners"

Volume 16: "The Terrifying Cats" and "The Submarine Cave"

Volume 17: "The Living Doll" and "The Disappearing Scientists"

Volume 18: "The Adventure of the Speckled Band" and "The Purloined Ruby"

Volume 19: "The Book of Tobit" and

"Murder Beyond the Mountains"

Volume 20: "The Manor House Case" and "The Adventure of the Stuttering Ghost"

Volume 21: "The Great Gandolfo" and "The Adventure of the Original Hamlet"

Volume 22: "Murder by Moonlight" and "The Singular Affair of the Coptic Compass"

Volume 23: "The Gunpowder Plot" and "The Babbling Butler"

Volume 24: "The Accidental Murderess" and "The Adventure of the Blarney Stone"

Volume 25: "The Night before Christmas" and "The Adventure of the Blarney Stone"
R: Nigel Bruce, Tom Conway, and Basil Rathbone

Volume 26: "The Haunting of Sherlock Holmes" and "The Baconian Cipher"

Gift Set Volume 1: Single Volumes 1–4

Gift Set Volume 2: Single Volumes 5–8

Gift Set Volume 3: Single Volumes 9–12

Gift Set Volume 4: Single Volumes 13–16

Gift Set Volume 5: Single Volumes 17–20

Night Shadows
A/R: Ron Ely
DOVE

Nightmare in Pink
A: John D. MacDonald
R: Darren McGavin
RH

No Night Is Too Long
A: Ruth Rendell (Writing as Barbara Vine)
R: Alan Cumming
PART

O Little Town of Maggody
A; Joan Hess
R: Jane Gabbert
PENG

Odds Against
A: Dick Francis
R: Ian McShane
HARP

The Old Fox Deceiv'd
A: Martha Grimes
R: Tim Curry
S&S

The Old Silent
A: Martha Grimes
R: Tim Curry
S&S

One Corpse Too Many
A: Ellis Peters
R: Sir Derek Jacobi
DURK

One Fearful Yellow Eye
A: John D. MacDonald
R: Darren McGavin
RH

One Lonely Night
A: Mickey Spillane
R: Stacy Keach
S&S

Out on the Rim
A: Ross Thomas
R: David Birney
DOVE

Over the Edge
A: Jonathan Kellerman
R: John Rubinstein
BDD

Pale Kings and Princes
A: Robert B. Parker
R: David Purdham
S&S

Paper Doll
A: Robert B. Parker
R: David Dukes
DOVE

Paradise Junction
A. Phillip Finch
DURK

Pastime
A: Robert B. Parker
R: David Dukes
DOVE

Perchance to Dream
A: Robert B. Parker
R: Elliott Gould
DOVE

The Perfect Murder
A: Jeffrey Archer
R: Rosalind Ayres and Martin Jarvis
DURK

Perry Mason—The Case of the Haunted Husband
A: Erle Stanley Gardner
R: William Hootkins
DURK

Perry Mason—The Case of the Reluctant Model
A: Erle Stanley Gardner
R: William Hootkins
DURK

Perry Mason—The Case of the Sulky Girl
A: Erle Stanley Gardner
R: William Hootkins
DURK

Playback
A: Raymond Chandler
R: Elliott Gould
DOVE

Playing for the Ashes
A: Elizabeth George
R: Derek Jacobi
BDD

Playing with Cobras
A/R: Craig Thomas
HARP

Playmates
A: Robert B. Parker
R: James Farentino
S&S

Pleading Guilty
A: Scott Turow
R: Stacy Keach
S&S

Plumbing for Willy
A: Mary Higgins Clark
R: Carol Higgins Clark
DOVE

Poirot Investigates
Volume II
A: Agatha Christie
R: David Suchet
DURK

Poirot Investigates
Volume III
A: Agatha Christie
R: David Suchet
DURK

Poodle Springs
A: Raymond Chandler and Robert B. Parker
R: Elliott Gould
DOVE

Pop. 1280
A: Jim Thompson
R: Will Patton
RH

Postmortem
A: Patricia D. Cornwell
R: Lindsay Crouse
HARP

Praying for Sleep
A: Jeffery Deaver
R: Anthony Heald
PENG

Private Eyes
A: Jonathan Kellerman
R: John Rubinstein
BDD

Proof
A: Dick Francis
R: Charles Dance
DURK

Puss in Boots
A: Ed McBain
R: Ken Howard
DOVE

The Quick Red Fox
A: John D. MacDonald
R: Darren McGavin
RH

A Quiver Full of Arrows
A: Jeffrey Archer
R: Peter Barkworth
DURK

Rat Race
A: Dick Francis
R: Simon Jones
HARP

Raymond Chandler's Philip Marlow: A Centennial Celebration
A: Edited by Byron Preiss
R: Elliott Gould
DOVE

Rear Window/Three O'Clock
A: Cornell Woolrich
R: Keir Dullea
DURK

Red Wind
A: Raymond Chandler
R: Elliott Gould
DOVE

Risk
A: Dick Francis
R: Michael York
HARP

RL's Dream
A: Walter Mosley
ART

Romance
A: Ed McBain
R: Len Cariou
HARP

Rumpole à la Carte
A: John Mortimer
R: Leo McKern
DURK

Rumpole at the Bar
A: John Mortimer
R: Leo McKern
DURK

Rumpole's Last Case
A: John Mortimer
R: Leo McKern
DURK

Rumpole's Return
A: John Mortimer
R: Leo McKern
DURK

Sacred Clowns
A; Tony Hillerman
R: Gil Silverbird
HARP

Santa Fe Rules
A: Stuart Woods
R: Tony Roberts
HARP

A Scandal in Bohemia
A: Sir Arthur Conan Doyle
R: Basil Rathbone
HARP

Self-defense
A: Jonathan Kellerman
R: John Rubinstein
BDD

See Jane Run
A/R: Joy Fielding
DOVE

The Seventh Commandment
A: Lawrence Sanders
R: Joanna Gleason
S&S

Shadow Man
A: John Katzenbach
S&S

Shadow Over Babylon
A: David Mason
R: Bob Peck
PENG

Shadow Prey
A: John Sandford
R: Ken Howard
HARP

Shattered
A: Richard Neely
R: Nick Mancuso
RH

She Walks These Hills
A: Sharyn McCrumb
BRILL

Sherlock Holmes Adventures
A: Sir Arthur Conan Doyle
R: John Wood
HARP

The Sherlock Holmes Audio Collection
A: Sir Arthur Conan Doyle
R: Basil Rathbone
HARP

Silent Partners
A: Jonathan Kellerman
R: John Rubinstein
BDD

Silent Prey
A: John Sandford
R: Ken Howard
HARP

Silver Blaze
A: Sir Arthur Conan Doyle
R: Basil Rathbone
HARP

Sing a Song of Sixpence
A: Agatha Christie
R: Michael Jayston
DURK

Single White Female
A: John Lutz
R: Morgan Fairchild
ART

Sisters in Crime
Volume I
A: Edited by Marilyn Wallace
R: Margaret Colin, Marsha Mason, and Kate Nelligan
TW

Skin Deep and Other Stories Featuring V. I. Warshawski
A: Sara Paretsky
DURK

Skinwalkers
A: Tony Hillerman
HARP

Smilla's Sense of Snow
A: Peter Hoeg
R: Rebecca Pidgeon
HARP

Smokescreen
A: Dick Francis
R: Edward Woodward
HARP

Snow White and Rose Red
A: Ed McBain
R: Ken Howard
DOVE

The Speckled Band
A: Sir Arthur Conan Doyle
R: Donald Pickering
DURK

Stalkers
A: Mystery Writers of American Anthology
R: Bess Armstrong, Joseph Campanella, David Dukes, and Arte Johnson
DOVE

Stalking Horse
A: Bill Shoemaker
R: Bruce Boxleitner
DOVE

Stardust
A: Robert R. Parker
R: Burt Reynolds
S&S

Stillwatch
A: Mary Higgins Clark
R: Carol Higgins Clark
DOVE

Stories from the Return of Sherlock Holmes
A: Sir Arthur Conan Doyle
DURK

The Stories of Sherlock Holmes
A: Sir Arthur Conan Doyle
R: Basil Rathbone
HARP

"Stowaway" and "Milk Run"
A: Mary Higgins Clark
R: Carol Higgins Clark
DOVE

Straight
A: Dick Francis
R: Simon MacCorkindale
HARP

A Stranger Is Watching
A: Mary Higgins Clark
R: Betty Buckley
S&S

Suitable for Framing
A: Edna Buchanan
R: Sandra Burr
BRILL

A Suitable Vengeance
A: Elizabeth George
R: Derek Jacobi
BDD

Sullivan Sting
A: Lawrence Sanders
R: Victor Garber
S&S

Swag
A: Elmore Leonard
R: Robert Lansing
DURK

Tales of the Unexpected
A: Saki
B: Derek Jacobi
DOVE

Tell Me No Secrets
A/R: Joy Fielding
HARP

The Tenth Commandment
A: Lawrence Sanders
R: Tony Goldwyn
S&S

Terror Stalks the Class Reunion
A: Mary Higgins Clark
R: Sally Kirkland
S&S

"That's the Ticket" and "Voices in the Coal Bin"
A: Mary Higgins Clark
R: Carol Higgins Clark
DOVE

A Thief of Time
A/R: Tony Hillerman
HARP

The Thirty-nine Steps
A: John Buchan
R: Sam Waterston
HARP

Thornyhold
A: Mary Stewart
R: Jenny Agutter
DOVE

Three Blind Mice
A: Agatha Christie
R: Denholm Elliott
DURK

Three Blind Mice
A: Ed McBain
R: Ken Howard
DOVE

Three-Dot Po
A: Sara Paretsky
MILLS

A Ticket to the Boneyard
A: Lawrence Block
R: Stephen Lang
HARP

Time Bomb
A: Jonathan Kellerman
R: John Rubinstein
BDD

Tomorrow's Crimes: Stories of Fantastic Suspense
A: Donald E. Westlake
DURK

The Tony Hillerman Audio Collection
A/R: Tony Hillerman
HARP

Traitor's Gate
A: Anne Perry
R: David McCallum
RH

A Treasury of Sherlock Holmes
A: Sir Arthur Conan Doyle
R: Ben Kingsley
DOVE

The Trials of Rumpole
A: John Mortimer
R: Leo McKern
DURK

"Triangle at Rhodes" and "The Incredible Theft"
A: Agatha Christie
R: David Suchet
DURK

Tripwire
A: Jay Brandon
R: Gregory Harrison
MILLS

Trouble Is My Business
A: Raymond Chandler
R: Elliott Gould
DOVE

True Betrayal
A: Nora Roberts
BRILL

Trust Me on This
A: Donald E. Westlake
R: Arte Johnson
DOVE

The Tuesday Club Murders
A: Agatha Christie
R: Joan Hickson
DURK

Twilight at Mac's Place
A: Ross Thomas
R: Robert Culp
DOVE

A Twist in the Tale
A: Jeffrey Archer
R: Nigel Havers
DURK

The Unbreakable Alibi
A: Agatha Christie
R: James Warwick
DURK

The Under Dog
A: Agatha Christie
R: David Suchet
DURK

A Vacation to Die For
A: Various
R: Angie Dickinson and Patrick MacNee
ART

Vanish with the Rose
A: Barbara Michaels
R: Deborah Lee Johnson
S&S

The Veiled Lady and the Third-Floor Flat
A: Agatha Christie
R: Roger Rees
HARP

Vengeance Is Mine
A: Mickey Spillane
R: Stacy Keach
S&S

Vespers
A: Ed McBain
R: Len Cariou
HARP

A Walk Among the Tombstones
A: Lawrence Block
R: Stephen Lang
HARP

The Way Through the Woods
A: Colin Dexter
R: Simon Jones
DURK

Weep No More My Lady
A: Mary Higgins Clark
R: Elizabeth Ashley
S&S

Well-Schooled in Murder
A: Elizabeth George
R: Derek Jacobi
BDD

When the Bough Breaks
A: Jonathan Kellerman
R: John Rubinstein
BDD

Where Are the Children
A: Mary Higgins Clark
R: Lindsay Crouse
S&S

While My Pretty One Sleeps
A: Mary Higgins Clark
R: Jessica Walter
S&S

White Butterfly
A: Walter Mosley
R: Paul Winfield
ART

Widows
A: Ed McBain
R: Len Cariou
HARP

Wild Horses
A: Dick Francis
R: Simon Jones
S&S

NONFICTION

War. Jazz. Antidepressants. Golf. Biographies of Groucho, Mommie Dearest, and Burns and Allen. Roseanne tells all. The Mafia. True crime. Memoirs from Orson Welles and Art Buchwald. Ross Perot rescues his corporate executives from an Iranian prison. Bill Graham and Janis Joplin bring back rock 'n' roll memories. There's even Annette Funicello, and the Bradys. There are opinions from Ice T, and Malcolm X. Bob Woodward examines the first year and a half of the Clinton presidency while Randy Shilts takes an historical look at gays and lesbians in the military.

There are two moving stories of the horrors of war represented by Anne Frank's *Diary of a Young Girl* and *Zlata's Diary,* by Zlata Filipovic, "the Anne Frank of Sarajavo." Magic Johnson gives us his frank *What You Can Do to Avoid AIDS,* while Paul Monette, in *Borrowed Time,* speaks eloquently of courageous attempts to cope with the effects of the virus when his friend is diagnosed with AIDS.

There is a sense of wonder experienced by naturalist John Muir upon encountering Yosemite. And John Winokur gives us a dizzying variety of fathers. John F. Kennedy, Jr., reads his own father's Pulitzer Prize–winning *Profiles in Courage.* And CBS reporter Charles Kuralt shares thirty years of life on the road.

An embarrassment of riches, from A to Z! Hear, Hear!

HIGHLY RECOMMENDED (★★★★)

The Agenda
The Art of Worldly Wisdom
The Autobiography of Malcolm X
Borrowed Time: An AIDS Memoir
Bound for Glory
D-Day
Diary of a Young Girl
Gracie: A Love Story
Having Our Say
The Ice Opinion
Leaving Home: A Memoir
The Lessons of History
Listening to Prozac
Live from the Battlefield
Marlene Dietrich
Profiles in Courage
This Is Orson Welles
Wild Swans
Woodsong
Zlata's Diary

The Agenda
Author: Bob Woodward
Reader: Kevin Spacey
★★★★

Meticulously researched and often disturbing, *The Agenda* is Woodward's take on the first year and a half of the Clinton presidency, which the Pulitzer Prize winner portrays as often chaotic, unfocused, and unable to make any real headway on economic policy. There are triumphs for President Clinton here, but there are also missed opportunities, mishandled situations, and maddening frustrations, as the rookie president and his staff struggle mightily to forge new policies for America.

2 css 2 hr Simon & Schuster Audio

Albatross
Authors: Deborah Scaling Kiley and Meg Noonan
Reader: Karen Allen
★★★

Kiley, a young woman who's "never turned down a dare in my life," finds herself aboard a fifty-eight-foot sailboat with four others, heading from New England to Florida. Along the way, they're swamped by a giant wave and spend the rest of the time in a fragile life raft, slowly wasting away from hunger and thirst, surrounded by sharks, and with nothing to signal the few ships they spot. The lengthy portion describing the wreck and its immediate aftermath, as they bob helplessly among giant waves, is especially riveting. Parents should note that a number of vulgarities are peppered throughout, probably rendering it unsuitable for family listening.

2 css 3 hr BDD Audio

The American Way of Birth
Author/Reader: Jessica Mitford
★★★

Thirty years after changing the way America looks at its funeral and burial practices with her *The American Way of Death,* Mitford returns with a look from the other end of things. All of the qualities present in the former book—including anecdotal evidence, thorough research, and strong opinion—are here as well, with Mitford arguing against state-of-the-art hospital techniques, deeming most of them unnecessary at best, and for more home births and midwives. Her British-accented narration helps give this audio book the proper ring of authority and, occasionally, restrained outrage.

2 css 3 hr Penguin HighBridge Audio

The Art of Worldly Wisdom
Author: Baltasar Gracian; translated by Christopher Maurer
Reader: Victor Garber
★★★★

Subtitled *A Pocket Oracle,* this selection of 300 aphorisms ("Always behave as though others were watching"; "Never stumble over fools"; "Leave people hungry") is taken from the longer work by Gracian, a seventeenth-century Jesuit priest praised by such philosophers as Friedrich Nietzsche and Arthur Schopenhauer. Each maxim is numbered and accompanied by a few lines of commentary from the original work. The translation combines both clear and poetic qualities, and a brief introductory segment explains the original purpose of the work and a few notes on its creator.

1 css 1 hr Bantam Audio

The Autobiography of Malcolm X
Authors: Malcolm X with Alex Haley
Readers: Roscoe Lee Brown and Joe Morton
★★★★

Through a life of passion, struggle, and change, Malcolm X became one of the most controversial figures in the 1960s. His famous autobiography recounts his journey from prison cell to Mecca, from hoodlum to minister. Time has not dimmed Malcolm X's message, and the strength of his words, the power of his ideas, continue to resonate more than a generation after they first appeared. This is not a cheap fictional account, filtered through someone else's beliefs and personal prejudices, but the message from the minister himself. Don't be fooled by imitations. Both Joe Morton and Roscoe Lee Brown are veteran actors and breathe the necessary fire into *The Autobiography of Malcolm X.*

4 css 4½ hr Simon & Schuster Audio

The Best of Alan Dershowitz
Author/Reader: Alan Dershowitz
★★

Alan Dershowitz is one of the great legal minds of this century. Just ask him, he'll tell you so. This tape is a mix of excerpts from his books *Contrary to Popular Opinion* and *Chutzpah*. He examines issues like anti-Semitism at home and abroad, free expression versus intolerance, and the state versus individual rights. The collection also contains previously unreleased recordings and proves Dershowitz saying exactly what's on his mind, is still unafraid of controversy.

2 css 3 hr Dove Audio

Bill Graham Presents
Authors: Bill Graham and Robert Greenfield
Readers: Robert Greenfield and Peter Wolf
★★★

A fascinating, anecdotal, sometimes vulgar chronicle of the greatest days of American rock music and the American rock scene, written by the man who founded the Fillmore West and East, the rock temples of the time. Whether relating stories of his youth in Europe during World War II or spinning tales about the Grateful Dead's attempts to sneak LSD into his system, the late Graham was a born raconteur. Here, Peter Wolf (of J. Geils Band fame) assumes the Graham role, with Robert Greenfield supplying the connective material between Graham's stories—just as he did in the book version of *Bill Graham Presents.*

2 css 3 hr Audio Literature

Blind Faith
Author: Joe McGinniss
Reader: James Naughton
★★

The Marshall family had new cars, community esteem, and a permanent membership in the country club. Then Maria Marshall, ideal wife and mother, became the victim of a cold-blooded murder. As the investigation proceeded, nasty little facts about her husband began to surface. Best-selling true-crime writer Joe McGinniss brings out detail after horrifying detail about the murder of Maria Marshall.

2 css 3 hr Simon & Schuster Audio

Blue Highways: A Journey into America
Author: William Least Heat Moon
Reader: Keith Szarabajka
★★

Author Moon headed out in his van to drive along America's smaller roads, on a trip that carried him 13,000 miles and brought him in contact with a wild array of characters and locales. As a series of snapshots of small-town America, *Blue Highways* is excellent, but the reading leaves much to be desired.

2 css 3 hr Simon & Schuster Audio

Borrowed Time: An AIDS Memoir
Author/Reader: Paul Monette
★★★★

This is a love story about Paul Monette and his friend Roger Horowitz, and their courageous attempts to cope with the debilitating effects of the virus when Roger is diagnosed with AIDS. *Borrowed Time* tells how to live with AIDS, how to fight for life, and, finally, how to die with dignity and grace. Once in a long while comes a recording like this that is so full of life, love, and the searching to understand one's own mortality. The author reads with such clarity and understated passion that his own voice is as powerful and compassionate as his writing.

2 css 3 hr Caedmon Audio

Bound for Glory
Author: Woody Guthrie
Reader: Arlo Guthrie
★★★★

This true story of America's dispossessed is told with dead-on dialogue, keen observation, and a deep sense of compassion by the elder Guthrie, whose poet's soul shines through not only in his music, but in this wonderful chronicle. Woody's son Arlo reads this as though he wrote it himself, spicing the earthy narration with swatches of his father's songs. Although it's set in the Great Depression, when millions—including Woody—rode the boxcars and knocked at the back doors of America looking for work, *Bound for Glory* is a timeless audio document that has special resonance in the United States of the mid-nineties.

2 css 3 hr Audio Literature

Bulow Hammock
Author: David Rains Wallace
Reader: Edward Markmann
★★★

A collaboration between the Sierra Club and Audio Literature, *Bulow Hammock* (a "hammock," the author notes, is a woodland with hardwood groves) tells of Wallace's visits to a particular Florida wilderness spot, beginning when he's nine years old. He and narrator Markmann evoke smells and other sensory triggers in a nicely satisfying way, while at the same time conveying the feeling that this—and any—undeveloped wilderness is preferable to untrammeled civilization. Wallace's visits to the spot also serve as a springboard for some interesting biology-based philosophizing.

2 css 3 hr Audio Literature

Case Closed: Lee Harvey Oswald and the Assassination of JFK
Author/Reader: Gerald Posner
★★

Over the past thirty years there have been hundreds of books on and many investigations of the Kennedy assassination in Dallas. *Case Closed* cuts through the misinformation and distortions, brings in new interviews and secret files, and employs the latest computer enhancements of film and evidence. Posner brings a human element to one of the worst crimes in American history, and presents his own answers to the riddle of how and why Lee Harvey Oswald shot the president.

2 css 3 hr Audio Select

Charlie's Victory
Authors: Charlie and Lucy Wedemeyer with Gregg Lewis
Readers: Lucy and Kale Wedemeyer
★★★

A remarkable testimony to optimism and faith, *Charlie's Victory* is the story of high school coach Charlie Wedemeyer, who, victimized by Lou Gehrig's disease, continues to find joy in life even at the end of this story, when he's unable to speak and can barely move his lips. His wife, Lucy, narrates, along with their son Kale, and while neither is a professional, they get the job done with conviction. The message here seems to be that not only Charlie Wedemeyer, but everyone, is terminal, so no matter where we are in the process, we should be grateful to God for our blessings—including the gift of each new day. In these stingy and self-involved times, it's a message that should be heard.

2 css 3 hr Zondervan

Comeback
Authors: Dave Dravecky with Tim Stafford
Reader: Dave Dravecky
★★★

Dravecky, a major-league pitcher for several seasons, tells this miraculous story of his comeback from cancer, weaving into the narrative stories about the rigors of winter baseball in Colombia and his other struggles to become a major-leaguer. The tape begins with his discovery of a lump in his pitching arm and the slow realization that it's cancerous. It ends with his retirement from baseball—but not before he's come back from the disease to win a crucial game during a pennant drive. A born-again Christian, Dravecky never fails to give the credit and glory to God.

1 css 1 hr Zondervan

Conduct Unbecoming
Author: Randy Shilts
Readers: Robby Benson and Randy Shilts
★★★

Subtitled *Gays and Lesbians in the U.S. Military,* this is an exhaustive, historical look at what Shilts describes as "the persistent presence of gays in the military, and the equally persistent hostility toward them." Shilts offers numerous examples of gays who've excelled in the military and the way the services—both officially and unofficially—dealt with them. This is another of those audio books so thick with detail that those with only a casual interest in the subject will probably fall out a few times along the way; for others, it will be absorbing throughout. Benson's narration is calm and sincere.

4 css 6 hr The Publishing Mills AudioBooks

The Courage to Raise Good Men
Author: Olga Silverstein and Beth Rashbaum
Reader: Olga Silverstein
★★

Family therapist Silverstein takes on the idea of male role models, slamming the likes of Robert Bly and Sigmund Freud along the way. Like Bly (see *A Gathering of Men* on page 297), she believes something profound happened to fathers and sons with the advent of the Industrial Revolution; unlike Bly, she doesn't think boys need men around in order to become men themselves. In fact, she credits the upheaval of the Industrial Revolution with being responsible for Freud's whole idea of the Oedipus complex. It's Silverstein's contention that male role models are unnecessary in boys' lives—a radical and provocative notion, to say the least. Listeners are apt to find her less than wholly persuasive.

2 css 3 hr Penguin HighBridge Audio

D-Day
Author/Reader: Stephen E. Ambrose
★★★★

The *D-Day* audio book runs almost a quarter as long as the actual battle itself, a fact that speaks eloquently of the detail involved in this presentation. Beginning with a speech by General Dwight D. Eisenhower, followed by a recounting of the first Allied and Axis casualty on Normandy Beach, *D-Day* is an eminently thorough look at the famed battle. At times, it's as personal as a soldier's reminiscence. At other times, the men on both sides seem simply tiny pieces on a vast game board, as the warring commanders strategize, trying to second-guess their opponents. Ambrose's narration gets a touch professorial at times, but in all this is a riveting look at a hugely important time in world history. A detailed map of the battle area is included.

4 css 6 hr Simon & Schuster Audio

Den of Lions: Memoirs of Seven Years
Author: Terry Anderson
Readers: Terry Anderson and Madeline Anderson
★★★

In 1985, Associated Press chief Terry Anderson was kidnapped by Arab terrorists and imprisoned for almost seven years. This inspiring account of the hardships Anderson endured at the hands of his Shiite captors is amplified by Madeline Anderson's account of what it was like on the outside, waiting for news of his release. This story of two people caught in the web of worldwide politics is a gripping tale of triumph and struggle.

2 css 3 hr Audio Renaissance Tape

The Dharma Bums
Author: Jack Kerouac
Reader: Allen Ginsberg
★★★

Read with obvious joy and relish by Ginsberg, himself a major player in the Beat Movement of the 1950s, *The Dharma Bums* is a thinly veiled roman à clef detailing Kerouac's adventures with other poets and hipsters. They climb mountains, hop freights, give poetry readings, meditate, march drunkenly and happily down Main streets, and drink lots of wine, and all of it comes out strained through a consciousness punctuated with bursts of wild imagery and Buddhist spiritual insight. A great chronicle of the "holy goofs" of the Beat culture.

2 css 2 hr Audio Literature

Diary of a Young Girl
Author: Anne Frank
Reader: Claire Bloom
★★★★

It's a worldwide classic, the simple, sincere words of a young Jewish girl hiding from the Nazis in Amsterdam in the 1940s. Preserved purely by coincidence, Anne Frank's diary has torn at the hearts of generations. This timeless book, with a message that is as relevant today as it ever was, is brought to audio by famed actress Claire Bloom, veteran of stage and screen.

1 css 1 hr Caedmon Audio

Don't Know Much about Geography
Author/Reader: Kenneth C. Davis
★★★

The author of *Don't Know Much about History* returns with an audio book devoted to geography—which, as the listener soon finds, Davis sees as a subject encompassing many other sciences, including astronomy, meteorology, and history. After explaining why at least a rudimentary knowledge of geography is important for anyone (and citing test results that show how uneducated Americans are on the subject), Davis segues to a question-and-answer format that ranges from the development of man on earth to the mysteries of the cosmos. Obviously, this is a serious amount of ground to cover in three hours, but the author does a decent job of it.

2 css 3 hr Bantam Audio

Don't Know Much about History: Everything You Need to Know about American History but Never Learned
Author: Kenneth C. Davis
Readers: Introduction by Kenneth C. Davis; Dick Rodstein
★★

In print this volume spent more than six months on the *New York Times* best-seller list, and in audio it continues its mission—that of debunking many long-cherished misconceptions about American history in such a charming way that even the most reluctant late-blooming student is drawn in. In this entertaining presentation, you'll meet the personalities who helped shape our nation and see the wheels within the wheels that brought us to where we are today. Davis's specialty is bringing life to the human side of history, which the textbooks neglect.

2 css 3 hr Bantam Audio

A Dream Is a Wish Your Heart Makes
Authors: Annette Funicello with Patricia Romanowski
Reader: Annette Funicello
★★★

It may be a bit of a shock to old *Mickey Mouse Club* fans to hear Funicello's mature (but still charming) voice narrating this tape. In it, she brings back gentle images of a bygone era, when teens were listening to songs like her "Tall Paul" and Dick Clark's Caravan of Stars was first crossing the country, giving many audiences their first look at an integrated live show. In addition to her work with Disney on both television and the big screen, Annette was a star of the early sixties *Beach Party* movies, and she makes some interesting observations about them (including the reason she didn't wear bikinis onscreen). She also tells of her teenage romance with Paul Anka, and relates her later struggles with multiple sclerosis, doing the latter without an ounce of self-pity.

2 css 3 hr Time Warner AudioBooks

Fathers
Authors: Various; compiled and edited by Jon Winokur
Readers: Allen Hamilton, Isabel Monk, Peter Moore, and Greta Schwerner; introduction by Jon Winokur
★★★

A dizzying variety of fathers, from Pretty Boy Floyd to Nathaniel Hawthorne, are remembered by sons and daughters in the scrapbooklike collection of remembrances. Collected under such headings as "Heroes," "Golden Moments," and "Quality Time," the entries range from single sentences to full-blown, near-mythic tales. (Yul Brynner's son, for instance, tells how his father sewed together a gash in his famous bald head with fishing line to keep from cutting short a family water-skiing trip.) Winokur has done a fine job of compiling these reminiscences from both primary and secondary sources, although many entries will leave the listener wishing for more.

1 css 1½ hr Penguin HighBridge Audio

Fire in the Belly: On Being a Man
Author/Reader: Sam Keen
★★

A contribution to the fading men's movement, *Fire in the Belly* offers the millions of restless, questioning men that are supposedly thronging America a new way to approach real manhood. All the main buzzwords are here: woundedness, self-actualizing, alienate, spiritually grounded, empowering, enriching. For most listeners, this material will seem dated.

2 css 2 hr Bantam Audio

From Beirut to Jerusalem
Author/Reader: Thomas L. Friedman
★★★

"Beirut was always a city that provoked more questions than answers," says Thomas Friedman, "for those who live there and those who do not." Winner of the 1989 National Book Award for nonfiction, Friedman uses anecdotes, history, and personal observation to bring vivid life to two of the most enigmatic, violent, and misunderstood cities in the world. Right at the heart of the Arab-Israeli conflict, no two cities have ever been as hotly debated, and no reporter has covered them in such depth. His reportage can serve as a framework to build an understanding of the situation and conflict in this region.

2 css 3 hr Harper Audio

Golf in the Kingdom
Author: Michael Murphy
Reader: Mitchell Ryan
★★★

Murphy, a philosophy student on his way to India to study, stops by a Scottish golf course and finds all the philosophy he can handle with a golf guru named Shivas Irons. The listener first encounters Irons trailing "the smell of eucalyptus and baking bread" and kicking at the ceiling of a clubhouse. A couple of hours later, after many stories, mots, and bits of wisdom, Murphy pushes on, leaving his mentor behind, waving sullenly from a train station. A book best appreciated by those who treasure both the discipline of golf and the discipline of philosophy.

2 css 3 hr Audio Literature

Gracie: A Love Story
Author/Reader: George Burns
★★★★

The magical glow of a vanished show-biz era, as well as the chronicle of an enduring love affair, is told here in George Burns's familiar anecdotal style. Less a full-blown autobiography than a series of amusing reminiscences, *Gracie* features stories about Burns and Gracie Allen's early days in vaudeville as well as tales from the days of their long-running radio and television series. Along the way, there are good ones about Jack Benny, George Jessel, and less famous, but no less interesting, members of the families of George and Gracie. Although the running time is listed as three hours, the actual time is closer to two. Or maybe it's just that Burns's narration is so breezy that *Gracie* seems shorter than it really is.

2 css 3 hr Simon & Schuster Audio

Growing Up Brady
Author: Barry Williams and Chris Kreski
Reader: Barry Williams
★★

Here it is! The ultimate insider's guide to *The Brady Bunch,* that wacky early-seventies blended-family sitcom that continues winning new fans in syndication. The thing that makes *Growing Up Brady* so entertaining is not only the subject matter, but Williams's good-natured, direct narration, beginning with a recounting of his driving ambition to be a movie star while still a young child. *Brady Bunch* fans—and there are millions out there—will relish his detailed, often humorous, reminiscences of shooting the series, including the behind-the-scenes romances, adventures, and practical jokes.

2 css 3 hr The Publishing Mills AudioBooks

Harvey Penick's Little Red Book
Authors: Harvey Penick with Bud Shrake
Reader: Jack Whitaker
★★★

Words of praise from high-octane pro golfers Tom Kite, Ben Crenshaw, and Kathy Whitworth provide a ringing endorsement of the skill of author Penick, an octogenarian whose teaching skills have become so legendary that the Golf Teachers Association's annual award is named after him. Here, he shares both tips and anecdotes culled from his life in golf, with Emmy-winning sports broadcaster Jack Whitaker narrating in a no-nonsense fashion. A treasure trove for golfers at all skill levels.

1 css 1½ hr Simon & Schuster Audio

Having Our Say: The Delany Sisters' First 100 Years
Authors: Sarah and A. Elizabeth Delany with Amy Hill Hearth
Reader: Whoopi Goldberg
★★★★

Sadie Delany is 104. Her sister Bessie is 102. Both are daughters of a freed slave who became America's first elected black Episcopal bishop. "When you get old, honey, you lay it all on the table," said Bessie. "There's an old saying: 'Only little children and old folks tell the truth.' " And here is more than a century's worth of hard truth, recounted honestly: the era of Jim Crow, of lynchings and legal segregation, of the sisters' success as two of the first black women professionals out of Harlem. This is an oral history of Americana that can never be replaced, and the kind of insight that can never be found in history books.

2 css 3 hr Audio Renaissance Tapes

The Hidden Life of Dogs
Author: Elizabeth Marshall Thomas
Reader: Swoosie Kurtz
★★

The listener interested in getting answers to the question "What do dogs want?" will be the perfect audience for this often fascinating tape, which is, as the author notes, a work about "dog consciousness." Using examples from her own life as a dog lover and owner, anthropologist-ethnologist Thomas comments on social equilibrium, group communication, and learned behaviors among canine pets, ending with a noble, sad story. Kurtz does a good job here, although at times she seems to be threatening to burst into tears.

2 css 3 hr Time Warner AudioBooks

Hollywood vs. America
Author/Reader: Michael Medved
★★

Subtitled *Popular Culture and the War on Traditional Values,* this overlong tape certainly has its points, but they end up being bludgeoned home by the humorless, often self-aggrandizing approach of film critic Medved—who notes that a movie industry friend advised him that he would become "the most hated man in Hollywood" if he went ahead with this project. Really. Medved espouses the notion that the film industry has lost touch with mainstream America, thanks to an overriding obsession with sex, violence, vulgarity, and general ugliness, and he calls for a return to wholesome values. Listeners may recall Medved as the coauthor of the best-selling *Golden Turkey Awards,* which made savage fun of films and filmmakers he didn't like. This, at least, is a step up.

2 css 3 hr 20 min Harper Audio

How Does Aspirin Find a Headache?
Author: David Feldman
Readers: David Feldman, Alison Fraser, Rusty Magee, and Jack Minfold
★★

This entry in the *Imponderable* series of audio books features narrator/writer Feldman throwing out twenty-two trivia questions, ranging from the sublime (the question in the book's title) to the pretty goofy (a series of questions about McDonald's restaurants, including "Why are the burgers upside down when you unfold the wrapper of a McDonald's hamburger?"). A man, a woman, and a child are featured after each question, giving contradictory (and rather long-winded) answers, after which time the listener has ten seconds to determine which response is correct. This one will probably be entertaining enough on car trips, but the relatively small number of questions and the large amount of time devoted to each make it all seem a bit insubstantial.

1 css 1 hr Harper Audio

The Ice Opinion
Author/Reader: Ice T
★★★★

Ice T is without question one of the most articulate and engaging of the "gangsta rappers." He became famed, and hated by many, for his song "Cop Killer." Responding to that pressure, he has become a powerful advocate of free speech and a strong voice of America's ghettos. If you can't stand rap music but have an interest in what's stirring up the violence and hatred in the ghetto, *The Ice Opinion* is the way to get answers. He wrote the book, he says, "in an attempt to inspire a conversation. . . . I know there are enough of you out there who will read this and understand that we're not all that different." As a gangsta rapper, he's won all the awards that count. As a communicator from the ghettos, he has no peer.

2 css 3 hr The Publishing Mills AudioBooks

In the Arena
Author/Reader: Richard M. Nixon
★★★

Written after Watergate, at a time when he was trying to return to public life, Nixon again showed the optimism that had made him the first American president to visit Beijing's Great Hall of the People, and displayed the inner strength that carried him through a life of triumph and defeat. His worst defeat is also vividly described here, the morning he sat gripped in despair facing the first-ever presidential resignation. This is an intensely intimate memoir from a man who had a pivotal role in shaping our times.

2 css 3 hr Simon & Schuster Audio

JFK: Reckless Youth
Author/Reader: Nigel Hamilton
★★

Another warts-and-all biography of the Kennedy family, focusing first on JFK and secondarily on father Joseph, *JFK: Reckless Youth* is a competent if not particularly lively work. It's not much helped by the British author's narration, which often seems to have a slightly contemptuous sheen to it. While there are a few new revelations here, there's not a lot that hasn't been at least hinted at before, including the more negative aspects of Joe's character and the constant striving for perfection that characterized the prepresidential Jack.

2 css 3 hr The Publishing Mills AudioBooks

Leading with My Heart: My Life: Virginia Kelley
Authors: Virginia Kelley with James Morgan
Reader: Rue McClanahan
★★

From growing up poor in Hope, Arkansas, through five marriages to four men, to a bout with breast cancer, here is the autobiography of the late Virginia Kelley, Bill Clinton's colorful and outspoken mother. Reader Rue McClanahan, best known for her role as Blanche in TV's *The Golden Girls,* brings an unmistakable passion for the material to her voice.

2 css 3 hr Simon & Schuster Audio

Leaving Home: A Memoir
Author/Reader: Art Buchwald
★★★★

Art Buchwald never saw his mother. She was ill with chronic depression and they were separated almost at birth. Buchwald's childhood was filled with strangers, shelters, and orphanages. In many ways he never even had a home to leave. But through his pain came humor, and he grew into a man who has made America laugh for forty years. *Leaving Home* is his own story, in his own voice—a moving and remarkable memoir of painful honesty.

2 css 3 hr Dove Audio

The Lessons of History
Authors: Will and Ariel Durant
Reader: Russ Holcomb
★★★★

Essentially a reflection by the famed historians following the completion of their eleven-volume *Story of Civilization, The Lessons of History* begins by questioning the benefits of studying history and ends with a recounting of some of its unique joys. In between, the Durants take a look at human nature in a historical context, covering, among many topics, inequality among people and nations, rationalism versus religion, and the benefits of capitalism. Profound but accessible, *The Lessons of History* transcends the partisan button-pushing that passes for political and historical discourse in today's America, offering a studied intelligence instead.

2 css 3 hr 15 min Audio Editions

A Life on the Road
Author/Reader: Charles Kuralt
★★★

For more than thirty years, Charles Kuralt, longtime CBS reporter and anchorman, has traveled the world. Here, he retraces the journey that began when he was a young newsman covering events in South America, Vietnam, and even the Okefenokee Swamp. Kuralt knows the world, and he also knows its people, from former Nazi POWs to luminaries like Marlon Brando and Nikita Khrushchev.

2 css 3 hr Simon & Schuster Audio

Lincoln: A Biography
Authors: Philip B. Kunhardt, Jr., Philip B. Kunhardt III, and Peter W. Kunhardt
Reader: Frank Langella
★★★

The current wave of interest in Civil War history has made Abraham Lincoln stand out more sharply in the public eye now than at any time since the day he was killed. This comprehensive biography presents a Lincoln we have never seen before. Drawing on letters, diaries, and other primary sources, *Lincoln* presents a close-up view of the president as a boy and as a grassroots politician, family man, president, and military leader. This extraordinary look at the man behind the presidency is augmented considerably by the excellent reading given by Frank Langella.

2 css 3 hr Random House AudioBooks

Listening to Prozac
Author/Reader: Peter D. Kramer, M.D.
★★★★

Psychiatrist Kramer takes an unblinking, measured look at the antidepressant Prozac, pondering its ability to "alter an internal mechanism" in users and exploring the behavioral as well as the moral consequences of the drug. Using case histories as illustration, he likens the effect of Prozac on contemporary society to the effect Freud's theories of psychoanalysis had upon their introduction. Although Kramer is far from an alarmist, the listener may be left thinking that something rather disturbing has been introduced into the bloodstreams of millions.

2 css 3 hr Simon & Schuster Audio

Live from the Battlefield
Author/Reader: Peter Arnett
★★★★

From Vietnam to Baghdad, Peter Arnett spent thirty-five years chasing the news in the world's war zones. His first assignment was Vietnam in 1962, and his frontline coverage, which helped educate the nation about its role in this small, distant country, infuriated President Lyndon Johnson, and won Arnett a Pulitzer Prize. Since then Arnett has covered the turmoil in Cyprus, the Jonestown massacre, the Iranian hostage crisis, the invasion of Afghanistan, and the ongoing conflict in Beirut. When the war broke out in the Persian Gulf, Arnett was there, too. This tape contains a lifetime of behind-the-scenes stories from a man who was at the front lines.

2 css 3 hr Simon & Schuster Audio

Love, Groucho
Authors: Groucho Marx; edited by Miriam Marx Allen
Readers: Frank Ferrante; commentary by Miriam Marx Allen; foreword by Dick Cavett
★★★

This text, read by Marx portrayer Ferrante, is taken from a series of letters written by the famed comedian to his daughter over a period of almost thirty years. The bulk of the correspondence is from the forties and fifties, when Groucho's best film years were over but *You Bet Your Life* was taking off on radio and, later, TV. While often humorous, these letters also reveal a stern parental side of Groucho, especially when he writes his daughter about her drinking problem or about her conflicts with his new wife. A tape more illuminating than hilarious, it's recommended for fans of Marx and the whole forties and fifties show-biz scene.

1 css 1½ hr The Publishing Mills AudioBooks

Love, Janis
Author: Laura Joplin
Reader: Debra Winger
★★★

A rather gentle portrait of the famed blues-rock singer, *Love, Janis* was penned by Joplin's younger sister and is read with sincerity by movie star Winger. The work traces Joplin's progress from Port Arthur, Texas, beatnik to Haight-Ashbury hippie darling, dealing fairly with, but without a lot of emphasis on, Janis's addictions to liquor and, later, heroin. The story of Joplin's appearance at a high school reunion is both sad and memorable, and the letters that form the narrative bridge show a childlike and enthusiastic Joplin—a much different persona from the one she created for her public.

2 css 3 hr Audio Literature

Many Lives, Many Masters
Author/Reader: Brian L. Weiss, M.D.
★★★

In calm, near-boyish tones, Weiss tells the story of a fear-racked patient who, even after eighteen months of intensive therapy, doesn't get any better. Then, she's hypnotized, and the process reveals a number of the woman's past lives. Weiss is led to the conclusion that there are many different souls on many different planes out there, and not only his patient's life is changed, but his as well. If nothing else, *Many Lives, Many Masters* ends up as a persuasive argument for the existence of an afterlife.

1 css 1½ hr Simon & Schuster Audio

Marlene Dietrich: Life and Legend
Author: Steven Bach
Reader: Roddy McDowall
★★★★

A first-rate biography of the star of such classic pictures as *The Blue Angel, Destry Rides Again,* and *Golden Earrings, Marlene Dietrich* begins with author Bach focusing on the director who "revealed" Dietrich, Josef von Sternberg, as he searches in Berlin for a star for his new Hollywood picture. That movie becomes *The Blue Angel,* launching Dietrich on a career that includes trouble with Hollywood's production code and a period when she's labeled "box-office poison." Of course, her complex private life is also delved into here. McDowall's narration is brisk and knowing—every once in a while, he even slips into a vocal impression of Dietrich's famed husky tones.

3 css 6 hr Dove Audio

Me
Author/Reader: Katharine Hepburn
★★★

Me features Ms. Hepburn in a feisty, often compelling recollection of events in her life. Along a more or less chronological pathway, the listener gets detailed portraits of her grandparents, parents, and other relatives; tales from her childhood; and stories of her stage and screen performances (she admits not knowing much about her costars' lives outside of the spotlight, noting that "getting my rest" was more important than after-hours socializing). The last part of the work deals extensively with the love of her life, Spencer Tracy, ending with a poignant letter to him.

2 css 3 hr Random House AudioBooks

Men at Work
Author: George F. Will
Reader: Bob Costas
★★★

The famed political columnist uses four major-league baseball stars—Oakland A's manager Tony LaRussa, Los Angeles Dodgers pitcher Orel Hershiser, Baltimore Orioles shortstop Cal Ripken, Jr., and San Diego Padres outfielder Tony Gwynn—as springboards to advance his theories and observations on the game of baseball. It's an insightful and interesting work, but all of the theorizing, postulations, and attention to the minutiae of baseball may be a bit much for anyone less than a dedicated fan. Costas does his usual good work as narrator.

2 css 3 hr Harper Audio

Miles
Authors: Miles Davis with Quincy Troupe
Reader: LeVar Burton
★★★

Jazz fans—of course—will be especially taken with this straightforward biography of the great trumpeter, read with conviction by noted actor Burton. Davis deals explicitly with a number of things here, from his heroin addiction (and cold-turkey withdrawal) to his desire to learn how to box, but one gets the feeling from this work that everything else was deeply subordinate to his music. It's the subject that draws the most passion from him in *Miles,* whether he's talking about technique and theory or about men—including Dizzy Gillespie and Charlie Parker—who made it with him. Those concerned about language should know that there's a significant amount of vulgarity and street talk throughout.

2 css 3 hr Audio Literature

Mommie Dearest
Author/Reader: Christina Crawford
★★★

The image of a square-shouldered Joan Crawford, her face contorted with rage as she flails away at her child with a coat hanger, has been forever branded onto the American psyche, thanks to the book and movie that preceded this audio book. Perhaps this version suffers a little from overfamiliarity with the image of Christina Crawford's abusive, erratic, alcoholic mother. Here, Christina narrates in wounded tones, and a transcription of a 1949 radio interview is included, adding to the verisimilitude of the presentation.

2 css 3 hr Listen for Pleasure

My Life
Authors: Earvin "Magic" Johnson with William Novak
Reader: Danny Glover
★★★

Magic Johnson stunned the world when he announced in 1991 that he was infected with the HIV virus. His life story begins with a moment of love and triumph, the 1991 All-Star Game in Orlando, Florida, where he was carried off the floor by his friends and fellow players. From his Michigan boyhood to his triumphs on the basketball court, and his current battle with HIV, his story is a powerful one. Danny Glover's reading is nothing short of astounding.

2 css 1 hr Random House AudioBooks

My Lives
Author/Reader: Roseanne Arnold
★

By turns depressing, tedious, vulgar, and distasteful, this autobiographical work revolves around the author's struggles against practically everyone, from the writers and producers of her hit TV show *Roseanne* to her family—who, she maintains, abused her so much that she had to develop multiple personalities just to cope. Just about the only person—besides herself—who comes off sympathetically here is writer-comic Tom Arnold, whom she married and has subsequently divorced. Fans of *Roseanne* may enjoy this; even they should be warned, though.

2 css 3 hr Random House AudioBooks

On Wings of Eagles
Author: Ken Follett
Reader: Ron Rifkin
★★★

This is the true-life tale of the rescue of captured Americans by a volunteer group of corporate executives able to penetrate an Iranian prison. Well told by Follett, best known for penning *Eye of the Needle,* this adventure helped catapult Ross Perot—who financed the whole affair—into the limelight. However, colorful ex–Green Beret Bull Simons emerges as the star of the story.

2 css 3 hr Durkin Hayes Audio

One More Mission
Authors: Oliver L. North and David Roth
Reader: Oliver North
★★

North, a decorated Vietnam vet before his Iran-Contra days, returns to Vietnam to examine the reasons that the war still scars the American psyche. Some of his observations are obvious ones. Others, such as the idea that Lyndon Johnson's Great Society was more or less responsible for the "sons of the working poor" being disproportionately represented in the war, aren't. Those who can separate North from his political image as the embattled darling of America's far right will find this interesting, as will those who embrace his public persona.

2 css 3 hr Zondervan

Out of the Madness
Author: Jerrold Ladd
Reader: Tyrin Turner
★★

Out of the Madness opens with an agonizingly sad scene: A hungry, sick young boy, lies, with sweats and chills, on a filthy mattress while the heat of the Dallas summer rages. Metaphorically at least, the fever never leaves Jerrold Ladd, as he tells of his harrowing life in the projects and the heroin-addict mother whose life he despises but whose love he craves. Throughout, his hatred burns, aimed at the thieves, addicts, and murderers all around him; at white society for keeping him and his race down; even at the church. It's an angry, effective work, with actor Turner stumbling over some of Ladd's phrases, but giving the audio book an air of authenticity.

2 css 3 hr Time Warner AudioBooks

The Plumber
Authors: Joseph Salerno and Stephen J. Rivele
Reader: Robert Foxworth
★★★

Gangster Nicodemo Scarfo made the Philadelphia Mafia into a power that was truly something to be reckoned with. Prosecutors, police, government commissions, and the courts tried to bring Scarfo down but couldn't. Then one night, a plumber witnessed a murder—and that plumber, Joe Salerno, became a one-man wrecking crew who brought down the Philly mob. A fiery, true story told passionately by Robert Foxworth, this tape details a heroism that few can match.

2 css 3 hr The Publishing Mills AudioBooks

Profiles in Courage
Author: John F. Kennedy
Reader: John F. Kennedy, Jr.
★★★★

The Pulitzer Prize–winning book, written by Kennedy well before he ascended to the presidency of the United States, remains a compelling work, steeped in principle and character, and fueled by the idea that courage "is that most admirable of all human values." Stories include Sam Houston's unsuccessful fight to keep Texas from joining the Confederacy, John Quincy Adams's life of voting his conscience, and Andrew Jackson's impeachment trial. A wise, earnest book, it teaches, among other things, that today's poll-driven, finger-to-the-wind politicos are hardly a new development in American politics.

2 css 3 hr Caedmon Audio

The Quiet Room
Authors: Lori Schiller and Amanda Bennett
Reader: Mary Beth Hurt
★★★

Veteran actress Hurt gives quiet urgency to this true, first-person story of a woman's struggle with schizophrenia. Seventeen years old and a summer-camp counselor, Lori Schiller begins to hear voices telling her she must die. She wakes up in her bunk and leaps out the door, trying to outrace the demons. She'll keep running for almost fifteen years, through hospital stays, a cocaine addiction, and, interestingly enough, her employment as a mental health professional. While some, including the writer of the back-cover copy, will see Schiller as finally "triumphant," there's a definite element of stalemate at the conclusion.

2 css 3 hr Time Warner AudioBooks

The Real Man Inside
Author/Reader: Vern Becker
★★★

Author Becker couldn't understand it when his wife left him. After all, wasn't he one of those "nice Christian guys, faithful to their wives and families"? Then, he began finding other men to whom the same thing had happened, and in the process went from blaming women to discovering that his own approach to life was flawed. This interesting work—which talks of the vaguely disturbing "rattle inside" many men on the threshold of middle age—offers advice on how males can find their emotional and spiritual centers, and puts a different spin on the "men's movement."

2 css 3 hr Zondervan

Reba
Authors: Reba McEntire with Tom Carter
Reader: Reba McEntire
★★

Starting out on the defensive—upset by a *Star* tabloid feature on her and her husband's ex-spouses—McEntire sets a bit of a chip-on-the-shoulder tone that her familiar, bouyant, down-home voice never quite overcomes. Those who have followed her career from the beginning may also detect a bit of revisionist history in certain places. Otherwise, it's an interesting, well-written work, full of stories, observations, and reminiscences that will draw and hold the attention of most country fans.

2 css 3 hr Simon & Schuster Audio

Rogue Warrior
Author/Reader: Richard Marcinko
★★

Richard Marcinko, leader of the military's ultrasecret Seal Team Six, "makes Arnold Schwartzenegger look like Little Lord Fauntleroy," said *The New York Times Book Review.* The real action and the occasional humor is recounted by the man who actually did the fighting.

2 css 3 hr Simon & Schuster Audio

See, I Told You So
Author/Reader: Rush Limbaugh
★★

More liberal bashing, pontification, and right-wing yucks from America's best-known radio commentator, hot on the heels of his best-selling *The Way Things Ought to Be* (see page 248). After congratulating himself heartily for surviving the election of a Democratic president (as though he didn't know that it was giving him so many new targets), Limbaugh wastes no time getting into his favorite topic: himself, and his views on what's wrong with America. As in *The Way Things Ought to Be,* his bombastic, relentlessly self-congratulatory style will either amuse listeners or drive them away.

2 css 3 hr Simon & Schuster Audio

Sir Charles: The Wit and Wisdom of Charles Barkley
Authors/Readers: Charles Barkley with Rick Reilley
★

Here, Reilley sets things up by explaining just what a great interview pro basketball player Barkley is, and then goes about proving it by conducting a lengthy, occasionally vulgar, talk with Barkley that lets him sound off on everything from athletes as role models to threats from racist fans. At the end, the listener is left feeling that the whole thing has just been a long attempt to put a good spin on Barkley's controversial image—which it does fairly well, revealing Barkley as a pretty bright, pretty witty, guy.

1 css 1 hr Time Warner AudioBooks

Sleeping with the Devil
Author/Reader: Suzanne Finstad
★★★

This work of true crime tells the story of Barbra Piotrowski, a beautiful and accomplished woman whose lifelong ambition was to become a doctor. Then she met Richard Minns, a Texas millionaire and bodybuilder who took over her life, moved her to Houston, where he already had a wife, and hired assassins to kill her. A riveting book of obsession, possession, and violence.

2 css 3 hr The Publishing Mills AudioBooks

The Sound of Wine
Authors: Various
Reader: Eric Brotman
★★★

Wine aficionados will enjoy this paean to the joys and benefits of their favorite beverage, in which the fermented grape is celebrated in twelve articles and book excerpts, along with a couple of interviews. In the latter, Julia Child gives her thoughts on the subject—including what wine she thinks goes best with a hamburger—and winemaker Robert Mondavi discusses the whole question of alcoholic beverages in society. Judging from this tape, wine fans and wine writers are all sensible, moderate people who believe their beverage to be responsible for a whole slate of positive things, from better health to more interesting lives.

1 css 1½ hr Audio Library

The Tears of My Soul
Author: Kim Hyun Hee
Reader: Sun Yung Cho
★★

Only nineteen years old, lovely Kim Hyun Hee was drafted by North Korea's Communist party and trained in the skills of a master spy. Lethally proficient in martial arts, she only abandoned what she considered a good fight after triggering the death of more than a hundred people in the crash of Korean flight 858.

Reader Sun Yun Cho is a Broadway veteran who imparts the torment in Kim Hyun Hee's soul.

2 css 3 hr Harper Audio

There Are No Children Here
Author: Alex Kotlowitz
Reader: Whoopi Goldberg
★★

Lafayette and Pharoah Rivers live in Chicago's Henry Horner Homes, a public housing complex disfigured by crime and neglect. Here, in the bleak heart of the other America, Lafayette and Pharoah fight the odds, growing up where growing up is an achievement. Whoopi Goldberg reads here, and after a rather perfunctory introduction to the material, negotiates this tale with sincerity, but oddly enough her character voices are sometimes flat and indistinguishable from her narrative voice.

2 css 3hr The Publishing Mills AudioBooks

The Things That Matter Most
Author/Reader: Cal Thomas
★★★

Early on, columnist Thomas defines his target audience: people who believe that the American system has failed, whose access to major media is blocked, who have been ignored by the experts. In Thomas's opinion, "overtaxed Americans" have been betrayed by the "cultural and academic elite," who are busy trying to fulfill what he feels are the false promises of the sixties. Those not within his target audience may at least admire his approach, which, while being thoroughly conservative and reactionary, is delivered with sincerity and none of the sneer that audiences have come to expect from conservative commentators in the Age of Limbaugh.

2 css 3 hr Harper Audio

Think Big
Authors: Ben Carson, M.D., with Cecil Murphey
Reader: Ben Carson, M.D.
★★★

A positive-thinking treatise by Carson, a man who rose from a youth in a black ghetto to become a top pediatric neurosurgeon, *Think Big* is an anecdote-stuffed work full of incidents from Carson's own life. As the Zondervan imprint suggests, Carson is a man of faith, which figures into his life and his advice. Using the words "think big" as acronyms, he finds importance in the word each letter represents, from "talent" to "God." This is calm and rational counsel that always recommends a striving for excellence, no matter what the field of endeavor.

2 css 2½ hr Zondervan

This is Orson Welles
Authors/Readers: Orson Welles and Peter Bogdanovich
★★★★

Recorded over a period of ten years (you can actually hear Bogdanovich's voice change occasionally), this fascinating work was culled from some twenty hours of tape-recorded conversations between young director Bogdanovich and old lion Welles. What emerges is not only Welles's riveting commentary on Hollywood and his career, as well as his variety of moods, but the fact that his *unmade* films—including an adaptation of Joseph Conrad's *Heart of Darkness* (later the inspiration for Francis Ford Coppola's *Apocalypse Now*) and the story of Jesus Christ done as a period western—were as interesting as the ones he made. Originally recorded for a proposed written biography of Welles, the sound quality varies a bit, and there are a few moments of awkwardness from interviewer Bogdanovich, but none of that really gets in the way of Welles's wonderful commentary. In fact, it gives it a bit of vérité—you can even hear Welles puffing on his cigar!

4 css 4 hr Caedmon Audio

The Way of Art
Author/Reader: Joseph Campbell
★★

"The way of the mystic and the way of the artist are very much alike, except that the mystic does not have a craft." So says Joseph Campbell, noted mythologist, author, and lecturer. Drawing together observations made by Buddha, James Joyce, and others, Campbell—in this live recording from the Theater of the Open Eye in New York City—examines the way of the mystic, the way of the artist, mythology and metaphor, and the essence of the aesthetic experience.

1 css 55 min Mystic Fire Audio

The Way Things Ought to Be
Author/Reader: Rush Limbaugh
★★

Taking the thesis familiar to anyone who's listened to his radio program—that "disguised liberal movements" are attacking the American way of life—the self-described "harmless, lovable little fuzzball" levels his big cannon at the usual suspects. That he's perceived as scoring some direct hits is illustrated by the runaway popularity of this book in both its print and audio forms, and by the millions who listen to his broadcasts. There's really no middle ground with Limbaugh, nor with *The Way Things Ought to Be,* which is essentially a distillation of his radio programs, with some personal and biographical material thrown in. Listeners who are not fans of Limbaugh will be either disgusted or mortified.

2 css 2½ hr Simon & Schuster Audio

What Are People For?
Author/Reader: Wendell Berry
★

Wendell Berry, a professor of literature as well as a farmer, has been called "one of the clearest thinkers in America." Included here are discussions on ecology and the environment, commentaries on culture, and ruminations on the plight of the small farmer. Unfortunately, Berry's voice is very rough and untrained, and after a while, it really grates.

2 css 3 hr Audio Literature

What You Can Do to Avoid AIDS
Author: Earvin "Magic" Johnson
Readers: Robert O'Keefe; introduction by Magic Johnson
★★★

This Grammy-winning audio is a frank and comprehensive exploration of AIDS and its prevention. It offers a graphic yet sensitive approach to drugs, safer sex, and condoms and other preventive measures, as well as HIV testing and topics like abstinence and how to talk about sex with potential partners. Magic Johnson gives an honest and touching introduction, then turns the helm over to Robert O'Keefe, who, in a knowledgeable, informative style, discusses HIV. All net profits from the sale and licensing of this audio are donated to the Magic Johnson Foundation for prevention, education, research, and care in the battle against AIDS.

1 css 1 hr Random House AudioBooks

What's It All About?
Author/Reader: Michael Caine
★★★

Born in the charity wing of an English hospital, and afflicted with rickets and Saint Vitus' dance as an infant, Michael Caine went on to become one of the world's best-known actors. (The title of the audio book is taken from a line in the theme song to *Alfie,* his 1966 breakthrough film.) *What's It All About?* takes Caine through a childhood that runs through World War II, into his days as a TV actor and active participant in London's swinging sixties scene, and finally to Hollywood, where he reflects on his roles in such box-office smashes as *Educating Rita* and *Dressed to Kill.* An in-depth, personal work, told with considerable charm.

2 css 3 hr Random House AudioBooks

Why Do Clocks Run Clockwise?
Author: David Feldman
Readers: David Feldman, Maggie Albright, Rusty Magee, and Louise Williams
★★

Another adaptation of Feldman's popular *Imponderables* books (with "imponderables" defined as "those little mysteries of life that drive you nuts"), this takes the usual format of Feldman as quiz master, posing a question to three panelists, two of who try to bluff the listener. The questions range from the truly puzzling ("What happens to the tread that wears off tires?") to the somewhat lame ("Why are there both brown and white chicken eggs?"). It's a good play-along tape for road trips, but some listeners may wish for more imponderables and less cute banter among the panelists.

1 css 1 hr Caedmon Audio

Wild Swans
Author: Jung Chang
Reader: Anna Massey
★★★★

This is the true story of three women—Jung Chang, her mother, and her grandmother—whose fortunes mirror the tumultuous history of twentieth-century China. Anna Massey (*Peeping Tom* and *Frenzy*) is everything a storyteller should be—sharp-edged, focused, easy to follow, with a soft, haunting quality to her voice that makes the material unfold like a detailed tapestry.

4 css Durkin Hayes Audio

Woodsong
Author/Reader: Gary Paulsen
★★★★

Author Paulsen (*The Winter Room, Dogsong*) tells an enthralling tale of the northern wilderness and the life within it, wrapping his observations around a narrative of his intensive training for the seventeen-day Alaskan dog race known as the Iditarod. The compelling nature of the tape, however, comes less from the race itself and more from Paulsen's detailed recollections of natural forces in action. It can be unbelievably brutal, as in the tale of wolves bringing down a deer. It can be amusing. And it can even be chilling, as in his and the team's discovery of a "ghost" in the starless night. Always, Paulsen's quiet, earnest voice rings with the sense of discovery and adventure—and, sometimes, danger.

2 css 2 hr 20 min Bantam Audio

The Yosemite
Author: John Muir
Reader: Michael Zebulon
★★★

An audio version of the late nineteenth-century book, *Yosemite* is full of the sense of wonder and majesty experienced by Muir upon first encountering the Yosemite area of east central California. With the joy of discovery, Muir hops over rocks and around falls, better to see and comment on the natural beauty that floods his vision. *Yosemite* will appeal mainly to armchair explorers, as well as those concerned with the preservation of America's natural resources. The Sierra Club and Audio Literature first issued this in 1990, in conjunction with Yosemite National Park's centennial celebration.

1 css 1½ hr Audio Literature

Zlata's Diary
Authors: Zlata Filipovic; translated by Robert Laffont
Readers: Dorota Puzio; introduction by Janine di Giovanni
★★★★

"The Anne Frank of Sarajevo" was eleven years old, with her thoughts turned to a new school year, when her diary was begun. Soon, the war crept into her writing, eventually all but taking it over as she wrote about surviving snipers, losing running water and electricity, and even the death of some of her friends. As with Anne Frank's World II diaries, *Zlata's Diary* shows once again the horrible randomness and awful, unwanted intimacy of war, as well as the resiliency of the human spirit even under the most horrific of circumstances.

1 css 1½ hr Penguin HighBridge Audio

Abduction: Human Encounters with Aliens
A: John Mack, M.D.
R: Josef Sommer
S&S

About Face
A: David Hackworth and Julie Sherman
R: David Hackworth
S&S

Accidentally on Purpose
A/R: Michael York
DOVE

All's Fair
A/R: James Carville and Mary Matalin
S&S

The American West
A: Dee Brown
AUDLIT

Among the Porcupines
A/R: Carol Matthau
MILLS

Amy Fisher: My Story
A: Amy Fisher and Sheila Weller
R: Carolyn McCormick and Ari Meyers
S&S

Anaïs Nin Herself Reads Selections from Her Diaries
A/R: Anaïs Nin
PART

Anaïs Nin Reads
A/R: Anaïs Nin
HARP

And If You Play Golf, You're My Friend
A: Harvey Penick with Bud Shrake
R: Jack Whitaker
S&S

And the Band Played On
A: Randy Shilts
R: Willem Dafoe
S&S

And the Sea Will Tell
A: Vincent Bugliosi with Bruce B. Henderson
R: Richard Crenna
S&S

Anguished English: An Anthology of Accidental Assaults upon Our Language
A/R: Richard Lederer
S&S

Ann-Margret: My Story
A: Ann-Margret with Todd Gold
R: Ann-Margret; introduction by George Burns
S&S

Anne Frank: The Diary of a Young Girl
A: Anne Frank
R: Julie Harris
PART

Anne Frank: The Diary of a Young Girl (The Definitive Edition)
A: Anne Frank
R: Winona Ryder

Ari: The Life and Times of Aristotle Onassis
A: Peter Evans
R: Sarah Miles
DOVE

The Art of Eating
A: M.F.K. Fisher
R: Diane Baker
PART

Aspire to the Heavens
A/R: Mary Higgins Clark
DOVE

At Dawn We Slept
A: Gordon W. Prange
R: Tony Roberts
PENG

The Autobiography of Mark Twain
A: Mark Twain
R: Will Geer
HARP

Backlash: The Undeclared War against American Women
A/R: Susan Faludi
MILLS

Backstage Passes
A/R: Angela Bowie
HARP

Bailey White: An Interesting Life (An NPR Presentation)
A/R: Bailey White
DOVE

Barbara Bush: A Memoir
A/R: Barbara Bush
S&S

Baseball
A: Geoffrey C. Ward and Ken Burns
R: Ken Burns
RH

Be My Baby: How I Survived Mascara, Miniskirts, and Madness, or My Life as a Fabulous Ronette
A: Ronnie Spector with Vince Waldron
R: Ronnie Spector
MILLS

The Beauty Myth
A/R: Naomi Wolf
HARP

Behind the Mask
A: Dave Pallone with Alan Steinberg
R: Dave Pallone
DOVE

The Bell Curve: Intelligence and Class Structure in American Life
A: Richard J. Bernstein and Charles Murray
R: Charles Murray
S&S

Berry, Me and Motown
A/R: Raynoma Gordy Singleton
MILLS

The Best and the Brightest
Twentieth Anniversary Edition
A: David Halberstam
R: David Clennon
RH

The Best of the Old Farmer's Almanac: The First 200 Years
A: Judson Hale
R: Robert Blackburn and Ron Frazier
RH

Beyond Love
A: Dominique Lapierre
R: Michael York
DOVE

Beyond Reason
A: Ken Englade
R: Michael McConnohie
ART

Beyond Uhura
A/R: Nichelle Nichols
RH

Black Boy
A: Richard Wright
R: Brock Peters
HARP

Black Elk: The Sacred Pipe
A: Joseph Epes Brown
R: Fred Contreras; accompanied by the drums and chants of Chemo Candelaria
AUDLIT

Black Elk Speaks
A: John G. Neihardt
R: Fred Contreras
AUDLIT

Black Holes and Baby Universes and Other Essays
A: Stephen Hawking
R: Simon Prebble
BDD

Black Widow
A: R. Robin McDonald
R: Michael McConnohie
ART

Blue Thunder: How the Mafia Owned and Finally Murdered Cigarette Boat King Donald Aronow
A: Thomas Burdick and Charlene Mitchell
R: Robert Foxworth
S&S

The Book of Virtues Audio Library, Volume I
A: William J. Bennett
R: William and Elayne Bennett and others
S&S

The Book of Virtues Audio Library, Volume II
A: William J. Bennett
R: William and Elayne Bennett and others
S&S

Bootlegger's Boy
A/R: Barry Switzer
DOVE

Boss of Bosses: The Fall of the Godfather: The FBI and Paul Castellano
A: Joseph F. O'Brien and Andris Kurins
R: James Naughton
S&S

The Boy Who Would Be King
A: Earl Greenwood with Kathy Tracy
MILLS

The Boys
A/R: Skip Bayless
S&S

Breaking the Silence
A: Mariette Hartley with Anne Commire
R: Mariette Hartley
MILLS

The Bridge Across Forever: A Love Story
A: Richard Bach
R: Richard Bach and Leslie Parrish-Bach
ART

A Brief History of Time
A: Stephen W. Hawking
R: Michael Jackson
DOVE

The Broken Cord
A/R: Michael Dorris
HARP

By Myself
A/R: Lauren Bacall
RH

By Way of Deception: The Making and Unmaking of a Mossad Officer
A/R: Victor Ostrovsky and Claire Hoy
ART

The Cannibal Queen
A/R: Stephen Coonts
S&S

Captain History
A: Michael Viner and Allan Katz
R: Mel Blanc and Gary Owens
DOVE

Carl Sandburg Reading a Lincoln Album
A/R: Carl Sandburg
HARP

The Cat and the Curmudgeon
A/R: Cleveland Amory
S&S

The Cat Who Came for Christmas
A/R: Cleveland Amory
RH

The Cat Who Went to Paris
A: Peter Gathers
R: Anthony Heald
RH

Cellar of Horror
A: Ken Englade
R: Michael McConnohie
ART

Chaos
A: James Gleick
R: Michael Jackson
DOVE

Chicago Days, Hoboken Nights
A/R: Daniel M. Pinkwater
DOVE

Chief: My Life in the L.A.P.D.
A: Daryl Gates with Diane K. Shah
R: Daryl Gates
DOVE

China Calls: Paving the Way for Nixon's Historic Journey to China
A: Anne Collins Walker
R: Joseph Campanella
DOVE

Chutzpah
A/R: Alan M. Dershowitz
DOVE

A Circle of Nations: Voices and Visions of American Indians
A: Edited by John Gattuso
R: Joy Harjo and Simon Ortiz
AUDLIT

The City of Joy
A: Dominique Lapierre
R: Michael York
DOVE

The Civil War
A: Geoffrey C. Ward with Ric Burns and Ken Burns
R: Ken Burns
RH

Close Encounters
A/R: Mike Wallace and Gary Gates
DOVE

The Closing of the American Mind
A/R: Allan Bloom
S&S

Coming into the Country
A/R: John McPhee
RH

Coming of Age in the Milky Way
A/R: Timothy Ferris
DOVE

Communion
A: Whitley Strieber
R: Roddy McDowall
DOVE

Como Hablar En Publico Como un Profesional (Osgood on Speaking)
(Spanish)
A: Charles Osgood
DOVE

A Company of Adventurers
A: Peter C. Newman
R: Gordon Pinsent
DURK

Compassion in Action
A/R: Ram Dass and Mirabai Bush
MILLS

Connections
A/R: James Burke
ART

Contract Killer
A: William Hoffman and Lake Headley
R: Joseph Campanella
RH

Contract with America
A: Newt Gingrich and Dick Armey
R: Larry Robinson
RH

Contrary to Popular Opinion
A/R: Alan M. Dershowitz
DOVE

The Control of Nature
A/R: John McPhee
RH

The Cosby Wit
A: Bill Adler
R: Gary Owens
DOVE

Crazy English
A/R: Richard Lederer
S&S

Creating Character Voices for Fun and Profit
A/R: Patrick Fraley
PART

The Creators
A: Daniel J. Boorstin
R: Michael Jackson
MILLS

Cruel Doubt
A: Joe McGinniss
R: Stacy Keach
S&S

Dances with Wolves
A/R: Michael Blake
PART

The Dancing Wu Li Masters
A/R: Gary Zukav
ART

Darkness Visible
A/R: William Styron
RH

The Day the Universe Changed
A/R: James Burke
ART

Days of Grace
A: Arthur Ashe and Arnold Rampersad
R: Joe Morton
RH

Deadly Medicine
A: Kelly Moore and Dan Reed
R: Michael McConnohie
ART

Debbie: My Life
A: Debbie Reynolds and David Patrick Columbia
R: Debbie Reynolds
DOVE

December 7, 1941
A: Gordon W. Prange
R: Tony Roberts
PENG

Den of Thieves
A: James B. Stewart
R: John Hockenberry
S&S

Diana: Her True Story
A: Andrew Morton
R: Stephanie Beacham
S&S

Dirty Little Secrets: Military Information You're Not Supposed to Know
A: James F. Dunnigan and Albert A. Nofi
R: James F. Dunnigan
DOVE

The Discoverers
A: Daniel J. Boorstin
R: Christopher Cazenove
MILLS

A Dog's Life
A: Peter Mayle
R: Simon Jones
RH

Dolly: My Life and Other Unfinished Business
A/R: Dolly Parton
HARP

Don't Know Much About History
A: Kenneth C. Davis
R: Dick Rodstein; introduction by Kenneth C. Davis
BDD

Double Cross: The Explosive, Inside Story of the Mobster Who Controlled America
A: Sam Giancana and Chuck Giancana
R: Jerry Orbach
HARP

The Downing Street Years
A/R: Margaret Thatcher
HARP

Dreamlovers
A: Dodd Darin
R: Allison Smith and Steven Weber
TW

Driving Under the Affluence
A/R: Julia Phillips
HARP

Eagles over the Gulf: Desert Storm—the Pilots' Stories
A: Louisville Productions
ART

Earth in the Balance
A/R: Vice President Al Gore
DOVE

Eat Smart, Think Smart
A/R: Robert Haas
MILLS

The Education of Little Tree
A: Forrest Carter
R: Peter Coyote
AUDLIT

Eight Seconds
A: Monte Merrick
R: Luke Perry
HARP

Eleanor Roosevelt, Volume I
A/R: Blanche Wiesen Cook
DOVE

Elizabeth and Philip
A: Charles Higham and Roy Moseley
R: Michael Jackson
DOVE

Elizabeth Taylor: The Last Star
A: Kitty Kelley
R: Susan Strasberg
DOVE

Elvis: An Audio Scrapbook
Westwood One
R: Elvis Presley
S&S

The Emperor's New Mind, Volumes I and II
A: Roger Penrose
R: Michael Jackson
DOVE

Enjoying Opera: An Inside Look at *La Bohème, Carmen, La Traviata,* and *The Magic Flute*
A: Dale Harris
PENG

Enter Talking
A/R: Joan Rivers
DOVE

The Era
A: Roger Kahn
R: Mel Allen
ART

Everest, "A Sound History, 1922–1983"
R: Early Pennington
DURK

Every Living Thing
A: James Herriot
R: Christopher Timothy
ART

Every Living Thing, Part II
A: James Herriot
R: Christopher Timothy
ART

Every Living Thing: The Complete Audio Edition
A: James Herriot
R: Christopher Timothy
ART

Every Spy a Prince
A/R: Dan Raviv
MILLS

Everybody Loves Oprah!
A: Norman King
R: Ruby Dee
DOVE

Everything She Ever Wanted
A: Ann Rule
R: Betty Buckley
S&S

The Executioner's Song
A: Norman Mailer
R: Michael McConnohie
ART

Explore the World of Classical Music
Produced by Commuter College
PART

The Family Heart: A Memoir of Our Son's Coming Out
A: Robb Forman Dew
R: Stockard Channing
S&S

The Fatal Shore
A/R: Robert Hughes
RH

Fatal Vision
A: Joe McGinniss
R: Christopher Reeve
S&S

The Feminine Force
A/R: Georgette Mosbacher
S&S

The Fifties
A: David Halberstam
R: Edwin Newman
RH

Final Cut
A: Steven Bach
R: Roddy McDowall
DOVE

Final Exit
A/R: Derek Humphry
DOVE

Fire with Fire: The New Female Power and How It Will Change the 21st Century
A/R: Naomi Wolf
RH

First Lady from Plains
A/R: Rosalynn Carter
S&S

500 Nations
A: Alvin M. Josephy, Jr.
RH

Flashbacks
A/R: Timothy Leary
DOVE

For All Those Who Love the Game: Lessons and Teaching for Women
A: Harvey Penick and Bud Shrake
S&S

Forty Days
A/R: Bob Simon
MILLS

The Fountain of Age
A/R: Betty Friedan
S&S

Friday Night Lights
A: H. G. Bissinger
R: Alex Karras
MILLS

Fuzzy Thinking: The New Science of Fuzzy Logic
A: Bart Kosko
AUDLIT

Gal: A True Life
A: Ruthie Bolton
R: C. C. H. Pounder
AUDLIT

Gangland: How the FBI Broke the Mob
A: Howard Blum
R: Jerry Orbach
S&S

Genius: The Life and Science of Richard Feynman
A: James Gleick
R: F. Murray Abraham
RH

Gilligan, Maynard and Me
A/R: Bob Denver
DOVE

Girl, Interrupted
A/R: Susanne Kaysen
RH

Goldwyn, A Biography
A: A. Scott Berg
R: Roddy McDowall
DOVE

The Good Calorie Diet: The Revolutionary New Diet Program Based on Inhibiting Fat Formation
A/R: Philip Lipetz, Ph.D.
HARP

The Good Times
A: Russell Baker
R: Arte Johnson
DOVE

A Good Walk Spoiled: Days and Nights on the PGA Tour
A: John Feinstein
TW

Goodbye Jumbo, Hello Cruel World
A/R: Louie Anderson
PENG

Grace
A: Robert Lacey
R: Donna Mills
DOVE

Great American Women's Speeches
A: Edited by Sharon Donovan
R: Eileen Heckart, Claudia McNeil, and Mildred Natwick
HARP

Great Black Speeches
A: Edited by John Graham
R: Claudia McNeil and Norman Matlock
HARP

The Great Getty
A: Robert Lenzner
R: Liz Smith
DOVE

The Great One: The Life and Legend of Jackie Gleason
A: William A. Henry III
R: Frank Ferrante
MILLS

The Grimaldis of Monaco
A: Anne Edwards
R: Roddy McDowall
DOVE

Growing Up
A: Russell Baker
R: Mason Adams
PART

The Haldeman Diaries
A: H. R. Haldeman
MILLS

Hardball: A Season in the Projects
A: Daniel Coyle
R: Giancarlo Esposito
HARP

The Harvey Penick Boxed Set
A: Harvey Penick with Bud Shrake
R: Ben Crenshaw, Tom Kite, Jack Whitaker, and Kathy Whitworth
S&S

The Heart of Justice
A: William J. Coughlin
BRILL

Henry Miller's People
R: Mitchell Ryan
AUDLIT

Henry Rollins: Get in the Van
A/R: Henry Rollins
TW

Here on Gilligan's Island
A: Russell Johnson and Steve Cox
R: Russell Johnson
DOVE

The Hero with a Thousand Faces, Volume I: The Adventure of the Hero
A: Joseph Campbell
R: Ralph Blum; commentary by Joseph Campbell
ART

The Hero with a Thousand Faces, Volume II: The Cosmogonic Cycle
A: Joseph Campbell
R: Ralph Blum; commentary by Joseph Campbell
ART

Hoffa
A: Ken Englade
R: Jerry Orbach
HARP

Holographic Golf
A/R: Larry Miller
HARP

The Hot Zone
A: Richard Preston
S&S

How We Die
A/R: Sherwin B. Nuland, M.D.
RH

I Had a Hammer
A: Hank Aaron with Lonnie Wheeler
R: Courtney Vance
HARP

I Know Why the Caged Bird Sings
A/R: Maya Angelou
RH

I Love Paul Revere, Whether He Rode or Not
A: Richard Shenkman
R: Gary Owens
DOVE

I Love This Game: My Life and Baseball
A: Kirby Puckett
R: Paul Calderon
HARP

I Never Played the Game
A/R: Howard Cosell
DOVE

I Send a Voice
A: Evelyn Eaton
R: Ellen Burstyn
AUDLIT

If You Really Loved Me
A/R: Ann Rule
S&S

Illiberal Education
A: Dinesh D'Souza
R: Joseph Campanella
DOVE

In Cold Blood
A: Truman Capote
R: Michael McConnohie
ART

An Incomplete Education
A: Judy Jones and William Wilson
R: Jane Gennaro and Dennis Predovic
RH

Indian Heroes and Great Chieftains
A: Charles Eastman
AUDLIT

The Intimate Sex Lives of Famous People
A: Irving, Sylvia, and Amy Wallace and David Wallechinsky
R: Robin Leach
DOVE

Iron John
A/R: Robert Bly
RH

Isaac Asimov's Guide to Earth and Space
A: Isaac Asimov
R: Michael Jackson
DOVE

It Doesn't Take a Hero
A: General H. Norman Schwarzkopf with Peter Petre
R: General H. Norman Schwarzkopf
BDD

It Would Be So Nice If You Weren't Here
A/R: Charles Grodin
DOVE

It's Always Something
A/R: Gilda Radner
S&S

JFK: Conspiracy
A: Public Interest Affiliates
R: Edwin Newman
ART

Jaguar Woman
A/R: Lynn V. Andrews
HARP

Jazz Cleopatra: Josephine Baker in Her Time
A: Phyllis Rose
R: Lynn Whitfield
ART

John Chancellor Makes Me Cry
A: Anne Rivers Siddons
R: Dana Ivey
HARP

John Muir: The Spirit of Wilderness
A/R: Lee Stetson
PART

Kaffir Boy
A: Mark Mathabane
R: Howard Rollins
DOVE

The Kennedy Women
A: Laurence Leamer
BRILL

The Kennedys
A: Peter Collier and David Horowitz
R: Joseph Campanella
DOVE

The Kid Stays in the Picture
A/R: Robert Evans
DOVE

King, Warrior, Magician, Lover
A/R: Robert Moore and Douglas Gillette
HARP

King Talk: The Secrets of Good Conversation—How to Talk to Anybody, Anytime, Anywhere
A: Larry King with Bill Gilbert
R: Larry King
RH

Koop: The Memoirs of America's Family Doctor
A/R: Dr. C. Everett Koop
DOVE

The Language and Music of the Wolves
R: Robert Redford
PART

Larry King: Champions
A: Larry King
R: Larry King and guests
S&S

Larry King: Laughs
A: Larry King
R: Larry King and guests
S&S

Larry King: Legends
A: Larry King
R: Larry King with guests
S&S

The Last Brother
A: Joe McGinniss
R: Cotter Smith
S&S

Last Chance to See
A: Douglas Adams and Mark Carwardine
R: Douglas Adams
RH

The Last Great Ride
A/R: Brandon Tartikoff
DOVE

Last Train to Memphis: The Rise of Elvis Presley
A: Peter Guralnick
R: J. Charles
BRILL

The Last Tsar: The Life and Death of Nicholas II
A: Edvard Radzinsky
R: David McCallum
BDD

Legacies: A Chinese Mosaic
A/R: Bette Bao Lord
MILLS

Legends, Lies and Cherished Myths of American History
A: Richard Shenkman
R: Gary Owens
DOVE

Legends, Lies and Cherished Myths of World History
A: Richard Shenkman
R: Arte Johnson
DOVE

Leslie Nielsen: The Naked Truth
A: Leslie Nielsen and David Fisher
R: Leslie Nielsen
S&S

Letters to a Young Poet
A: Rainer Maria Rilke; translated by Stephen Mitchell
R: Stephen Mitchell
AUDLIT

A Liar's Autobiography
A/R: Graham Chapman
DOVE

Life, Liberty and the Pursuit of Happiness
A/R: Peggy Noonan
RH

Life Wish and Life Lines
A: Jill Ireland
R: Jenny Seagrove
DOVE

Lightningbolt
A: Hyemeyohsts Storm
R: Hyemeyohsts and Swan Storm
HARP

Lincoln at Gettysburg
A/R: Garry Wills
DOVE

A Little House Sampler
A: Laura Ingalls Wilder and Rose Wilder
R: Judy Collins
HARP

Little Man: Meyer Lansky and the Gangster Life
A: Robert Lacey
R: Ron Silver
DOVE

The Long Gray Line
A: Rick Atkinson
R: Bruce Weitz
DOVE

Long Walk to Freedom
A: Nelson Mandela
R: Danny Glover
TW

Looking for a Ship
A/R: John McPhee
RH

Losing Jessica
A: Robby DeBoer with Jane Marks
R: Robby DeBoer
BDD

Lost Moon: The Perilous Voyage of Apollo 13
A: Jim Lovell and Jeffrey Kluger
R: Introduction by Jim Lovell
S&S

Love, Alice: My Life as a Honeymooner
A: Audrey Meadows with Joseph A. Daley
R: Audrey Meadows
RH

Love and Friendship
A: Allan Bloom
R: Nicholas Kepros
S&S

Love Can Build A Bridge
A: Naomi Judd with Bud Schaetzle
R: Naomi Judd
RH

Love, Love and Love
A/R: Sandra Bernhard
S&S

Love, War and the Art of Politics
A/R: James Carville and Mary Matalin
S&S

Ludlum on Ludlum
A/R: Robert Ludlum
BDD

Maggie's American Dream: The Life and Times of a Black Family
A: James P. Comer
R: Ossie Davis and Ruby Dee
PENG

Makes Me Wanna Holler: A Young Black Man in America
A/R: Nathan McCall
RH

Malcolm X
(An NPR Presentation)
DOVE

The Man Who Stayed Behind
A: Sidney Rittenberg and Amanda Bennett
R: Josef Sommer
S&S

Mark It and Strike It
A/R: Steve Allen
DOVE

Medicine Woman
A/R: Lynn V. Andrews
HARP

Meeting of Minds
Volume I: Theodore Roosevelt, Thomas Paine, Thomas Aquinas and Cleopatra
R: Steve Allen
DOVE

Meeting of Minds
Volume II: Ulysses S. Grant, Marie Antoinette, Sir Thomas More and Karl Marx
R: Steve Allen
DOVE

Meeting of Minds
Volume III: Charles Darwin, Emily Dickinson, Galileo and Attila the Hun
R: Steve Allen
DOVE

Meeting of Minds
Volume IV: The Marquis de Sade, Cesare Beccaria, Empress Tz'u-hsi and Frederick Douglass
R: Steve Allen
DOVE

Meeting of Minds
Volume V: Martin Luther, Voltaire, Plato and Florence Nightingale
R: Steve Allen
DOVE

Meeting of Minds
Volume VI: Sir Francis Bacon, Susan B. Anthony, Emiliano Zapata and Socrates
R: Steve Allen
DOVE

Meeting of Minds
Volume VII: St. Augustine of Hippo, Empress Theodora of the Byzantine Empire, Thomas Jefferson and Bertrand Russell
R: Steve Allen
DOVE

Meeting of Minds
Volume VIII: Sun Yat-Sen, Machiavelli, Elizabeth Barrett Browning
R: Steve Allen
DOVE

Meeting of Minds
Volume IX: William Shakespeare's Most Enigmatic Characters
R: Steve Allen
DOVE

Meeting of Minds
Volume X: Margaret Sanger, Mahatma Gandhi and Adam Smith
R: Steve Allen
DOVE

Meeting of Minds
Volume XI: Niccolo Paganini, William Blake and Leonardo da Vinci
R: Steve Allen
DOVE

Meeting of Minds
Volume XII: Daniel O'Connell, Oliver Cromwell and Catherine the Great
R: Steve Allen
DOVE

Memo from Darryl F. Zanuck
A: Edited and annotated by Rudy Behlmer
R: Richard D. Zanuck
DOVE

Menendez Murder Trial Courtroom Cassette #1
Mutual Broadcasting System
Actual courtroom testimony
S&S

Mid-Life Confidential: The Rock Bottom Remainders Tour America with Three Chords and an Attitude
A/R: Stephen King, Amy Tan, Dave Barry, Roy Blount, Jr., Ridley Pearson, Dave Marsh, Barbara Kingsolver, and others
PENG

Midnight in the Garden of Good and Evil
A: John Berendt
R: Anthony Heald
RH

Midterm Report: The Class of '65
A: David Wallechinsky
R: David Wallechinsky, Tony Bill, Gloria Loring and Lynne Moody
DOVE

The Mind's Sky: Human Intelligence in a Cosmic Context
A/R: Timothy Ferris
DOVE

Miracle at Midway
A: Gordon W. Prange
R: Tony Roberts
PENG

More Memories
A: Ralph Emery with Tom Carter
R: Ralph Emery
S&S

Mortal Error
A: Bonar Menninger
R: John Hockenberry
S&S

Move On: Adventures in the Real World
A/R: Linda Ellerbee
HARP

Moving Beyond Words
A/R: Gloria Steinem
S&S

Murder in Boston
A: Ken Englade
R: Michael Rider
ART

Murder in Little Egypt
A: Darcy O'Brien
R: Gregory Snegoff
ART

Mutant Message Down Under
A: Marlo Morgan
HARP

My Breast
A/R: Joyce Wadler
S&S

My Favorite Summer, 1956
A: Mickey Mantle and Phil Pepe
R: Phil Pepe
MILLS

My Life in Three Acts
A: Helen Hayes with Katherine Hatch
R: Helen Hayes
ART

My Life with Martin Luther King, Jr.
A/R: Coretta Scott King
HARP

My Lucky Stars
A/R: Shirley MacLaine
BDD

The Myth of Male Power
A/R: Warren Farrell
S&S

Native Son
A: Richard Wright
R: James Earl Jones
HARP

A Natural History of Love
A/R: Diane Ackerman
MILLS

A Natural History of the Senses
A/R: Diane Ackerman
MILLS

The Next Century
A: David Halberstam
R: E. G. Marshall
DOVE

Nice Couples Do
A: Joan E. Lloyd
R: Maggie Albright
TW

Nixon: A Life
A: John Aitken
R: Alan Rachins
DOVE

The Nobel Lecture in Literature, 1993
A/R: Toni Morrison
RH

Nobody Nowhere
A: Donna Williams
R: Debra Winger
AUDLIT

Not Without My Daughter
A: Betty Mahmoody with William Hoffer
R: Julie Just
ART

Now
A/R: Lauren Bacall
RH

October 1964
A: David Halberstam
RH

October Surprise
A: Gary Sick
R: Joe Regalbuto
MILLS

Old Friends
A/R: Tracy Kidder
PENG

Old Songs in a New Cafe
A/R: Robert Waller
S&S

On the Line
A: Larry King
R: Larry King with Mark Stencel
MILLS

On the Pulse of Morning
A/R: Maya Angelou
RH

On Writing Well
A/R: William Zinsser
HARP

One Frog Can Make a Difference: Kermit's Guide to Life in the '90s
A: Robert P. Riger as told by Kermit
R: Kermit the Frog; special appearance by Miss Piggy
S&S

One Lifetime Is Not Enough
A/R: Zsa Zsa Gabor
S&S

The Osgood Files
A/R: Charles Osgood
S&S

Oswald's Tale
A: Norman Mailer
R: Norman Mailer and Norris Chuck Mailer
RH

Out of Africa
A: Isak Dinesen
R: Julie Harris
PART

Papa Hemingway
A: A. E. Hotchner
R: Robert Stack
DURK

Paper Lion
A/R: George Plimpton
DURK

Parables and Portraits
A/R: Stephen Mitchell
AUDLIT

The Path to Power
A/R: Margaret Thatcher
HARP

Pearl Harbor
A: Gordon W. Prange
R: Tony Roberts
PENG

Perfect Victim
A: Christine McGuire and Carla Norton
R: Amanda Plummer
DOVE

Peripheral Visions: Learning Along the Way
A: Mary Catherine Bateson
HARP

Peter Mayle's Provence
(Contains *Toujours Provence* and *A Year In Provence*)
A: Peter Mayle
R: Peter Mayle and Patrick MacNee
ART

The Physics of Immortality
A: Frank J. Tipler
BDD

The Pilgrim Saga
A: Edited by Philip L. Barbour
R: Alan Howard, Barry Stanton, and full cast
HARP

The Popcorn Report
A/R: Faith Popcorn
S&S

Possessed: The True Story of an Exorcism
A: Thomas Allen
BDD

Powershift
A: Alvin Toffler
R: Introduction by Alvin Toffler
BDD

Prairyerth
A: William Least Heat-Moon
R: Cotter Smith
S&S

Pride: The Charley Pride Story
A: Charley Pride with Jim Henderson
R: Charley Pride
MILLS

Princess: A True Story of Life behind the Veil in Saudi Arabia
A: Jean P. Sasson
R: Valerie Bertinelli
ART

Princess Sultana's Daughters
A: Jean P. Sasson
BDD

The Prize: The Epic Quest for Oil, Money and Power: The Battle for World Mastery
A: Daniel Yergin
R: Bob Jamieson
S&S

A Prophet with Honor
A: William Martin
R: Joseph Campanella
DOVE

Pryor Convictions
A: Richard Pryor
R: Charles Dutton
RH

P. S. Jack Paar
A/R: Jack Paar
DURK

Pure Baseball: Pitch by Pitch for the Advanced Fan
A/R: Keith Hernandez
HARP

Race Matters
A/R: Cornel West
PART

The Ragman's Son
A/R: Kirk Douglas
S&S

Random Acts of Kindness
A: Chuck Wall
BDD

Read It Again!: How to Read Aloud to Kids
A/R: Patrick Fraley
PART

Real Men Don't Bond
A: Bruce Feirstein
R: John Hockenberry and Keith Szarabajka
S&S

Right Reason
A/R: William F. Buckley, Jr.
PART

Rise and Walk
A/R: Dennis Byrd
HARP

Rising from the Plains
A: John McPhee
R: John and Yolanda McPhee
RH

Rivethead: Tales from the Assembly Line
A: Ben Hamper
R: Joe Don Baker
DOVE

Robert Frost: Fire and Ice
A: Jane August and Arthur Peterson
R: Arthur Peterson
PART

Rogue Warrior Two: Red Cell
A: Richard Marcinko and John Weisman
R: Richard Marcinko
S&S

Room for Danny
A: Danny Thomas with Bill Davidson
R: Milton Berle, Red Buttons, Sid Caesar, and Jan Murray; anecdotes by George Burns and Bob Hope
ART

Run with the Hunted: A Charles Bukowski Reader
A/R: Charles Bukowski
HARP

Ryan White: My Own Story
A: Ryan White and Ann Marie Cunningham
R: Lukas Haas
DOVE

Schindler's Legacy: True Stories of the List Survivors
A: Elinor J. Brecher
R: Full cast
PENG

A Season for Justice
A: Morris Dees with Steve Fiffer
R: Morris Dees
MILLS

Secret Ceremonies
A: Deborah Laake
R: Meredith MacRae
DOVE

Secret Soldier: The Autobiography of Israel's Greatest Commando
A: Muki Betzer with Robert Rosenberg
HARP

Secrets of a Sparrow
A/R: Diana Ross
RH

Serving in Silence
A: Margarette Cammermeyer with Chris Fisher
R: Lee Meriwether
PENG

A Seven Storey Mountain
A: Thomas Merton
R: Sidney Lanier
AUDLIT

Shelley Two: The Middle of My Century
A/R: Shelley Winters
S&S

Shot in the Heart
A: Mikal Gilmore
R: Will Patton
BDD

Silent Spring
A: Rachel Carson
R: Ellen Burstyn
DURK

Small Sacrifices
A/R: Ann Rule
S&S

Son of the Morning Star
A: Evan S. Connell
R: Joseph Campanella
MILLS

Songs of the Doomed
A/R: Hunter S. Thompson
S&S

Standing Firm: A Vice-Presidential Memoir
A/R: Dan Quayle
HARP

Star Trek Memories
A: William Shatner and Chris Kreski
R: William Shatner
HARP

Stephen Hawking's Universe
A: John Boslough
R: Michael Jackson
DOVE

Stephen W. Hawking's Life Works: The Cambridge Lectures
A/R: Stephen W. Hawking
DOVE

Still Talking
A/R: Joan Rivers
DOVE

Stranger at the Gate: To Be Gay and Christian in America
A/R: Mel White
S&S

The Stranger Beside Me
A/R: Ann Rule
S&S

Sudden Fury
A: Leslie Walker
R: Michael McConnohie
ART

Suetonius: The Twelve Caesars
A: Suetonius; translated by Robert Graves
R: Fritz Weaver
PENG

Summer of '49
A: David Halberstam
R: Mel Allen
DOVE

Talking Back to Prozac
A: Peter Breggin, M.D., and Ginger Ross Breggin
MILLS

The Tao of Physics
A: Fritjof Capra, Ph.D.
R: Michael McConnohie
ART

Target Tokyo
A: Gordon W. Prange
R: Tony Roberts
PENG

A Taste of Power
A/R: Elaine Brown
HARP

Tell Me More
A: Larry King
R: Larry King and Peter Occhiogrosso
MILLS

Telling: Confessions, Concessions, and Other Flashes of Light
A/R: Marion Winik
RH

The Tempting of America
A/R: Robert H. Bork
DOVE

A Terrible Liar
A/R: Hume Cronyn
S&S

They Can Kill You but They Can't Eat You . . . and Other Lessons from the Front
A/R: Dawn Steel
S&S

They Made a Monkee Out of Me
A/R: Davy Jones
DOVE

Thinking Out Loud: On the Personal, the Political, the Public and the Private
A/R: Anna Quindlen
S&S

Thoreau and Emerson: Nature and Spirit
A: Henry David Thoreau and Ralph Waldo Emerson
R: Russ Barnett, Howard Mumford Jones, and Kenneth S. Lynn
PART

365 Ways You Can Save the Earth
A: Michael Viner with Pat Hilton
R: Ed Begley, Jr.
DOVE

To Be a Slave
A: Julius Lester
R: Julius Lester, Ossie Davis, Ruby Dee, and full cast
HARP

To Be Loved
A/R: Berry Gordy
TW

To Life!: A Celebration of Jewish Being and Thinking
A/R: Harold S. Kushner
RH

To the Stars: The Autobiography of Star Trek's Mr. Sulu
A/R: George Takei
S&S

The Total Zone
A: Martina Navratilova with Liz Nickels
BRILL

Touched by Angels
A: Eileen Elias Freeman
R: Lindsay Crouse
TW

Toujours Provence
A: Peter Mayle
R: Patrick MacNee
ART

Transformation
A: Whitley Strieber
R: Roddy McDowall
DOVE

The Transformed Cell
A: Steven A. Rosenberg, M.D., Ph.D., and John M. Barry
R: Ron Rifkin
S&S

Traveling Trivia
A: Pamela Acuff
RH

The Tribe of Tiger: Cats and Their Culture
A/R: Elizabeth Marshall Thomas
S&S

Truman
A/R: David McCullough
S&S

The Trunk Murderess: Winnie Ruth Judd
A: Jana Bommersbach
R: Jane Alexander
S&S

Two of a Kind: The Hillside Stranglers
A: Darcy O'Brien
R: Michael McConnohie
ART

Unanswered Cries
A: Thomas French
R: Michael McConnohie
ART

Under the Streets of Nice
A: Ken Follett and Rene L. Maurice
R: Roddy McDowall
DOVE

Unto the Sons
A: Gay Talese
R: Daniel J. Travanti
RH

Valvano: They Gave Me a Lifetime Contract, and Then They Declared Me Dead
A: Jim Valvano and Curry Kirkpatrick
R: Jim Valvano
S&S

Veil: The Secret Wars of the CIA, 1981–1987
A: Robert Woodward
R: John Hockenberry
S&S

Volunteer Slavery
A/R: Jill Nelson
TW

Walden
A: Henry David Thoreau
R: Archibald MacLeish
HARP

Wasted: The Preppie Murder
A: Linda Wolfe
R: Gregory Snegoff
ART

The Way I See It
A/R: Patti Davis
DOVE

We Were Soldiers Once . . . and Young
A: Lieutenant General Harold G. Moore and Joseph Galloway
R: Joseph Galloway
HARP

West with the Night
A: Beryl Markham
R: Julie Harris
PART

Whad'ya Know?
A/R: Michael Feldman
S&S

What I Saw at the Revolution
A/R: Peggy Noonan
DOVE

What's in It for Me?: How an Ex-Wiseguy Exposed the Greed, Jealousy and Lust That Drive Arizona Politics
A: Joseph Stedino with Dary Matera
R: Joseph Stedino
HARP

When Heaven and Earth Changed Places
A: Le Ly Hayslip with Jay Wurtz
R: Nancy Kwan
DOVE

When You're from Brooklyn, Everything Else Is Tokyo
A/R: Larry King
S&S

The Wild West
A: Editors of Time-Life
R: Jack Lemmon
S&S

Wisdomkeepers
A: Steve Wall and Harvey Arden
R: Fred Gonyea, Ray Gonyea, Tammy Rahr, and Michael Toms
AUDLIT

The Woman Warrior
A/R: Maxine Hong Kingston
RH

Women on Top
A/R: Nancy Friday
S&S

Wordstruck
A/R: Robert MacNeil
S&S

The World Is My Home
A: James A. Michener
R: George Grizzard
RH

Wouldn't Take Nothing for My Journey Now
A/R: Maya Angelou
RH

A Year in Provence
A/R: Peter Mayle
ART

You Are Special
A/R: Fred Rogers
PENG

PLAYS AND POETRY

The dramatic voice and the poetic voice are very closely aligned. While both voices live in different homes (the voice of drama in plays, the voice of poetry in poems), they both live to achieve similar goals. Both voices aim to delineate character, express a certain slant on reality, unleash truth. Ranging from the voice of Hamlet questioning his role both in his play and in his life, to the voice of the West Indian Homer of Derek Walcott's poem recounting his epic story in his native inflections, these diverse voices are a basic core of the works they control. They all speak to the listener and vie for his attention. These drama and poetry tapes are filled with voices vying for our attention. Some capture that attention more quickly and hold it longer than others.

In the drama tapes, the attention-grabbing and -sustaining voices are most often those of the actors who have mastered the delicate art of creating a character solely through their vocal instrument. No gestures, no stances, no hands, no eyes—just voice. It is a subtle talent, in the absence of which bombastic articulation or affected vocal quirks can result; unfortunately, there are instances of those problems on some of these tapes. It is interesting to note that these problems seem to be more prevalent on the newer tapes. Kenneth Branagh's *Romeo and Juliet* and *Hamlet* tapes, both from the early nineties, though produced with superior production values, suffer from inflated readings. No matter how fine the sound effects, background music, quality of sound, are on these tapes, if the performers do not draw the listeners in, the audio experience is not fully satisfying. This is a major reason why some of the older drama tapes (*Death of a Salesman, The Glass Menagerie,* the Bloom/Finney *Romeo and Juliet*) are more satisfying. They have simpler production values, but somehow this forces the performers to use their voices for maximum artistic effect.

In the case of the poetry readings, another factor is evident. If the poets are reading their own works, what is needed is not great performance art or a reasonant voice, but the poet's ability to shed light on the poem through the poet's delivery. There are examples on these tapes of poets with fine speaking voices and poets with less than perfect instruments, but except for one case, each poet, no matter what the quality of voice, is able to bring the listener into the world of his poem through his delivery. (Note the special "Poets Reading Their Own Poems" section beginning on page 276.) A poet's connection to his poem, in most cases, gives his voice the ability to convey clarity through nuance, inflection, tone. This ability serves as a firm grasp on the listener's attention. Performers reading a poet's poems seems to stand or fall on just those vocal performance qualities that were discussed in the drama section above. A Julie Harris or an Alexander Scourby has learned the art of shading and emphasis that draws us into the poem, so we can become familiar with it.

What seems to be of most importance when it comes to evaluating the drama and poetry tapes is the centrality of the human voice. Does it have the ability, the quality, the power, to capture the listener and make him share the moment? This ability, quality, etc., has very little to do with the beauty of the instrument and everything to do with the speaker's connection to the material being presented. Even if he has not written the material he is speaking, he needs to *know* it and not *mouth* it.

PLAYS

HIGHLY RECOMMENDED (★★★★)

Ages of Man
Death of a Salesman
The Glass Menagerie
Lucifer's Child
Mark Twain Tonight
The Normal Heart
Romeo and Juliet*

Ages of Man
Author: William Shakespeare
Performer: Sir John Gielgud
★★★★

The Grammy-winning recital of Shakespeare's most exquisite soliloquies, sonnets, and speeches is performed by the preeminent Shakespearean actor of our era. These readings present a tremendous gallery of the great dramatic figures of Shakespeare. Included are selections from *As You Like It, Merchant of Venice, Hamlet, Macbeth,* and *King Lear. Ages of Man* made its New York stage debut on December 28, 1958, and played to SRO for its entire run. It also had a very popular international run. This tape perfectly captures the mellifluous and stirring voice of Gielgud. He uses his voice like a musician uses his instrument; he carefully breathes the words and his readings become sumptuous melodies.

2 css   1 hr 15 min   Caedmon Audio

*Caedmon Audio

Cyrano de Bergerac
Author: Edmond Rostand
Performers: Anna Massey, Sir Ralph Richardson, and others
★★★

This classic love story cries out for a larger-than-life performance in the title role. Cyrano is a man whose words and gestures match the grandiosity of his nose. To sustain the poetry, the humor, and the heartbreak of this play, the lead must have romance, comedy, and pathos in his voice. Sir Ralph Richardson has the last two items of this triumvirate in abundance; it is only the first of these—the romance—that escapes him. Still, he definitely gives a robust and memorable reading and the rest of the company matches his vigor.

2 css   2½ hr   Caedmon Audio

Death of a Salesman
Author: Arthur Miller
Performers: Lee J. Cobb, Mildred Dunnock, Dustin Hoffman, Michael Tolan, and others
★★★★

Death of a Salesman burst upon the scene in 1949, and is as fresh and meaningful today as it was when it opened on Broadway and won the Pulitzer Prize. Lee J. Cobb and Mildred Dunnock re-create their original roles here with intense power and clarity. In addition to these two towering performances, this tape offers an eloquent, mood-setting introduction by the author and a supporting performance by the young Dustin Hoffman as Bernard, the neighbor's son. The contrast set up by the booming gravel and defeat in Cobb's voice and the chirping delicacy and steel heartbreak in Dunnock's reading captures the essence of the salesman's tragedy. This tape is a must for people interested in a moving reproduction of a classic American drama.

2 css   2 hr 15 min   Caedmon Audio

The Glass Menagerie
Author: Tennessee Williams
Performers: Montgomery Clift, Julie Harris, Jessica Tandy, and David Wayne
★★★★

Few plays have explored the byways of the human heart as poignantly as Tennessee Williams's *The Glass Menagerie.* In this touching audio, we meet the embattled Wingfield family: Amanda—faded southern belle, abandoned wife, dominating mother; Laura—lame and painfully shy daughter; and Tom—the son and sole support of the family, who eventually leaves home to become a writer. The sound medium is a perfect way to convey the essence of this memory-play. "In memory everything seems to happen to music." And the sounds of this tape (the tinkling of Laura's glass figurines, the wistful menagerie musical motif) contribute to the lyrical power of this most poetic of American dramas.

2 css   2½ hr   Caedmon Audio

Hamlet
Author: William Shakespeare
Performers: Kenneth Branagh, Judi Dench, Sir John Gielgud, Derek Jacobi, and others
★★★

Three generations of legendary leading actors gather here to perform the rarely heard complete (three-and-a-half-hour) version of the play. This is a full-blown, meticulously detailed production with rousing music, clangorous sound effects, and two energetically articulated but emotionally static performances by Kenneth Branagh as Hamlet and Derek Jacobi as Claudius. Judi Dench's Gertrude and Sir John Gielgud's Ghost bring true conviction to their readings. On the whole, this Renaissance Theatre Company production is a worthy undertaking with stirringly effective production values.

4 css 3½ hr BBD Audio

Julius Caesar
Author: William Shakespeare
Performers: Alan Bates, John Mills, Sir Ralph Richardson, Anthony Quayle, and others
★★

Julius Caesar, the first of Shakespeare's greater tragedies, is a compact study of the minds and motives of a group of Roman historical figures who surround the assassination of their leader. Considering the cast assembled, this is a strangely lifeless reading. The actors seem detached in their scenes together, as if they were reciting their lines in separate rooms. Even the great Sir Ralph Richardson seems plagued by this remote delivery. Also, the production, as a whole, lacks a sense of atmosphere and nuance.

2 css 2 hr 40 min Caedmon Audio

Lucifer's Child
Author: William Luce
Performer: Julie Harris
★★★★

This is a one-woman play based on the life and writings of Isak Dinesen (pen name of Karen Blixen-Finecke), author and heroine of *Out of Africa.* Through her fanciful pact with Lucifer, Dinesen becomes a defiant spirit, an eccentric storytelling sorceress—passionate and wickedly witty. In preparation for this role, Julie Harris studied the one recording available of Isak Dinesen's voice. Harris captures the cadence and drama of the author in a spellbinding performance. Especially effective and moving are the stories told of Africa. In these sections, the actress conveys the haunting power the African landscape and its people had over the Danish author. Harris's performance is much enhanced by the evocative original score composed by Charles Gross.

2 css 1 hr 45 min Audio Editions

Mark Twain Tonight
Author: Mark Twain
Performer: Hal Holbrook
★★★★

Hal Holbrook's one-man show *Mark Twain Tonight* sold out in New York, traveled across the United States and abroad, and appeared on television. In this extraordinary theatrical achievement, Holbrook becomes truly transformed, re-creating the incisive mind and scalding tongue of the legendary man from Missouri. The actor spent twelve years researching Mark Twain's voice and movements, using the recollections of people who knew Twain personally. This tape recaptures the great humorist's voice, timing, and very thinking in a live performance of the Hal Holbrook show. This audio is an important addition to the small collection of live recordings of legendary performances.

2 css 1 hr 40 min Audio Editions

The Normal Heart
Author: Larry Kramer
Performers: Eric Bogosian, Stockard Channing, D. W. Moffett, John Turturro, and others
★★★★

The Normal Heart, Larry Kramer's explosive, polemical drama of the early years of the AIDS epidemic, opened in April 1985. Eight years later, as the plague raged on, a group of the stage's most celebrated talents joined forces in a benefit reading of the play to raise money and awareness in the ongoing fight against AIDS. This special presentation of the Broadway Benefit Reading of *The Normal Heart* captures this legendary night of theater. From the urgency of Barbra Streisand's opening remarks, to the sincerity of the performances, to the spontaneous outpouring of emotion at the final curtain, this is a powerful example of audio drama and an inspiring tribute to the power of theater.

3 css 2 hr 10 min Simon & Schuster Audio

Romeo and Juliet
Author: William Shakespeare
Performers: Claire Bloom, Dame Edith Evans, Albert Finney, and others
★★★★

Romeo and Juliet was Shakespeare's first great play and this tape does full justice to the youthful ardor of the story. The production values are simple, but the performances are eloquent. Claire Bloom and Albert Finney, playing the title characters, are able to capture not only the youthful sound of the star-crossed lovers but also the vocal dexterity and dramatic eloquence required by the Shakespearean line. Dame Edith Evans is a real treasure as the nurse; her quavering but precise inflections emphasize the humor but also the heartbreak in the nurse's role.

2 css 3 hr Caedmon Audio

Romeo and Juliet
Author: William Shakespeare
Performers: Samantha Bond, Kenneth Branagh, Judy Dench, Sir John Gielgud, Derek Jacobi, and others
★★★

The Renaissance Theatre Company and BBC radio present another richly textured and detailed tape of a Shakespearean drama. The overall production values, as in the same company's version of *Hamlet,* are more impressive than the actors' performances which, except in a few cases, sound too much articulated and too little felt. Samantha Bond's performance is one of the exceptions. Her Juliet is an honest, unfussy reading of the part. The music (the original score by Patrick Doyle owes more than a passing nod to Prokofiev's ballet music set to the same literary source) and the sound effects do much to enhance the listener's interest in the drama. However, the less richly mounted 1960s Caedmon version of the same play (above) is a much more dramatically effective tape.

3 css 3 hr 25 min BDD Audio

Twelfth Night
Author: William Shakespeare
Performers: Siobhan McKenna, Vanessa Redgrave, Paul Scofield, and others
★★★

This Shakespeare Recording Society production of Shakespeare's happiest and more lyrical comedy is an uneven reading of this delightful romp of deception and romance. The two exceptions are the impeccable performances of Paul Scofield as Malvolio and Vanessa Redgrave as Olivia. They alone of the leads capture the sound and the sense of the lines. On the other hand, Siobhan McKenna's affected reading of Viola annoys rather than enchants, and the comic parts (Sir Toby, Sir Andrew, Feste, Maria) are given a lackluster reading. This is a distinct disappointment, since these characters are probably the greatest group of clowns in all Shakespearean comedy.

2 css 2 hr 10 min Caedmon Audio

All's Well That Ends Well
A: William Shakespeare
R: Claire Bloom, Eric Portman, and full cast
HARP

As You Like It
A: William Shakespeare
R: Max Adrian, Keith Mitchell, Vanessa Redgrave, and full cast
HARP

Benjamin Franklin, Citizen
A: Fredd Wayne
R: Live performance by Fredd Wayne
AUDLIT

Catskills on Broadway
Original Broadway Production
DOVE

The Comedy of Errors
A: William Shakespeare
R: Alec McCowen, Anna Massey, and full cast
HARP

Coriolanus
A: William Shakespeare
R: Richard Burton, Jessica Tandy, and full cast
HARP

The Crucible
A: Arthur Miller
R: Jerome Dempsey, Stuart Pankin, and full cast
HARP

Great Scenes from Antony and Cleopatra
A: William Shakespeare
R: Pamela Brown, Anthony Quayle, and full cast
HARP

Hamlet
A: William Shakespeare
R: Paul Scofield, Diana Wyngard, and full cast
HARP

Heartbreak House
A: George Bernard Shaw
R: Jessica Tandy, Tony Van Bridge, and full cast
HARP

Hedda Gabler
A: Henrik Ibsen; translated by Michael Meyer
R: Joan Plowright, Anthony Quayle, and full cast
HARP

The Importance of Being Earnest
A: Oscar Wilde
R: Alec McCowen, Lynn Redgrave, and full cast
HARP

King Henry the Fourth, Part I
A: William Shakespeare
R: Dame Edith Evans, Anthony Quayle, and full cast
HARP

King Lear
A: William Shakespeare
R: Cyril Cusack, Rachel Roberts, Paul Scofield, and full cast
HARP

King Richard the Second
A: William Shakespeare
R: Sir John Gielgud, Keith Mitchell, and full cast
HARP

King Richard the Third
A: William Shakespeare
R: Dame Peggy Ashcroft, Robert Stephens, and full cast
HARP

Long Day's Journey into Night
A: Eugene O'Neill
R: Geraldine Fitzgerald, Stacy Keach, and full cast
HARP

Love's Labour Lost
A: William Shakespeare
R: Jeremy Brett, Geraldine McEwan, and full cast
HARP

Macbeth
A: William Shakespeare
R: Stanley Holloway, Anthony Quayle, and full cast
HARP

The Master Builder
A: Henrik Ibsen; edited by Emlyn Williams
R: Sir Michael Redgrave, Maggie Smith, and full cast
HARP

A Midsummer Night's Dream
A: William Shakespeare
R: Joy Parker, Paul Scofield, and full cast
HARP

A Moon for the Misbegotten
A: Eugene O'Neill
R: Salome Jens, Michael Ryan, and full cast
HARP

Much Ado about Nothing
A: William Shakespeare
R: Rex Harrison, Rachel Roberts, and full cast
HARP

Murder in the Cathedral
A: T. S. Eliot
R: Cyril Cusack, Paul Scofield, and full cast
HARP

Othello
A: William Shakespeare
R: Cyril Cusack, Frank Silvera, and full cast
HARP

Private Lives and Present Laughter
A: Noël Coward
R: Paul Scofield and full cast
PART

Pygmalion
A: George Bernard Shaw
R: Lynn Redgrave, Sir Michael Redgrave, and full cast
HARP

A Raisin in the Sun
A: Lorraine Hansberry
R: Ossie Davis, Ruby Dee, and full cast
HARP

A Streetcar Named Desire
A: Tennessee Williams
R: James Farentino, Rosemary Harris, and full cast
HARP

The Taming of the Shrew
A: William Shakespeare
R: David Dodimead, Trevor Howard, Margaret Leighton, and full cast
HARP

The Tempest
A: William Shakespeare
R: Hugh Griffith, Sir Michael Redgrave, Vanessa Redgrave, and full cast
HARP

Tennessee Williams Reads the Glass Menagerie
A/R: Tennessee Williams
HARP

The Three Sisters
A: Anton Chekhov
R: Siobhan McKenna, Zena Walker, and full cast
HARP

Titus Andronicus
A: William Shakespeare
R: Maxine Audley, Anthony Quayle, and full cast
HARP

To Be Young, Gifted and Black
A: Lorraine Hansberry
R: Barbara Baxley, James Earl Jones, Claudia McNeil, and full cast
HARP

The Two Gentlemen of Verona
A: William Shakespeare
R: John Laurie, Peter Wyngarde, and full cast
HARP

Ulysses
A: James Joyce
R: Barbara Jefford, Milo O'Shea, and full cast
HARP

Under Milk Wood
A: Dylan Thomas
R: Dylan Thomas, Dion Allen, and full cast
HARP

Will Rogers' USA
R: James Whitmore
PART

POETRY

HIGHLY RECOMMENDED (★★★★)

Anne Sexton Reads
The Caedmon Treasury of Modern Poets Reading Their Own Poetry
Poems and Letters of Emily Dickinson

POETS READING THEIR OWN POEMS

"On the Pulse of Morning"
Author/Reader: Maya Angelou*
★★★

An eloquent and elegant reading by Maya Angelou of the poem she wrote for President Clinton's inauguration. The author prefaces her reading with a short presentation of the three elements she used in the poem (a rock, a river, a tree), which she took from Black American spirituals. This is definitely an instance where it is a must to have the poet read her own material. It would be hard for another reader to get the same sunny majesty out of the last two words of the poem: "Good Morning."

1 css 10 min Random House AudioBooks

* This section is arranged alphabetically by author's name.

The Caedmon Treasury of Modern Poets Reading Their Own Poetry
Authors/Readers: W. H. Auden, Marianne Moore, Ezra Pound, Gertrude Stein, Wallace Stevens, William Carlos Williams, and others
★★★★

This tape is a choice gathering of some of the twentieth century's greatest poems read by the twentieth century's greatest poets. Hearing poets ranging from W. B. Yeats to Richard Wilbur read their own work illustrates how important their interpretations are to a full comprehension of the poems. The ministerial intonations of T. S. Eliot, the passionate orchestrations of Dylan Thomas, the very precise formulations of e. e. cummings, the easy conversational inflections of Robert Frost, lend subtle clarification to our full understanding and appreciation of the poems. Adding to the many treasures of this audio is the fact that it includes the voice of Yeats, which is something of a miracle. In the early 1930s, when the thought of recording poets occurred to few, Yeats himself made several recordings for radio broadcast. Consequently, for the first time his rich and melodious voice can be heard by a new generation.

2 css 1 hr 35 min Caedmon Audio

Run with the Hunted: A Charles Bukowski Reader
Author/Reader: Charles Bukowski
★★★

Charles Bukowski has achieved international fame with his forty-five books of prose and poetry, including the novels *Post Office, Factotum,* and *Woman,* and the screenplay for the film *Barfly.* To his legions of fans, the author is a counterculture icon. From his odd jobs and wanderings to his drunken debauches and literary successes, the cult personality of Bukowski comes alive. Here, in the first and only audio anthology of his writing, the author, in his inimitable zonked-out style, reads memorable selections of his work. With his gift of observation and his view from the rough and the raw side of life, this recording gives us the dark, literary explorations of this unique writer. The tape includes poems and selections from *consummation of grief, Less Delicate Than the Locust,* and *The Genius of the Crowd.*

1 css 1 hr Caedmon Audio

e. e. cummings Reads
Author/Reader: e. e. cummings
★★★

e. e. cummings's experimental poetry made him famous, or at least notorious. These recorded poems demonstrate cummings's fervid affirmation of life as well as his iconoclastic style. The poet described himself as someone "whose only happiness is to transcend himself, whose every agony is to grow." Cummings's beautifully modulated voice brings great clarity to the twists and turns of his playful and thorny poems.

1 css 55 min Caedmon Audio

T. S. Eliot Reads
Author/Reader: T. S. Eliot
★★★

The work of one of the most influential poets of the twentieth century, T. S. Eliot's highly intellectual, allusion-filled poetry has been both a joy and a horror to many readers. Whatever one thinks of Eliot's poetry, and the opinions vary greatly, listening to this historic recording made in 1947 is quite an experience. What amazes the listener is how the dry, detached voice of Eliot is able to capture the voices in his epic, doom-laden, fun-house poem of the twentieth century: *The Waste Land.* Toothless Cockney slatterns and bored bloodless English gentlemen come popping out of the poet's mouth in such quick succession that he sounds liked a reserved schoolmaster with a few snorts in him. For anyone even slightly interested in this modern master, this is a must-hear.

2 css 1 hr 45 min Caedmon Audio

Robert Frost Reads
Author/Reader: Robert Frost
★★★

These two cassettes capture the masterful New England poet at two different periods and two different places in his life. Tape 1 was recorded in 1956 in the poet's home in Cambridge, Massachusetts. Tape 2 was recorded at the Poetry Center of the 92nd Street YM–YWCA in 1950, 1951, and 1952. Frost's flat New England sound sharply conveys the harsh life and simple yet profound feelings of his rural characters. On the first cassette, Frost's readings are often tentative and his voice is somewhat weak. On the second cassette, made a few years earlier, his delivery is more energetic. However, the sound on this cassette is not as sharp and full as on the first.

2 css 1 hr 40 min Caedmon Audio

Langston Hughes Reads
Author/Reader: Langston Hughes
★★★

This tape is a combination poetry reading and chatty autobiographical textural commentary by the African American poet, Langston Hughes. The author's affable personality shines through even in his recounting of prejudicial treatment. His style is that of a great host, a perfect bartender, and an acutely observant street-corner chronicler. He opens the doors of his Harlem neighborhood and gives us a glimpse into the world of the African American; his most emphatic poems deal with the recollections of those blacks who moved up to the northern cities from the South after World War II. Their harrowing memories of oppression and their poignant recountings of displacement are a testament to the durability of the human spirit.

1 css 50 min Caedmon Audio

Becoming Light
Author/Reader: Erica Jong
★★

Although she is most famous for her best-selling fiction, including *Fear of Flying* and *Any Woman's Blues,* Erica Jong started her publishing career as a poet and has an international reputation for her verse. *Becoming Light* includes early poems previously uncollected in book form, selections from her previous books, and many new poems. Jong's poetry, while often accessible and vigorous, is sometimes predictable, lacking a sense of wonder or discovery. Her commentary tends to add to the lack of surprise in the poems. She tells you what the poem means and then the poem tells you what the poem means. Jong's fans will certainly find much in this tape to enjoy, but it certainly helps to be a fan. Otherwise, move on.

2 css 2 hrs Dove Audio

Parables and Portraits
Author/Reader: Stephen Mitchell
★★★

Stephen Mitchell has produced several popular and critically acclaimed works, including translations of *The Book of Job, The Selected Poetry of Rainer Maria Rilke,* and *Letters to a Young Poet* (all available on audio). This tape concentrates on his original work, which is fresh, profound, funny, and full of Zen references. The poet's delivery is open and unaffected, complementing the spiritual smile that seems to be at the center of the poems.

1 css 45 min Audio Literature

Sylvia Plath Reads
Author/Reader: Sylvia Plath
★★★

Of the many American poets who reached their zenith in the past few decades, perhaps none looms so large as the legendary Sylvia Plath. Her stormy but luminous poetry is both sharp and poignant. Since her suicide in 1963, her life has been as much discussed and analyzed as her poetry. This invaluable tape, recorded in 1960–1962, gives the listener the voice of Plath reading twenty-three of her poems. It is the voice of an East Coast 1950s coed, with a slightly affected, Grace Kelly–ish finishing-school accent, but there are no Grace Kelly twinkles in the eyes or hearts of these poems. This finishing-school girl is finished and she is going to give you every last, bloody detail of her demise.

1 css 50 min Caedmon Audio

Carl Sandburg Reads
Author/Reader: Carl Sandburg
★★

Carl Sandburg, known as "the poet of the people," recorded these tapes in 1951–1952. On this unique collection is Sandburg's dedication to America's sixteenth president. Included are "Fog," *The People, Yes,* and "The Windy City."

Although the poet reads with superb understatement, nuance, and phrasing, the poems themselves are dated, very much a product of their times. They almost seem to demand background music by Aaron Copland to fill them out. The sentiments expressed call to mind the WPA, Capra films, *The Grapes of Wrath.* These are not bad images in themselves; it's just that the images seem to invoke a 1930s black-and-white documentary without speaking on their own to a 1990s audience. This tape is an interesting curiosity.

2 css 1 hr 35 min Caedmon Audio

Anne Sexton Reads
Author/Reader: Anne Sexton
★★★★

On this recording, made shortly before her death in 1974, Sexton, the 1967 Pulitzer Prize–winning poet, reads twenty-four poems selected from different periods in her creative life, all in a dramatic, resonant voice that complements the deeply personal quality of her dark, poetic explorations. Sexton had a wonderfully unique literary vision, often brutally honest, often controversial—always thought-provoking. These poems are a haunting reminder of how a deeply disturbed mind can create great beauty through the power of artistic shaping.

1 css 50 min Caedmon Audio

Derek Walcott Reads
Author/Reader: Derek Walcott
★★★

Derek Walcott, the 1992 recipient of the Nobel Prize in literature, maintains a permanent residence in his native Saint Lucia, in the West Indies. Collected here are many of his best-known shorter pieces as well as key excerpts from his epic narrative works, *Omeros* and *The Odyssey.* The poet's voice is filled with the musical inflections of the islands and the rolling, resonant tones of the native storyteller. The richness of the poetic images and the richness of the poet's voice make this tape a real audio treat.

1 css 1½ hr Caedmon Audio

William Carlos Williams Reads
Author/Reader: William Carlos Williams
★★

Although the ordinary, the commonplace, and the matter of fact are the stuff of William Carlos Williams's poetry, he never idealizes or romanticizes. Williams offers his images as he sees them in their everyday commonplaceness and asks us to know them for their poetry. Though he is a truly influential and revolutionary poet, his reading does not do justice to the sensuousness of the particular that is embedded in his poetry. Except for an appropriately homespun quality in his delivery, there is not much in the poet's reading to bring the poems closer to the reader. The sound quality is also a problem, since there is much background noise (traffic sounds, rustling, and turning of pages) to distract the listener from the artless art of these poems.

1 css 45 min Caedmon Audio

POETRY READ BY OTHERS

The Big Book for Our Planet
Authors: Various
Readers: Ed Begley, Jr., Robby Benson, Shelly Hack, and others
★★

Over twenty-five of the best-loved authors of children's books have pooled their talents to honor one very special planet—the earth. Here are stories and poems, essays and limericks, all sharing a belief that humans must live in harmony with their environment. The readers make this tape a pleasant enough experience, but it is hard to gauge for what audience. This is certainly an admirable project; I am sorry I can't get that enthusiastic about the finished product.

1 css 1 hr 40 min The Publishing Mills AudioBooks

Dickinson and Whitman: Ebb and Flow
Authors: Emily Dickinson and Walt Whitman
Readers: Nancy Wickwire and Alexander Scourby
★★★

The essence of poetry—the ebb and flow of language, the ebb and flow of the human spirit—is captured in these distinguished readings of fifty-three poems from two of America's greatest poets. Emily Dickinson, a recluse in Amherst, Massachusetts, unpublished and unknown at the time of her death in 1886, stands today at the front rank of American poets. Though Nancy Wickwire's readings are subtle and inspired, the musical accompaniment is not. It tends to act intrusively and it often underscores or repeats a verbal phrase in a much too obvious manner. Walt Whitman, poet, journalist, lover of freedom, published his great tribute to America, *Leaves of Grass,* in 1855. Whitman continued to revise and expand it until his death in 1892. Today *Leaves of Grass* is universally recognized as one of the masterpieces of world literature. Alexander Scourby captures all the unbridled effusiveness of the Whitman voice in these excellent readings.

2css 2 hr 20 min Audio Partners

Eighty-One Famous Poems
Authors: Various
Readers: Bramwell Fletcher, Alexander Scourby, and Nancy Wickwire
★★★

This collection of timeless British and American poems are presented in the order they appear in *The Norton Anthology of Poetry*, 3rd ed.; thirty-nine poets are included, from Shakespeare, Blake, and Wordsworth to Keats, the Brownings, Whitman, Dickinson, and Yeats. The three classically trained actors give clear, natural, and eloquent readings of these poetic masterpieces. This tape should prove helpful to student and teacher alike.

2 css 2 hr 20 min Audio Partners

The Enlightened Heart: An Anthology of Sacred Poetry
Authors: Various
Readers: Coleman Barks, Peter Coyote, Ram Dass, and others
★★★

Stephen Mitchell, poet and translator, has edited this collection of spiritual poetry. The selection includes sections of the Upanishads, the book of Psalms, and the "Bhagavadgita," as well as the writings of Francis of Assisi, Dante, Blake, and Yeats. The works presented in this sacred anthology have been chosen with fine taste and purpose. The interpretations by the nine readers are simple and inspired. There is a distinct sense of joy, wisdom, and humor in this collection.

2 css 2½ hr Audio Literature

Footprints
Author: Margaret Fishback Powers
Readers: Joan Windmill Brow and Ben Kingsley
★★

The true story behind the poem that inspired millions. *Footprints* was composed by Margaret Fishback, a young woman searching for direction at the crossroads in her life. The creation of the poem, its subsequent loss, and its astonishing rediscovery are intertwined with a life full of challenge, adversity, and joy. The readers struggle to give life to a style of narration that is more at home stamped on plaques, cards, calendars, and posters.Inspirational in the worse sense of the word.

1 css 1½ hr Dove Audio

Great American Poetry
Authors: Various
Readers: Eddie Albert, Ed Begley, Helen Gahagan Douglas, Julie Harris, and Vincent Price
★★★

This is an anthology of thirty-one American poems written by fourteen poets, ranging from the poetry of the earliest published American poet, Anne Bradstreet, to the poetry of Emily Dickinson and Stephen Crane. The readers are quite a diverse group, starting with the singer-actress-congresswoman Helen Gahagan Douglas reading Bradstreet, and continuing to include Ed Begley [the original Joe Keller in Arthur Miller's *All My Sons*] reading Whitman. The clash of interpretations adds to the fun of this collection.

2 css 1 hr 45 min Audio Partners

Like This: More Poems of Rumi
Authors: Jalal-ud-din Rumi; translated by Coleman Barks
Reader: Coleman Barks
★★★

Jalal-ud-din Rumi (1207–1273), a saint of the Islamic world, is now recognized in the West as one of the greatest poets of all time. His words are charged with an unequaled blend of literary genius and spiritual wisdom. This program includes twenty-two of Rumi's most beautiful poems, primarily selected from *Like This.* Coleman Barks, accompanied by two musicians, gives a relaxed yet evocative reading to these hypnotic poems.

1 css 1 hr 25 min Audio Literature

Love and Desire: An Anthology of Love Poems
Authors: Various
Readers: David Birney, Jane Lapotaire, Lee Remick, Robert Stephens, and Michael York
★★★

This romantic selection from history's most prominent poets includes the poetry of Auden, Burns, Dickinson, Keats, and Shakespeare, as well as many others. The poems are divided into four sections: "Love Found"—poems of falling in love; "Poems of Courtship, Seduction, and Desire"; "Love Transformed"—poems of marriage; and "Love Lost"—poems of loss and regret. Here are some delightful readings and some that do not come close. Michael York and Robert Stephens are the standouts in this collection. Both of these readers are able to effortlessly make the switch from lush love verse to satiric light verse without turning the lush into mush or the light into slight.

2 css 1 hr 15 min Dove Audio

The Love Poems of John Donne
Author: John Donne
Reader: Richard Burton
★★★

From the timeless pen of English poet John Donne, twenty monologues spoken by the lover to his beloved are read by Richard Burton. These poems describe a real and experienced love, a joyous union of body and soul, poured out in the heat of the moment. Burton's fiery and resonant tone is well suited to the great sense of immediacy evident in all of these poems.

1 css 35 min Caedmon Audio

Poems and Letters of Emily Dickinson
Author: Emily Dickinson
Reader: Julie Harris
★★★★

Kown as "the myth of Amherst" for her withdrawal from society while still a young woman, Emily Dickinson (1830–1886) had an inner life that was deeply emotional and intense. She broke with tradition and was criticized for her experiments with unorthodox phrasing, rhyme, and broken meter, within concise forms, thus becoming an innovator and forerunner of modern poets. This collection of Emily Dickinson's poems is interspersed with her luminous letters, all read by Julie Harris, who received a Tony Award for her portrayal of Emily Dickinson in *The Belle of Amherst.* One of the many joys of this reading is the special way Harris creates a new world in her reading of each short poem. This ability enables the reader to grasp Emily Dickinson's breathtaking talent of squeezing an entire universe into a few lines.

1 css 50 min Caedmon Audio

Poems of Kabir
Authors: Kabir; translated by Robert Bly
Reader: Robert Bly
★★★

Kabir, fifteenth-century Indian spiritual master, embraced both the Hindu and the Sufi traditions. His poems are at the same time irreverent and intensely religious. Robert Bly, who recites here his own versions of Kabir poems, is one of America's most respected and influential poets and translators. In the past, audiences throughout the nation have responded with tremendous enthusiasm to his Kabir recitations, accompanied by these superb musicians, David Whetstone on sitar and Marcus Wise on tabla. Bly's chantlike readings of his translations of Kabir can either strike one as an accurate approximation of the master's style and intention or a monotonous singsong. It is a matter of taste.

2 css 2 hr Audio Literature

Poems of Rumi
Authors: Jalal-ud-din Rumi; translated by Robert Bly and Coleman Barks
Readers: Robert Bly and Coleman Barks
★★★

Jalal-ud-din Rumi (1207–1273) is unquestionably one of the greatest spiritual poets of the world. Speaking from the heart of the Sufi tradition, his astonishing expressions of unfathomable love transcend the boundaries of culture. Robert Bly and Coleman Barks are widely known for their translations of spiritual poetry. In this program, each reads from his own versions of Rumi, accompanied by a group of musicians who give playfulness and ground to the works. The two readers give a needed variety to the mystical dialogue of words. Coleman Barks's gentle country sound contrasts nicely with Robert Bly's more chantlike delivery.

2 css 2 hr 20 min Audio Literature

Poetry of James Kavanaugh
Author: James Kavanaugh
Reader: William Conrad
★★★

James Kavanaugh has been a Roman Catholic priest, teacher, and marriage counselor. He is a nationally known author of some twenty books, including *Will You Be My Friend?* and *Faces in the City,* from which selections were chosen for this audio program. His poetry challenges us to find joy and fulfillment in today's often perplexing world. Original guitar and percussion arrangements enhance William Conrad's expressive reading of Kavanaugh's unique blend of compassion and humor.

1 css 1 hr 5 min Dove Audio

Rilke: Selected Poems
Author: Rainer Maria Rilke
Reader: Stephen Mitchell
★★★

Rilke has been called the most significant and compelling poet of spiritual experience of the twentieth century. His influence and popularity in America have never been greater than they are today. The poems in this reading are from *The Selected Poetry of Rainer Maria Rilke,* edited and translated by Stephen Mitchell. Mitchell's reading is an effective blending of a relaxed tone with a hushed intensity. His interpretation and his translations do justice to Rilke.

2 css 2 hr Audio Literature

Beowulf and Other Poetry (In Old English)
A: Various
R: William Butler Yeats and J. B. Bessinger, Jr.
HARP

The Best Loved Poems of Longfellow
A: Henry Wadsworth Longfellow
R: Hal Holbrook
HARP

Carl Sandburg Reading "Cool Tombs" and Other Poems
A/R: Carl Sandburg
HARP

Carl Sandburg Reading "Fog" and Other Poems
A/R: Carl Sandburg
HARP

Dylan Thomas: "In Country Heaven"—the Evolution of a Poem
A: Dylan Thomas
R: Dylan Thomas, Hugh Griffith, Basil Jones, and others
HARP

Dylan Thomas Reading "A Visit to America"
A/R: Dylan Thomas
HARP

Dylan Thomas Reading from His Work and the Works of Sean O'Casey and Djuna Barnes
A: Dylan Thomas, Sean O'Casey, and Djuna Barnes
R: Dylan Thomas
HARP

Dylan Thomas Reading His Poetry
A/R: Dylan Thomas
HARP

Dylan Thomas Reading "Over Sir John's Hill" and Other Poems
A/R: Dylan Thomas
HARP

Dylan Thomas Reading *Quite Early One Morning*
A/R: Dylan Thomas
HARP

Dylan Thomas Reads
A/R: Dylan Thomas
HARP

Dylan Thomas Reads *A Child's Christmas in Wales and Five Poems*
A/R: Dylan Thomas
HARP

Dylan Thomas Reads a Personal Anthology
A/R: Dylan Thomas
HARP

Dylan Thomas Reads "And Death Shall Have No Dominion" and Other Poems
A/R: Dylan Thomas
HARP

e. e. cummings Reads His Collected Poetry, 1943–1958
A/R: e. e. cummings
HARP

Edgar Allan Poe: Poetry Collection
A: Edgar Allan Poe
DOVE

Emily Dickinson: A Self-Portrait
A: Emily Dickinson
R: Julie Harris
HARP

Emily Dickinson's Poetry
A: Emily Dickinson
DOVE

English Romantic Poetry
A: Various
R: Claire Bloom, Anthony Quayle, and Sir Ralph Richardson
HARP

An Evening with Dylan Thomas
A/R: Dylan Thomas
HARP

Ezra Pound Reads
A/R: Ezra Pound
HARP

Frost on the Window
A: Mary Stewart
R: Jenny Seagrove
DOVE

Gertrude Stein Reads from Her Poetry
A/R: Gertrude Stein
HARP

Great Voices Boxed Audio Collection
A/R: Various
HARP

Gwendolyn Brooks Reading Her Poetry
A/R: Gwendolyn Brooks
HARP

James Dickey Reads His Poetry and Prose
A/R: James Dickey
HARP

Jimmy Stewart and His Poems
A/R: Jimmy Stewart
RH

Margaret Atwood Reads
A/R: Margaret Atwood
HARP

May Sarton Reading Her Poetry
A/R: May Sarton
HARP

More Carl Sandburg Reads
A/R: Carl Sandburg
HARP

More T. S. Eliot Reads
A/R: T. S. Eliot
HARP

News of the Universe: Poems of Twofold Consciousness
A: Various; selected by Robert Bly
R: Robert Bly
AUDLIT

Nonlecture Six: I and Am and Santa Claus
A/R: e. e. cummings
HARP

Nonlecture Three: I and Selfdiscovery
A/R: e. e. cummings
HARP

Old Possum's Book of Practical Cats
A: T. S. Eliot
R: Sir John Gielgud and Irene Worth
HARP

One Poem at a Time
A: Samuel Hazo
BRIL

Pablo Neruda Reading His Poetry
(In Spanish)
A/R: Pablo Neruda
HARP

The People, Yes
A/R: Carl Sandburg
HARP

The Poetry and Voice of Galway Kinnell
A/R: Galway Kinnell
HARP

The Poetry and Voice of James Wright
A/R: James Wright
HARP

The Poetry of Byron
A: Lord Byron
R: Tyrone Power
HARP

The Poetry of Coleridge
A: Samuel Taylor Coleridge
R: Sir Ralph Richardson
HARP

Poetry of Edna St. Vincent Millay
A: Edna St. Vincent Millay
R: Dame Judith Anderson
HARP

The Poetry of Thomas Hardy
A: Thomas Hardy
R: Richard Burton
HARP

The Poetry of Wordsworth
A: William Wordsworth
R: Sir Cedric Hardwicke
HARP

A Poet's Bible: Rediscovering the Voices of the Original Text
A: David Rosenberg
R: Michael York
DOVE

The Rape of Lucrece and Other Poems
A: William Shakespeare
R: Richard Burton, Dame Edith Evans, and Sir Donald Wolfit
HARP

Robert Frost: Fire and Ice
A: June August and Arthur Peterson
R: Arthur Peterson
PART

Robert Frost in Recital
A/R: Robert Frost
HARP

Robert Frost Reads His Poetry
A/R: Robert Frost
HARP

Robert Graves Reads
A/R: Robert Graves
HARP

Robert Lowell Reads His Poetry
A/R: Robert Lowell
HARP

Robert Penn Warren Reads Selected Poems
A/R: Robert Penn Warren
HARP

Sir John Betjeman Reading His Poetry
A/R: Sir John Betjeman
HARP

Sonnets of William Shakespeare
A: William Shakespeare
R: Sir John Gielgud
HARP

T. S. Eliot Reading Four Quartets
A/R: T. S. Eliot
HARP

T. S. Eliot Reading *The Waste Land* and Other Poems
A/R: T. S. Eliot
HARP

Theodore Roethke Reads His Poetry
A/R: Theodore Roethke
HARP

There Are Men Too Gentle to Live among Wolves
A/R: James Kavanaugh
DOVE

A Treasury of Christmas Stories and Poems
R: Jane Alexander
BDD

W. H. Auden Reads His Poetry
A/R: W. H. Auden
HARP

W. S. Merwin Collected Poems
A/R: W. S. Merwin
HARP

Wallace Stevens Reads
A/R: Wallace Stevens
HARP

RADIO DRAMA AND DOCUMENTARIES

It's been called by many the Theater of the Mind, a tag it picked up years ago, when it seemed to be everywhere. It's radio drama, an art form requiring only an actor or two and some sound effects to take listeners anywhere in the universe, anyplace in time. And although it's been around for decades, it seems especially refreshing and invigorating these days, when million dollar special effects have become the reigning component of much of our popular entertainment, showing us in mind-numbing detail full-blown spectacles constructed from the blueprint of someone else's imagination.

In radio drama, the creator's imagination is also important—but so is the listener's. It's a collaboration, with the listener fleshing out the characters and the details of the settings they move through, using auditory information supplied by the creator. Like reading, radio drama stimulates active mental participation, and the more imagination a listener brings to it, the better it is.

A generation ago, radio drama was a lot easier to find. In fact, you could find it every evening, a rich variety of it, by simply punching a button or two and adjusting a few dials on the family radio. All the genres familiar to the television age were there—mystery, romance, adventure, comedy, musical—along with the more highbrow stuff, beaming into living rooms all over the world. The golden age of the radio drama began in the late twenties, peaked somewhere around the beginning of World War II, and finally died away in the fifties, supplanted—like so many other popular entertainments of the time—by television, which brought sound *and* pictures into the home.

But radio drama was too good to die off completely.

In several other countries, notably Britain, radio drama has remained a staple of broadcasting, although at a far lower level than it was in the thirties, forties, and early fifties. Here in America, we seem to periodically rediscover it. Some disc jockey with a yen to do something different will begin playing old radio-show episodes late at night, or at some other relatively dead time, and listeners will light up the switchboard, wanting more. Another station may find that broadcasts of thirties and forties radio programs fit perfectly into a big-band and nostalgia format. And occasionally, a national sponsor will come along that's willing to back a whole new series of dramas, and for a year or two we'll have a fresh new batch of dramas with today's stars and state-of-the-art recording.

The fact that radio drama still lives—and, indeed, may be undergoing a bit of a renaissance—is amply demonstrated by the tapes in this section, which includes an example or two of dramatic radio's cousin, the radio documentary. The documentary form has survived nicely through the years—these days, it's most often heard as syndicated combinations of music, interviews, and commentary, radio "specials" that appear often in virtually every musical format.

Of course, there were no cassettes or portable tape players during radio's golden age. If a show was popular enough (as in this section's "Sorry, Wrong Number" and "The Hitch-Hiker" from the *Suspense* program), it was rebroadcast. Otherwise, it was gone, at least as far as the average listener was concerned.

Now, technology—which essentially killed radio drama by giving birth to television—has helped resurrect radio's golden days. Once again, the rich, exciting, and boundless Theater of the Mind stage is accessible to anyone with a cassette deck.

Here, then, are stories old and new, tales first spun ages ago, and works as fresh as the latest best-sellers. They come from the past, from across the Atlantic, from long-gone studios in New York and Chicago and Hollywood, where all it took to create a World War I battlefield, an Old West shoot-out, or an exploding world was a good special effects technician and a few props, along with some actors willing to sustain a beautiful illusion. The tapes listed here will take some back to sweet evenings spent with the family around an old Atwater Kent radio, the tubes inside it glowing reassuringly in the darkness. They'll take others to times and places never before visited. It may not be easy to get this stuff on the radio anymore, but anyone can still get it. All it takes is the punch of a different button, the twist of a different dial.

DRAMA

HIGHLY RECOMMENDED (★★★★)

The African Queen
The Glass Menagerie
It's A Wonderful Life
Miracle on 34th Street
Our Town
Proof
"Sorry, Wrong Number" and "The Hitch-Hiker"

Note: *The African Queen, The Glass Menagerie, It's a Wonderful Life, Miracle on 34th Street, Our Town,* and "Sorry, Wrong Number" and "The Hitch-Hiker" can be found packaged together in a miniature crate, offered by The Mind's Eye.

The African Queen
Authors: C. S. Forester; script by James Agee
Performers: Humphrey Bogart and Greer Garson
★★★★

Bogart had already won the Academy Award for his film portrayal of dissolute but decent African trader Charlie Allnutt when this radio adaptation was aired on *Lux Radio Theatre.* Instead of the movie's Oscar-nominated costar, Katharine Hepburn, Greer Garson plays the missionary who accompanies Allnutt on a harrowing journey through the African backwaters, and does it with more reserve but less haughtiness than Hepburn. Garson comes off well during the curtain-call segment of the program, too, while Bogey endearingly screws up a plug for his upcoming *Battle Circus.*

1 css 1 hr The Mind's Eye

Cape Cod Radio Mystery Theater
Volume III
Author: Stephen Thomas Oney
Performers: George McConville, Carol McManus, Stephen Russell, and others
★★

"It's a foggy night on old Cape Cod—a perfect night for a mystery. . . ." The catchphrase almost says it all for *Cape Cod Radio Mystery Theater,* a public radio series of dramatized mystery and ghost stories. What sound conveys better is the series' devotion to old-time radio, especially to radio's ability to conjure sinister fogs and shadows in the listener's mind. The best stories are those of evil doings aboard ship and overboard—"The Buoy" and "Five Fathom Rip." But the second cassette gives way to "The Case of the Murdered Miser," which is overlong to the point of gathering barnacles.

2 css 2½ hr Penguin HighBridge Audio

Dracula
Author: Bram Stoker
Reader: Robert Powell
★★

Veeeeelcome to the Carpathians—again. This is BBC radio's nip at Stoker's vampire classic, a thoroughly professional but just not very exciting visit to that castle where they check in, but they don't check out. Robert Powell's able narration is nonetheless thin blood compared to Donald Pickering's in the Durkin Hayes version (see page 162).

2 css 3 hr Bantam Audio

The Glass Menagerie
Author: Tennessee Williams
Performers: Helen Hayes, Montgomery Clift, Karl Malden, and Katharine Bard
★★★★

Hayes, as the giddy, desperate matriarch Amanda Wingfield, and Clift, as her equally desperate son, make a formidable team in this radio premiere of the famed play, originally presented on *The Theatre Guild on the Air.* Malden is also good as the hail-fellow-well-met gentleman caller, tricked into a tête-à-tête with the innocent Laura Wingfield, whom Bard plays with a little less of the nervous vulnerability we've come to expect in that character. It's a little disconcerting to hear the live audience laughing uproariously at a few of Tom's and Amanda's lines.

1 css 1 hr The Mind's Eye

Great Expectations
(A BBC Audio Drama)
Author: Charles Dickens
Performers: Multiple Cast
★★★

Pip has been raised on the moors by his sister and her husband, the blacksmith. Pip has dreams of grandeur, which are fueled by the eccentric Miss Havisham, a wealthy neighbor. This is a full-cast, dramatized performance of the novel. Music and sound effects contribute to the theatrical slant. Well acted, this may be your spot of tea . . . then again. . . . The sound effects and music, at least to my mind, are nearly superfluous and, without the visuals, tend to take away from the acting. It's almost like hearing a film sound track rather than a radio drama.

4 css 5 hr 40 min BDD Audio

It's a Wonderful Life
Authors: Frances Goodrich, Albert Hackett, and Frank Capra
Performers: James Stewart, Donna Reed, and Victor Moore
★★★★

Stewart and Reed reprise their roles from the 1946 Christmas release that has since become, thanks to literally thousands of TV showings, a seasonal classic. The radio adaptation keeps many of the movie's darker undercurrents, focusing more on the relationship between George Bailey (Stewart) and his guardian angel, Clarence (played here by Moore, rather than the movie's Henry Travers). The program includes a sweet curtain call with Stewart, Reed, and *Lux Radio Theatre* host William Keighley.

1 css 1 hr The Mind's eye

Miracle on 34th Street
Authors: Valentine Davies; script by George Seaton
Performers: Edmund Gwynn, Maureen O'Hara, John Payne, and Natalie Wood
★★★★

One of the great feel-good movies of all time makes a nice little radio drama, as Macy's department-store Santa (Gwynn)—who may or may not be the real item—changes the life of a pragmatic mother (O'Hara), her precocious daughter (Wood), and the lawyer who loves them both (Payne), all the while infusing big business with the Christmas spirit. This *Lux Radio Theatre* production, featuring the film's main cast, eliminates a lot of the romantic parrying between O'Hara and Payne, resulting in more of a focus on Santa and his good works.

1 css 1 hr The Mind's Eye

Our Town
Author: Thornton Wilder
Performers: Frank Craven, William Holden, Martha Scott, Fay Bainter, Beulah Bondi, Thomas Mitchell, Guy Kibbee, and Stuart Erwin
★★★★

Famed Hollywood director Cecil B. DeMille hosted the *Lux Radio Theatre* from 1936 to early 1945, and here he introduces that program's hour-long adaptation of the classic statge play, bantering with the narrator (Craven) before turning things over to the excellent ensemble cast. Even in an audio version, Wilder's quietly powerful words shine through, and listeners will likely find themselves choking up once or twice as this tale of the life cycle in a small New Hampshire town unfolds. The main cast, including a very young Holden, also made the 1940 movie, released a few weeks after this broadcast.

1 css 1 hr The Mind's Eye

Proof
Author: Dick Francis
Performers: Nigel Havers, George Parsons, and Jennifer Piercey
★★★★

Proof features the same cover as the Dick Francis novel, which might lead one to believe that it's a reading rather than a dramatization. But it's actually a well-done BBC radio adaptation, minus beginning and end credits, that finds Francis's protagonist Tony Beach, a failed horseman who now runs a wine shop, drawn into a web of murder and liquor smuggling after a fatal accident occurs at a party for the horsey set. As is the case with the Francis novels, some of the British racetrack slang falls oddly on Stateside ears, but it can usually be figured out in context.

2 css 3 hr BDD Audio

"Sorry, Wrong Number" and "The Hitch-Hiker"
Author: Lucille Fletcher
Performers: Agnes Moorehead and Orson Welles
★★★★

Probably the two most famous episodes of the long-running *Suspense* program (which began in 1942 and lasted well into the mid-fifties), "Sorry, Wrong Number" and "The Hitch-Hiker" still pack a pretty good wallop. Both are essentially one-person shows: In "Sorry," Moorehead is an unpleasant invalid who encounters phone company and police bureaucracy—and worse, when she overhears a murder plot. "Hitch-Hiker" features Welles (who also offers an amusing introduction) as a cross-country traveler dogged by the image of a rain-spattered hitchhiker.

1css 1 hr Jabberwocky

Ulysses
(A BBC Audio Drama)
Author: James Joyce
Performers: Multiple Cast
★★

This is a lavish production of Joyce's towering novel. It's a cross between a theater performance and a vintage radio show, full of music and sound effects. Generally well performed, this dramatization is a bit hard to follow and some of the power of Joyce's language is overshadowed by the theatricality.

4 css 6 hr BDD Audio

Sherlock Holmes on Audio

HIGHLY RECOMMENDED (★★★★)

The New Adventures of Sherlock Holmes

Memoirs of Sherlock Holmes
Author: Sir Arthur Conan Doyle
Performers: Clive Merrison and Michael Williams
★★★

Those accustomed to the Basil Rathbone and Nigel Bruce Holmes and Watson may feel some slight disorientation upon encountering this set of four

Holmes adventures, originally presented on BBC radio in England. In these adaptations of the original Conan Doyle stories, "Silver Blaze," "The Yellow Face," "The Stockbroker's Clerk," and "The 'Gloria Scott,' " Holmes is often distracted, detached, and not particularly likeable, and Watson is a man far younger and crankier than Bruce's lovable old English doctor. During the unraveling of the cases, the two bicker as much as they agree. It's likely that true Holmes buffs will prefer these to the gentler, more Americanized, Holmes and Watson of the forties movies and radio shows; it's also likely it will take the average listener substantially longer to warm up to the Merrison and Williams portrayals.

2 css 2 hr 55 min BDD Audio

The New Adventures of Sherlock Homes
Authors: Anthony Boucher and Denis Green (occasionally adapting a Sir Arthur Conan Doyle story)
Performers: Basil Rathbone and Nigel Bruce
★★★★

In 1986, Simon & Schuster began issuing cassettes of *The New Adventures of Sherlock Holmes,* a popular radio drama from the forties that featured actors Basil Rathbone and Nigel Bruce, the same duo that had begun making the Sherlock Holmes film series in 1939. As in the pictures, Bruce plays Watson as a sputtering bumbler, a perfect foil for Rathbone's razor-edged delivery. The radio dramas themselves—again, like the movies—play out swiftly and economically, without so much as a wasted line. While some of *The New Adventures of Sherlock Holmes* were "suggested" by a story or an incident in a story by Conan Doyle, most of them sprang full-blown from the minds of writers Anthony Boucher and Denis Green, a duo as responsible for the high entertainment value of these dramas as the two stars.

Simon & Schuster has chosen to present these shows in full form, with all commercials (usually for Petrie wines), war-related announcements, and bantering between Bruce (as Watson) and the show's announcers intact. It's a good choice. The company has also taken the extra step of enlisting people associated with the show to do new wraparound commentary.

The New Adventures of Sherlock Holmes series comes packaged in two different ways, as two-episode volumes and as multi-volume gift sets. The single-volume audios that follow are a sampling of what is available. Each consists of one cassette and is one hour long. See page 219 for a complete listing.

Volume 1

While not marked as such, this is the first release in the series, featuring "The Unfortunate Tobacconist" and "The Paradol Chamber." In the former, operators of a tobacco shop are being rubbed out at an alarming rate. In the latter, Holmes and Watson encounter an inventor and his alleged "matter transporter," a meeting that leads to a murder plot. These 1945 programs are introduced by radio actor Ben Wright, who played Holmes later in the show's run.

The New Adventures of Sherlock Holmes
Volume 2

"The Viennese Strangler" finds Holmes and Watson in a Vienna boardinghouse chock-full of eccentric artists—one of whom is a murderer. In "The Notorious Canary Trainer," a pair of dead canaries leads to the unraveling of a bogus suicide. Glenhall Taylor, the show's first director, offers some interesting commentary about the show's production schedule.

The New Adventures of Sherlock Holmes
Volume 3

Originally broadcast on April 1, 1946, "The April Fool's Day Adventure" focuses on a prank pulled on Holmes—by poor Dr. Watson, of course—that goes badly awry. "The Strange Adventure of the Uneasy Easy Chair" is a locked-room mystery featuring not one but two corpses. Mary Green, widow of the series' cowriter, supplies good wraparounds, which include a poignant story about Nigel Bruce's death.

The New Adventures of Sherlock Holmes
Volume 4

Two of the more horrific—and clever—entries in the series comprise this package, as an actor in the stage production of *Sweeney Todd* begins to believe that he's actually a murderer ("The Strange Case of the Demon Barber"), and a beheaded monk becomes the prime suspect in a fresh murder ("The Mystery of the Headless Monk"). Ben Wright is back with commentary.

The New Adventures of Sherlock Holmes
Volume 20

The newer volumes continue packaging mid-forties episodes, and quality in all departments remains high. Here, "The Manor House Case" is one of the series' most unusual entries—it emphasizes the deductive abilities of Watson, rather than Holmes. In "The Adventures of the Stuttering Ghost," the duo descends into London's catacombs, following a message from a dead jewel thief. Harry Bartell, one of the program's original announcers, introduces the episodes.

The New Adventures of Sherlock Holmes
Volume 23

Listeners get some deftly presented history as well as a mystery in "The Gunpowder Plot," which concerns a murder scheme that unravels on the English holiday Guy Fawkes Day. And there's something unusual—beyond the wild stories of the titular character—in "The Babbling Butler": Tom Conway, best known for his portrayal of the Falcon in RKO's popular B-movie series of the forties (and for being George Sanders's brother), plays Holmes in this one. By the time "The Babbling Butler" was originally broadcast, in early 1947, Rathbone had left the Holmes radio and movie series, motivated at least partially by a desire to break away from the character. Harry Bartell handles the wraparounds.

The New Adventures of Sherlock Holmes
Volume 24
It's back to 1945 and 1946, respectively, for these two adventures. In "The Accidental Murderess," Holmes visits the English countryside, gets winged by a stray bullet, and uncovers a murder plot. In "The Adventure of the Blarney Stone," Holmes and Watson see a man fall to his death after kissing Ireland's Blarney Stone, and they set off to determine if the fall was accidental. Commentary is by Sarah Marshall, daughter of famed Hollywood director Herbert Marshall. She's here because her mother, Edna Best, directed *The New Adventures of Sherlock Holmes* after Glenhall Taylor was promoted to supervising producer.

The four-volume gift sets that follow are again a sampling. Each consists of four cassettes and is four hours long.

The New Adventures of Sherlock Holmes
Audio Gift Set, Volume 1
This boxed collection repackages the first four volumes of *The New Adventures of Sherlock Holmes.*

The New Adventures of Sherlock Holmes
Audio Gift Set, Volume 3
Included here is the radio adaptation of one of Conan Doyle's most famous Holmes tales, "A Scandal in Bohemia"—in which Holmes first meets, and is apparently bested by, his adversary/love interest, the opera singer Irene Adler—along with its Boucher and Green–penned sequel, "The Second Generation" (which originally aired a week after the first). Peggy Webber, an actress in the series, comments on the two productions. On Tape 2, actor Ben Wright introduces "In Flanders Fields," which takes Holmes and Watson to the front lines of World War I, and "The Eyes of Mr. Leyton," which finds them in London's sordid Limehouse district, searching for a murderer. Tape 3 features Harry Bartell, reminiscing briefly about auditioning for the *New Adventures* announcing job before leading into "The Tell Tale Pigeon Feathers" and "The Indiscretion of Mr. Edwards," two 1946 adventures. Finally, Tape 4 features more Bartell commentary and two good 1945 episodes: "The Problem of Thor Bridge," with Holmes investigating the murder of a mining magnate, and "The Double Zero," set in a gambling casino.

The New Adventures of Sherlock Holmes
Audio Gift Set, Volume 4
"Murder in the Casbah" finds the indefatigable duo going to bat for an accused murderer in North Africa, and "The Tankerville Club" concerns a young pal of Watson's who faces death in a duel. Ben Wright handles the intros. On Tape 2, it's Harry Bartell introducing a reliable killer-in-the-wax-museum tale, "The Strange Case of the Murderer in Wax," and a ghostly husband in "The Man with

the Twisted Lip." Wright's back for "The Guileless Gypsy" and "The Camberwell Poisoners" on Tape 3, followed by Bartell with "The Terrifying Cats," featuring a young American opera singer named Lizzie Borden (!), along with "The Submarine Caves." In the former, Eric Snowden—who played Watson in 1949, the last year of the series—warms up by filling in for an ailing Nigel Bruce. His Watson is calmer than Bruce's, and a bit less phlegmatic.

DOCUMENTARY

HIGHLY RECOMMENDED (★★★★)

The Home Front: 1938–1945
Pop Chronicles of the '40s

A Gathering of Men
Narrator: Bill Moyers; featuring Robert Bly
★★★

Here's audio documentation of the much-talked-about men's movement, with veteran journalist Moyers providing expert questions and commentary on the phenomenon and its central figure, poet Robert Bly. The listener hears several Bly poems and stories, many of them recorded live at a men's gathering. There's also lots of commentary from the poet, who asserts that the movement didn't start as a reaction to the women's movement but instead to events that began during the Industrial Revolution, which took fathers out of their homes and away from their sons. Interesting material taken quite seriously by all involved.

1 css 1 hr 25 min Mystic Fire Audio

The Home Front: 1938–1945
Writers/Narrators: Edward Brown, Frank Gorin, and William B. Williams
★★★★

A fully realized, recently produced radio documentary, this is subtitled *The Drama of the War Years.* It's an apt description, with the drama captured nicely in a collage of well-chosen music and sound bites for those years, stitched together with sure-handed commentary from the three narrators, all broadcast veterans. America's reluctance to be drawn into World War II is only one of the topics dealt with frankly but fairly, and many specific historic incidents—the national panic over Orson Welles's *War of the Worlds* broadcast, for instance—can be better understood and appreciated when heard in the rich and enthralling context of this five-hour-plus radio special.

4 css 5 hr 20 min The Mind's Eye

Legends
Writer/Narrator: Larry King
★★★

In volume two of the made-for-audio series *The Best of the Larry King Show,* the celebrated commentator/interviewer shows off some of his most impressive guests: Frank Sinatra, Sammy Davis, Jr., James Stewart, Shirley Temple Black, Kirk Douglas, and Shirley MacLaine. The hour flows quickly—almost *too* quickly. The listener may end up wishing for more, and for less of a scattershot approach to the conversational topics. King also does a bit of interrupting in an attempt to keep things moving.

1 css 1 hr Simon & Schuster Audio

Pop Chronicles of the '40s
Author: Compiled by John Gilliland
Performers: Various
★★★★

This is the original *Pop Chronicles* radio series, featuring rare interviews, commentary, and music from the 1940s. The first half was originally broadcast in 1972, and the second half in 1976—and since then this sparkling, ambitious archive has been a lost treasure. Tape 1 covers 1940 and 1941, up until Pearl Harbor. Tape 2 features music through V-J Day. Tape 3 spins up to 1947, and Tape 4 swings with Broadway's golden age, 1948 and 1949. The roster of musicians and talents included on these tapes is far too long to list, but it's safe to say that anybody who was anybody in music—and that includes writers, producers, and performers—is here, telling their own stories their own way.

4 css 6½ hr The Mind's Eye

Agatha Christie's Poirot (A BBC Radio Dramatization)
A: Agatha Christie
BDD

Aging Aircraft
(An NPR Presentation)
DOVE

America's Disappearing Wetlands
(An NPR Presentation)
DOVE

Astronaut's Journal
(An NPR Presentation)
R: Jeffrey Hoffman
DOVE

The Best of Daniel Pinkwater: Everyday Life
(An NPR Presentation)
R: Daniel Pinkwater
DOVE

The Best of the Stan Freberg Shows
A/R: Stan Freberg
PENG

Brazilian Rain Forests: A Correspondent's Personal Expedition
(An NPR Presentation)
DOVE

Cape Cod Radio Mystery Theater
Volume I
A: Steven Thomas Oney
R: Full Cast
PENG

Cape Cod Radio Mystery Theater
Volume II
A: Steven Thomas Oney
R: Full Cast
PENG

Cape Cod Radio Mystery Theater
Volume IV
A: Steven Thomas Oney
R: Full Cast
PENG

Caring for Aging Parents
(An NPR Presentation)
DOVE

Children of Alcoholics
(An NPR Presentation)
DOVE

Churchill in His Own Voice and the Voices of His Contemporaries
A/R: Winston Churchill
HARP

Daniel Pinkwater: Of Dogs and Men
(An NPR Presentation)
R: Daniel Pinkwater
DOVE

Dick Tracy Radio Classics
PENG

Dr. Who: The Evil of the Daleks
(A BBC Radio Dramatization)
BDD

Dr. Who: The Macra Terror
(A BBC Radio Dramatization)
BDD

Dracula
A: Bram Stoker
R: Robert Powell
BDD

The Eagle Has Landed
(A BBC Radio Dramatization)
A: Jack Higgins
BDD

Eisenhower
A: Edited by Jim Wessel
R: Dwight D. Eisenhower and others
HARP

El Cuidado de los Padres Ancianos (Caring for Aging Parents)
(Spanish)
(An NPR Presentation)
DOVE

The Elvis Tapes
(Press Conferences with Elvis Presley)
R: Elvis Presley
MILLS

Emma
(A BBC Radio Dramatization)
A: Jane Austen
R: Angharad Rees
BDD

The Empire Strikes Back
Produced by National Public Radio, with the cooperation of Lucasfilm, Ltd.
PENG

Entrenando al Cerebro (Training the Brain)
(Spanish)
(An NPR Presentation)
DOVE

The Family Radio
A/R: Garrison Keillor
PENG

Fawlty Towers
A: John Cleese and Connie Booth
R: John Cleese
BDD

The First Season
A/R: Garrison Keillor
PENG

Four Decades with Studs Terkel
A/R: Studs Terkel
PENG

Getting into College
(An NPR Presentation)
DOVE

God's Trombones: Seven Negro Sermons in Verse
A: James Weldon Johnson
R: Full Cast
PENG

Gospel Birds and Other Stories of Lake Wobegon
A: Garrison Keillor
PENG

Great American Speeches: 1931–1947
A: Edited by John Graham
R: Oliver Wendell Holmes, Jr., Will Rogers, Franklin D. Roosevelt, and others
HARP

Great American Speeches: 1950–1963
A: Edited by John Graham
R: William Faulker, John F. Kennedy, Carl Sandburg, and others
HARP

Great Black Speeches
A: Edited by John Graham
R: Claudia McNeil and Norman Matlock
HARP

Guy Noir
(Nine Live Radio Skits from *A Prairie Home Companion*)
PENG

H. L. Mencken Speaking
A/R: Henry L. Mencken
HARP

Hamlet
(A BBC Radio Dramatization)
A: William Shakespeare
R: Kenneth Branagh
BDD

Healing and the Mind (Soundtrack to PBS Series)
A: Bill Moyers
BDD

Helen Hayes: First Lady of the American Theater
(An NPR Presentation)
DOVE

The Hobbit
(A BBC Radio Dramatization)
A: J.R.R. Tolkien
BDD

Infant Learning
(An NPR Presentation)
DOVE

JFK: The Kennedy Tapes: Original Speeches of the Presidential Years, 1960–1963
R: John F. Kennedy
MILLS

John F. Kennedy: A Self-Portrait
A/R: John F. Kennedy
HARP

King Lear
(A BBC Radio Dramatization)
A: William Shakespeare
R: Kenneth Branagh and Sir John Gielgud
BDD

Lake Wobegon, U.S.A.
A/R: Garrison Keillor
PENG

Lake Wobegon USA Singles Series: Fertility
A: Original radio monologues by Garrison Keillor
R: Garrison Keillor
PENG

Lake Wobegon USA Singles Series: Patience
A: Original radio monologues by Garrison Keillor
R: Garrison Keillor
PENG

Lake Wobegon USA Singles Series: Rhubarb
A: Original radio monologues by Garrison Keillor
R: Garrison Keillor
PENG

Lake Wobegon USA Singles Series: Youth
A: Original radio monologues by Garrison Keillor
R: Garrison Keillor
PENG

Little Chills
Volume I
(An NPR Presentation)
DOVE

Little Chills
Volume II
(An NPR Presentation)
DOVE

Little Chills
Volume III
(An NPR Presentation)
DOVE

Little Chills
Volume IV
(An NPR Presentation)
DOVE

The Lord of the Rings
(A BBC Radio Dramatization)
A: J.R.R. Tolkien
R: Ian Holm
BDD

Lorraine Hansberry Speaks Out: Art and the Black Revolution
A/R: Lorraine Hansberry
HARP

Los Hijos de los Alcoholicos (Children of Alcoholics)
(Spanish)
(An NPR Presentation)
DOVE

Middlemarch
A: George Eliot
R: Ronald Pickup
BDD

Murder on the Orient Express
(A BBC Radio Dramatization)
A: Agatha Christie
BDD

My Life with Martin Luther King, Jr.
A/R: Coretta Scott King
HARP

The Mystery of the Blue Train
(A BBC Radio Dramatization)
A: Agatha Christie
BDD

The News from Lake Wobegon: 1974–1994: A 20th Anniversary Collection
A/R: Garrison Keillor
PENG

Pain and Medicine
(An NPR Presentation)
DOVE

Parenting—the World's Toughest Job
(An NPR Presentation)
DOVE

Prairie Home Comedy: Radio Songs and Sketches
A/R: Garrison Keillor
PENG

Prairie Home Companion: Anniversary Album: The First Five Years
A/R: Garrison Keillor
PENG

Prairie Home Companion: The Final Performance
A/R: Garrison Keillor
PENG

Prairie Home Companion: The Fourth Annual Farewell Performance
A/R: Garrison Keillor
PENG

Prairie Home Companion: The Second Annual Farewell Performance
A/R: Garrison Keillor
PENG

Prairie Home Companion: Tenth Anniversary Show
A/R: Garrison Keillor
PENG

Prairie Home Companion: Third Annual Farewell Performance
A/R: Garrison Keillor
PENG

Prairie Home Companion: Tourists
A: Garrison Keillor
R: Garrison Keillor; music by the Butch Thompson Trio and the Klezmer Conservatory Band
PENG

Quitting Smoking with Rod MacLeish
(An NPR Presentation)
R: Rod MacLeish
DOVE

Retrospective on the Gulf: The Questions of War
(An NPR Presentation)
DOVE

RFK: Selected Speeches
A: Edited by Edwin Guthman and C. Richard Allen
R: Robert Kennedy
PENG

Romeo and Juliet
(A BBC Radio Dramatization)
A: William Shakespeare
R: Kenneth Branagh
BDD

Rumpole on Trial: Selections
A: John Mortimer
R: Sir Michael Hordern
PENG

Sad Cypress
(A BBC Radio Dramatization)
A: Agatha Christie
BDD

Senseless Cruelty and Other Comedies
Duck's Breath Mystery Theatre
PENG

The Skull Beneath the Skin
(A BBC Radio Dramatization)
A: P. D. James
R: Great Scacchi
BDD

Spirits of the Present
Produced by the Native American Public Broadcasting Consortium and Radio Smithsonian
PENG

Star Wars
The Original Radio Drama
Produced by National Public Radio, with the cooperation of Lucasfilm, Ltd.
PENG

Thirteen at Dinner
(A BBC Radio Dramatization)
A: Agatha Christie
BDD

Training the Brain
(An NPR Presentation)
DOVE

Twenty Years with NPR
(An NPR Presentation)
DOVE

An Unsuitable Job for a Woman
(A BBC Radio Dramatization)
A: P. D. James
BDD

A Visit to Mark Twain's House
A/R: Garrison Keillor
PENG

Will Rogers' America
A/R: Will Rogers
HARP

The Wit and Wisdom of Will Rogers
A/R: Will Rogers
HARP

RELIGION

What unites every one of the following audio books is their overriding concern with the spiritual nature of humanity. Most of this section is taken up with works of and about faith—"the substance of things hoped for, the evidence of things not seen," as the Apostle Paul wrote in his Letter to the Hebrews. Here, the listener will find stories, aphorisms, and meditations to enrich and strengthen the life of the soul: audio books ranging from accessible versions of ancient spiritual wisdom—from the writings of the Old Testament to anthropomorphic tales attributed to the Buddha—to modern-day stories of joyous faith in the face of sometimes overwhelming adversity. Some of this material, too, will be controversial in some circles, as it questions some basic beliefs and strives to recast some long-accepted truths.

Certainly, other sections of *The Listener's Guide to Audio Books* feature tapes with some religious content, particularly the "Spirituality" and "Self-Help" sections. But the ones chosen for this particular section were picked because faith is their focus. Whether Buddhist, Jewish, or Christian in nature, all offer illuminating, inspiring, and sometimes challenging messages of spirituality.

HIGHLY RECOMMENDED (★★★★)

The Book of Job
The Cloud of Unknowing
Exodus
Genesis
Instructive Moments with the Savior
The Legend of the Baal-Shem
Sayings of the Buddha

The Book of Job
Author: Translated by Stephen Mitchell
Reader: Peter Coyote
★★★★

Brilliantly and empathetically read by actor Coyote—who conveys the wonder, anger, and suffering inherent in the Old Testament text—*The Book of Job* also benefits from a fine contemporary-language translation. Dealing with the age-old question of why good people suffer, it tells how Job, a man of God, endures horrible reversals of fortune but sticks to his faith, despite the words of well-meaning family members and friends. "We have accepted good fortune from God," he says in Mitchell's translation. "Surely we can accept bad fortune, too." A rich and inspirational work with a first-rate presentation.

1 css 1 hr 10 min Audio Literature

Boundaries
Authors/Readers: Dr. Henry Cloud and Dr. John Townsend
★★★

Using a fictional thirty-five-year-old wife, mother, and career person named Sherry, the authors—who are both psychologists and Christians—show how an inability to take control of one's own life (which, among other things, involves occasionally saying no to people demanding one's time) can lead to stressed-out feelings and ineffective living. An interesting blend of psychological and biblical principles, *Boundaries* shows how one can keep from being taken advantage of or otherwise unfairly used by others—without sacrificing a kind spirit.

2 css 2 hr 20 min Zondervan

Churches That Abuse
Author/Reader: Ronald M. Enroth
★★★

What does one do when he is abused by a church or other Christian organization? When spiritual leaders violate trust and pervert their power? Enroth gives some answers here for those he calls "battered believers," most of whom come from fundamentalist institutions outside the mainstream of America's evangelical churches. Essentially, what he's talking about here are cults, many of which are preoccupied by such things as demon possession, lust, and paranoia, and are often run by oddballs who claim divine inspiration. It's well researched, and some of the anecdotal evidence gets pretty scary.

2 css 3 hr Zondervan

The Cloud of Unknowing
Author: Translated by James Walsh
Reader: Alan Jones
★★★★

Written in the fourteenth century by an anonymous Christian, this guide to a contemplative as well as an active faith is both practical and mystical. The author believes that one can progress through four degrees of Christianity—ordinary, special, singular, and perfect—with the last stage reserved for the afterlife. Still, he believes the foundation for the final degree can be laid in this world. The writer exhorts Christians to be always open to the Truth, so that they might grow by degrees closer to the source of that Truth. Jones, Dean of Grace Cathedral in San Francisco, provides a reasoned, English-accented reading.

2 css 3 hr Audio Literature

Devotions for Growing Strong in the Seasons of Life
Author/Reader: Charles R. Swindoll
★★★

A million-seller as a book, *Devotions for Growing Strong in the Seasons of Life* is presented here in abridged form, with the good-natured narration of the author—president of Dallas Theological Seminary—taking the listener through anecdote-filled meditations. It's Swindoll's contention that people should "learn the answers to new questions, learn to sing the new melodies," as they approach each new season of their lives. These gentle, insightful bits of wisdom will enrich the daily routines of believers.

1 css 1½ hr Zondervan

Exodus
Reader: Joe Morton
★★★★

A companion to BDD's *Genesis* (see below), this reading of the second book of the Holy Bible chronicles the tribulations and triumphs of the Israelites under Moses, the Ten Commandments, and the building of God's tabernacle. Much of *Exodus* is taken up with the story of the flight from Egypt, and the time Moses and his flock spent in the wilderness; there's also a lengthy passage describing rules for building the tabernacle. A book of narrative as well as a book of law, it is, like *Genesis,* taken from the New Jerusalem translation.

4 css 4½ hr BDD Audio

Genesis
Reader: Joe Morton
★★★★

Of all the books of the Holy Bible, none has given the world more enduring tales than the Book of Genesis, read here in its entirety by actor Joe Morton in appropriately reverent tones. Beginning with the earth's very creation, and ending with the death of Joseph, who'd survived his brothers' selling him into slavery to become ruler of Egypt, *Genesis* relates the stories of such famous historical characters as Noah, Abraham, Adam and Eve, and Cain and Abel. The audio version is taken from the New Jerusalem Bible, a translation that lends itself well to the spoken word.

4 css 4 hr BDD Audio

The Gospel According to Jesus
Reader: Stephen Mitchell
★★★

A work of deep feeling as well as scholarship, *The Gospel According to Jesus* is also controversial. Mitchell's avowed purpose is to go into the Scriptures and strip away what he sees as bogus quotations—words ascribed to Jesus Christ that were instead created by others involved with the writing and transcribing of the four Gospels. For this, Mitchell takes the lead of Thomas Jefferson, who attempted the same thing—without, as Mitchell points out, the sophisticated research methods on hand today. The author notes that there are ultimately "no proofs, only probabilities," but he makes strong cases for the words he believes actually came from the mouth of Christ.

2 css 3 hr Audio Literature

Instructive Moments with the Savior
Author: Ken Gire
Readers: Jean Reed Bahle and Tom Casaletto
★★★★

Combining music, good writing, and solid narration, this version of one of Gire's *Moments with the Savior* series of books uses the audio book medium about as well as it can be used. Each of the several entries takes one of Jesus' parables and surrounds it with commentary and rich imagery, re-creating the setting for listeners and guiding them toward meaning. It is, as one of the readers notes, "a fresh look at the parables" that helps listeners in their search for God's messages.

2 css 3 hr Zondervan

Jataka Tales
Author: Noor Inayat Khan
Reader: Ellen Burstyn
★★★

"And while the Buddha sat, and all around him listened, these are the stories he told. . . ." So begins *Jataka Tales,* a series of eighteen anthropomorphic fables using animals to illustrate the virtues of self-sacrifice, compassion, and nonviolence. In their original form, these stories were said to have been related by the Buddha concerning things he observed in his previous, nonhuman, lives. Burstyn, herself a student of Sufi spiritual philosophy, narrates in a voice full of wonder and warmth, spinning stories of quail and dogs and monkeys learning how to live together and keep from falling prey to their enemies.

1 css 1½ hr Audio Literature

The Legend of the Baal-Shem
Author: Martin Buber
Reader: Theodore Bikel
★★★★

Actor-singer Bikel gives subtle, persuasive life to these stories—and sometimes, stories within stories—about the life and times of Israel ben Eliezer, who founded Hasidic Judaism in the early eighteenth century. (He was known as the Baal-Shem Tov, which translated to "Master of God's Name.") Working from legends and tales passed down for centuries, the noted scholar and philosopher Buber has done an excellent job of making the stories clear and direct even as they resonate with profound meaning.

2 css 2 hr 50 min Audio Literature

Little Lamb, Who Made Thee?
Author/Reader: Walter Wangerin, Jr.
★★★

A storyteller whose intensity, use of metaphor, and prairie inflections may remind the listener of Garrison Keillor, Wangerin extols the virtues here of being childlike throughout life, tying the attitude to a Christian perspective on childrearing. Examples from his own life as a minister's child, and later as a parent, are given in vivid and persuasive detail, and the advice that weaves his anecdotes together is solidly grounded in scriptural principles. Some later stories about adult children and their aging parents are especially touching.

2 css 3 hr Zondervan

Mourning into Dancing
Author/Reader: Walter Wangerin, Jr.
★★★

In this thoughtful, compelling tape, Wangerin deals with what he variously calls "the terrible guest" and "the cause of all our sadness"—death—in both its final, accepted sense, and in the sense of smaller deaths, caused by such things as abuse, divorce, neglect, loneliness, and despair. Using a blend of anecdotes, spiritual philosophy, and moral teachings, he shows the listener how grief over the daily forms of death can be transformed into joy and hope, and how the final victory over death is at the center of the Gospel of Jesus Christ.

2 css 2½ hr Zondervan

A Poet's Bible
Author: David Rosenberg
Reader: Michael York
★★★

With both a scientist's eye and a poet's ear, his words conveyed by the cultured tones of British star York, Rosenberg turns most ideas of the Bible's authorship upside down, claiming—as he did in his earlier *The Book of J*—that the Old

Testament was written in large part by professional Hebrew poets, both male and female. He even suggests that many of them didn't take the religious portions with complete reverence, occasionally going so far as to make puns involving the name of the Deity. Lively examples of Rosenberg's own translations from the Hebrew underscore his thesis.

2 css 3 hr Dove Audio

Reliving the Passion
Author/Reader: Walter Wangerin, Jr.
★★★

A series of thirty-seven meditations leading up to Easter, *Reliving the Passion* takes for its text the Gospel of Mark, specifically those parts regarding Jesus' trial, death, and resurrection. An opening segment, in which the author describes the feeling of being pulled into the Calvary scene as a child, is wildly emotional, contrasting with later calm and explanatory material. Wangerin's delivery during a few stretches will probably strike some as excessive, but it's undeniably effective at conveying the transcendent agony and horror of the Crucifixion, and the wonder of the Resurrection as well.

2 css 3 hr Zondervan

Sayings of the Buddha
Author: Translated by Thomas Byron
Reader: Jacob Needleman
★★★★

Translated from the Dhammapada, which is said to be taken directly from the words of the Buddha, *Sayings of the Buddha* provides an excellent introduction to the beliefs and teachings of Buddhism and its emphasis on spiritual growth through denial of self. Reader Needleman includes an illuminating essay of his own comparing Buddhism to other religions, concluding by calling for a wider acceptance of Buddhistic principles in modern society.

1 css 1½ hr Audio Literature

The Seven Storey Mountain
Author: Thomas Merton
Reader: Sidney Lanier
★★★

Although *The Seven Storey Mountain* is outwardly a biography, beginning with the late author's birth in Europe while World War I rages around him, and continuing through his education and life in a monastery, it's actually more the story of what happens inside Thomas Merton—an internal biography, if you will, by a man who felt "the necessity of a vital faith [and] the need for an interior life." Like the text itself, narrator Lanier—a former Episcopal priest—is both rational and persuasive.

2 css 2½ hr Audio Literature

A Shepherd Looks at Psalm 23
Author/Reader: Phillip Keller
★★★

The best-known psalm in the Bible begins with the words "The Lord is my shepherd, I shall not want." Keller begins his audio book on that psalm with a question: "Who is the Lord, and does he really have the authority to be my shepherd?" From there on, he takes the extended metaphor of shepherd and sheep from Psalm 23 and explores it from the perspective of a shepherd, noting that both sheep and people can be balky and spiritless and usually need constant care. The idea of being responsible for a flock comes into play here as well.

1 css 1 hr Zondervan

A Touch of His Peace
Author/Reader: Charles Stanley
★★★

Set up as a series of short meditations on God's peace, *A Touch of His Peace* features Baptist minister Stanley conveying each message in the familiar meditation format of Bible verse, commentary, and prayer. Very much Scripture- and Christ-centered, messages of God's forgiveness, grace, and unchanging love form the core of every message here.

2 css 2 hr Zondervan

A Touch of His Wisdom
Author/Reader: Charles Stanley
★★★

Like *A Touch of His Peace* (see above), *A Touch of His Wisdom* is a series of Bible-based reflections and meditations by Stanley, whose soft southern voice is familiar to fans of the *In Touch* radio and television programs. This time, each meditation is based on a verse or two from the Book of Proverbs, with Stanley adding commentary and prayers. There's more talk of the devil and sin in this volume than in *A Touch of His Peace,* but there's the same sure belief that God is at the center and in control.

2 css 2 hr Zondervan

When Is It Right to Die?
Author/Reader: Joni Deareckson Tada
★★★

Narrated by quadriplegic Tada in a conversational, frequently emotional, but never bathetic manner, *When Is It Right to Die?* finds her at odds with most of the philosophy of the right-to-die movement, which she feels embraces a seductive premise that's evil at the core. No one, she believes, is immune from the pull of death as an antidote to suffering. But instead, Tada encourages the listener to reach out in faith and hope, both to God and to other people, no matter what the circumstances. It's an approach illustrated convincingly by her own life.

2 css 2½ hr Zondervan

Where Is God When It Hurts?
Author/Reader: Philip Yancey
★★★

Narrating his own book in a warm, ministerial voice, Yancey takes on the timeless question of why God allows so much suffering in the world. He doesn't shy away from the question's uglier ramifications, either, at one point going as far as to use one of Elie Wiesel's harrowing concentration camp stories as an illustration of how horrible life can get. Yancey's answers have to do with putting suffering in context with the hope of eternal peace and with the life of the spirit. He also calls upon his listeners to give more help to those who suffer.

2 css 2 hr Zondervan

Aim High: An Olympic Decathlete's Inspiring Story
A: Dave Johnson with Verne Becker
R: Dave Johnson
ZON

Amazing Grace
R: Judy Collins
RH

Angels: God's Secret Agents
A/R: Billy Graham
RH

Becoming a Contagious Christian
A: Bill Hybels and Mark Mittelberg
R: Bill Hybels
ZON

The Be-Happy Attitudes
A/R: Robert Schuller
RH

Being a Wild, Wonderful Woman for God
A/R: Becky Tirabassi
ZOND

Believe and Be Happy
A/R: Dr. Robert H. Schuller
S&S

Believe in the God Who Believes in You
A: Dr. Robert H. Schuller
BDD

The Bible: The New Testament
R: Gregory Peck
DOVE

The Book of Psalms
R: Michael York
DOVE

Born for Love
A/R: Leo Buscaglia, Ph.D.
RH

The Bride: Renewing Our Passion for the Church
A/R: Charles R. Swindoll
ZOND

Character and Destiny: A Nation in Search of Its Soul
A: D. James Kennedy with James Nelson Black
R: D. James Kennedy
ZON

Come Before Winter and Share My Hope
A/R: Charles R. Swindoll
ZON

Crow and Weasel
A/R: Barry Lopez
RH

Footprints
A: Margaret Fishback Powers
R: Joan Winmill Brown
DOVE

Gift from the Sea
A: Anne Morrow Lindbergh
R: Claudette Colbert
RH

The Heart of It: World Religions
A/R: Dr. Elizabeth McNamer
DOVE

A History of God: The 4000-Year Quest of Judaism, Christianity, and Islam
A: Karen Armstrong
HARP

The Holy Bible
R: Dame Judith Anderson
DOVE

Joshua
A: Joseph F. Girzone
BDD

Joshua and the Children
A: Joseph F. Girzone
BDD

Joshua in the Holy Land
A: Joseph F. Girzone
BDD

The Joys of Yiddish
A/R: Leo Rosten
HARP

Kwanzaa Folktales
A: Gordon Lewis
R: Multiple Voice Presentation
TW

Never Forget: The Riveting Story of One Woman's Journey from Public Housing to the Corridors of Power
A: Kay Coles James
ZON

The Physics of Immortality
A: Frank J. Tipler
BDD

The Power of Myth
A: Joseph Campbell with Bill Moyers
PENG

- **Program 1: The Hero's Adventure**
- **Program 2: The Message of the Myth**
- **Program 3: The First Storytellers**
- **Program 4: Sacrifice and Bliss**
- **Program 5: Love and the Goddess**
- **Program 6: Masks of Eternity**

The Presence of Christmas
R: Bruce Heighley; music by Harry Nilsson
DOVE

The President's Angel
A/R: Sophy Burnham
RH

The Sermon on the Mount: Living Outside Life's Struggle
A: Emmet Fox
HARP

The Sermon on the Mount: The Golden Keys to Successful Living
A: Emmet Fox
HARP

Sharing Christmas
A: Edited by Deborah Raffin
DOVE

The Shepherd
A: Joseph F. Girzone
BDD

Silence of Adam
A: Larry Crabb with Don Hudson and Al Andrews
R: Larry Crabb
ZOND

The Simple English Gospels
R: Pat Boone
DOVE

Success Is Never Ending, Failure Is Never Final
A: Dr. Robert H. Schuller
BDD

Super Sheep Audio
A: Ken Davis
ZON

Surprised by the Voice of God
A/R: Jack Deere
ZOND

The Twelfth Angel
A: Og Mandino
R: Og Mandino and others
RH

- **Volume I: The Soul of the Ancients**
- **Volume II: The Wisdom of the East**
- **Volume III: The Western Way**

Well Done: The Common Guy's Guide to Success
A: R. David Thomas with Ron Beyma
ZON

What Jesus Would Say To: Rush Limbaugh, Madonna, Bill Clinton, Michael Jordan, Bart Simpson, Etc. and You
A/R: Lee Strobel
ZOND

Words of Comfort and Wisdom
BDD

The World of Joseph Campbell
A: Joseph Campbell
PENG

SCIENCE FICTION AND FANTASY

Science fiction is a literature of ideas, and unlike many other fiction categories, it does not easily lend itself to pictures. Perhaps that is why science fiction and fantasy work best on the printed page—though audio has proven to be a notable exception.

Welcome to imagination done right.

Listeners can find a range of science fiction and fantasy tapes, from hard science to whimsy, usually all together on the same shelf in the bookstore. But this can also be a confusing category.

More than any other audio category, science fiction is peppered with sequels, prequels, trilogies, and series of books that go on and on, some practically impossible to understand except by starting at the beginning.

Isaac Asimov's *Foundation* series, for example, spans almost fifty years in its writing, and the last books connect *Foundation* with his earlier series of *Robot* stories. No matter how inviting the last book in a series might seem, it is usually better to start with number one.

Not to be confused with a series of books are "related" books. The science fiction shelf is apt to be loaded with TV and movie novelizations and spin-offs—most notably, the *Star Trek* books.

Sometimes science fiction listeners have a choice of the same books on tape or pricier compact discs. CD sound is sharper, not as strikingly better as music on CD. But, say, is this idea a natural or what?—science fiction on silver saucers.

HIGHLY RECOMMENDED (★★★★)

The Chronicles of Narnia
Do Androids Dream of Electric Sheep?
The Ender Wiggins Saga
The Hobbit*
The Lord of the Rings
Neuromancer
Star Trek: The Next Generation: Q-Squared
The Stories of Ray Bradbury

All the Weyrs of Pern
Author/Reader: Anne McCaffrey
★★

A talky start makes slow going of this late entry in McCaffrey's best-selling *Pern* series, at least for listeners anxious to get the dragons off the ground. But in fairness, this prolific author has built a following who would just as soon hear about her characters' tangled relationships. Pern is one of science fiction's most fully envisioned worlds—one of fire-breathing, telepathic dragons and brave dragon-riders, who live in *weyrs.* The new story element this time is a twenty-five-century-old artificial intelligence. McCaffrey reads with prim enjoyment, like a schoolteacher having a great time.

2 css 3 hr The Publishing Mills AudioBooks

Another Fine Myth
Author: Robert Asprin
Reader: Tony Roberts
★★★

The title sets the tone for this first book in Asprin's *Myth* series of comic fantasies. If Woody Allen were to write about wizards and unicorns, he might come up with a story like this one—the tale of a magician's apprentice and a purple-tongued demon named Aahz. So it's fitting that the book is read by Tony Roberts, an actor familiar to moviegoers for his roles in several of Allen's films, including *Annie Hall.* Especially good is the voice Roberts comes up with for Aahz, like a cross between Humphrey Bogart and the grump who runs your favorite deli counter. (See *Myth Conceptions,* and *Myth Directions* on page 319.)

2 css 3 hr Durkin Hayes Audio

* Both The Mind's Eye and the Bantam Audio editions are highly recommended.

Batman: The Complete Knightfall Saga
Author: DC Comics
Performers: Bob Sessions, Kerry Shale, and others
★★★

Dying worked out so well for Superman (see *Superman Lives!* on page 330), DC Comics gave Batman an extra share of troubles, too. Batman is crippled, and troubled Gotham City finds a new savior called Azrael, who takes the job maybe a little too seriously. It won't make you any smarter, but this comic-book-brought-to-sound is great fun, much like old-time radio drama loaded with hissing threats and squealing tires. Perfect for a dark and stormy night.

2css 3 hr Time Warner AudioBooks

The Chronicles of Narnia
Author: C. S. Lewis
Readers: Claire Bloom, Anthony Quayle, Ian Richardson, and Michael York
★★★★

Four children go to live with an old professor in the country, where little Lucy wanders into a wardrobe that leads her into Lewis's land of wonders, Narnia. The series is a Christian allegory in which Lewis recasts biblical happenings as they might have transpired in an altogether different world—for example, the Christ-like death and resurrection of Aslan, the lion. But that description makes Lewis's writing sound stuffy and pious, whereas the hard-drinking, pipe-puffing writer shared with his Oxford friend J.R.R. Tolkien the belief that a good story didn't need to be loaded with lessons. Seven books comprise the series: *The Lion, The Witch and the Wardrobe, Prince Caspian, The Voyage of the Dawn Treader, The Silver Chair, The Horse and His Boy, The Magician's Nephew,* and *The Last Battle.* The first, published in 1950, remains the series' best known, but this tape set is a chance to discover the whole of Lewis's Narnia stories, read by a superlative cast.

7 css 7 hr Harper Audio

Crystal Singer
Author: Anne McCaffrey
Reader: Adrienne Barbeau
★★★

Among Anne McCaffrey's best books, *Crystal Singer* is the story of singer Killashandra Ree's adventures in the crystal mines of planet Ballybran. The tape package says she hopes to become "a sought-after soloist," just like any other hopeful on the Milky Way to Nashville. Somebody wasn't listening. Ballybran is not a planet of music buffs; it is a place where only singers like Killashandra can find and cut the rare crystals that are vital to interstellar communication, and the mines ruin their health. Adrienne Barbeau's tough-edged reading is a neat match to Killashandra's character.

2 css 3 hr Dove Audio

Do Androids Dream of Electric Sheep?
Author: Philip K. Dick
Readers: Calista Flockhart and Matthew Modine
★★★★

This is the quintessential Philip K. Dick novel. He wrote many, but this one became Dick's best known when director Ridley Scott made it into the movie *Blade Runner* (1982). If you've only seen the movie, though—rich in visual invention—you haven't experienced all the mind power the book delivers. Dick's concern is with the difference between androids, who look human, and humans, who act like machines, told as the story of a bounty hunter assigned to eliminating androids on the loose. An effective touch is the sound production's teaming of Matthew Modine with Calista Flockhart for reading the book's edgy man-woman dialogue.

2 css 3 hr Time Warner AudioBooks

Doctor Who: The Evil of the Daleks
Author: David Whitaker
Performers: Patrick Thoughton and others
★★

A treasure or a scratchy old radio show: The difference depends on how attached you are to this distinctively British science fiction hero, Doctor Who. Step aboard the good doctor's time-traveling *Tardis* to rediscover a long-lost BBC radio drama, *The Evil of the Daleks.* Armed with their own means of time travel, the Daleks set a trap. The doctor and his traveling companion, Jamie, wind up prisoners in a Victorian mansion. The sometimes fuzzy sound demands close attention, but the reward is a story that was lost for so long, it's like new again.

2 css 3 hr BDD Audio

Doctor Who: The Macra Terror
Author: Ian Stuart Black
Performers: Patrick Thoughton and others
★★

As above, this is a BBC radio drama from the early sixties. *Doctor Who* has been on the British scene almost as long as steak-and-kidney pie, and, like that venerable dish, tends to be an acquired taste. *The Macra Terror* finds Doctor Who checking into a resort spa where sinister goings-on happen late at night. Radio can conjure sets and monsters far more elaborate than those offered by the low-budget *Dr. Who* television series; but, again, the sound quality is a bit lacking.

2 css 2½ hr BDD Audio

The DragonLance Chronicles: Dragons of Spring Dawning
Authors: Margaret Weis and Tracy Hickman
Reader: Peter MacNicol
★★

Volume three of the *DragonLance Chronicles,* which began with *Dragons of Autumn Twilight, Dragons of Spring Dawning* finds the Companions of the Lance taking up their dragonlances. Not only are there dragons to fight, but there is also the five-headed dragon goddess. Peter MacNichol is the perfect choice to read these tales of flashing blades and mystic glades; he has the musical voice of a bard, as well as having starred in the movie *Dragonslayer.*

2 css 3 hr Random House AudioBooks

The DragonLance Chronicles: Dragons of Winter Night
Authors: Margaret Weis and Tracy Hickman
Reader: Peter MacNichol
★★

In *Dragons of Winter Night,* volume two of the *DragonLance Chronicles,* our heroes run into trouble in their quest for the dragon orb, not to mention the dragonlance, while the Dark Queen plots against them. No surprise that it sounds like a role-playing game; the books are from TSR, Inc., a game publisher. Fun on that level.

2 css 3 hr Random House AudioBooks

The Ender Wiggins Saga
Author: Orson Scott Card
Reader: Mark Rolson
★★★★

This is a boxed set of Orson Scott Card's three Ender novels: *Ender's Game, Speaker for the Dead,* and *Xenocide.* The first two each won the Hugo and Nebula awards, the science fiction equivalent of an Academy Award sweep plus a marching band. Card's subject is rite of passage, and his gift is the rare ability to weave challenging moral issues into slam-bang adventure. Actor Mark Rolston reads all three books, even though *Xenocide* credits Card himself as the narrator. *Ender's Game* begins with six-year-old Ender Wiggins's forced entry into military training in a time of intergalactic chaos. In *Speaker for the Dead,* the young warrior must confront his guilt at having wiped out an alien race, and *Xenocide* finds him at odds with a killer virus and a psychic girl. (These tapes are available separately, too, but it's cheaper to buy the whole set.)

6 css 9 hr Audio Renaissance Tapes

Friday
Author: Robert Heinlein
Reader: Samantha Eggar
★★

As if to send his worst critics—those who called him sexist—into frothing fits of objection, Heinlein wrote *Friday.* Friday is a hot-to-trot secret courier with a "trick belly button," in which she carries her secrets. This is minor writing compared to grand master Heinlein's classic *Starship Troopers* or *Stranger in a Strange Land.* But just as the book gained more than it deserved from Michael Whelan's seductive cover painting, so the tape gains from Eggar's sexy, hard-boiled reading.

2 css 3 hr Listen for Pleasure

Forward the Foundation
Author: Isaac Asimov
Reader: David Dukes
★★★

The landmark success of Isaac Asimov's *Foundation* series launched the career of this incredibly productive writer. The first three books—*Prelude to Foundation, Foundation and Empire,* and *Second Foundation*—were put together from a series of short stories that date to the 1940s, starting from Asimov's general idea of retelling the fall of the Roman Empire on a galactic scale. Forty years later, he began adding to the original trilogy, delivering a series of uncharacteristically thick novels. *Forward the Foundation,* the last of them, was finished just before his death. Absolutely not the place to start, it is Asimov tying up loose ends and moving his *Foundation* story into the future. It might sound a little sad, too—not in Dukes's strong reading, but in the sense of a great man nearing the end of his life, writing that one last book. It's not his best (Asimov's all-time best would be hard to name; he wrote hundreds), but it's a must-have, or must-hear, for anyone who has followed his *Foundation* series to this point.

4 css 6 hr BDD Audio

The Hobbit
Author: J.R.R. Tolkien
Performers: Bernard Mayes, Ray Reinhardt, and others; narrated by Gail Chugg
★★★★

"In a hole in the ground, there lived a hobbit." And with these words, the British writer J.R.R. Tolkien began the saga that was to become fantasy's masterwork (see *The Lord of the Rings* on page 319). *The Hobbit* is a children's story in the same way that *Alice in Wonderland* is, a tale that can be heard over and over again, speaking in some new way to each new generation. Bilbo Baggins is an extra-peaceful hobbit (a little guy, smaller than a dwarf) who leaves his cozy hole to join the wizard Gandalf in an adventure that leads them to the lair of the terrible dragon, Smaug, in a far-off time of "less noise and more green." This faithful audio version works magic that even Gandalf might envy.

6 css 6 hr The Mind's Eye

The Hobbit
Author: J.R.R. Tolkien
Cast: Multi
★★★★

Bilbo Baggins never liked to make hard choices, so he wouldn't have liked deciding between this and The Mind's Eye version (see above) of Tolkien's first-published book (1937). Gandalf might conjure up the resources to buy both. This one is BBC radio's production, marking the centenary of Tolkien's birth. It plays a little looser in its adaptation, but with just the right balance of humor, affection, and reverence to Tolkien's classic. For instance, Bilbo himself interrupts the veddy-veddy British narrator at the story's beginning to clear up that business about living in a hole: "My hole was a hobbit-hole, and that means comfort."

4 css 4 hr Bantam Audio

In Pursuit of the Green Lion
Author: Judith Merkle Riley
Reader: Juliet Mills
★★★

Except for a touch of alchemy, this lighthearted medieval adventure belongs more under the heading of, well . . . lighthearted medieval adventure. Margaret of Ashbury is exactly the sort of spunky, stubborn heroine to inspire exclamations of "My God! What a woman!" and the like from strong men in varying degrees of attraction, exasperation, and dismay. Here, she is on a quest to rescue her captive husband from an archfiend and, worse, bad poet. Juliet Mills's reading keeps the tale bubbling along.

2 css 3 hr The Publishing Mills AudioBooks

Isaac Asimov Audio Collection
Author: Isaac Asimov
Readers: Isaac Asimov, William Shatner
★★★

The sheer length of Asimov's Foundation series can make it daunting to start. But here's a well-produced sampler that will give you some of the tone and the fascination. The author, who predicted the advent of the hand-held computer, reads two sections—"Foundation's Edge" and "The Mayors from Foundation." William Shatner deftly reads Asimov's "Foundation: The Psychohistorians," a story that works like a primer to explain what psychohistory is. After listening, even a math failure can calculate the prospect of enjoying this series as a whole.

3 css 4 hrs Harper Audio

Isaac Asimov's Science Fiction Magazine
Authors: Isaac Asimov and Frederik Pohl
Readers: Ed Bishop and Peter Marinker
★★

Asimov lent his name to a monthly magazine that has become a regular home for science fiction award winners, often a showcase for cutting-edge writers in this genre. However, this tape is not the cutting edge; it is a look back. Asimov contributes two stories—"Strikebreaker" and "It's Such a Beautiful Day"—from the 1950s, and Frederik's Pohl's "Sitting Around the Pool, Soaking Up the Rays" is from 1984.

2 css 2½ hr Listen for Pleasure

The Lord of the Rings
Author: J.R.R. Tolkien
Performers: Ian Holm, Michael Horndern, and others
★★★★★

Our rating system only goes as high as four stars, but we've called on elfin magic to forge a fifth star for this mammoth BBC radio production of Tolkien's epic. And what's that hammering sound in the woods?—maybe a sixth star. *The Lord of the Rings* is three books: *The Fellowship of the Ring, The Two Towers,* and *The Return of the King.* Begun as merely a sequel to *The Hobbit,* this trilogy takes on Shakespearean thunder as Frodo the hobbit, Gandalf the wizard, and a not-so-brave party of other elves and men set out to destroy the One Ring of the Dark Lord—a perilous journey that takes them to the evil Land of Mordor, where the shadows lie. The story lends itself to many interpretations, including that Tolkien was writing about the horrors and heroics of twentieth-century warfare and the losses that come to all, win or lose. But this work stands as the milestone of modern fantasy.

13 css 20 hr BDD Audio

Myth Conceptions
Author: Robert Asprin
Reader: Tony Roberts
★★★

Skeeve, the magician apprentice from Robert Asprin's earlier *Another Fine Myth* (see page 313), again teams up with the golden-eyed demon Aahz, this time to defend the embattled Kingdom of Possiltum. A good part of the fun here is Tony Roberts's reading, like telling a joke that he knows will pay off. Roberts's good nature makes up for what listeners are missing when they don't see the book in print. As the title hints—or maybe warns—there are puns in these woods, some hard to catch on tape: wordplay and words that just look funny in print. Hopped a good D-Hopper lately?

2 css 3 hr Durkin Hayes Audio

Myth Directions
Author: Robert Asprin
Reader: Tony Roberts
★★★

Skeeve and a shapely demon named Tanda go birthday shopping for Aahz, in a dimension where the greatest prize of all is an ugly sports trophy. More laughs in a genre that doesn't laugh much.

2 css 3 hr Durkin Hayes Audio

Neuromancer
Author/Reader: William Gibson
★★★★

It blew minds like a literary power surge ten years ago, this burning chrome book that changed what science fiction is all about. The first sentence signaled a whole new kind of story: "The sky above the port was the color of television tuned to a dead channel." And it's still cutting edge, inspiring this top-rate sound production. Few authors have the right voice to match the tone of their own words, but Gibson does, telling his fevered dreams of "live-wire voodoo" like a marathon coffeehouse poetry reading. The story is about a hustler named Case who must plug into lethal cyberspace one last time, and remember: there was no such thing as cyberspace to plug into until Gibson invented it.

4 css 6 hr Time Warner AudioBooks

Nightwings
Author: Robert Silverberg
Reader: Fritz Weaver
★★★

One of Robert Silverberg's best novels, *Nightwings* is the lyrical tale of the Watcher, whose mission is to scan the skies for sight of alien invaders; and Avluela the Flier, the winged girl who roams the world's ancient cities with him. A portion of *Nightwings* won the Hugo Award for best science fiction novella in 1969. The sixties were a turn-around time in Silverberg's career, when he switched gears from sci-fi guy to thoughtful science fiction writer, applying mainstream techniques to themes that really mattered to him. The reward for that sort of change is that, someday, an actor with Fritz Weaver's commanding skills might read your work out loud.

2 css 3 hr Listen for Pleasure

Powers That Be
Authors: Anne McCaffrey and Elizabeth Ann Scarborough
Reader: Marina Sirtis
★★

Well, thought Yana. An hour on the planet and intrigue starts already. And so it does, in ways that ought to please staunch fans of these two award-winning collaborators, Anne McCaffrey and Elizabeth Ann Scarborough, as well as those of actress Marina Sirtis from *Star Trek: The Next Generation.* Yana is a sickly combat veteran assigned to making sense of mysterious happenings on the frozen planet Petaybee. (But on the subject of truth in packaging—how can we say this within the bounds of political correctness?—listen, you guys, don't be fooled by the sloe-eyed, buxom bimbo on the cover. It ain't that kinda tape.)

2 css 3 hr Dove Audio

Ruby: The Adventures of a Galactic Gumshoe
Author: M. Fulton
Readers: Laura Esterman and "a stellar cast of supporting androids, etc."
★★

Promising "a narrative hybrid of *The Maltese Falcon* and *Star Wars,*" *Ruby* is a hyperactive comedy that brings to mind Sydney Greenstreet's line in *The Maltese Falcon:* "It—it's lead! It's lead!" Ruby is a galactic detective who goes around shooting genetically engineered assassins called Slimies, then gasping, "Peeee-yew! Nuthin's worse'n a burnt Slimie." Peeee-yew! is right, but some of the sound effects are entertaining.

2 css 3 hr Audio Editions

Second Foundation
Author: Isaac Asimov
Reader: David Dukes
★★★

The classic *Foundation* trilogy (see *Forward the Foundation* on page 000) concludes with a galactic search for the Second Foundation, where man's best knowledge might have survived centuries of barbarism. This is old-time science fiction, the sort with lots of talk and not much action from its cast of one-dimensional characters, but they are talking fantastic ideas. In particular, there is protagonist Hari Seldon's concept of psychohistory: prediction by means of statistics. David Dukes's clear, confident reading makes it all sound user-friendly, even for techno-know-nothings.

2 css 3 hr BDD Audio

Star Trek

Star Trek is a phenomenon. From a low-rated, three-season TV series that started in 1966, it has grown to inspire and encompass galaxies of intensely loyal fans, three other TV series (*Star Trek: The Next Generation, Deep Space Nine,* and *Voyager*), seven big-screen movies, more than a hundred hardcover and paperback books—and books on tape. The readers are *Star Trek* cast members, and the sound is enhanced with authentic, *Enterprise*-sounding beeps and tweeps. Like the movies that followed the original TV series, these books tend to assume that you already know and care deeply about the starship *Enterprise,* its mission, and the series' characters, but it's not hard to get up to speed on them. Just say, "Warp five." Here are some of the *Star Trek* books available for listening with pointy ears. Note that the *Star Trek: Deep Space Nine* and *The Next Generation* series follow the *Star Trek* titles listed below.

Star Trek: Best Destiny
Author: Diane Carey
Reader: James Doohan
★★★

The story of a then-young Captain James T. Kirk's first flight into space with his estranged father, *Best Destiny* has more going for it than most *Star Trek* adventures—more makings of a real novel—confronting Kirk with the question that everyone has to ask one time or another, whether in space or in Omaha: What should I do with my life? And that question is far more challenging than any Klingon attack.

2 css 3 hr Simon & Schuster Audio

Star Trek: Conversational Klingon
Authors: Barry Levine and Marc Okrand
Instructors: Marc Okrand and Michael Dorn
★★★★

Our four-star rating system goes out the starboard port on this one. Truth is, we don't know a better guide to conversational Klingon, or, for that matter, a worse one. Michael Dorn (resident Klingon Lieutenant Worf on TV's *Star Trek: The Next Generation*) lends his booming bass voice to the enterprise, advising, "Speak Klingon boldly." Otherwise, it's much the same as any other learn-a-language tape, except that students are warned they are apt to spit a lot.

1 css 1 hr Simon & Schuster Audio

Star Trek: Faces of Fear
Author: Michael Jan Friedman
Reader: Bibi Besch
★★

Kirk has a war to stop on Alpha Malurian Six, while Spoke has Klingon trouble on Beta Canzandia Three. Standard fare, read by Bibi Besch. Star Trek trivia buffs can take turns guessing which role Besch played: (A) Mudd's woman, (B) the Horta, or (C) the role of Dr. Carol Marcus in *Star Trek II: The Wrath of Khan.*

2 css 3 hr Simon & Schuster Audio

Star Trek: Power Klingon
Authors: Barry Levine and Marc Okrand
Instructors: Marc Okrand and Michael Dorn
★★

Wait no more, here is advanced Klingon for the determinedly well-spoken warrior. It really is a functional language that can be swapped in guttural glee with fellow combatants. Dorn advises, "Klingon is a language of controlled fury," so no wonder this lingo is studded with such power words as *HIv!* (meaning "Attack!") and *DeSveth yIv!* ("Chew that arm!"). The tape comes with a handy printed guide to tough talking. (See *Star Trek: Conversational Klingon*, above.)

1 css 1 hr Simon & Schuster Audio

Star Trek: Probe
Author: Margaret Wander Bonanno
Reader: James Doohan
★★

A sequel to the movie *Star Trek IV: The Voyage Home* (1986), this story finds Captain Kirk and his crew swooshing across the galaxy to nab that troublesome probe last seen in the movie—the one that nearly destroyed earth, and now it has popped up again in Romulan territory. (Truth is, we don't remember much about this probe from the movie, let alone ever wondering what happened to it.

What happened to the whales?) *Star Trek IV* is one of the best—certainly funniest—in *Star Trek*'s big-screen series, and a hard act to follow.

2 css 3 hr Simon & Schuster Audio

Star Trek: Sarek
Author: A. C. Crispin
Reader: Mark Lenard
★★

Actor Mark Lenard reads this talky episode that centers on Spock's all-Vulcan father, Sarek, the character Lenard played. Spock and Sarek have to set aside their differences to foil a plot against the Federation. Lenard's soft, sinuous voice is the essence of Sarek, but it's a bit unsettling when Captain Kirk and other characters start sounding the same way.

2 css 3 hr Simon & Schuster Audio

Star Trek: Spock's World
Author: Diana Duane
Readers: Leonard Nimoy and George Takei
★★★

When producer Gene Roddenbury launched *Star Trek,* one of his brighter ideas was to call on real, published science fiction writers for scripts. Diane Duane show the book series benefits from that same thinking. Here, Spock's home planet, Vulcan, is threatening to quit the Federation, the *Enterprise* crew is supposed to make peace, and Spock is caught in the middle. Leonard Nimoy reads the part of Spock as he would play it on screen; George Takei (Helmsman Sulu) reads the rest with a broadcaster's aplomb.

2 css 3 hr Simon & Schuster Audio

Star Trek: The Kobayashi Maru
Author: Julia Ecklar
Reader: James Doohan
★★

The Kobayashi Maru is a simulated space crisis that is inflicted on cadets at Starfleet Academy. Nobody is supposed to win. It gives Scotty and other frustrated test-takers something to talk about years later, say, when they are trapped in a drifting shuttle craft "in the hours they had before rescue—or death." James Doohan (Scotty) reads the narrative parts without Scotty's accent, a reminder that he appeared on other TV series, even *Peyton Place,* before he and Scotty took over the starship *Enterprise*'s ever-troubled engine room.

1 css 1½ hr Simon & Schuster Audio

Star Trek: 25th Anniversary Audio Collection
Authors: Vonda N. McIntyre, Margaret Wander Bonanno, and Diane Carey
Readers: Leonard Nimoy, James Doohan, and George Takei; introduction by William Shatner
★★★

Hailing frequencies, hailing frequencies, the gang's all here. William Shatner introduces this CD collection of three *Star Trek* adventures: *Enterprise: The First Adventure* by Vonda N. McIntyre; *Strangers from the Sky* by Margaret Wander Bonanno, and *Final Frontier* by Diane Carey, read by cast members Leonard Nimoy, James Doohan, and George Takei. One of the best parts is Shatner's recitation of alternative *Star Trek* openings that were considered and, happily, photon-torpedoed just before the first TV series began. Instead of proclaiming the starship *Enterprise* on a "five-year mission to seek out new life and new civilizations," Captain Kirk might have found himself announcing a mere "five-year patrol," like a space cop in a planetary prowl car.

4 CDs 9½ hr Simon & Schuster Audio

Star Trek: Memories
Authors: William Shatner with Cris Kreski
Reader: William Shatner
★★★

Shatner lends his familiar voice to some unfamiliar glimpses of life behind the scenes when he starred as Captain James T. Kirk in the original *Star Trek* series. He makes it sound conversational, confessional, even conspiratorial, as he lets the cat out of the transporter beam, saying he never really understood the show's popularity. "For me, it had always been first and foremost, a job." Best is the book's conclusion, as Shatner gamely records his fellow cast members' gripes against him, trying to make peace—at least with himself. Brace yourself for a meteor storm of *Star Trek* memoirs as the original cast members warp into retirement; but unless and until Leonard Nimoy joins the parade with his own book, we predict Shatner's will stand as the best. Well done, Captain.

4 css 4½ hr Harper Audio

Star Trek: Deep Space Nine: Fallen Heroes
Author: Dafydd ab Hugh
Reader: Rene Auberjonois
★★

This busy time in deep space finds alien warriors knocking on Commander Sisko's door, demanding the return of a prisoner he doesn't know is aboard the *Deep Space Nine* station. Meantime, Quark and security chief Odo zip three days into the future, where they discover the station has gone ker-blooey. *Deep Space Nine* must be the only thing in the universe more constantly on the verge of destruction than the starship *Enterprise*'s dicey antimatter engines. Rene Auberjonois plays Odo on TV.

2 css 2 hr Simon & Schuster Audio

Star Trek: Deep Space Nine: The Emissary
Author: J. M. Dillard
Reader: Nana Visitor
★★

J. M. Dillard's game novel is based on a teleplay by Michael Piller, based on a story by Piller and Rick Berman, based on an idea that just plain isn't as interesting as the first two *Star Trek* series. Instead of boldly going in search of new life and new civilization, Commander Sisko and his crew boldly sit aboard their space station, keeping watch over their wormhole, and wait for new life and whatever else to come their way. As Captain Kirk might have said it, give us a tall ship.

2 css 3 hr Simon & Schuster Audio

Star Trek: The Next Generation: All Good Things . . .
Author: Michael Jan Friedman
Reader: Jonathan Frakes
★★★

A novelization of the series' last episode (based on the teleplay by Ronald D. Moore and Brannon Braga), *All Good Things . . .* finds Captain Jean-Luc Picard coming unstuck in time much like Billy Pilgrim in Kurt Vonnegut's *Slaughterhouse Five.* Sometimes, he is reliving his past; sometimes, he is caught in the future. Either way, he is struggling to make sense of it. Jonathan Frakes (Commander William Riker on TV) delivers a number-one reading, although his take on Worf is a bit growly.

2 css 3 hr Simon & Schuster Audio

Star Trek: The Next Generation: Contamination
Author: John Vornholt
Reader: Michael Dorn
★★

Klingon Lieutenant Worf and Counsellor Denna Troi investigate the murder of a famed scientist in a mystery read by Worf himself, actor Michael Dorn. The usually blunt-spoken Klingon is uncommonly erudite this time around, noting the late scientist "had recently exhibited . . . irrational behavior, but nothing of this magnitude," which calls for "a thorough psychological examination." Worf, is that you? *'IwlIj jachjaj!* Still, when a Klingon reads, you'd better listen.

1 css 1½ hr Simon & Schuster Audio

Star Trek: The Next Generation: Dark Mirror
Author: Diane Duane
Reader: John De Lancie
★★

This one is a spin-off from the old Star Trek episode, "Mirror, Mirror"—the one in which Kirk and Co. slip over the wrong dimensional line, and they wind up confronting evil duplicates of themselves: *Star Trek*'s take on the even older premise of the evil twin. The package cover gives away the none-too-surprising update this time around: A scowling Captain Jean-Luc Picard glowers against a ruddy dark sky to the left, while a paternal Picard commands a starry sky of benevolent blue to the right.

2 css 3 hr Simon & Schuster Audio

Star Trek: The Next Generation: Imzadi
Author: Peter David
Reader: Jonathan Frakes
★★

Dependable Peter David scores points for even attempting a story that centers on the hinted-at affair between Commander Riker (Frakes's role) and Counsellor Troi that happened on Betrazoid. Frankly, the second series could use a little more mush. But these two characters are an unlikely match. David wisely moves Riker into a more two-fisted adventure.

2 css 3 hr Simon & Schuster Audio

Star Trek: The Next Generation: Q-in-Law
Author: Peter David
Readers: Majel Barrett and John De Lancie
★★

Peter David warms up for his much better *Q* novel (see following listing) with this report on wedding troubles aboard the *Enterprise.* Counsellor Troi's naggy mother, Lwaxana, would be enough to make any captain long for those easier times of the Kobayashi Maru. But then—even worse—Q crashes the party. What is love? Q wants to know, having already answered the question of what is annoyance. Majel Barrett (Mrs. Gene Roddenberry) and John De Lancie play Lwaxana and Q, respectively, on TV, as well as here.

2 css 1½ hr Simon & Schuster Audio

Star Trek: The Next Generation: Q-Squared
Author: Peter David
Reader: John De Lancie
★★★★

Like the *Star Trek* TV series, *Star Trek* books by and large hold to a respectable standard, now and then rising well above the norm. This book is one of those high points. Read by John De Lancie, the actor who plays the enigmatic superbeing Q in *Star Trek: The Next Generation,* the story is a chance to learn some of Q's secrets—instead of just watching him play his maddening mind games with Captain Jean-Luc Picard, although he does that, too. Author Peter David is a practiced professional with a background that includes writing comics, but this time he also proves to have a mainstream novelist's grasp of conflict and character.

2 css 3 hr Simon & Schuster Audio

Star Trek: The Next Generation: The Devil's Heart
Author: Carmen Carter
Reader: Gates McFadden
★★★

The Devil's Heart is a mystery object that propels Captain Jean-Luc Picard and his crew into a search for the ancient talisman, perhaps better left unfound. Not only would this have made a good TV episode, but it also nonchalantly answers the question, What does Captain Picard wear to sleep? Give up? Pajamas. Gates McFadden plays Dr. Beverly Crusher on TV.

2 css 3 hr Simon & Schuster Audio

Star Wars

Star Wars creator George Lucas finished his movie trilogy in 1983, but the movies' fans were nowhere close to quitting. *Star Wars* (1977), *The Empire Strikes Back* (1980), and *Return of the Jedi* (1983) left a Forceful demand for more stories about the young hero Luke Skywalker, hotshot adventurer Han Solo, Princess Leia, and the films' array of other human and otherworldly heroes and bad guys. No problem: May the tape player be with you. *Star Wars* tapes benefit from movielike sound effects and the movies' thundering theme music. Unlike the *Star Trek* tapes, however, they aren't all read by *Star Wars* cast members.

Star Wars: The Courtship of Princess Leia
Author: Dave Wolverton
Reader: Anthony Heald
★★

Say, how did headlong Han Solo and the feisty Princess Leia come to tie the knot, anyway? Here is the *Star Wars* answer to romance, opening with Han already thinking of Leia as more than a good shot—in fact, longing "for the taste of Leia's kisses, the caress of her hand." But she is in line for a purely political marriage to a rich prince. Is elopement the answer? Maybe so. At least, a spaceship beats a stepladder.

2 css 3 hr BDD Audio

Star Wars: Dark Empire
Author: Based on *Dark Horse Comics* by Tom Veitch
Performers: Billy Dee Williams, Lando Calrissian; John Cygan, Luke Skywalker; Joe Hacker, Han Solo; and others
★★

"Battle sequences explode in Dolby Surround!" the package proclaims—and, sure enough, they do. A set of head speakers will have you convincingly caught in the cross fire. In between space battles, however, the story is more of the usual as Luke Skywalker, Han Solo, and Princess Leia confront yet another threat from the evil Empire. Actors including Billy Dee Williams as Lando Calrissian (his screen role in *The Empire Strikes Back*) must battle not only Imperial bad guys but also lumps of expository dialogue as hairy as a Wookie. When some enemy tie-fighters roar past, guess what Leia says to Han: (a) "Wow!" (b) "Damn!", or (c) "They must be joining forces with one of the Imperial factions fighting for the throne."

2 css 2½ hr Time Warner AudioBooks

Star Wars: The Original Trilogy
Authors: George Lucas, Donald F. Glut, and James Kahn
Reader: Tony Roberts
★★★

If you haven't seen the Star Wars movies by now, you must have spent the last eighteen years on the desert planet Tatooine. Why hear the same stories again? This collection proves they are more than just stories—they are myths. They not only survive retelling, they gain from it. The first book is the prize here: *Star Wars: A New Hope* by George Lucas, the movies' creator. It has details that aren't in the movie, including exactly how tall Darth Vader is (two meters—the same as Chewbacca, the wookie) and what to call that weird mask on his face. (It's a "bizarre black metal breath screen.") The sequels are *Star Wars: The Empire Strikes Back* by Donald F. Glut and *Star Wars: Return of the Jedi* by James Kahn, based on Lucas' screen stories. Tony Roberts delivers excellent readings of all three, especially when he booms into the role of Lord Vader.

6 css 9 hrs Time Warner AudioBooks

Star Wars: Tales of the Jedi
Author: Based on *Dark Horse Comics* by Tom Veitch
Performers: David Scott Gordon, Skip Lackey, Mark Feuerstein, and others
★★

Ages before Luke Skywalker carved his niche with a light saber, the Jedi Knights were "the most powerful, most respected force in the galaxy," according to this tape's windy prologue. But you'd never guess it from hearing these clunky adventures of the young knights Ulic Qel-Droma and Nomi Sunrider, and their teacher, Master Arca, an Obi-Wan Kenobi wanna-be. (Typical dialogue: "Sorry to interrupt your pleasure with business, boys, but I've got a flight of giant birds on a collision trajectory." ". . . What kind of crazy birds would—" ". . . Those aren't birds! They're Beast Riders!")

2 css 2½ hrs Time Warner AudioBooks

Star Wars: The Three-Book Cycle by Timothy Zahn
Author: Timothy Zahn
Readers: Denis Lawson and Anthony Daniels
★★★

Hugo Award winner Timothy Zahn's three best-selling *Star Wars* novels proved there *is* life after *The Return of the Jedi*—in fact, five years after, as we find Han Solo and Princess Leia married, about to be hearing the patter of little Jedi feet around the house, while Luke is the first of the new Jedi Knights. The story begins with Zahn's subtitled *Heir to the Empire,* continuing with *Dark Force Rising,* and *The Last Command.* Book one is read by Denis Lawson, the actor who played Wedge Antilles. Anthony Daniels steps in for books two and three, doing far more with voice and emotion than he could on screen as the fussy robot, C3PO.

6 css 9 hr BDD Audio

Star Wars: The Truce at Bakura
Author: Kathy Tyers
Reader: Anthony Heald
★★

Obi-Wan Kenobi warns Luke that he must go to the troubled planet Bakura to make peace with the sinister reptilians who live there. As usual, the whole galaxy hangs in the balance.

2 css 3 hr BDD Audio

The Stories of Ray Bradbury
Author/Reader: Ray Bradbury
★★★★

The tapes are hard to pry out of the package, but after that—pure joy. Bradbury reads nine of his classic stories the same way that he has described his writing: "exactly one half terror, exactly one half exhiliration." These are from his milestone collection of the same title in print (1980), and include "The Emissary," "The Strawberry Window," and "The Happiness Machine." Some are science fiction, some horror, some whimsy, some hard to define. They all have what counts, though. They spark with Bradburian magic.

2 css 2 hr 45 min Random House AudioBooks

Superman Lives!
Author: DC Comics
Performers: Lorelei King, Stuart Milligan and others
★★★

You've dutifully bought all the jillions of comics it took to tell the story of Superman's fatal slugfest with that bone-plated cosmic case of bad news, Doomsday. You've read the hardback novel version. What's left? The best telling of all is this dramatized audio extravaganza, complete with sound effects including the nifty rocket swoosh of Superman in flight, and Doomsday's rip-roaring rampage. Sure, it's kinda dopey, this whole death-of-Superman-whoops!-he's-back saga, but still . . . that's one heck of a neat-sounding *ka-powww!* when the gun goes off, proving again that Superman is faster than a speeding bullet.

2 css 2½ hr Time Warner AudioBooks

The Wheel of Time
Author: Robert Jordan
Reader: Mark Rolston
★★★

Starting with *The Eye of the World* in 1990, Robert Jordan has been building this fantasy epic that is based on his premise of the Wheel of Time. Often compared to J.R.R. Tolkien, Jordan is nonetheless his own man, writing from a southern background that includes being a graduate of The Citadel military academy in Charleston, South Carolina, a Vietnam veteran, and a history buff. On tape, the series is well read and bound together by a single narrator, Mark Rolston. Books in the series include *The Eye of the World, The Dragon Reborn, The Great Hunt, The Shadow Rising,* and *The Fires of Heaven.* The books can be heard as separate novels, but in print, they have been accumulating a sizable glossary. If you don't know your Three Oathes from a *kaf* stain, better head for square one.

2 css each book 3 hr each The Publishing Mills AudioBooks

Alien 3
A: Novelization by Alan Dean Foster
R: Lance Henricksen
DOVE

Batman
A: Screenplay by Sam Hamm and Warren Skaaren; novelization by Craig Shaw Gardner
R: Roddy McDowall
DOVE

Battles of Dune
A/R: Frank Herbert
HARP

Best of Science Fiction and Fantasy
A: Arthur C. Clarke, Kristine K. Rusch, Ben Bova, Greg Bear, Susan Schwartz, Fritz Leiber, Jane Yolin, Connie Willis, and Dan Simmons
DOVE

The Book of Merlyn: King Arthur and Merlyn's Animal Council
A: T. H. White
R: Christopher Plummer
HARP

The Call of Earth
A: Orson Scott Card
R: Mark Rolston
ART

Chronicles of Pern: First Fall
A: Anne McCaffrey
R: Meredith MacRae
DOVE

The City Who Fought
A: Anne McCaffrey and S. M. Stirling
R: Constance Towers
DOVE

Conqueror's Pride
A: Timothy Zahn
BRILL

Crisis on Doona
A: Anne McCaffrey and Jody Lynn Nye
DOVE

The Crystal Cave
A: Mary Stewart
R: Nicol Williamson
DOVE

Death Dream
A: Ben Bova
BRILL

Dirk Gently's Holistic Detective Agency
A/R: Douglas Adams
S&S

The Dolfins of Pern
A: Anne McCaffrey
MILLS

A Dragon Lover's Treasury of the Fantastic
A: Edited by Mary Weiss
R: Glynnis G. Talken and John F. Cygan
TW

The Dragon Reborn
(Book Three of *The Wheel of Time*)
A: Robert Jordan
R: Mark Rolston
MILLS

Dragonflight and Dragonquest
A: Anne McCaffrey
R: Adrienne Barbeau
DOVE

Dragonsdawn and The Renegades of Pern
A: Anne McCaffrey
R: Adrienne Barbeau
DOVE

Dragonsdrums and The White Dragon
A: Anne McCaffrey
R: Adrienne Barbeau
DOVE

Dragonsong and Dragonslinger
A: Anne McCaffrey
R: Adrienne Barbeau
DOVE

The Druid of Shannara
A: Terry Morse
R: Theodore Bikel
DOVE

The Elf Queen of Shannara
A: Terry Brooks
R: Theodore Bikel
DOVE

Empire Builders
A: Ben Bova
BRILL

Ender's Game
A: Orson Scott Card
R: Mark Rolston
ART

The Eye of the World
(Book One of *The Wheel of Time*)
A: Robert Jordan
R: Mark Rolston
MILLS

The Fires of Heaven
A: Robert Jordan
MILLS

The Forest House
A: Marion Zimmer Bradley
BRILL

Foundation
A/R: Isaac Asimov
BDD

Foundation: The Psychohistorians
A: Isaac Asimov
R: William Shatner
HARP

Foundation and Earth
A: Isaac Asimov
R: David Dukes
BDD

Foundation and Empire
A: Isaac Asimov
R: David Dukes
BDD

Foundation's Edge
A: Isaac Asimov
R: David Dukes
BDD

God Emperor of Dune
A/R: Frank Herbert
HARP

The Great Hunt
(Book Two of *The Wheel of Time*)
A: Robert Jordan
R: Mark Rolston
MILLS

The Handmaid's Tale
A: Margaret Atwood
R: Julie Christie
DURK

Heretics of Dune
A/R: Frank Herbert
HARP

The Hitchhiker's Guide to the Galaxy
A/R: Douglas Adams
DOVE

The Hitchhiker's Guide to the Galaxy
A: Douglas Adams
R: Multi-voice production
TW

The Hobbit and the Fellowship of the Ring
A/R: J.R.R. Tolkien
HARP

The Hollow Hills
A: Mary Stewart
R: Nicol Williamson
DOVE

Isaac Asimov Himself Reads Five Complete Stories
A/R: Isaac Asimov
PART

The J.R.R. Tolkien Audio Collection Centenary Edition
A/R: J.R.R. Tolkien
HARP

Johnny Mnemonic
A: Terry Bisson, based on the short story by William Gibson
R: Jack Noseworthy
S&S

The Last Enchantment
A: Mary Stewart
R: Nicol Williamson
DOVE

Life, The Universe and Everything
A/R: Douglas Adams
DOVE

Logan's Run
A: William F. Nolan and George Clayton Johnson
R: William F. Nolan
DOVE

The Long Dark Tea-Time of the Soul
A: Douglas Adams
R: Simon Jones
S&S

Lord of Chaos
A: Robert Jordan
MILLS

The Lord of the Rings: The Two Towers and The Return of The King
A/R: J.R.R. Tolkien
HARP

Low-Flying Aircraft
A: J. G. Ballard
R: Jonathan Frakes
DURK

Lyon's Pride
A: Anne McCaffrey
BRILL

Mack Bolan: Stony Man Doctrine
A: Don Pendleton
R: George Maharis
DURK

The Martian Chronicles
A/R: Ray Bradbury
PART

The Memory of Earth
A: Orson Scott Card
R: Mark Rolston
ART

The Merlin Trilogy: The Crystal Cave, The Hollow Hills and The Last Enchantment
A: Mary Stewart
R: Nicol Williamson
DOVE

Mostly Harmless
A/R: Douglas Adams
DOVE

Moving Mars
A: Greg Bear
BRILL

Nemesis
A: Isaac Asimov
R: Peter MacNicol
BDD

Pegasus in Flight and To Ride Pegasus
A: Anne McCaffrey
R: Adrienne Barbeau
DOVE

People of the Earth
A: W. Michael Gear and Kathleen O'Neal Gear
R: George American Horse
ART

People of the Fire
A: W. Michael Gear and Kathleen O'Neal Gear
R: George American Horse
ART

People of the River
A: W. Michael Gear and Kathleen O'Neal Gear
R: Wes Studi
ART

People of the Wolf
A: W. Michael Gear and Kathleen O'Neal Gear
R: Wes Studi
ART

Prelude to Foundation
A: Isaac Asimov
R: David Dukes
BDD

Ray Bradbury Himself Reads Nineteen Complete Stories
A/R: Ray Bradbury
PART

The Restaurant at the Edge of the Universe
A/R: Douglas Adams
DOVE

Robot City Book I: Odyssey
A: Isaac Asimov
R: Peter MacNicol, John Hickey, Constance Boardman, and full cast
HARP

Scanners II
A: Professor James Kimball
R: Roddy McDowall
DOVE

The Scions of Shannara
A: Terry Brooks
R: Theodore Bikel
DOVE

Shadow Moon
A: George Lucas and Chris Claremont
BDD

The Shadow Rising
(Book Four of *The Wheel of Time*)
A: Robert Jordan
R: Mark Rolston
MILLS

The Ship Who Searched
A: Anne McCaffrey and Mercedes Lackey

The Ship Who Won
A: Anne McCaffrey
R: Constance Towers
DOVE

Shuttle
A: David C. Onley
R: Robert Lansing
DURK

So Long, and Thanks for All the Fish
A/R: Douglas Adams
DOVE

Speaker for the Dead
A: Orson Scott Card
R: Mark Rolston
ART

Star Trek: Ashes of Eden
A/R: William Shatner
S&S

Star Trek: Cacophony: A Captain Sulu Adventure
A: Peter David
R: George Takei and others
S&S

Star Trek: *Enterprise*, The First Adventure
A: Vonda McIntyre
R: Leonard Nimoy and George Takei
S&S

Star Trek: Federation
A: Judith and Garfield Reeves-Stevens
S&S

Star Trek: Final Frontier
A: Diane Carey
R: James Doohan and Leonard Nimoy
S&S

Star Trek: Prime Directive
A: Judith and Garfield Reeves-Stevens
R: James Doohan
S&S

Star Trek: Shadows on the Sun
A: Michael Jan Friedman
R: James Doohan
S&S

Star Trek: Strangers from the Sky
A: Margaret Wander Bonanno
R: Leonard Nimoy and George Takei
S&S

Star Trek: The Entropy Effect
A: Vonda McIntyre
R: Leonard Nimoy and George Takei
S&S

Star Trek: The Lost Years
A: J. M. Dillard
R: James Doohan and Leonard Nimoy
S&S

Star Trek: The Next Generation: Gulliver's Fugitives
A: Keith Sharee
R: Jonathan Frakes
S&S

Star Trek: The Next Generation: Relics
A: Michael Jan Friedman
R: LeVar Burton and James Doohan
S&S

Star Trek: The Next Generation: Reunion
A: Michael Jan Freidman
R: Gates McFadden
S&S

Star Trek: Time For Yesterday
A: A. C. Crispin
R: James Doohan and Leonard Nimoy
S&S

Star Trek: Transformations: A Captain Sulu Adventure
A: David Stern
R: Daniel Gerroll, Dana Ivey and George Takei
S&S

Star Trek: Voyager: Caretaker
A: L. A. Graf
R: Robert Picardo
S&S

Star Trek: Web of the Romulans
A: M. S. Murdock
R: Leonard Nimoy and George Takei
S&S

Star Trek: Windows on a Lost World
A: V. E. Mitchell
R: Walter Koenig
S&S

Star Trek: Yesterday's Son
A: A. C. Crispin
R: James Doohan and Leonard Nimoy
S&S

Star Trek IV: The Voyage Home
A: Vonda McIntyre
R: Leonard Nimoy and George Takei
S&S

Star Trek V: The Final Frontier
A: J. M. Dillard
R: Leonard Nimoy and George Takei
S&S

Star Trek VI: The Undiscovered Country
A: J. M. Dillard
R: James Doohan
S&S

Star Trek Deep Space Nine: Warped
A: K. W. Jeter
S&S

Star Wars: Ambush at Corellia, Volume I of the Corellian
A: Roger MacBride Allen
R: Anthony Heald
BDD

Star Wars: Assault at Selonia, Volume II of the Corellian
A: Roger MacBride Allen
R: Anthony Heald
BDD

Star Wars: Children of the Jedi
A: Barbara Hambley
BDD

Star Wars: The Crystal Star
A: Vonda McIntrye
BDD

Star Wars: The Jedi Academy Trilogy Volume I: Jedi Search
A: Kevin J. Anderson
R: Anthony Heald
BDD

Star Wars: The Jedi Academy Trilogy Volume II: Dark Apprentice
A: Kevin J. Anderson
R: Anthony Heald
BDD

Star Wars: The Jedi Academy Trilogy Volume III: Champions of the Force
A: Kevin Anderson
R: Anthony Heald
BDD

The Star Wars Audio Boxed Set
A: Timothy Zahn
R: Anthony Daniels and Denis Lawson
BDD

The Sword of Shannara
A/R: Terry Brooks
HARP

The Sword of Shannara, The Elftones of Shannara, and **The Wishsong of Shannara**
A: Terry Brooks
R: Theodore Bikel
DOVE

The Talismans of Shannara
A: Terry Brooks
R: Rene Auberjonois
DOVE

Tarzan of the Apes
A: Edgar Rice Burroughs
R: Ben Kingsley
DOVE

Teklords
A/R: William Shatner
S&S

Tekwar
A/R: William Shatner
S&S

The Time Machine
A: H. G. Wells
R: Ben Kingsley
DOVE

To the Stars: The Autobiography of *Star Trek*'s Mr. Sulu
A/R: George Takei
S&S

20,000 Leagues Under the Sea
A: Jules Verne
R: James Mason
HARP

2001: A Space Odyssey
A/R: Arthur C. Clarke
HARP

Virtual Light
A: William Gibson
BDD

War of the Worlds
A: H. G. Wells
DURK

War of the Worlds
A: H. G. Wells
R: Leonard Nimoy
HARP

The White Plague
A: Frank Herbert
R: Bradford Dillman
DURK

William Shatner and Leonard Nimoy Read
Four Science Fiction Classics
A: Various
R: William Shatner and Leonard Nimoy
HARP

Xenocide
A: Orson Scott Card
R: Mark Rolston
ART

SELF-HELP

Self-help books have been on the move during the past decade and audio has certainly kept up the pace. This is one of the most popular of the genres, with a tremendous amount of titles intended to foster self-improvement and personal empowerment covering everything from stopping smoking to addictions recovery to improving your vocabulary to better communications skills to utilizing the mind for self-healing to better sex and so on and so on.

Unlike most of the other genres on audio, where professional actors are more frequently used to perform or read, self-help tapes are primarily recorded by clinicians or self-help gurus who in most instances have authored the work. In some cases, such as with John Bradshaw, M. Scott Peck, and Shirley MacLaine (who of course is also a seasoned actress), this adds a dimension of intimacy, personalization, and connection to the material that gives a depth and understanding that might have been missed with an actor. However, in other instances, such as with Karen Goldman, Larry Crabb, and Harold Kushner, an actor may have given the work just the extra oomph needed to create a more engaging recording.

But in this section especially, the material is the key and, unlike in other genres, people listen to self-help tapes over and over, especially ones with an inspirational message. So turn the tape player on and listen to learn.

HIGHLY RECOMMENDED (★★★★)

Creating Love
Further along the Road Less Traveled
The Girls with the Grandmother Faces
Going Within
Homecoming
Lighting the Path
Peace, Love and Healing
The Road Less Traveled

Ageless Body, Timeless Mind:
The Quantum Alternative to Growing Old
Author/Reader: Deepak Chopra, M.D.
★★★

Dr. Chopra shows that, contrary to traditional beliefs, we can learn to direct the way our bodies and minds metabolize time and actually reverse the aging process—thereby retaining vitality, creativity, memory, and self-esteem. For those of us concerned about aging, this is the perfect tape, and for those of us who don't care about growing old, it still holds great value. With a friendly, illuminating mode of social intercourse, Chopra transcends any difficulty the listener may have adjusting to his accent and teaches us about the power we hold within ourselves to keep our bodies and minds healthy at any point of our lives.

2 css 3hr Random House AudioBooks

Anatomy of an Illness:
A Guide to Healing and Regeneration
Author: Norman Cousins
Readers: Introduction by Norman Cousins; Jason Robards, Jr.
★★★

When *Saturday Review* editor Cousins contracted an obscure disease, the doctors held no hope. Cousins decided to take his cure into his own hands, relying on his own research, his sense of humor, and his indomitable will to live. This is the story of his success and his insights into the nature of disease and wellness. After a choppy introduction by author Cousins, Robards picks up the pace with style, clarity, and a dynamism that allows us to absorb the material.

2 css 2 hr 45 min Dove Audio

The Angel Book:
A Handbook for Aspiring Angels
Author: Karen Goldman
Performer: Judy Collins
Bomb

The Angel Book teaches us how to find the angel in ourselves and others—through inspirations and reflections that provide a pathway to the higher realms within us. It shows what it means to fly, how to make miracles, and how to get our own wings. Unfortunately, Collins can't make us believe what she's saying, and the reverb effects make this hokey and insipid.

1 css 1 hr Audio Renaissance Tapes

Born for Love:
Reflections on Loving
Author/Reader: Leo Buscaglia
★★★

Here is a tender and supportive collection of thoughts that gently encourages us all to continue our search for that most precious of emotions. Buscaglia presents a series of pesonal reflections that orient us toward our own capacity for loving. He offers that love is far less concerned with what's past than with what's next and that there is no better time to love than right now! Buscaglia's role is one of compatriot on this shared journey and his sensitivity and sense of humor shine through.

1 css 1 hr Random House AudioBooks

Care of the Soul:
A Guide for Cultivating Depth and Sacredness in Everyday Life
Author: Thomas Moore
Reader: Peter Thomas
★★★

This is a path-breaking lifestyle guide that shows how to add spirituality, depth, and meaning to modern-day life by nurturing the soul. It points the way to a therapeutic way of life that is not a self-improvement project. Instead, it shows you how to look more deeply into emotional problems and sense the sacredness in ordinary things. There is a bit of distance in Thomas's reading, as if he is almost halfheartedly communicating someone else's writing to the listener, yet the material is engrossing.

2 css 3 hr Harper Audio

Change Your Mind, Change Your Life
Authors/Readers: Gerald G. Jampolsky, M.D., and Diane V. Cirincione
★★

Here are dozens of real-life stories about people who have used the power of Attitudinal Healing to change the world they experience simply by changing their thoughts and attitudes. On this program, you'll learn how to use Attitudinal Healing in parenting, teaching, business, sports, legal matters, and more. The authors provide a step-by-step, eighteen-week program to eliminate stress, fear, and conflict. The authors impart this intriguing information with mixed results: While Jampolsky tends to be empowering, Cirincione seems to speak with a loftiness that might control rather than liberate the listener.

2 css 2 hr BDD Audio

The Courage to Live Your Dreams, Volume III
Author/Reader: Les Brown
★★★

In this third lecture of a six-tape series, Brown (host of TV's *The Les Brown Show*) motivates you to pursue your goals wholeheartedly. He insists you need the right people in your life. People who will empower and enrich you. Brown charges you up in a positive way and his intelligible voice is easy to follow. The only quibble is wondering how he supports some extravagant facts and figures, such as "One negative comment is sixteen times more powerful than a positive comment." . . . Not fifteen?

1 css 50 min Harper Audio

Creating Love:
The Next Great Stage of Growth
Author/Reader: John Bradshaw
★★★★

John Bradshaw has touched millions of lives through his PBS series and best-selling books. In *Creating Love,* he provides a new way to understand our most crucial relationships: with parents and children, with friends and coworkers, with ourselves, and with God. Combining live audio footage from the "Creating Love" workshop and exclusive studio material that offers the tools to help listeners bring hope and new direction to their lives, he shows us how we have been literally "entranced" by past experiences of counterfeit love, how we can break these destructive patterns, and how we can open ourselves to the soul-building work of real love. As usual, Bradshaw's vibrant personality emerges to make us feel present and nurtured by his material.

4 css 4 hr Bantam Audio

The Dance of Anger:
A Woman's Guide to Changing the Patterns of Intimate Relationships
Author/Reader: Harriet Goldhor Lerner, Ph.D.
★★★

Menninger Clinic psychologist and psychotherapist Lerner teaches how to stop choosing between having a relationship and having a self: *The Dance of Anger* is about both. Includes: "Circular Dances in Couples," "Anger at Our Impossible Mothers," "Up and Down the Generations," and "Using Anger as a Guide." The complex material is presented in a wonderfully direct and comprehensible way, but another Lerner is not a particularly dynamic speaker and occasionally loses the high-powered energy of the dance.

2 css 3 hr Caedmon Audio

Finding the Miracle of Love in Your Life
(Based on *A Course in Miracles*)
Authors/Readers: Gerald G. Jampolsky, M.D., and Diane V. Cirincione
★★★

Authors Jampolsky and Cirincione draw on the decades they have devoted to revealing the essential truths of *A Course in Miracles.* In this boxed set, they offer four complete audio workshops, including *Introduction to* A Course in Miracles (see page 343), *Teach Only Love, To Give Is to Receive,* and *Forgiveness Is the Key to Happiness.* The authors present the valuable information in a pragmatic style and their unaffected voices let us get at the heart of the material. A favorite quote: "We should only have one goal in life—peace of mind."

4 css 4 hr Bantam Audio

M. Scott Peck, M.D., Speaks On: Further Along the Road Less Traveled

★★★★

The *Further Along the Road Less Traveled* series are live-talk recordings given by M. Scott Peck, M.D., one of the forerunners in self-help education, and are Simon & Schuster Audio originals—not available in book form. In this series of live lectures, Peck fosters a sense of equality with the listener. His honesty and openness about his own life, and his evident sense of humor, put us at ease as he explores various recovery issues. It is also an added pleasure to hear live recordings with good sound quality.

Addiction: The Sacred Disease

Peck explores the misguided tendency of individuals to substitute an addiction for a true relationship with the Divine. Citing the community-building themes of Alcoholics Anonymous and other recovery groups, he demonstrates how the tremendous spiritual potential of the addictive personality can be harnessed productively instead of destructively.

1 css 50 min Simon & Schuster Audio

Blame and Forgiveness

All of us feel angry at times—but few people can deal well or honestly with this very human emotion. Often we blame others when bad things happen, or we learn to deny our disappointment. Peck uncovers our immense power to understand our anger—and shows us how the processes of blaming and forgiving are essential to our spiritual health.

1 css 50 min Simon & Schuster Audio

Consciousness and the Problem of Pain

How many of us are truly adults in the fullest sense of the word? Peck suggests that today most adults are mere children in grown-up clothing—unwilling to make the painful odyssey that leads to spiritual and psychological maturity. By differentiating between "productive pain" and "unproductive pain," there is the opportunity to grow stronger, wiser, and more courageous.

1 css 1 hr Simon & Schuster Audio

The Issue of Death and Meaning

In today's society, death is kept in the closet; we don't talk about it, try not to think about it, and even pretend it won't happen to us. Peck believes that by exploring and accepting the subject of death and by developing a relationship with the end of our existence, we can overcome the fear and meaninglessness in our lives.

1 css 1 hr Simon & Schuster Audio

Self-Love versus Self-Esteem

Do you know yourself? Do you value yourself? Peck believes that it is not possible to always "feel good about ourselves." He stresses the roles that self-doubt and humility play in total happiness. He explains we can like ourselves despite our failings and value ourselves for everything we can be.

1 css 50 min Simon & Schuster Audio

Sexuality and Spirituality

From promiscuity to chastity, from being obsessed with our lovers to being afraid to love, Peck draws on modern psychology, religious literature, and his own experience to examine our most pressing concerns. He demonstrates that the sexual urge is the urge for wholeness—and that we can be sexually fulfilled only as we become spiritually alive.

1 css 1 hr Simon & Schuster Audio

Togetherness and Separateness in Marriage and the Family

Peck focuses on the tensions between our quest for personal growth and the idealized view of marriage and the family given to us by society. He tackles the hard, hurtful issues that can lead to family breakups and spiritual stagnation. With insight and humor, we are given perspective on the family frictions we all face.

1 css 1 hr Simon & Schuster Audio

Getting the Love You Want:
A Guide for Couples
Author/Reader: Harville Hendrix, Ph.D.

★★★

In a clear, friendly voice, Hendrix, marriage therapist and pastoral counselor, offers advice for transforming an intimate relationship into a lasting source of love and companionship. This therapeutic course offers a series of step-by-step exercises that lead to insight, resolution, and revitalization.

1 css 1 hr Sound Editions

The Girls with the Grandmother Faces
Author/Reader: Frances Weaver

★★★★

The author is a freelance columnist whose writing career began in her fifties. She maintains that boredom is mainly self-inflicted at any age. Any person who has no new interest of his own is of no interest to anyone else. People over fifty-five have 20 percent of their lives ahead of them. But this is a world for self-starters! With wonderful animation and enthusiasm, Weaver coaxes mature women back into life and directs them to take responsibility for personal fulfillment.

2 css 3 hr The Publishing Mills AudioBooks

Going Within:
Meditations for Relaxation and Stress Reduction
Author/Reader: Shirley MacLaine
★★★★

In this companion to her book *Going Within,* Shirley MacLaine shows you how to free your mind and body from everyday worries and tensions through age-old meditation and relaxation techniques long practiced in the Far East and India. With remarkable emotional capability, MacLaine offers tools to a more balanced, peaceful inner life. We found her meditations exceptionally relaxing and healing, and a comforting presence is felt from her as she escorts you on your journey within.

1 css 1½ hr Bantam Audio

The Higher Self:
The You Inside of You
Author/Reader: Deepak Chopra, M.D.
★★★

Why are you here? What do you really need? How can you get it? Inside you there's a "you" who knows the answers to these questions—a "higher self" that resides in each of us that is naturally boundless, totally intelligent, and completely free. Although Chopra's voice carries a lackluster quality in this recording, he is able to clearly articulate the power that our "higher selves" can have in our lives and enables the listener to begin the process of personal empowerment.

2 css 2 hr Simon & Schuster Audio

Homecoming: Reclaiming and Championing Your Inner Child
Author/Reader: John Bradshaw
★★★★

Born into a troubled family, and abandoned by his alcoholic father, Bradshaw has become one of the primary figures in recovery and dysfunctional families. In this special adaptation of *Homecoming,* he presents the highlights of the inner child workshops that he calls "the most powerful work I have ever done," and leads listeners through the healing meditations and exercises that enable them to bring the power of inner child work into their lives. Accompanied by the soothing music of Stephen Halpern, this presentation shows you how to validate your inner child through meditations and affirmations. With his inviting, clear, and natural delivery, Bradshaw immediately connects us to his process and makes this a very personal experience.

3 css 3½ hr Bantam Audio

How We Die: Reflections on Life's Final Chapter
Author/Reader: Sherwin B. Nuland
★★

In *How We Die,* Sherwin B. Nuland, a surgeon and teacher of medicine, tells some stories of dying that reveal not only why someone dies but how. He offers a portrait of the experience of dying that makes clear the choices that can be made to allow each of us his own death. Nuland reads effectively, though mouth noises sometimes break concentration.

2 css 3 hr Random House AudioBooks

Introduction to *A Course in Miracles:*
Insights into Love, Forgiveness, and Inner Peace
Authors/Readers: Gerald G. Jampolsky, M.D., and Diane V. Cirincione

★★

A Course in Miracles allows us to see beyond life's surface to the changeless truths of God's love. The authors reveal the essential truths that have sustained and guided the devoted followers of *A Course in Miracles* for the past twenty years. But Jampolsky and Cirincione's languid conversation fails to ignite much interest in the acclaimed course.

1 css 1 hr BDD Audio

Journey of the Heart:
Intimate Relationship and the Path of Love
Author/Reader: John Welwood

★★

Journey of the Heart shows us how to meet the challenge of intimate relationships and how the greatest difficulties in those relationships also provide the most opportunity for growth and awareness. Dr. Welwood's unique blend of Eastern philosophy and Western psychology provides a means for helping us cope with modern life. Would that his reading were less monotone, revealing the obvious depth of his feeling.

1 css 3 hr Audio Literature

Lighting the Path:
Meditations on the Twelve Steps
Author/Reader: Melody Beattie

★★★★

In this original audio program, Beattie, a recovering person, offers a unique opportunity to experience the comfort and hope of the Twelve Steps in a whole new way. Through guided imagery, affirmations, and soothing music, she creates an aural environment for healing. With a polished, easy manner, Beattie is able to engross the listener and engender peace and stability.

1 css 1½ hr Simon & Schuster Audio

Marianne Williamson: On Relationships
(Lectures Based on *A Course in Miracles*)
Author/Reader: Marianne Williamson

★★★

Provided here are the spiritual keys for coping with romantic delusions. We are shown how friendships and all of our relationships are processes through which we grow and move toward God. Williamson tells you how to learn from the problems in your relationships and create a more peaceful and loving world for yourself and those you love. After sprinting through what could have been a relaxing meditation, Williamson settles into a spiritual groove and gets her points across with honest knowledge of the subject.

1 css 1 hr 15 min Harper Audio

Marianne Williamson: On Self-Esteem
(Lectures Based on *A Course in Miracles*)
Author/Reader: Marianne Williamson
★★★

In these interpretive lectures, Williamson tells us that we can love ourselves and find emotional fulfillment by looking beyond old patterns and past mistakes to the fact that we are all, in essence, perfect creations of God. Rather than looking to things outside ourselves to confirm our worth, we achieve self-esteem through self-awareness and cultivation of a relationship with God. On this tape, Williamson is lively and engaging and her enthusiasm creates a positive experience.

1 css 1 hr Harper Audio

Men and Women:
Enjoying the Difference
Author/Reader: Dr. Larry Crabb
★★

How do you go about making a marriage work for a lifetime? This is the topic Crabb tackles. He includes answers to such questions as: What's the biggest obstacle to building truly good relationships? How does anger figure in? (No, it's not the biggest obstacle.) What is your greatest need? Unfortunately, Dr. Crabb races along at inappropriate moments, spoiling the reflective experience he expects us to share with him. He even cuts words off in his haste, making us strain to understand him.

2 css 3 hrs Zondervan

Men Are from Mars, Women Are from Venus
Author/Reader: John Gray, Ph.D.
★★★

Once upon a time, Martians and Venusians met and fell in love, all the while respecting and accepting their differences. Then they came to Earth and amnesia set in: They forgot they were from different planets. Using this metaphor, Gray explains how these differences can come between the sexes and prohibit mutually fulfilling relationships. He gives advice on how to counteract these differences in communication styles to promote a greater understanding between partners. Author Gray is skilled at conveying a clear understanding of the differences between men and women.

1 css 1½ hr Harper Audio

Nice Couples Do:
How to Turn Your Secret Dreams into Sensational Sex
Author: Joan Elizabeth Lloyd
Reader: Maggie Albright
★★

Combined here are three books by author Lloyd (a high school math teacher and emergency medical technician): *Come Play with Me, If It Feels Good,* and *Nice Couples Do.* This is a tour of highly erotic stories and a treasury of solid advice. It leads the way to sexual adventures that couples may have fantasized about but haven't had the courage or communications skills to try. Reader Albright is funny, sexy, serious, and informative by turn, lending her clear, pure voice to fairly obvious sensationalism as opposed to sensational revelations.

2 css 3 hr Time Warner AudioBooks

Peace, Love and Healing: The Bodymind and Path to Self-Healing: An Exploration
Author/Reader: Bernie S. Siegel, M.D.
★★★★

With a sensitive, grounded presentation, Siegel (*Love, Medicine and Miracles*) shows us how to listen to our bodies—to learn how to talk to our inner selves and give ourselves healing messages through meditation, visualization, and relaxation. Includes: "Who Is the Healer, Who Is the Healed?" "The Doctor-Patient Relationship," "Finding Your True Self," "Communicating with Your Body," and a meditation created especially for this recording. By sharing his personal experience with patients who beat the odds, Siegel gives a wonderful lesson about the power of love and the responsibility each of us must take in the healing process.

2 css 3 hr Caedmon Audio

Positive Plus:
The Practical Plan for Liking Yourself Better
Author/Reader: Dr. Joyce Brothers
★★

Positive Plus shows us the way to effect positive changes in our behavior. Dr. Brothers takes negative personality traits like nagging, perfectionism, and compulsive behavior and shows how to turn these negatives into positives. She provides a plan for sensible behavior modification through the use of her "Psychological Tool Kit." Dr. Brothers could have integrated the experience between author and listener by not coming on as a teacher, but by leaving the pedestal to communicate as equals.

2 css 3 hr Dove Audio

The Power of the Mind to Heal: Renewing Body, Mind, and Spirit
Author/Reader: Joan Borysenko, Ph.D.
★★

According to Harvard-trained Joan Borysenko, the process of healing is one of self-realization—a peeling away of the fears and negativity that obscure the light of our own true nature and our innate essence of compassion and love. Here she leads you to develop a spiritual framework that can transform your life and relationships, and she teaches you a three-part meditation on gratitude and loving kindness. There are two barriers here to involvement in Borysenko's spiritual quest: terrible mouth noises that could have been lessened had she had plenty of water during the recording . . . and a rather condescending delivery that seems to be aimed more at children than adults.

2 css 2 hr Simon & Schuster Audio

Quantum Healing:
Exploring the Frontiers of Mind/Body Medicine
Author/Reader: Deepak Chopra, M.D.
★★★

Can positive emotions alone, or simply the will to live, produce spontaneous healing? Drawing on many fascinating case histories, Chopra brings together the insights of Indian Ayurvedic medical treatment and the most recent Western research in medicine, neuroscience, and physics. This topic was captivating, and Chopra's manner of communication held a polished and relaxed quality that made it easy to digest the substance of his vision.

1 css 1 hr BDD Audio

A Return to Love:
Reflections on the Principles of *A Course in Miracles*
Author/Reader: Marianne Williamson
★★

This is Williamson's account of the life-changing principles of *A Course in Miracles.* In *A Return to Love,* Williamson insincerely discusses the principles and practice of miracles; the releasing of fear, which blocks our awareness of love; and the forgiveness of ourselves and others, which sets us free. Williamson's colorless, hurried manner of speaking leaves the impression that she doesn't care as much about the material as she professes to.

2 css 2 hr 40 min Harper Audio

The Road Less Traveled
Author/Reader: M. Scott Peck, M.D.
★★★★

Personably and candidly, Peck cuts through powerful, timeless myths to bring us to a deep understanding of ourselves, and motivates us into action that demands of us courage and discipline. These are very powerful educational tools.

Part I: Discipline

Peck's crucial premise—that life is hard—is challenging for even the strongest among us, but his art lies in his ability to lead us to accept, and ultimately transcend, this idea. He presents the four principles of discipline needed for a healthy life: delaying gratification, accepting responsibility, dedication to reality, and balancing.

1 css 1½ hr Simon & Schuster Audio

Part II: Love

M. Scott Peck explores love, our key to personal growth and fulfillment. He offers case histories and personal experiences in an attempt to define what it is we mean by love, and to clarify the confusion and misconceptions that arise in our thinking about it.

1 css 1½ hr Simon & Schuster Audio

Part III: Religion and Grace

Peck shares his unique insights on two concepts that are crucial to enjoying life in our secular world. He demonstrates how everyone has a religion—a set of beliefs that defines an understanding of life—and how the cultivation of one's own religion is the key to achieving spiritual and pscyhological self-fulfillment. To grow, however, one must be open to the amazing force of grace—those miraculous moments that everyone experiences but often fails to appreciate.

1 css 1½ hr Simon & Schuster Audio

Secrets About Men Every Woman Should Know
Author/Reader: Barbara DeAngelis, Ph.D.
★★

Love expert DeAngelis offers candid, provocative information that will help you understand the men in your life—your husband, your boyfriend, your boss (or that man you hope to meet!). You'll learn such secrets as the five biggest mistakes women make with men, why men always want to be right, secret fears men have that women never know about, and how to get the man you love to open up. The information is valuable (and doesn't bash men!), but DeAngelis speeds through this and doesn't allow us time to assimilate her point of view.

1 css 1 hr Bantam Audio

Shame and Grace:
Healing the Shame We Don't Deserve
Author/Reader: Lewis B. Smedes
★

This is a personal, story-filled Christian exposition of the difference between good shame and bad shame. It explains how a real experience of grace can be the healing of shame and how we can let ourselves be grace based instead of shame based. Smedes overdramatizes this sensitive subject, leaving us feeling chastised by his zealous, breathy delivery.

2 css 3 hr Zondervan

Soul Mates:
Honoring the Mysteries of Love and Relationships
Author/Reader: Thomas Moore
★★★

A companion piece to *Care of the Soul* (see page 000), this explores how relationships of all kinds—with all their difficulties—deepen our lives and help fulfill the needs of the soul. For insight, he appeals to figures such as Emily Dickinson, Black Elk, and Sufi poets. Utilizing a warm, hospitable style, Moore welcomes the listener into this meaningful recording.

2 css 3 hr Harper Audio

Teaching Your Children Values
Authors/Readers: Linda and Richard Eyre
★★★

In this practical, month-by-month program based on the number-one *New York Times* best-seller, the authors present a number of proven methods for teaching values to kids of all ages. With games, family activities, and value-building exercises, their program can help you develop a family relationship that is strong, caring, and supportive. The Eyres are easy to listen to, since they seem involved and interested in imparting their experience in social education.

2 css 2½ hr Simon & Schuster Audio

That's Not What I Meant!:
How Conversational Style Makes or Breaks Relationships
Author/Reader: Deborah Tannen, Ph.D.
★★

Conversation is the key to any relationship and, as acclaimed sociolinguistics expert Tannen reveals, style is the key to any conversation. Here Tannen helps you recognize your own conversational style and understand the styles of others, and includes dramatized vignettes to illustrate those differences. Whether you are dealing with a person who's too quiet or someone who's a conversational bulldozer, learning to understand conversational style will help you deal with any situation. Pleasantly read by Tannen, who makes the most of the clever vignettes.

1 css 1½ hr Simon & Schuster Audio

Three Steps to a Strong Family
Authors: Linda and Richard Eyre
Readers: Linda and Richard Eyre and their children
★★

The Eyres, who served on the President's Advisory Council for Education, help parents answer the question, How can we build strong families in a world where social problems threaten to tear apart the very fabric of their existence? with three simple steps: step one—a family legal system; step two—a family economy; and step three—family traditions. This three-step plan allows parents significant opportunities to praise and reward their children while conserving time and promoting communication. The inclusion of their children on the tape helps to complete a full family portrait, and the Eyres deliver their points with conviction.

2 css 3 hr Time Warner AudioBooks

Unconditional Life:
Mastering the Forces That Shape Personal Reality
Author/Reader: Deepak Chopra, M.D.
★★★

Deepak Chopra's new inquiry begins with the urgent questions of a physician who cares deeply for his patients' humanity: Why do some patients "do all the right things" and still not improve? Why do the terminallly ill often seem relieved, almost happy, as if dying were teaching them how to live for the first time? Can human beings learn only through suffering or is there another way to find meaning and fulfillment? This was engrossing and enlightening, as Chopra communicated his points in an amiable, melodious fashion.

2 css 2 hr Bantam Audio

When Bad Things Happen to Good People
Author/Reader: Harold Kushner
★★

Based on the nationally acclaimed best-seller, inspired by the death of Rabbi Kushner's fourteen-year-old son and his family's shared ordeal, this tape tells how to deal spiritually with an unfair loss or tragedy. It was really disappointing to hear this well-respected piece sounded out with a flat, rather disconnected interpretation by author Kushner.

1 css 40 min Sound Editions

Why Men Are the Way They Are
Author/Reader: Warren Farrell, Ph.D.
★★★

In his warm and compassionate voice, Warren Farrell engages in a dialogue to explore this provocative topic. His purpose is to point out the male experience of powerlessness and open a dialogue between the sexes so that real communication and love can take place. Farrell is the only man ever elected three times to the board of NOW in New York City. The book has been updated by the author for this tape.

2 css 2 hr 50 min Audio Editions

A Woman's Worth
Author/Reader: Marianne Williamson
★★★

Williamson explores the many facets of contemporary womanhood—family, work, sex, love, power—and investigates the distinctive contours of women's spiritual and emotional lives. She also examines the enduring power of female archetypes, from women healers to women who run with wolves. Williamson's challenging observations and insights into dilemmas women face today are sparked by her trademark one-liners. While the material is inspiring, we finished the tape feeling that Williamson didn't quite match it's intensity with her sometimes distant delivery.

2 css 3 hr Random House AudioBooks

Women and Self-Esteem:
Understanding and Improving the Way We Think and Feel about Ourselves
Authors: Linda Tschirhart Sanford and Mary Ellen Donovan
Reader: Linda Tschirhart Sanford

★★★

This program offers support and guidance for any woman who knows the pain of low self-esteem. The authors explain how women's self-attitudes are shaped by family relationships, schools, religion, the workplace, and the media. Then they provide step-by-step exercises for building higher self-esteem and, ultimately, for living a fulfilling life. How refreshing to feel that Sanford really believes in what she is saying. This is a treat for women (and men, too).

2 css 3 hr Penguin HighBridge Audio

Wordbuilders
Volume I: The Sixty-Minute Program for Building a More Powerful Vocabulary
Author: Audio University
Performers: Various

★

Wordbuilders features words you often hear used in conversations or read in magazines, books, and newspapers but which most people skip, finding them difficult to define or pronounce with any accuracy. Using mnemonic devices, dramatized vignettes, and exercises to aid retention, this program purports to teach you how to pronounce, define, and *use* a new selection of common but hard-to-use words. (Comes with a wallet-sized card that contains words and definitions and a pronunciation key.) This is a bit of a quiz show from hell. The games are pretty silly and sometimes unnecessarily complicated, the two hosts drip honey, and the recording is noisy. You're better off with a thesaurus.

1 css 1 hr Bantam Audio

A World Waiting to Be Born
Civility Rediscovered
Author/Reader: M. Scott Peck, M.D.

★★★

We are a deeply ailing society. Our illness is incivility. Morally destructive patterns of self-absorption, callousness, manipulativeness, and materialism are so ingrained in our routine behavior that we often do not recognize them. Using examples from his own life, case histories of patients who sought his psychiatric counsel, and dramatic scenarios of businesses that have made a conscious decision to bring civility to their organizations, as well as his expertise and winning personality, Peck demonstrates where we have gone wrong and how change can be effected.

4 css 5 hr BDD Audio

You Just Don't Understand: Women and Men in Conversation
Author/Reader: Deborah Tannen, Ph.D.
★★

From Tannen's number-one best-seller comes this audio program in which she shows how the best intentions can so easily go painfully astray between spouses, family members, coworkers, and friends, and offers vignettes that illustrate the misunderstandings that can result. The information presented could be interesting and enlightening, but due to Tannen's monotone delivery, it was a strain to stay involved with the subject matter.

1 css 1½ hr Simon & Schuster Audio

All You Can Do Is All You Can Do
A/R: A. L. Williams
RH

Allies in Healing: When the Person You Love Was Sexually Abused as a Child
A/R: Laura Davis
HARP

The American Cancer Society's "Freshstart": Twenty-one Days to Stop Smoking
A: The American Cancer Society
R: Robert Klein
S&S

Amor Obsesivo (Obsessive Love)
(Spanish)
A: Dr. Susan Forward
DOVE

The Angry Marriage
A/R: Bonnie Maslin, Ph.D.
HARP

Are You the One for Me?: Knowing Who's Right and Avoiding Who's Wrong
A/R: Barbara DeAngelis, Ph.D.
ART

The Art of Breathing and Centering
A/R: Gay Hendricks, Ph.D.
ART

The Art of Exceptional Living
A/R: Jim Rohn
S&S

The Art of Loving
A: Erich Fromm
R: Jeff David
PART

The Art of Meditation
A/R: Daniel Goleman, Ph.D.
ART

Awaken the Giant Within
A/R: Anthony Robbins
S&S

Awakening the Heroes Within: Twelve Archetypes to Help Find Us
A/R: Carol Pearson
HARP

Awakenings
A/R: Oliver Sacks
HARP

Betting on Yourself
A/R: Dr. Robert Anthony
RH

Between the Words: Hidden Meanings in What People Say
A: Gerald I. Nierenberg and Henry Calero
R: Gerald I. Nierenberg
S&S

Beyond Therapy, Beyond Science: A New Model for Healing the Whole Person
A: Anne Wilson Schaef
R: Mary Beth Hurt
HARP

Black Pearls: Daily Meditations, Affirmations and Inspirations for African-Americans
A: Eric V. Copage
R: Ben Vereen
HARP

The Celebration of Life
A: Norman Cousins
R: Norman Cousins and Michael Jackson
DOVE

Changing for Good
A/R: J. Prochaska, C. DiClemente and J. Norcross
S&S

The Co-dependent Parent
A/R: Barbara Cottman Becnel
HARP

The Codependents' Guide to the Twelve Steps
A/R: Melody Beattie
S&S

Como Hablar en Publico Como un Profesional (Osgood on Speaking)
(Spanish)
A: Charles Osgood
DOVE

The Complete Guide to Higher Consciousness
A/R: Ken Keyes, Jr.
ART

Composing a Life
A: Mary Catherine Bateson
R: Dana Ivey
PENG

Conquering Stress in Daily Life
A: Pat Hilton
R: Constance Towers
DOVE

Control Your Destiny or Someone Else Will: How Jack Welch Is Making General Electric the World's Most Competitive Company
A/R: Noel Tichy and Stratford Sherman
HARP

Controlling Your Dreams
A/R: Stephen LaBerge, Ph.D.
ART

Couples and Money
A/R: Dr. Victoria Felton-Collins
PART

The Courage to Heal
A/R: Ellen Bass and Laura Davis
HARP

The Courage to Heal, Part II: Changing Patterns
A/R: Ellen Bass and Laura Davis
HARP

The Courage to Live Your Dreams Volume I: Reinvent Your Life and Say Yes to Your Dreams
A/R: Les Brown
HARP

The Courage to Live Your Dreams Volume II: Powerful Goals and a Commitment to Happiness
A/R: Les Brown
HARP

The Courage to Raise Good Men
A: Olga Silverstein and Beth Rashbaum
R: Olga Silverstein
PENG

Creative Affirmations
A/R: Jerry Gillies
ART

The Dance of Deception: Pretending and Truth-Telling in Women's Lives
A/R: Harriet G. Lerner, Ph.D.
HARP

The Dance of Intimacy
A/R: Harriet G. Lerner, Ph.D.
HARP

Dialogues on Death and Dying
A: Elisabeth Kubler-Ross, M.D.
R: Carol Bilger
ART

The Different Drum
A/R: M. Scott Peck, M.D.
S&S

Discovering the Power of Self-Hypnosis
A: Stanley Fisher, Ph.D., with James Ellison
R: Stanley Fisher, Ph.D.
HARP

The Divine Child
A: Robert Bly and Marion Woodman
AUDLIT

Dr. Spock's Baby and Child Care: The Parent's Part
A/R: Benjamin Spock, M.D., and Michael B. Rothenberg, M.D.
S&S

Doing What You Love, Loving What You Do
A/R: Dr. Robert Anthony
RH

Don't Say Yes When You Want to Say No
A: Herbert Fensterheim, Ph.D., and Jean Baer
R: Herbert Fensterheim, Ph.D.
ART

Drama of the Gifted Child
A: Alice Miller
R: Mary Beth Hurt
HARP

Edward de Bono's Smart Thinking
A/R: Edward de Bono
ART

Effective Listening
A/R: Kevin J. Murphy
S&S

The Egoscue Method of Health through Motion: A Revolutionary Program of Stretching and Exercises for a Pain-Free Life
A: Pete Egoscue with Roger Gittines
R: Pete Egoscue
HARP

Eight Steps to a Healthy Heart
A/R: Robert E. Kowalski
S&S

The Eight-Week Cholesterol Cure
A/R: Robert E. Kowalski
S&S

Empowerment
A/R: David Gershon and Gail Straub
AUDLIT

Everyone's a Coach: You Can Inspire Anyone to Be a Winner
A/R: Ken Blanchard and Don Shula
HARP

Excess Baggage
A/R: Judith Sills, Ph.D.
PENG

Exercisewalking
A/R: Gary Yanker
S&S

Experience High Self-Esteem
A/R: Nathaniel Branden, Ph.D.
S&S

Facing Co-dependence: What It Is, Where It Comes from, How It Sabotages Our Lives
A: Pia Mellody with Andrea Wells Miller
R: Pia Mellody
HARP

Feel the Fear and Do It Anyway
A/R: Susan Jeffers, Ph.D.
S&S

The Female Advantage
A/R: Sally Helgesen
BDD

Female Rage: Unlocking the Secrets, Claiming the Power
A: Mary Valentis, Ph.D., and Anne Devane, Ph.D.
HARP

Fifty-two Minutes to Turning Your Life Around
The David Viscott Library
ART

Finding Joy: Ways to Free Your Spirit and Dance with Life
A/R: Charlotte Davis Kasl, Ph.D.
HARP

Fire Your Shrink!: Fast, Lasting Solutions for All Kinds of Problems
A/R: Michele Weiner-Davis
S&S

The Fit or Fat Woman
A/R: Covert Bailey
PART

Five Classic Meditations
A/R: Shinzen Young
ART

Flow: The Psychology of Optimal Experience
A/R: Mihaly Csikszentmihalyi
S&S

Fly Fishing through the Midlife Crisis
A: Howell Raines
BDD

Focusing
A/R: Eugene T. Gendlin, Ph.D.
ART

Forever Young
A: Stuart M. Berger, M.D.
R: Joseph Campanella
DOVE

Further Along the Road Less Traveled
A/R: M. Scott Peck, M.D.
S&S

Volume VI: The Taste for Mystery

Volume X: The New Age Movement: What in God's or Satan's Name Is It? Further Along the Road Less Traveled: The Unending Journey toward Spiritual Growth

Gathering Power through Insight and Love
A/R: Ken Keyes, Jr., and Penny Keyes
ART

Getting Better: Inside Alcoholics Anonymous
A: Nan Robertson
R: Michael Learned
DOVE

Guerrilla Dating Tactics
A/R: Sharyn Wolf
PENG

Guilt is the Teacher, Love Is the Lesson
A/R: Joan Borysenko, Ph.D.
RH

Handbook to Higher Consciousness
A/R: Ken Keyes, Jr.
ART

The Harville Hendrix Audio Workshop for Couples
Volume I: The Purposes and Problems of Romantic Love
A/R: Harville Hendrix
HARP

Having It All
A/R: Helen Gurley Brown
DOVE

He: Understanding Masculine Psychology
A: Robert A. Johnson
R: Introduction by Robert A. Johnson; Ralph Blum and Marsha Mason
ART

He Says, She Says: Closing the Communication Gap between the Sexes
A/R: Lillian Glass, Ph.D.
HARP

The Healing Heart
A: Norman Cousins
R: William Conrad
DOVE

The Hero Within
A/R: Carol Pearson
HARP

Hidden Passions
A/R: Steve Pieczenik
HARP

How Can I Get Through to You?: Breakthrough Communication—Beyond Gender, Beyond Therapy, Beyond Description
A: D. Glenn Foster and Mary Marshall
HARP

How to Argue and Win Every Time
A/R: Gerry Spence
ART

How to Be a No-Limit Person
A/R: Dr. Wayne Dyer
S&S

How to Be an Assertive (Not Aggressive) Woman
A/R: Jean Baer
ART

How to Be an Exceptional Patient
A: Bernie S. Siegel, M.D.
HARP

How to Be Your Own Nutritionist
A: Stuart M. Berger, M.D.
R: Betsy Palmer
DOVE

How to Be Your Own Therapist
The David Viscott Library
ART

How to Improve Your Memory
A/R: Harry Lorayne
RH

How to Live Between Office Visits
A/R: Bernie S. Siegel, M.D.
HARP

How to Make Love All Night (and Drive Your Woman Wild): The Male Multiple Orgasm and Other Secrets of Prolonged Lovemaking
A/R: Barbara Keesling, Ph.D.
HARP

How to Make Love to a Man (Safely)
A: Alexandra Penney
R: Meredith MacRae
DOVE

How to Meditate
A/R: Lawrence LeShan, Ph.D.
ART

How to Read a Person Like a Book
A: Gerald I. Nierenberg
RH

How to Satisfy a Woman Every Time
A/R: Naura Hayden
PENG

How to Start a Conversation
A/R: Don Gabor
RH

How to Stop Worrying and Start Living
A: Dale Carnegie and Associates, Inc.
R: Andrew MacMillan
S&S

How to Use the Silva Mind Control Method
A/R: Hans DeJong
ART

How to Win Friends and Influence People
A: Dale Carnegie and Associates, Inc.
R: Andrew MacMillan
S&S

Hymns to an Unknown God
A/R: Sam Keen
BDD

I Love You, Let's Work It Out
The David Viscott Library
ART

If You Meet the Buddha on the Road, Kill Him
A/R: Sheldon B. Kopp, Ph.D.
ART

If You Want to Write
A: Brenda Ueland
R: Pat Carroll
PENG

I'm OK, You're OK
A: Thomas A. Harris, M.D.
R: Sophie Hayden
HARP

In the Company of My Sisters: Black Women and Self-esteem
A/R: Julia Boyd
S&S

Innocence and Betrayal
A/R: Dr. Susan Forward
DOVE

Inocencia y Traición (Innocence and Betrayal)
(Spanish)
A: Dr. Susan Forward
DOVE

Instant Rapport
A/R: Michael Brooks
SS

It's Not What You're Eating, It's What's Eating You
A/R: Janet Greeson, Ph.D.
S&S

Jenny Craig's *What Have You Got to Lose?*
A/R: Jenny Craig with Brenda L. Wolfe, Ph.D.
DOVE

Jung: Interpreting Your Dreams
A/R: James A. Hall, M.D.
ART

Keeping the Love You Find
A/R: Harville Hendrix
S&S

The King Within
A: Robert Moore and Douglas Gillette
R: David Dukes
DOVE

La Viudez: Como Hacerle Frente a la Perdida (Widowed: How to Cope with Loss)
(Spanish)
A: Dr. Joyce Brothers
DOVE

The Language of Feelings
The David Viscott Library
ART

The Late Show: A Semi-Wild but Practical Survival Plan for Women over Fifty
A/R: Helen Gurley Brown
DOVE

Leadership When the Heat's On
A/R: Danny Cox
PART

Learn How to Learn
A/R: Sheila Ostrander and Lynn Schroeder
ART

Learned Optimism
A/R: Martin E. P. Seligman, Ph.D.
S&S

The Lessons of Love
A: Melody Beattie
HARP

Liberating the Adult Within: Moving from Childish Responses to Authentic Adulthood
A/R: Helen Kramer
S&S

Life Zones: How to Win in the Game of Life
A: Richard Corriere, Ph.D., and Patrick M. McGrady, Jr.
R: Richard Corriere, Ph.D.
DOVE

Light Her Fire
A/R: Ellen Kreidman
ART

Light His Fire
A/R: Ellen Kreidman
ART

Live Your Dreams
A/R: Les Brown
HARP

Lose Weight through Self-Hypnosis
A/R: Harold Bloomfield, M.D., and Sirah Vettese, Ph.D.
HARP

Love Is Never Enough: How Couples Can Overcome Misunderstandings, Resolve Conflicts, and Solve Relationship Problems through Cognitive Therapy
A: Aaron T. Beck, M.D.
R: Walter Charles
HARP

Love, Medicine and Miracles
A/R: Bernie S. Siegel, M.D
HARP

Loving Your Child Is Not Enough
A/R: Nancy Samalin
PENG

Make the Most of Your Mind
A/R: Tony Buzan
S&S

Making People Talk
A/R: Barry Farber
DOVE

The Man Who Mistook His Wife for a Hat
A/R: Oliver Sacks
HARP

Managing Your Fears and Phobias
A/R: Christopher J. McCullough, Ph.D.
ART

Many Roads, One Journey: Moving Beyond the Twelve Steps
A/R: Charlotte Davis Kasl, Ph.D.
HARP

Marianne Williamson Audio Collection
A/R: Marianne Williamson
HARP

Marianne Williamson: On Communication
A/R: Marianne Williamson
HARP

Marianne Williamson: On Dealing with Anger
A/R: Marriage Williamson
HARP

Marianne Williamson: On Death and Dying
A/R: Marianne Williamson
HARP

Marianne Williamson: On Forgiving Your Parents
A/R: Marianne Williamson
HARP

Marianne Williamson: On Intimacy
A/R: Marianne Williamson
HARP

Marianne Williamson: On Love
A/R: Marianne Williamson
HARP

Marianne Williamson: On Money
A/R: Marianne Williamson
HARP

Marianne Williamson: On Success
A/R: Marianne Williamson
HARP

Marianne Williamson: On Work and Career
A/R: Marianne Williamson
HARP

Mars and Venus in the Bedroom
A/R: John Gray
HARP

Master the Magic Power of Self-Image Psychology
A/R: Maxwell Maltz, M.D.
ART

Master True Self-Esteem
A: Nathaniel Branden
BDD

Mastering the Gentle Art of Verbal Self-Defense
A/R: Suzette Haden Elgin
S&S

Measure of Our Success: A Letter to My Children and Yours
A/R: Marian Wright Edelman
HARP

Medical Makeover
A: Robert Giller, M.D., and Kathy Matthews
R: Bob Seagren
DOVE

***Meditation* by Edgar Cayce**
A: Mark Thurston
R: Stanley Ralph Ross
ART

Meditations for New Mothers
A: Beth Wilson Saavedra
R: Tyne Daly
HARP

Meditations for Women Who Do Too Much
A: Anne Wilson Schaef
R: Kathryn Walker
HARP

Meditations from the Road
A: M. Scott Peck, M.D.
R: Introduction by M. Scott Peck, M.D.
S&S

Mega Memory
A/R: Kevin Trudeau
S&S

Mind/Body Communication: The Secrets of Total Wellness
A/R: Robert B. Stone
S&S

Minding the Body, Mending the Mind
A/R: Dr. Joan Borysenko
S&S

***Money* Magazine's Guide to Personal Finance in the 90s**
A: Editors of *Money* Magazine
R: Annie Bergen and Bill Jerome
RH

More Meditations for Women Who Do Too Much
A: Anne Wilson Schaef
R: Sophie Hayden
HARP

More than Meets the Eye
A: Joan Brock and Derek Gill
R: Joan Brock
HARP

Mother Daughter Revolution
A: Elizabeth Debold, Marie Wilson, and Idelisse Malave
BRILL

Motherless Daughters
A/R: Hope Edelman
HARP

Napoleon Hill's *A Year of Growing Rich:* Fifty-two Steps to Achieving Life's Rewards
A: Napoleon Hill; foreword by W. Clement Stone
PENG

Never Be Nervous Again
A: Dorothy Sarnoff with Gaylen Moore
R: Dorothy Sarnoff
S&S

New Passages
A/R: Gail Sheehy
RH

NLP: The New Method of Achievement
A: NLP Comprehensive
R: Charles Faulkner, Tim Hallbom, Robert McDonald, M.S.W., and Suzi Smith
S&S

Now that I Have Cancer . . . I Am Whole
A/R: John Robert McFarland
HARP

Obsessive Love
A/R: Dr. Susan Forward
DOVE

On Death and Dying
A: Elisabeth Kubler-Ross, M.D.
R: Carol Bilger
ART

On Writing Well
A/R: William Zinsser
HARP

Osgood on Speaking
A/R: Charles Osgood
DOVE

Overcoming Fearful Flying
A/R: Captain T. W. Cummings
S&S

Overcoming the Pain of Childhood
The David Viscott Library
ART

Para Abatir el Stress en la Vida Cotidiana (How to Cope with Stress in Everyday Life)
(Spanish)
A: Pat Hilton
DOVE

Peak Learning
A/R: Ron Gross
ART

People of the Lie
A/R: M. Scott Peck, M.D.
S&S

- **Volume I: Toward a Psychology of Evil**
- **Volume II: The Hope for Healing Human Evil**
- **Volume III: Possession and Group Evil**

Personal Meditations
A: Richard O'Connor
R: Rick Kleit
ART

Personal Mythology
A: David Feinstein and Stanley Krippner
R: David Feinstein
ART

Personal Reflections and Meditations
A/R: Bernie S. Siegel, M.D.
HARP

The Pocket Powter
A/R: Susan Powter
S&S

The Power of Visualization
A/R: Lee Pulos
S&S

The Power of Your Voice
A/R: Dr. Carol Fleming
S&S

Power Thoughts: Positive Messages for Everyday Life
A/R: Robert Schuller
HARP

Predictive Parenting
A/R: Shad Helmstetter
DOVE

Psycho-Cybernetics
A/R: Maxwell Maltz, M.D.
ART

Psycho-Cybernetics and Self-Image Psychology (Contains *Psycho-Cybernetics* and *Master the Magic Power of Self-Image Psychology*)
A/R: Maxwell Maltz
ART

Psycho-Cybernetics 2000
A: Bobbe Sommer, Ph.D., with Mark Falstein
R: Bobbe Sommer
S&S

Pulling Your Own Strings
A/R: Dr. Wayne W. Dyer
HARP

Raise Your Self-Esteem
A: Nathaniel Branden
BDD

Real Magic: Creating Miracles in Everyday Life
A/R: Dr. Wayne W. Dyer
HARP

Real Moments
A/R: Barbara DeAngelis, Ph.D.
BDD

Real Moments for Lovers
A/R: Barbara DeAngelis
BDD

Recovery: A Guide for Adult Children of Alcoholics
A/R: Herbert L. Gravitz and Julie D. Bowden
S&S

The Relaxation Response
A/R: Herbert Benson, M.D.
DOVE

Remarkable Recovery
A: Caryle Hirshberg and Marc Ian Barasch
R: Caryle Hirshberg
TW

Revolution from Within
A/R: Gloria Steinem
DOVE

Richard Simmons' *Never Give Up:* Inspirations, Reflections, Stories of Hope
A/R: Richard Simmons
ART

The Right-Brain Experience
A/R: Marilee Zdenek
ART

Risking
The David Viscott Library
ART

Safe People: How to Find Relationships That Are Good for You and Avoid Those That Aren't
A: Henry Cloud and John Townsend
ZOND

***Self-Hypnosis* by Edgar Cayce**
A: Mark Thurston
R: Stanley Ralph Ross
ART

The Self-Talk Solution
A/R: Shad Helmstetter
DOVE

She: Understanding Feminine Psychology
A: Robert A. Johnson
R: Introduction by Robert A. Johnson; Ralph Blum and Marsha Mason
ART

The Silent Passage
A/R: Gail Sheedy
HARP

The Silva Method: Unlocking the Genius Within
A/R: Robert B. Stone
S&S

Silva Mind Control for Success and Self-confidence
A/R: Hans DeJong
ART

Silva Mind Control for Super-Memory and Speed Learning
A/R: Hans DeJong
ART

The Silva Mind Control Method of Mental Dynamics
A: Jose Silva and Burt Goldman
R: Burt Goldman
S&S

Six Promises for Emotional Well-Being
A/R: Dr. Susan Forward
DOVE

Sixty Minutes to Super-Creativity
A/R: Tony Buzan
ART

Sixty Minutes to Unlocking Your Intuition
A/R: Philip Goldberg
ART

Smart Speaking
A: Laurie Schloff and Marcia Yudkin
R: Laurie Schloff
PENG

The Sound of Your Voice
A/R: Dr. Carol Fleming
S&S

Staying on Top When Your World Turns Upside Down
A/R: Kathryn Cramer
S&S

Stop Smoking through Self-Hypnosis
A/R: Harold Bloomfield, M.D., and Sirah Vettese, Ph.D.
HARP

Stop the Insanity!
A/R: Susan Powter
S&S

Success Runs in Our Race: The Next Challenge for African-Americans—Networking for Information, Influence, and Resources
A/R: George C. Fraser
HARP

Success through Self-confidence
A/R: Beverly Nadier
RH

Super Learning
A: Sheila Ostrander and Lynn Schroeder
RH

Super Learning 2000: New, Triple-Fast Ways You Can Learn, Earn, and Succeed in the 21st Century
A: Sheila Ostrander and Lynn Schroeder
RH

Superself
A/R: Charles J. Givens
S&S

Talk to Win: Seven Steps to a Successful Vocal Image
A/R: Lillian Glass, Ph.D.
HARP

Talking Back to Prozac
A: Peter Breggin and Ginger Ross Breggin
R: Peter Breggin
MILLS

The Tao of Pooh
A/R: Benjamin Hoff
HARP

The Te of Piglet
A/R: Benjamin Hoff
HARP

Teach Only Love
A: Gerald G. Jampolsky, M.D.
BDD

Thin for Life: Ten Keys to Success from People Who Have Lost Weight and Kept It Off
A/R: Anne M. Fletcher
HARP

Thomas Moore Boxed Audio Collection
A: Thomas Moore
R: Thomas Moore and Peter Thomas
HARP

To Build the Life You Want, Create the Work You Love
A/R: Marsha Sinetar
PART

To Give Is to Receive
A: Gerald G. Jampolsky, M.D., and Diane V. Cirincione
BDD

Tough Marriage
A: Paul A. Mickey, Ph.D., with William Proctor
R: Pat Boone
DOVE

Transformation: The Next Step for the No-Limit Person
A/R: Wayne Dyer
S&S

Undercurrents: A Therapist's Reckoning with Depression
A/R: Martha Manning
HARP

Unlimited Wealth
A/R: Paul Zane Pilzer
RH

The Updated Pritikin Program
A: Nathan Pritikin
R: Carl Reiner
DOVE

Visualization: Directing the Movies of Your Mind
A: Adelaide Bry with Marjorie Bair
R: Julie Just
ART

Webster's New World Power Vocabulary Volume I
A: Elizabeth Morse-Cluley and Richard Read
R: Elizabeth Morse-Cluley
S&S

Webster's New World Power Vocabulary Volume II
A: Elizabeth Morse-Cluley and Richard Read
R: Elizabeth Morse-Cluley
S&S

Webster's New World Power Vocabulary Volume III
A: Elizabeth Morse-Cluley and Richard Read
R: Elizabeth Morse-Cluley
S&S

Webster's New World Power Vocabulary Volume IV
A: Elizabeth Morse-Cluley and Richard Read
R: Elizabeth Morse-Cluley
S&S

What Every Woman Ought to Know about Love and Marriage
A/R: Dr. Joyce Brothers
DOVE

What You Can Change, and What You Can't
A/R: Martin E. P. Seligman, Ph.D.
S&S

What Your Doctor Didn't Learn in Medical School
A: Stuart M. Berger, M.D.
R: Joseph Campanella
DOVE

What Your Mother Couldn't Tell You and Your Father Didn't Know
A/R: John Gray
HARP

When Food Is Love
A/R: Geneen Roth
PENG

When Opposites Attract
A: Rebecca Cutter
PENG

Wherever You Go, There You Are: Mindfulness Meditation in Everyday Life
A/R: Jon Kabat-Zinn
ART

Why Me, Why This, Why Now
A/R: Robin Norwood
ART

Widowed—How to Cope with Loss
A/R: Dr. Joyce Brothers
DOVE

Winning
The David Viscott Library
ART

Wishcraft: How to Get What You Really Want
A/R: Barbara Sher
ART

Women Who Love Too Much
A: Robin Norwood
R: Julie Just
ART

Word Power
A/R: Peter Funk
RH

Wordbuilders
A: Audio University
BDD

Volume II

Volume III

Volume IV

Volume V

Volume VI

Volume VII

Volume VIII

Volume IX

Volume X

Volume XI

Volume XII

Wordbuilders Audio Boxed Set
A: Audio University
BDD

Words at Work
A/R: Deborah Tannen, Ph.D.
S&S

The World of Words
A/R: Lillian Glass, Ph.D.
HARP

Writing the Natural Way
A/R: Gabriele Rico, Ph.D.
ART

You and Your Baby's First Years
A: Sirgay Sanger, M.D., and John Kelly
R: Sirgay Sanger, M.D.
DOVE

You Are the Message
A: Roger Ailes with Jon Kraushar
R: Roger Ailes
S&S

You Can Become the Person You Want to Be
A/R: Dr. Robert H. Schuller
S&S

You Can If You Think You Can
A/R: Dr. Norman Vincent Peale
S&S

You'll See It When You Believe It: The Way to Your Personal Transformation
A/R: Wayne Dyer
S&S

Your Erroneous Zones
A/R: Dr. Wayne W. Dyer
HARP

Your Inner Child of the Past
A: W. Hugh Missildine, M.D.
R: Arthur Bernard, Ph.D.
ART

Your Mythic Journey
A/R: Sam Keen and Anne Valley-Fox
BDD

SPIRITUALITY

Hear the wisdom of the ancients from *The Bhagavad-Gita* to *The Tibetan Book of the Living and Dying* to Lao Tsu's *Book of the Way*, or *Tao Te Ching*. Or hear Kahlil Gibran's modern masterpiece, *The Prophet.*

Spirituality abounds on cassette, often with contemplative underscoring to set the mood and allow one to meditate and ponder the words and their wisdom. The best pieces are read in soothing, inviting tones by modern spiritual spokespersons who have an affinity with and a knowledge of the material that they present.

A wealth of spiritual history and application can be found in such programs as the *Ramayana,* the interesting compendium *The Enlightened Mind,* and the numerous discourses on Zen. This is a section for those already on a spiritual path, as well as those looking to discover one.

HIGHLY RECOMMENDED (★★★★)

Alchemy of the Heart
The Bhagavad-Gita
The Enlightened Mind
The Tibetan Book of Living and Dying

Alchemy of the Heart
Author/Reader: Reshad Feild
★★★★

Reshad Feild has studied spiritual philosophy in Zen monasteries and with Sufi (Mevlevi) dervishes. This program is a collection of teachings from classes and workshops given by Feild. Whether the subject is pain, death, consciousness, or the divine order, his is a message of the acceptance of love as the only truth. With a calm yet firm directness, Feild shares his experience of grace in the face of life's chaos.

2 css 3 hr Audio Literature

The Bhagavad-Gita
Author: Translated by Barbara Stoler Miller
Reader: Jacob Needleman
★★★★

This sacred text is a beautiful, rhythmic poem. Hearing the *Bhagavad-Gita,* rather than reading it, helps one understand why many cultures to this day refuse to commit their sacred texts to writing, believing that script would profane them. This unabridged recording is a wonderful representation of this timeless classic, and Needleman, a bold, dramatic interpreter, imbues this classic with a marvelous immediacy.

2 css 2½ hr Audio Literature

Choose Once Again: Selections from *A Course in Miracles*
Reader: Charles Tart
★★

A Course in Miracles, through its unique blend of Christian spirituality and practical psychology, shows how an individual can change his life through a miraculously simple reorientation of the mind. Tart has a hypnotic quality to his reading, but at times he seems self-conscious and lofty.

2 css 2 hr Audio Literature

Compassion in Action: Setting Out on the Path of Service
Authors/Readers: Ram Dass and Mirabai Bush
★★★

This program gives practical methods to discover what we have to offer (skills and resources) and shows how to match our resources with the needs of others.

The authors seem genuinely connected with the subject matter and keep us interested throughout.

2 css 3 hr The Publishing Mills AudioBooks

Crazy Wisdom
Author/Reader: Wes "Scoop" Nisker
★

Wes "Scoop" Nisker, editor of *Inquiring Mind,* the Buddhist journal, and San Francisco Bay area radio personality, attempts to bring the element of humor into today's spiritual milieu. From Socrates to Native American coyote legends to Taoism to Dada, Nisker traces the thread of crazy wisdom throughout human history. Nisker goes over the top, however, with his crazy one-note delivery. Interest flagged for us, but this may tickle someone else's spiritual funny bone.

2 css 3 hr Audio Literature

The Dream of the Earth
Author/Reader: Thomas Berry
Bomb

Drawing upon the timeless wisdom of nature and the insights of thinkers ranging from Buddha and Plato to Teilhard de Chardin and E. F. Schumacher, and from ancient Chinese philosophers to Native American elders, Berry defines a restorative, creative relationship with the natural world. Berry suggests that we "listen" to what the earth has to tell us about itself as an emergent process governed by what he calls the "primodial dream" whence all things come into being. Berry's voice unfortunately wavers unpleasantly. And his heavy unidentifiable accent and vocal pattern gives weight where sensitivity is required. Imagine if you will the "Godfather" trying to turn you on to esoteric wisdom. Please! If we had it our way, Berry would wake up in the morning with a horse's head next to him.

2 css 3 hr Audio Literature

Embraced by the Light
Author/Reader: Betty J. Eadie
★★

During a near-death experience after routine surgery, Betty Eadie was given knowledge of the afterlife that would make even the greatest skeptic think twice. She explains the reasons we have chosen to be on this earth at this time in history, and how all of our actions are growing experiences for our immortal spirits. Eadie's lethargy is catching and proves to keep the listener detached from the compelling material.

4 css 3½ hr Simon & Schuster Audio

The Enlightened Mind: An Anthology of Sacred Prose
Author: Edited by Stephen Mitchell
Readers: Ram Dass, Robert Hass, Stephen Mitchell, Jacob Needleman, and Huston Smith
★★★★

Gathered here are some of the most luminous expressions by the world's masters of wisdom. These selections of sacred prose from the Old Testament, the Upanishads, the Buddha, Jesus of Nazareth, Muhammad, Rumi, and other sources are presented as guides to instruct and inspire the listener. This is a wonderful compendium that is read well and threaded together with the intricacy of a tapestry.

2 css   3 hr   Audio Literature

The Future of Humanity
Authors/Readers: Jiddu Krishnamurti and David Bohm
★★

The Future of Humanity is a dialogue between Krishnamurti and Bohm that took place in Brockwood Park, England, in 1983. The conversation embarks on the incredible journey of the unconditioned mind and asks if the consciousness of mankind can be changed through time. An illuminating exchange of ideas.

1 css   1 hr 10 min   Mystic Fire Audio

History Ends in Green: Gaia, Psychedelics and the Archaic Revival
Author/Reader: Terence McKenna
★★

The coming together of dreams, film, and psychedelics in the twentieth century set the stage for the "archaic revival." McKenna speaks of a wrong turn taken ever since the abandonment of our relationship to ecstasy induced by plants, of the ancient goddess-oriented religions, where the dimensions of the self directly interface nature and allow a kind of symbiosis between human beings and the biosphere.

6 css   7½ hr   Mystic Fire Audio

I Send a Voice
Author: Evelyn Eaton
Reader: Ellen Burstyn
★

In this firsthand account of what actually takes place in the Native American healing rituals, Eaton speaks from the heart of a tradition that is now a source of hope and inspiration to our troubled world. Reading in all too reverential tones, Burstyn pontificates from on high rather than from the heart. How about sending another voice?

2 css   3 hr   Audio Literature

The Prophet
Author: Kahlil Gibran
Reader: Paul Sparer
★★★

Cherished by millions and translated into more than twenty languages, *The Prophet* is the masterpiece of Lebanese poet, philosopher, and artist Kahlil Gibran. (Why does this tape begin with the chirpy Random House piece music, which collides like a freight train with the following flute music?) Sparer has a cultured resonant voice that is used at times too dramatically for the simplicity of Gibran's words to be felt.

1 css 1 hr 20 min Random House AudioBooks

Ramayana
Authors: Valmiki; retold by William Buck
Reader: Ram Dass
★★

Created over two thousand years ago by the poet-sage Valmiki, this tale of cosmic adventure from India emerses us in a world of people and gods and demons. This adaptation by William Buck is considered to be the definitive English version. A foreword by Ram Dass and a list of characters are included in the enclosed booklet. Ram Dass is spirited throughout and what he lacks in dramatic nuance he makes up in heartfelt exposition.

4 css 6 hr Audio Literature

Recovering the Soul: A Scientific and Spiritual Approach
Author/Reader: Larry Dossey, M.D.
★★

This is an exploration at the crossroads of mysticism and healing, religion, and physics, which challenges modern Western ideas with an alternative view of human consciousness—a theory of mind independent of physical matter, time, and space. Larry Dossey, former chief of staff of Medical City Dallas Hospital, is committed to exploring the convergence of science and religion. Dossey gives a compelling, upbeat lecture, but this live recording is noisy.

1 css 55 min Mystic Fire Audio

The Secret Path
Author: Paul Brunton
Reader: Christopher Reeve
★★

When Christopher Reeve was asked what books he would want with him if he were marooned on a desert island, Brunton's works were at the top of his list. Brunton is generally recognized as having introduced yoga and meditation to the West, and *The Secret Path* is a practical guide to the spiritual wisdom of the East. Reeve sometimes declines to color the material, as if it were all of one breath, and though this is hypnotic, it is also less engaging than a more well-modulated presentation.

1 css 1 hr 10 min Audio Literature

A Separate Reality: Further Conversations with Don Juan
Author: Carlos Castaneda
Reader: Peter Coyote
★★

In this second volume in the Don Juan series, Castaneda's teacher demonstrates the seriousness and danger of the sorcerer's way. With astonishing and inescapable logic, he provides us with insight into the meaning of death. Others have written about the hero's journey, but Castaneda leads to it. Coyote is a smooth reader, but his style is closer to that of a reporter than that of a spiritual adventurer.

2 css 3 hr Audio Literature

The Spiritual Light of Ralph Waldo Emerson
Author: Ralph Waldo Emerson
Reader: Richard Kiley
★★★

These passages from the writings of Ralph Waldo Emerson on religion and spiritual philosophy reveal a metaphysical thought that is quintessentially American and universally relevant to the spiritual needs of today's world. In his words, we hear echoes of the great truths of Christianity, Buddhism, Hinduism, and the wisdom of the Greeks. This works well on audio, with Kiley's rich voice letting us ruminate on Emerson's integrated world.

2 css 2½ hr Audio Literature

Tao Te Ching
Authors: Lao Tsu; translated by Gia-fu Feng and Jane English
Reader: Jacob Needleman
★★★

This program presents one of the world's most revered sources of spiritual wisdom. The two-part program contains an unabridged reading of the text on Tape 1, while Tape 2 presents Jacob Needleman's commentary on the *Tao Te Ching* (*Book of the Way*). Needleman uses his rich dark voice to paint visual pictures of the *Tao,* while Stephen Mitchell (in the *Tao* reviewed below) uses a quiet, meditative approach to his reading. Both are different and both work.

2 css 2 hr 10 min Audio Literature

Tao Te Ching: A New English Version
Authors: Lao-Tsu; translated by Stephen Mitchell
Reader: Stephen Mitchell
★★★

Dating from the sixth century B.C., the *Tao Te Ching* (*Book of the Way*) looks at the basic predicament of being alive, giving advice that imparts balance and perspective and a serene and generous spirit. This recording includes the entire eighty-one chapters as well as Michell's introduction to the new translation, an excellent way to enter into these basic principles of the universe. Mitchell has a quiet, calm voice and this is a very thoughtful production, with space between chapters conducive to meditation and replenishment.

2 css 2 hr Caedmon Audio

The Teachings of Don Juan: A Yaqui Way of Knowledge
Author: Carlos Castaneda
Reader: Peter Coyote
★★★

Carlos Castaneda has come to be seen as an anthropologist of the soul, showing us that the inner world has its own inaccessible mountains, forbidding deserts, and awesomely beautiful dangers that we are all called to confront. Coyote makes us listen to Don Juan's vision with fresh ears; he enlivens this mystical search with a sense of mystery and poetry.

2 css 3 hr Audio Literature

The Teachings of Zen Master Dogen
Author: Kazuaki Tanahashi
Reader: Gary Snyder
★★★

Dogen founded the Soto school of Zen Buddhism in Japan and his teachings are the embodiment of the paradoxical blend of mystery and clarity that characterizes Zen. Gary Snyder, poet, cultural hero, and practitioner of Zen Buddhism for more than thirty years, here selects teachings from *Moon in a Dewdrop.* Snyder's pleasing tenor voice allows full concentration on the material, and the recording itself is very clean.

2 css 3 hr Audio Literature

The Tibetan Book of Living and Dying
Author: Sogyal Rinpoche
Readers: Sogyal Rinpoche, Lisa Brewer, Charles Tart, and Michael Toms
★★★★

This spiritual masterpiece interprets Tibetan Buddhism for the West. Rinpoche presents a radically new vision of living and dying. He shows how to go beyond our fear and denial of death to discover what it is in us that survives death and is changeless. Rinpoche explains simple yet powerful practices that anyone can do to transform his life, prepare for death, and help the dying. Very nicely read by this sensitive ensemble.

4 css 6 hr Audio Literature

Touch the Earth
Author: T. C. McLuhan
Readers: Various Native Americans
★★★

This is a performance of words and music on the sacredness of land and life by fourteen distinguished Native American actors, musicians, artists, writers, and spiritual leaders, based on T. C. McLuhan's best-selling book *Touch the Earth.* Gratitude and respect for the living earth—and the land, animals, and objects that make up the territory in which Native Americans live—lies at the heart of this gathering of Native American voices from across North America. Stereo effects are well placed.

1 css 1 hr Mystic Fire Audio

Zen and the Art of the Controlled Accident
Author/Reader: Alan W. Watts
★★★

Alan Watts has popularized the philosophy and practice of Zen through his numerous books and public lectures. In these informal talks, recorded in California and Japan in 1965, Watts reads Zen poetry, including the work of Haiku poet Basho, and tells stories of Zen masters, including Zen teachers Vanca and Hakuin, and the great Zen painter Sengei. It's mesmerizing to hear Watts, especially reading poetry. Effective koto accompaniment.

2 css 1 hr 20 min Mystic Fire Audio

Zen Bones: On the Spirit of Zen
Author/Reader: Alan W. Watts
★★

This lecture was given by Alan Watts in 1967 at the Avalon Ballroom in San Francisco for the purpose of raising funds for the Tassajara Zen Center in northern California. He examines Zen Buddhism and shows how this ancient spiritual tradition makes it possible to live freely and naturally in the turmoil and tension of the modern world. Watts is powerful to hear, but unfortunately the ambience at this sixties lecture is tinny, echoey. . . . It detracts from but certainly does not destroy the mood.

1 css 55 min Audio Literature

Zen Mind, Beginner's Mind
Author: Shunryu Suzuki-roshi
Reader: Peter Coyote
★★★

As Suzuki, a direct spiritual descendant of the thirteenth-century Zen master Dogen, reveals the actual practice of Zen as a discipline for daily life, one begins to understand what Zen is really about. Coyote is an actor, so this may be a bit too dramatic for some purists, but he is clear and energetic.

2 css 3 hr Audio Literature

Addiction to Perfection
A: Marion Woodman
RH

Aim High: An Olympic Decathlete's Inspiring Story
A: Dave Johnson with Verne Becker
R: Mark Winston
ZOND

Alan Watts Live
A/R: Alan W. Watts
RH

Alan Watts Teaches Meditation
A/R: Alan W. Watts
ART

All I Really Need to Know I Learned in Kindergarten
A/R: Robert Fulghum
RH

***All I Really Need to Know I Learned in Kindergarten/It Was on Fire When I Lay Down on It* (Boxed Set)**
A/R: Robert Fulghum
RH

Angel Voices: The Advanced Audio Handbook for Aspiring Angels
A: Karen Goldman
R: Maryann Plunkett
S&S

The Art of War
A: Sun Tzu; translated by Thomas Cleary
RH

Attaining Inner Peace: Practical Applications of *A Course in Miracles*
A/R: Gerald G. Jampolsky, M.D., and Diane V. Cirincione
S&S

Awakening Osiris: The Egyptian *Book of the Dead*
A: Translated by Normandie Ellis
R: Jean Houston
AUDLIT

Awakening the Hidden Storyteller
A: Robin Moore
RH

Beauty, Pleasure, Sorrow and Love
A/R: J. Krishnamurti
HARP

Black Pearls: Daily Meditations, Affirmations and Inspirations for African-Americans
A: Eric V. Copage
R: Ben Vereen
HARP

The Book: On the Taboo against Knowing Who You Are
A: Alan W. Watts
R: Ralph Blum and recordings of Alan Watts
ART

The Book of Leadership and Strategy: Lessons of the Chinese Masters
A: Translated by Thomas Cleary
R: David Warrilow
RH

The Book of Qualities
A: J. Ruth Gendler
R: J. Ruth Gendler and Michael McConnohie
ART

The Celestine Prophecy: An Experimental Guide
A/R: James Redfield with Carol Adrienne
TW

Certain Trumpets: The Call of Leaders
A/R: Garry Wills
S&S

***Channeling Your Higher Self* by Edgar Cayce**
A: Mark Thurston
R: Stanley Ralph Ross
ART

Chogyam Trungpa Live
A/R: Chogyam Trungpa
RH

Chop Wood, Carry Water
A: Edited by Rick Fields with Peggy Taylor, Rex Weyler, and Rick Ingrasci
R: Richard Thomas
ART

The Cloud of Unknowing
A: Translated by James Walsh
R: Alan Jones
AUDLIT

Confidence: The Cornerstone of Success and Happiness
A/R: Alan Loy McGinnis
S&S

A Course in Miracles: Accept This Gift
R: Richard Thomas
ART

A Course in Miracles: A Gift of Healing
R: Richard Thomas
ART

A Course in Miracles: A Gift of Peace
R: Richard Thomas
ART

Denis Waitley's Psychology of Motivation
A/R: Denis Waitley
S&S

Developing Winner's Habits
A/R: Denis Waitley
S&S

The Enlightened Heart
A: Stephen Mitchell
R: Stephen Mitchell, Jacob Needleman, and others
AUDLIT

Family Secrets
A/R: John Bradshaw
BDD

Finding and Exploring Your Spiritual Path
A/R: Ram Dass
ART

Flextactics: The New Dynamics of Goal Setting
A/R: Denis Waitley
S&S

The Fourth Instinct: The Call of the Soul
A/R: Arianna Huffington
S&S

From Beginning to End
A/R: Robert Fulghum
RH

Golf in the Kingdom
A: Michael Murphy
R: Mitchell Ryan
AUDLIT

The Greatest Miracle in the World
A/R: Og Mandino
BDD

The Greatest Salesman in the World
A/R: Og Mandino
BDD

The Greatest Salesman in the World: Part II: The End of the Story
A/R: Og Mandino
BDD

The Greatest Secret in the World
A/R: Og Mandino
BDD

The Heart of Relationship
A: Ondres and Stephen Levine
RH

Hymns to an Unknown God
A/R: Sam Keen
BDD

Illuminata: Prayers for Everyday Life
A/R: Marianne Williamson
RH

In Search of Stones
A: M. Scott Peck
TW

In the Spirit
A/R: Susan L. Taylor
TW

Intuition Training with Helen Palmer
A/R: Helen Palmer
RH

It Was on Fire When I Lay Down on It
A/R: Robert Fulghum
RH

The Japanese Art of War
A: Thomas Cleary
RH

Journey of Awakening
A/R: Ram Dass
ART

Journey to the Heart
A/R: John Welwood
AUDLIT

Leaving My Father's House
A/R: Marion Woodman
RH

Legacy of the Heart
A/R: Wayne Muller
S&S

Life's Little Instruction Book Volume I
A: H. Jackson Brown, Jr.
R: H. Jackson Brown, Jr., and others
RH

Life's Little Instruction Book Volume II
A: H. Jackson Brown, Jr.
R: H. Jackson Brown, Jr., and others
RH

Lightningbolt
A: Hyemeyohsts Storm
R: Hyemeyohsts Storm and Swan Storm
ART

Like This: More Poems of Rumi
A: Translated by Coleman Barks
R: Coleman Barks; accompanied by Hamza El-Din on oud and Steve Coughlin on flute
AUDLIT

The Listening Book
A: W. A. Mathieu
RH

Live and Learn and Pass It On
A: H. Jackson Brown, Jr.
R: H. Jackson Brown, Jr., and others
RH

Lord Buckley Live
A/R: Lord Buckley
RH

The Magic of Believing
A: Claude M. Bristol
R: Various
S&S

Man, Nature, and the Nature of Man
A/R: Alan W. Watts
ART

Many Lives, Many Masters
A/R: Brian L. Weiss, M.D.
S&S

Maybe (Maybe Not): Second Thoughts on a Secret Life
A: Robert Fulghum
RH

Meditations for Men Who Do Too Much
A/R: Jonathon Lazear
S&S

Memories, Dreams, Reflections
A: C. G. Jung
RH

The Miracle of Mindfulness: A Manual on Meditation
A: Thich Nhat Hanh
HARP

Money and the Meaning of Life
A/R: Jacob Needleman
BDD

Notes to Myself
A/R: Hugh Prather
ART

Perfect Weight: The Complete Mind Body Program for Achieving and Maintaining Your Ideal Weight
A/R: Deepak Chopra
RH

Quiet Strength
A: Rosa Parks as told to Gregory Reed
R: Deforia Lane
ZOND

The Ravaged Bridegroom
A/R: Marion Woodman
RH

Reflections of Highly Effective People
A: Stephen R. Covey
R: Introduction by Stephen R. Covey; various
S&S

Restful Sleep: The Complete Mind Body Program
A/R: Deepak Chopra
RH

The Return of Merlin
A/R: Deepak Chopra
RH

Sayings of the Buddha: The Dhammapada
R: Jacob Needleman
AUDLIT

The Seat of the Soul
A/R: Gary Zukav
ART

Selections from *A Course in Miracles* (Includes *Accept This Gift, A Gift of Healing,* and *A Gift of Peace*)
R: Richard Thomas
ART

Shambhala: The Sacred Path of the Warrior
A: Chogyam
RH

Through Time into Healing
A/R: Brian L. Weiss, M.D.
S&S

The Tibetan Book of the Dead
A: Translated by Francesca Fremantle and Chogyam
RH

True Success
A/R: Tom Morris
S&S

Uh-Oh: Some Observations from Both Sides of the Refrigerator Door
A/R: Robert Fulghum
RH

Walden
A: Henry David Thoreau
RH

The Way of a Pilgrim
A: Unknown
AUDLIT

The Way of Zen
A: Alan W. Watts
R: Ralph Blum, and recordings of Alan Watts
ART

Well Done
A/R: Dave Thomas
ZOND

When All You've Ever Wanted Isn't Enough
A/R: Harold Kushner
S&S

Wherever You Go, There You Are
A/R: Jon Kabat-Zinn
ART

Who Needs God
A/R: Harold Kushner
S&S

The Winner Within: A Life Plan for Team Players
A/R: Pat Riley
S&S

The Wisdom of Baltasar Gracian
A: J. Leonard Kaye
R: F. Murray Abraham
S&S

The Words of Gandhi
A: Mohandas K. Gandhi
R: Ben Kingsley
HARP

The Wounded Woman
A: Linda Schierse Leonard
RH

Writing Down the Bones
A: Natalie Goldberg
RH

Zen in the Art of Archery
A: Eugene Herrigel
R: Ralph Blum
ART

Zen Lessons: The Art of Leadership
A: Translated and edited by Thomas Cleary
RH

Zen Practice, Zen Art
A: Alan W. Watts
R: Ralph Blum, and recordings of Alan Watts
ART

WESTERNS

The overall quality of western audios to choose from is quite high and there is a good selection available for western lovers. Simple seems to work best here and the villains and the good guys are easy to identify (even if you can't see who's wearing black and who's wearing white). John Randolph Jones creates a diverse set of characters beautifully; it was a pleasure to hear him on a number of Louis L'Amour titles. Along with these single-reader recordings, I found a nice selection of dramatized, multi-cast L'Amour recordings with quality production values, including vital music and exciting sound effects.

The intimacy of locale and immediacy of myths and legends are successfully assimilated by this dramatic medium. The sights and sounds of the Old West are easily conjured up by the drawl of a cowboy, the ring of a gunfight, the crackle of a roaring campfire, or the lonely twang of a guitar.

HIGHLY RECOMMENDED (★★★★)

Law of the Desert Born
Ride You Tonto Raiders and Law of the Desert Born
Strange Pursuit

Brules
Author: Harry Combs
Reader: Stacy Keach
★★★

A grizzled mountain man with chilling memories and few regrets, Brules loses his best friend to the Comanches and wages a one-man war against those who robbed him of his girl, his friend, and his heart. Stacy Keach has a nice clean sound to his voice. He understands pacing and modulation and brings the long descriptive passages of this book to life as well as differentiating the characters nicely. This is a bit different from most westerns in that it is taken at a leisurely pace with many psychological nuances to contemplate.

4 css 5 hr 10 min BDD Audio

Canyon Walls
Author: Zane Grey
Reader: Robert Foxworth
★

Outlaw Monty Bellew takes refuge at a ranch on the Utah border. Bellew wants the land and the beautiful daughter of the ranch owner. With the story's hard-shooting action, High Plains panoramas, and heart-and-guts characters, we know we're in Zane Grey territory. Robert Foxworth reads very well, his deep, sonorous voice suited to western fare. But he is overpowered by the over-the-top production values, the insistent sound effects and routine music taking center stage and leaving Foxworth out in the cold.

1 css 1½ hr Harper Audio

Dances with Wolves
Author/Reader: Michael Blake
★★★

This story, which was the basis of the blockbuster film of the same name, follows the life of John J. Dunbar, a young cavalry lieutenant who finds himself at the edge of the American frontier in the year 1863. Though circumstance has left him completely alone at one of the army's most isolated outposts, Dunbar is entranced by the wild, open country surrounding him, and the stage is set for one man's classic adventure with the free people of the plains in a time long past. Those familiar with the movie may be disappointed here; the author/reader just does not have the dramatic impetus to move such a sweeping epic along. Yet this is complete and unabridged, and for those who want to hear the book in its entirety, this should be a satisfactory listening experience.

5 css 7 hr 40 min Audio Editions

Dream Catcher
Author: Terry C. Johnston
Reader: John Randolph Jones
★★

A decade has passed since Confederate soldier Jonah Hook returned to find his wife and children gone—kidnapped by a man of unspeakable brutality. Driven by his eternal love for his wife, Hook will ride one last time with his firstborn son, Jeremiah, and his friend Two Sleep. However, Jonah alone must face the demon he has chased so long. . . . This is harrowing material with scenes of torture and sadism—yet it is a realistic picture. John Randolph Jones varies the book's many moods and characters in a dynamic reading.

2 css 3 hr Time Warner AudioBooks

Law of the Desert Born
Author: Louis L'Amour
Performers: Multiple Cast
★★★★

Against his better judgment, when Sheriff Gates forms his posse to track down a killer, he opens the jail and lets Lopez ride along. This is one of many L'Amour BDD dramatizations that works well on audio. There is an opening of gunshots, a death, a dog barking, then a guitar twang and we are suddenly swept into the glory days of the late 1800s. This is a compelling production that keeps you wanting to hear more.

1 css 1 hr BDD Audio

The Maverick Queen
Author: Zane Grey
Reader: James Whitmore
★★

When Linc Bradway rides into South Pass, Wyoming, looking for his partner's killer, he finds a town where vice is rampant and life is cheap. He also encounters the beautiful Maverick Queen, whose charm he finds difficult to resist. James Whitmore reads in a lively, aggressive manner, but the story hits and misses and there are unfortunate breaths and lip smacks that detract from the listening experience.

2 css 3 hr Listen for Pleasure

Ride You Tonto Raiders and Law of the Desert Born
Author: Louis L'Amour
Reader: John Randolph Jones
★★★★

This is one from the L'Amour/Jones series that works so well on audio. John Randolph Jones breathes the spirit of the Old West in his lively presentation of these L'Amour chestnuts. Predictable as the material is, with the characters in either white or black hats (with no gray on the horizon), if you enjoy L'Amour, this is a lively presentation, with Jones giving it his all and drawing memorable characterizations for both heroes and villains.

2 css 2½ hr Listen for Pleasure

St. Agnes' Stand
Author: Tom Eidson
Reader: Rob Campbell
★★

Nat Swanson killed a man in self-defense back in West Texas, but the dead man's buddies don't care about innocence or guilt. They'll track him from hell to breakfast to see him hang. Now Swanson's on the run, but his troubles are just beginning. After a nice guitar opening, Rob Campbell begins to read in a slow (you can hear him reading) drawl. But he emphasizes his words well and is clear and easy to follow. But there are not many sparks here.

2 css 3 hr Simon & Schuster Audio

Shane
Author: Jack Schaefer
Reader: Dick Cavett
★★

In this classic western tale, there is a lot of heartfelt human drama amid the suspense. Dick Cavett reads well enough in an easy, folksy vein; however, his voice is so identifiable from his late-night television show, it is hard to enter into the spirit of the Old West. Still, Cavett makes sense of the narrative and gives us some believable character voices along the trail.

2 css 3 hr Durkin Hayes Audio

Strange Pursuit
A Chick Bowdrie Story
Author: Louis L'Amour
Performers: Multiple Cast; introduction by Louis L'Amour
★★★★

For four years, Chick Bowdrie has been riding with the Texas Rangers. If they want a man, they get him. Bowdrie is smart, fast—and relentless—in tracking his prey across dusty cow towns and barren desert landscapes and through the canyons and pine forests of northern Arizona into deadly Apache territory. This is one of the fine BDD L'Amour dramatizations, with crisp production values and plenty of exciting sound effects and music, with actors who obviously enjoy sinking their teeth into this nicely patterned ensemble piece. L'Amour's introduction is a big plus for fans. He talks about tracking and following trails (tracking a person's mind, not only his footprints), and how the West itself is an actor in all his stories.

1 css 1 hr BDD Audio

The Third Bullet
Author: Max Brand
Reader: Barry Corbin
★★

Despite Christopher Ballantine's struggles to put his siblings through college, his efforts are met with greed and contempt, and the town ridicules him as a failure. It is time for a change, and he vows to show he is not someone to be taken for granted. . . . This is very western sounding; reader Barry Corbin pronounces phrases like "heavily mortgaged" as "heavily margaged," yet his delivery fits the bill. Unfortunately, while he nails the accents, he reads along at the same pace, so that a certain blandness emerges.

1 css 1½ hr Audio Renaissance Tapes

The Virginian
Author: Owen Wister
Reader: Patrick Duffy
★

In 1902, the cowboy became a fully realized article of American culture when Owen Wister published *The Virginian,* which established the conventions of the western. His classic characters moved in the raw, bracing atmosphere that generations of readers and moviegoers would come to expect from westerns. Patrick Duffy, while reading well enough, never quite ignites the sparks to make this horse opera sing.

2 css 3 hr The Publishing Mills AudioBooks

The Wild West
Authors: Mark Twain, Walter Van Tilburg Clark, Max Brand, Bret Harte, Tony Hillerman, T. V. Olsen, Robert Easton, and Ernest Haycox
Performers: Charles Dean and Jack Palance
★★★

These four audio cassettes housed in an attractive wooden box run the spectrum from Bret Harte's classic "The Outcasts of Poker Flat" to Tony Hillerman's contemporary western "The Great Taos Bank Robbery." This is a nice compendium with Jack Palance performing six stories in his trademark gravelly voice, appropriate to bringing these suspenseful tales to climax. Charles Dean has a good reach with characterization and reads two stories here. The one drawback: some tape hiss that might annoy the sensitive ear.

4 css 4 hr The Mind's Eye

Wyatt Earp
Author/Reader: Dan Gordon
★★

Wyatt Earp, the tough, mean, crafty sheriff whose career started on the wrong side of the tracks, strides into Tombstone to clean up the town. With his closest friend, the notorious Doc Holliday, Wyatt Earp prepares for a confrontation that will come to be known as the most famous gunfight in the history of the Old West. With a bite to his voice and an ability to convey good characterizations, author Gordon proves that the writer is also a performer. For those fans of Wyatt Earp, this should be provocative fare.

2 css 3 hr Time Warner AudioBooks

Battle's End
A: Max Brand
R: Barry Corbin
ART

The Best Bandit
A: Max Brand
R: Barry Corbin
ART

Best of the West
A: Gary McCarthy, Gordon Shirreffs, Jory Sherman, Matt Braun, Zane Grey, Loren D. Estleman, Bill Gulick, and Elmer Kelton
R: David Birney, Joseph Campanella, Ken Howard, and Arte Johnson
DOVE

Best of the West II
A: Gordon Shirreffs, Zane Grey, Jeanne Williams, Will Henry, Elmer Kelton, Bill Gulick, Lauran Paine, and Julie Alter
R: Ed Asner, Arte Johnson, Diane Ladd, and Richard Thomas
DOVE

Best of the West III
A: Jory Sherman, Terry C. Johnston, Robert Dyer, Judy Alter, Jeanne Williams, Alexandra Morgan, Zane Grey, and Betty Traylor Gyenes
DOVE

The Black Rock Coffin Makers
A Chick Bowdrie Story
A: Louis L'Amour
BDD

Black Thunder
A: Max Brand
R: Barry Corbin
ART

Bowdrie Follows a Cold Trail
A Chick Bowdrie Story
A: Louis L'Amour
BDD

Bowdrie Passes Through
A Chick Bowdrie Story
A: Louis L'Amour
R: Introduction by Louis L'Amour
BDD

Carcajou's Trail
A: Max Brand
R: Barry Corbin
ART

Carry the Wind
A: Terry C. Johnston
R: Ken Howard
TW

The *Chick Bowdrie* Audio Boxed Set
A: Louis L'Amour
BDD

Chip Champions a Lady
A: Max Brand
R: Barry Corbin
ART

Desert Death Song
A: Louis L'Amour
R: John Randolph Jones
DURK

Desert Death Song
A: Louis L'Amour
BDD

Down Sonora Way
A: Louis L'Amour
R: Full Cast
BDD

Down the Pogonip Trail
A: Louis L'Amour
BDD

Forgotten Treasure
A: Max Brand
R: Barry Corbin
ART

Four-Card Draw
A: Louis L'Amour
R: Introduction by Louis L'Amour
BDD

Home in the Valley
A: Louis L'Amour
R: Full cast
BDD

Horse Thief
A: Zane Grey
R: Robert Foxworth
HARP

A Job For a Ranger
A Chick Bowdrie Story
A: Louis L'Amour
BDD

Keep Travelin', Rider
A: Louis L'Amour
R: John Randolph Jones
DURK

The *Law of the Desert Born* Audio Boxed Set
A: Louis L'Amour
BDD

Lit a Shuck for Texas
A: Louis L'Amour
BDD

Lonigan
A: Louis L'Amour
R: Full cast
BDD

McNelly Knows a Ranger
A Chick Bowdrie Story
A: Louis L'Amour
BDD

McQueen of the Tumbling K
A: Louis L'Amour
R: John Randolph Jones
DURK

Merrano of the Dry Country
A: Louis L'Amour
BDD

A Mule for Santa Fe
A: Louis L'Amour
BDD

One for the Mohave Kid
A: Louis L'Amour
BDD

Outcast Breed
A: Max Brand
R: Barry Corbin
ART

Outlaws of Poplar Creek
A Chick Bowdrie Story
A: Louis L'Amour
BDD

The Race
A: Max Brand
R: Barry Corbin
ART

Rain on the Mountain Fork
A Chick Bowdrie Story
A: Louis L'Amour
BDD

Range Jester
A: Max Brand
R: Barry Corbin
ART

The Ranger
A: Zane Grey
HARP

***A Ranger Gets His Man:* The Audio Boxed Set**
A: Louis L'Amour
BDD

***A Ranger Rides Again:* The Audio Boxed Set**
A: Louis L'Amour
BDD

***A Ranger Rides for Justice:* The Audio Boxed Set**
A: Louis L'Amour
BDD

The Red Bandanna
A: Max Brand
R: Barry Corbin
ART

The *Riding for the Brand* Audio Boxed Set
A: Louis L'Amour
BDD

Showdown Trail
A: Louis L'Amour
R: Introduction by Louis L'Amour; Richard Crenna
BDD

That Triggernometry Tenderfoot
A: Louis L'Amour
R: Full cast
BDD

There's Always a Trail
A: Louis L'Amour
R: Full cast
BDD

The Three Crosses
A: Max Brand
R: Barry Corbin
ART

The Town No Guns Could Tame
A: Louis L'Amour
BDD

The Trail to Peach Meadow Canyon
A: Louis L'Amour
R: Introduction by Louis L'Amour; Robert Stack
BDD

A Trail to the West
A Chick Bowdrie Story
A: Louis L'Amour
R: Introduction by Louis L'Amour; full cast
BDD

Valley of Wild Horses
A: Zane Grey
R: Charles Haid
DURK

West of the Tularosas
A: Louis L'Amour
BDD

Where Buzzards Fly
A: Louis L'Amour
R: Full cast
BDD

GRAMMY AWARDS FOR BEST SPOKEN-WORD RECORDING (1958–1993)

Winners are listed first and noted in bold; nominated titles follow.

1958
***The Best of the Stan Freberg Shows,* Stan Freberg**
Great American Speeches, Melvyn Douglas, Vincent Price, Carl Sandburg, Ed Begley
Green Christmas, Stan Freberg
Improvisations to Music, Mike Nichols, Elaine May
The Lady from Philadelphia, Marion Anderson
Two Interviews of Our Time, Henry Jacobs, Woody Leafer

1959
***A Lincoln Portrait,* Carl Sandburg**
Ages of Man, Sir John Gielgud
Basil Rathbone Reads Sherlock Holmes, Basil Rathbone
Mark Twain Tonight, Hal Holbrook
New York Taxi Driver, Tony Schwartz

1960
***F.D.R. Speaks,* Franklin Delano Roosevelt**
Ages of Man, Vol. II, One Man in His Time, Part II, "Shakespeare," Sir John Gielgud
Voices of the Twentieth Century, Henry Fonda

1961
***Humor in Music,* Leonard Bernstein conducting New York Philharmonic**

The Coming of Christ, Alexander Scourby, Robert Russell Bennett, conducting
More of Hal Holbrook in Mark Twain Tonight, Hal Holbrook
Wisdom, Vol. I, Sandburg, Shapley, Nehru, Lipschitz
The World of Dorothy Parker, Dorothy Parker

1962
***The Story-Teller: A Session with Charles Laughton,* Charles Laughton**
Carl Sandburg Reading His Poetry, Carl Sandburg
Enoch Arder (music by R. Strauss; poem by Alfred Tennyson), Claude Rains, reader; Glenn Gould, pianist
First Performance: Lincoln Center for the Performing Arts, Leonard Bernstein conducting New York Philharmonic
Mama Sang a Song, Stan Kenton
Sir Michael Redgrave Reads "The Harmfulness of Tobacco," "A Transgression," and *"The First Class Passenger"* by Anton Chekhov, Sir Michael Redgrave
Six Million Accuse, Yehuda Lev, narrator
This Is My Beloved, Laurence Harvey

1963
***Who's Afraid of Virginia Woolf?* Uta Hagen, Arthur Hill**
The Badmen, Pete Seeger
Brecht on Brecht, Dane Clark, Anne Jackson
John F. Kennedy—the Presidential Years, David Teig, narrator
Strange Interlude, Betty Field, Jane Fonda
We Shall Overcome (the March on Washington, August 28, 1963), Martin Luther King, Jr.

1964
***BBC Tribute to John F. Kennedy: That Was the Week That Was,* cast**
Dialogue Highlights from "Becket," Richard Burton, Peter O'Toole
Dylan, original cast with Sir Alec Guinness, Kate Reid
The Kennedy Wit, John F. Kennedy; David Brinkley, narrator
Shakespeare: Hamlet, Richard Burton
Shakespeare: Othello, National Theatre of Great Britain

1965
***John F. Kennedy: As We Remember Him,* produced by Goddard Lieberson**
The Brontës, Margaret Webster
Much Ado about Nothing, National Theatre of Great Britain
A Personal Choice, Sir Alec Guinness
A Time to Keep: 1964, Chet Huntley
The Voice of the Uncommon Man, Adlai Stevenson

1966
***Edward R. Murrow, A Reporter Remembers*—Vol. I, *The War Years,* Edward R. Murrow**
Day for Decision, Johnny Sea
Death of a Salesman, Lee J. Cobb, Mildred Dunnock
History Repeats Itself, Buddy Starcher
The Stevenson Wit, Adlai Stevenson

1967
***Gallant Men,* Senator Everett M. Dirksen**

The Balcony, Patrick Magee, Cyril Cusack
The Earth, Rod McKuen
A Man for All Seasons, Paul Scofield, Wendy Hiller, Robert Shaw
Mark Twain Tonight, Vol. III, Hal Holbrook
An Open Letter to My Teenage Son, Victor Lundberg
Poems of James Dickey, James Dickey

1968
***Lonesome Cities,* Rod McKuen**
The Canterbury Pilgrams, Martin Starkie
I Have a Dream, Martin Luther King, Jr.
Kennedy-Nixon: The Great Debates, 1960, produced by Joel Heller
Murder in the Cathedral, Paul Scofield

1969
***We Love You, Call Collect,* Art Linkletter and Diane**
The Great White Hope, James Earl Jones
Home to the Sea, Jesse Pearson
Man on the Moon, Walter Cronkite
Robert F. Kennedy: A Memorial

1970
***Why I Oppose the War in Vietnam,* Martin Luther King, Jr.**
Everett Dirksen's America, Everett Dirksen
Grover Henson Feels Forgotten, Bill Cosby
In the Beginning: Apollo 8, 11, 12 *Astronauts,* Presidents Kennedy and Nixon
Poems and Ballads from 100-Plus American Poets
The Soft Sea, Jesse Pearson

1971
***Desidrata,* Les Crane**
Hamlet, Richard Chamberlain
I Can Hear It Now—the Sixties, Walter Cronkite
Long Day's Journey into Night, Stacy Keach, Robert Ryan, Geraldine Fitzgerald
Will Rogers' U.S.A., James Whitmore

1972
***Lenny,* original cast**
Angela Davis Speaks, Angela Davis
Cannonball Adderley Presents Soul Zodiac, Rick Holmes, narrator
The Word, Rod McKuen
Yevtushenko, Yevtushenko

1973
***Jonathan Livingston Seagull,* Richard Harris**
America, Why I Love Her, John Wayne
Slaughterhouse Five, Kurt Vonnegut, Jr.
Songs and Conversations, Billie Holiday
Witches, Ghosts and Goblins, Vincent Price

1974
***Good Evening, Peter Cook,* Dudley Moore**
An Ear to the Sounds of Our History, Eric Sevareid
"Autumn," Rod McKuen
Senator Sam at Home, Sam Ervin
Watergate, Vol. III, *"I Hope the President Is Forgiven,"* (John W. Dean III testifies)

1975
***Give 'Em Hell, Harry,* James Whitmore**

The Autobiography of Miss Jane Pittman, Claudia McNeil
Immortal Sherlock Holmes Mercury Theatre on the Air, Orson Welles
The Prophet, Richard Harris
Talk about America, Alistair Cooke
To Kill a Mockingbird, Maureen Stapleton

1976
***Great American Documents,* Orson Welles, Henry Fonda, Helen Hayes, James Earl Jones**
Asimov: Foundation, The Psychohistorians
Dickens: A Tale of Two Cities, James Mason
Fahrenheit 451, Ray Bradbury
Hemingway: The Old Man and the Sea, Charlton Heston

1977
***The Belle of Amherst,* Julie Harris**
Alex Haley Tells the Story of His Search for Roots, Alex Haley
For Colored Girls Who Have Considered Suicide/When the Rainbow Is Enuf, original cast
J.R.R. Tolkien: The Silmarillion of Beren and Luthien, Christopher Tolkien
The Truman Tapes, Harry Truman with Ben Gradus

1978
***Citizen Kane,* movie soundtrack**
John Steinbeck: The Grapes of Wrath, Henry Fonda
The Nixon Interviews with David Frost
Roots, TV soundtrack
Wuthering Heights, Dame Judith Anderson, Claire Bloom, James Mason

1979
***The Ages of Man (Readings from Shakespeare),* Sir John Gielgud**
An American Prayer, Jim Morrison
Apocalypse Now, movie soundtrack
Orson Welles/Helen Hayes at Their Best
The Ox-Bow Incident, Henry Fonda
Stare with Your Ears, Ken Nordine

1980
***Gertrude Stein, Gertrude Stein, Gertrude Stein,* Pat Carroll**
Adventures of Luke Skywalker, The Empire Strikes Back, original cast
A Curb in the Sky, James Thurber, Peter Ustinov
I Sing Because I'm Happy, Vols. I and II, Mahalia Jackson
Obediently Yours, Orson Welles

1981
***Donovan's Brain,* Orson Welles**
Justice Holmes' Decisions, E. G. Marshall
The McCartney Interview, Paul McCartney
'Twas the Night Before Christmas, track, Ed McMahon
Vladimir Nabokov: Lolita, James Mason

1982
Raiders of the Lost Ark: The Movie on Record
Charles Dickens' Nicholas Nickelby, Roger Rees
Foundation's Edge, Isaac Asimov
No Man's Island, Sir John Gielgud, Sir Ralph Richardson
2010—Odyssey Two, Arthur C. Clarke

1983
***Copland: Lincoln Portrait,* William Warfield**

Everything You Always Wanted to Know about Home Computers, Steve Allen, Jayne Meadows
Jane Fonda's Workout Record for Pregnancy, Birth and Recovery, Jane Fonda, Femmy De Lyser
Old Possum's Book of Practical Cats, Sir John Gielgud, Irene Worth
The Robots of Dawn, Isaac Asimov

1984
***The Words of Ghandi,* Ben Kingsley**
Heart Play (Unfinished Dialogue), John Lennon, Yoko Ono
Our Time Has Come, Rev. Jesse Jackson
The Real Thing (Original Cast Recording), Jeremy Irons, Glenn Close
The Story of Indiana Jones and the Temple of Doom (narration, dialogue, and music from the original motion picture soundtrack)

1985
***Ma Rainey's Black Bottom,* original cast**
Adventures of Huckleberry Finn, Dick Cavett
Catch-22, Alan Arkin
The Spy Who Came in from the Cold, John Le Carré
Zuckerman Bound, Philip Roth

1986
***Interviews from the Class of '55, Recording Sessions,* Carl Perkins, Johnny Cash, Roy Orbison**
Gulliver, Sir John Gielgud
Hard Headed Boys, Bill Cosby
Interview with the Vampire, F. Murray Abraham
The Stories of Ray Bradbury, Ray Bradbury

1987
***Lake Wobegon Days,* Garrison Keillor**
Lauren Bacall by Myself
"Lincoln Portrait," track from *Aaron Copland: Lincoln Portrait,* Katharine Hepburn
Star Trek IV: The Voyage Home, Leonard Nimoy
Whales Alive, Leonard Nimoy

1988
"Speech by Rev. Jesse Jackson, July 27,"* track from Aretha Franklin's *One Lord, One Faith, One Baptism
A Christmas Carol, Sir John Gielgud
A Prairie Home Companion: The 2nd Annual Farewell Performance, Garrison Keillor
The Screwtape Letters, John Cleese
Winters' Tales, Jonathan Winters

1989
***It's Always Something,* Gilda Radner**
All I Really Need to Know I Learned in Kindergarten, Robert Fulghum
I Want to Grow Hair, I Want to Grow Up, I Want to Go to Boise, Erma Bombeck
Sir John Gielgud Reads "Alice in Wonderland"
The War of the Worlds 50th Anniversary Production, Jason Robards, Steve Allen, and others

1990
***Gracie: A Love Story,* George Burns**
"Diane . . ." the Twin Peaks of Agent Cooper, Kyle MacLachlan
Jimmy Stewart and His Poems, Jimmy Stewart
A Prairie Home Companion: The 4th

Annual Farewell Performance, Garrison Keillor
Profiles in Courage, John F. Kennedy, Jr.

1991
***The Civil War,* Ken Burns**
The Hitchhiker's Guide to the Galaxy, Douglas Adams
A Life on the Road, Charles Kuralt
Me: Stories of My Life, Katharine Hepburn

1992
***What You Can Do to Avoid AIDS,* Earvin "Magic" Johnson, Robert O'Keefe**
A Christmas Carol, Patrick Stewart
Devout Catalyst, Ken Nordine
Fried Green Tomatoes at the Whistle Stop Cafe, Fannie Flagg
Stories, Garrison Keillor
This Is Orson Welles, Orson Welles, Peter Bogdanovich

1993
On the Pulse of Morning, Maya Angelou
Bound for Glory, Arlo Guthrie
Howards End, Emma Thompson
Miles: The Autobiography, LeVar Burton
Mr. and Mrs. Bridge, Paul Newman, Joanne Woodward

ORDERING INFORMATION

Audio books under the following imprints are reviewed or listed in this book. (The abbreviations used in the listings are in boldface.)

If your bookstore doesn't stock a title you are interested in, ask them to special order it for you, or contact the audio publisher directly, using the information that follows. Also contact the audio publisher directly if you wish to receive information on upcoming releases.

ART—See Audio Renaissance Tapes

Audio Editions—See The Audio Partners Publishing Corporation

Audio Literature **(AUDLIT)**
For ordering information call 800-841-BOOK or 510-845-8414; Audio Literature, P.O. Box 7123, Berkeley, CA 94707

The Audio Partners Publishing Corporation **(PART)**
To order, call 800-231-4261 or 916-888-7803; The Audio Partners Publishing Corporation, 1133 High Street, P.O. Box 6930, Auburn, CA 95604

Audio Renaissance Tapes **(ART)**
Consumers contact Audio Renaissance Tapes, 5858 Wilshire Boulevard, Suite 205, Los Angeles, CA 90036; 213-939-1840; fax: 213- 939-6436

AUDLIT—See Audio Literature

Bantam Audio—see Bantam Doubleday Dell Audio Publishing

Bantam Doubleday Dell Audio Publishing **(BDD)**
Customer Service Department: 800-323-9872 (708-827-1111 in Illinois) or 212-354-6500; Bantam Doubleday Dell Audio Publishing, 1540 Broadway, New York, NY 10036

BDD—See Bantam Doubleday Dell Audio Publishing

BDD Audio—See Bantam Doubleday Dell Audio Publishing

BRILL—See Brilliance Corporation/Nova

Brilliance Corporation/Nova **(BRILL)**
To order, call or fax 800-648-2312 or call 616-846-5256; Brilliance Corporation, 1810-B Industrial Drive, P.O. Box 887, Grand Haven, Michigan 49417

Caedmon Audio—See Harper Audio/Caedmon

Caedmon/Harper Audio—See Harper Audio/Caedmon

DOVE—See Dove Audio

Dove Audio **(DOVE)**
To order, call 800-328-DOVE (3683) or 310-273-7722; Dove Audio, 310 North Canon Drive, Beverly Hills, CA 90210

Dove Kids—See Dove Audio

Dove/Morrow—See Dove Audio

DURK—See Durkin Hayes Publishing, Ltd./Listen for Pleasure

Durkin Hayes Publishing, Ltd./Listen for Pleasure **(DURK)**
Order desk: (USA)—800-962-5200 or 716-298-5150; (Canada)—800-264-5224 or 716-298-5150; Durkin Hayes Publishing, Ltd., One Colomba Drive, Niagara Falls, NY 14305 (USA); 3375 North Service Road, Unit B7, Burlington ON L7N 3G2 (Canada)

Everyman Library Children's Classics—See Random House Audiobooks

HARP—See Harper Audio/Caedmon

Harper Audio/Caedmon **(HARP)**
To order, call 800-331-3761, 800-242-7737 or 212-207-7790; HarperCollins Publishers, P.O. Box 588, Scranton, PA 18512-0588

HighBridge Audio—See Penguin-HighBridge Audio

Jabberwocky—See The Mind's Eye

Listen for Pleasure—See Durkin Hayes Publishing, Ltd./Listen for Pleasure

MILLS—See The Publishing Mills Audio Books

MIND—See The Mind's Eye

The Mind's Eye **(MIND)**
To order, call 800-227-2020; The Mind's Eye, 4 Commercial Boulevard, Novato, CA 94949

Mystic Fire Audio—For ordering information call 212-941-0999; Mystic Fire, P.O. 422, Prince St. Station, New York, NY 10012

Newman—See Dove Audio

Nova—See Brilliance Corporation/Nova

Paperback Audio—See Durkin Hayes Publishing, Ltd./Listen for Pleasure

PART—See The Audio Partners Publishing Corporation

PENG—See Penguin AudioBooks-HighBridge Audio

Penguin AudioBooks-HighBridge Audio **(PENG)**
To order, call 800-755-8532 or 612-659-3700; HighBridge Audio,

P.O. Box 64541, St. Paul, MN 55164-0541

Penguin-HighBridge Audio—See Penguin Audiobooks-HighBridge Audio

The Publishing Mills Audio Books **(MILLS)**
To order, call Customer Service at 800-72-AUDIO or 213-467-7831; The Publishing Mills, P.O. Box 481006, Los Angeles, CA 90048

Random House Audiobooks **(RH)**
To order, call 800-733-3000; Random House, Inc., Order Entry Department, 400 Hahn Road, Westminster, MD 21157

RH—See Random House Audio

S&S—See Simon & Schuster Audio

Simon & Schuster Audio **(S&S)**
To order, call 800-223-2336; for inquiries, call 800-223-2348, or send a fax to 800-445-6991; Order Department, Simon & Schuster, 200 Old Tappan Road, Old Tappan, NJ 07675

Sound Editions—See Random House Audiobooks

Ten Speed Press—See Audio Literature

Time Warner AudioBooks **(TW)**
To order, call 800-759-0190 or 310-205-7421; Time Warner AudioBooks, 9229 Sunset Boulevard, Los Angeles, CA 90069

TW—See Time Warner AudioBooks

TW Kids—See Time Warner AudioBooks

ZOND—See Zondervan Publishing House

Zondervan Publishing House **(ZOND)**
To order, call Order Processing at 800-727-1309, or send a fax to 800-934-6381; for product information, call Customer Service at 800-727-1309, or send a fax to 616-698-3255; 5300 Patterson Avenue, SE, Grand Rapids, MI 49530

[illegible]

Penguin Highbridge Audio [illegible]

Sound Editions [illegible] Random House [illegible]

[illegible]

INDEX

9 780684 802398

Printed in the United States
By Bookmasters